Date Due

OCT 18			
DEC 5	JAN 4		
FEB 4			
FEB 18	JAN 1 1		
	DEC 2 0		
MAR 5	MAR 2 0		
MAR 2 0	OCT 2 6		
APR 3	JAN 1 1		
APR 1 7	DEC 13		
MAY 1	JAN 2		
MAY 14	DEC 18		
MAY 23	FEB 25		
NOV 5			
NOV 2 5			
JAN 2 0			
FEB 2 7			
MAR 13			
MAR 2 7			
OCT 2 1			
NOV 1 0			
OCT 8			
OCT 2 3			

No. 293   DEMCO-MADISON-WIS

GOD AND HIS CREATURES

Books by the Author

The Science of Correct Thinking
Reality and the Mind
The Domain of Being
From Aether to Cosmos
The Whole Man
Man and Morals

GOD AND
HIS CREATURES
THEODICY

CELESTINE N. BITTLE, O.F.M.Cap.

THE BRUCE PUBLISHING COMPANY
MILWAUKEE

NIHIL OBSTAT
Thomas Aquinas Heidenreich, O.F.M.Cap.
March 18, 1952

NIHIL OBSTAT
Berchmans Bittle, O.F.M.Cap.
March 19, 1952

IMPRIMI POTEST
Cyprian Abler, O.F.M.Cap., Minister Provincial
June 21, 1952

NIHIL OBSTAT
John A. Schulien, S.T.D., Censor librorum

IMPRIMATUR
✝ *Moyses E. Kiley, Archiepiscopus Milwauchiensis*
November 3, 1952

PREFACE

OF THE various departments constituting the general science of philosophy, theodicy (natural theology) is the most noble and most important.

It is the most noble. Its nobility stems from the pre-eminence of its subject-matter which is God Himself, the Supreme Being. God is the *summum bonum,* the supreme good, both in Himself and in His relation to creatures. He is the supreme truth and as such alone satisfies the undying craving of the human mind for a complete explanation of the world and of every being.

It is the most important. Nothing can be more important to man in time and eternity than to know God and to love Him. Life here on earth would have no meaning if God were removed from the key position of influencing man in his thought and action. Man must, therefore, be sure of God's existence and seek to inform himself thoroughly with regard to His nature and operations.

A survey of the American people has brought out the information that ninety-nine per cent believe in God; of these over ninety per cent are absolutely convinced of God's existence. Inasmuch as it has been currently assumed that Americans are rather 'materialistic' in their general attitude, this fact is both startling and heartening. Such a survey, however, could not be expected to bring out what the individuals thought about the real nature of the Supreme Being. If such a survey were made, it would probably show much confused thinking. That is practically unavoidable in convictions which are the result more of spontaneous thinking than of reflective reasoning. The matter of God's existence and nature is too important to be left to spontaneous thinking, especially so far as the educated classes are concerned.

The present book seeks to supply the information desired

by the reasoning mind of man. Its general standpoint is that of theism in its traditional form. Nothing new should be expected as regards the subject-matter under discussion. If there is anything new in the book, it is the manner of presentation.

Like the other books of the author, the present treatise is directed toward the undergraduate students in their endeavor to understand the many difficult problems connected with philosophical inquiry. Having been a teacher of undergraduates, the author realizes the necessity of simplification and clarification in so difficult a subject; this he has attempted to provide for the budding mentality of the students in writing a theodicy for their use.

The author has now completed the series of the various departments of philosophy. It is his fond hope that this book on theodicy will also enable the reader to understand the existence, nature, and operations of God, so that he will know Him and love Him more and more.

C. N. BITTLE, O.F.M.CAP.

CONTENTS

PREFACE v

PART I

THE EXISTENCE OF GOD

I. NOTION AND SCOPE 3
Theodicy — Natural Theology. Theodicy as a Science.
A Philosophical Science. Scope of Theodicy. Object
of Theodicy. The Method of Theodicy. Postulates
of Theodicy.

II. FIRST PRINCIPLES 14
First Principles. The Principle of Identity. The Principle of Contradiction. The Principle of Excluded
Middle. The Principle of Sufficient Reason. The
Principle of Causality. Basic Concepts and First Principles. Empiricism. Idealistic Monism. Pragmatism.

III. THE POSSIBILITY OF PROOF 36
Scientific Explanation. Deism and Agnosticism. Fideism and Traditionalism. Ontologism. Religious Experience. The Ontological Proof. The Necessity of
Proof. God's Existence Can Be Proved. Kant's Formalism. The Method of Proof.

IV. CHANGE 58
Parmenides, Heraclitus. Aristotle. Bergson. Change
and Causality. The Universality of Change. Extramundane Cause of Change. Unchangeable Cause.
The Argument of St. Thomas. Consequences.

V. DESIGN 80
Order and Design. Order and Chance. Chance and
Probability. Order and Intelligence. Order in the
World of Stars. Order in the World of Atoms. Order
in the World of Plants. Order in the World of Ani-

mals. Order in the World of Men. Conclusions. Proof
of God's Existence. The Argument of St. Thomas.

VI.   CONTINGENCY AND CAUSALITY 105

Necessity and Contingency. Contingency and the
World. Contingency and Organisms. Contingency
and Atoms. Contingency and Matter. Proof of God's
Existence. The Argument of St. Thomas. The Princi-
ple of Causality. The Fact of Causality. Finite or
Infinite Series of Causes. Infinite Series Impossible.
Circle of Causes Impossible. Proof for God's Existence.
The Proof of St. Thomas. Corollaries.

VII.   LIFE AND PERFECTION 131

The Problem of Life. Abiogenesis. The Origin of
Life. God, the Ultimate Cause of Life. God and
Evolution. God and Purposive Evolution. Notion of
Perfection. Grades of Perfection. Limitation of Per-
fection. God and Perfection. The Argument of St.
Thomas. Inferences.

VIII.   OPPOSING VIEWS 163

Objections of Transcendentalism. Refutation of Transcendentalism. Objections of Materialism. Refutation
of Materialism.

PART II

THE NATURE OF GOD

SECTION I: ABSOLUTE ATTRIBUTES

IX.   GOD'S ESSENCE 187

Man's Knowledge of God. Ways of Knowing God.
Analogical Knowledge of God. Notion of Essence
and Attribute. God's Metaphysical Essence. Evaluation of Theories. God, the Self-Subsistent Being. God's
Physical Essence.

X.   SIMPLICITY, INFINITY, UNICITY 214

Notion of Simplicity. The Problem of God's Simplicity. Proof of God's Absolute Simplicity. Notion of
Infinite Perfection. The Problem of God's Infinity.

Proof of God's Infinity. The Unicity of God. Distinctions in God.

XI. IMMUTABILITY, ETERNITY, IMMENSITY 240
Notion of Immutability. Proof of God's Immutability. Notion of Eternity. Proof of God's Eternity. Notion of Immensity. Proof of God's Immensity. Pantheism. Refutation of Pantheism.

XII. GOD'S INTELLECT AND WILL 266
Nature of God's Intellection. The Object of God's Knowledge. Kinds of Divine Knowledge. Existence of God's Knowledge. Nature of God's Will. Existence of God's Volition. Necessity and Freedom in God. Liberty and Immutability.

SECTION II: RELATIVE ATTRIBUTES

XIII. OMNIPOTENCE AND CREATION 292
The Notion of Omnipotence. Existence of God's Omnipotence. The Foundation of Possibles. The Notion of Creation. Opponents of Creation. Proof of Creation. God Alone Can Create. Eternity of Creation. Infinite Number of Creatures.

XIV. CONSERVATION AND CONCURRENCE 319
The Notion of Conservation. Proof of Divine Conservation. Notion of Divine Concurrence. Proof of Physical Concurrence. Mode of Divine Concurrence. The Answer of Bannesianism. The Answer of Molinism. The Defense of Thomism. The Defense of Molinism. Evaluation.

XV. PROVIDENCE AND GOVERNANCE 350
Notion of Providence. Notion of Governance. Proof of God's Providence. Physical Evil. Moral Evil. Fate and Chance. Optimism and Pessimism. Miracles. Miracles Are Possible. Miracles Can Be Known. God and Man.

GLOSSARY 381

BIBLIOGRAPHY 397

INDEX 405

GOD AND HIS CREATURES

PART I

THE EXISTENCE OF GOD

Chapter I

NOTION AND SCOPE

HISTORY and anthropology show that all peoples without exception worship some sort of divinity.

Many peoples worship more than one divinity — they are 'polytheistic.' Some worship idols; some, natural objects; some, gods who possess human traits in a superior degree. In every form of polytheism, many deities occupy a subordinate position, while others are superior to them in power and intelligence. In this hierarchy of deities, frequently one is supreme.

Other peoples worship but one God — they are 'monotheistic.' Jews, Christians, and Mohammedans profess monotheism. God, in their concept, is eternal, infinite; the beginning and end of all things; supreme intelligence; the creator and governor of the world.

No people has ever been discovered which, in the strict sense of the term, is 'atheistic.' Individuals may be atheists; but a people, never. This universal belief is a tremendous fact. Most persons, even when they abandon their Christian heritage, still retain the fundamental conviction of the existence of God. Apparently, then, belief in God or some sort of deity is a spontaneous and natural dictate of human reason.

The philosopher takes this universal fact as the starting-point of his investigation. He then seeks to determine, with reason as his guide, the truth-value of the idea of God — whether He actually exists, what His nature is, what His relation is to the world. This investigation gives rise to the philosophical science of *theodicy.*

Theodicy — Natural Theology

The department of philosophy treating of God usually is designated either 'theodicy' or 'natural theology.'

The name *theodicy* was introduced by Leibnitz (*Essais de Théodicée sur la bonté de Dieu, etc.*, 1710), and the literal meaning of 'theodicy,' as used by him, is 'the justification of God' (Gr., θεός, *God,* and δίκη, *right, trial, justification*). Leibnitz maintained that the existing order of the universe is the best which God in His omnipotence and providence could possibly devise. Many writers attacked this extreme optimism, pointing out that the many physical and moral evils present in the world disproved such an exaggerated position. He thereupon wrote his *Essais de Théodicée* as a 'justification of God,' attempting to show that the physical and moral evils of the world are no valid argument against the optimism he advocated. While Leibnitz' optimism has passed into the limbo of discarded philosophical opinions, his term 'theodicy' has survived in a different meaning.

In the course of time, the name 'theodicy' was given to any treatise or book which vindicated man's belief in God and sought to refute the manifold objections raised against this belief, whether these objections were urged against His existence, His providence, or any of His perfections. Gradually, then, the name was used to signify 'the science of God' as a distinct department of philosophy treating of God in His existence, His nature, His attributes, and the relation of creatures to Him. It is in this broadened meaning, as the *philosophical science of God,* that the term 'theodicy' is used in our day, and so it is used in this book.

Another name used to designate the philosophical science of God is *natural theology.* Strictly speaking, the term 'theology' should be sufficient for the purpose, because 'theology' means the science of God (Gr., θεός, *God,* and λόγος, *treatise, science*). However, the term 'theology' more frequently designates the application of reason and of the reasoning process to truths furnished by supernatural revelation. As a consequence, it has become customary to distinguish between 'dogmatic (supernatural) theology' and 'natural (philosophical) theology.' Many philosophers dislike the term 'theodicy,' claiming that it is too narrow in meaning. They prefer the term 'natural theology' as more expressive of the true meaning of this specific department of philosophy. On the other hand, many philosophers dislike the term 'natural theology' because of the possibility of confusion with dogmatic theology. Both terms, 'theodicy' and 'natural theology,' are current, and their meaning is identical. Names are of minor importance, so long as their signification is clear and unambiguous.

Theodicy as a Science

Briefly, theodicy or natural theology can be defined as the *science of God*. Since a 'science' is an organized body of distinct truths regarding some special object of thought, theodicy is rightly called a 'science.'

The special object treated in theodicy is *God*. Such an object involves many problems and the proper solution of them. The truths discovered, when arranged into a system, form a true science. Nowadays, it is customary to speak of 'the sciences' as referring almost exclusively to the physical sciences, but such a use of the term 'science' is too restrictive and therefore unwarranted. A science is distinguished from mere experience. Experience pertains to isolated facts and the truths immediately evident in these facts. A science is based on fundamental principles, and these principles are applied to the facts in question, so that the final result of the investigation is a body of proved truths concerning a general subject-matter, resting on fundamental principles and arranged into a system. Such is the nature of the physical sciences, and such is also the nature of theodicy.

As a rule, the popular knowledge of God is altogether too human in conception: it is steeped in 'anthropomorphism,' because God is endowed too much by man with purely human characteristics. Man's knowledge begins in the senses, and material things are the connatural object of his intellect. He is at home in the material world, and it is only with difficulty that he attains to the immaterial. It is the purpose of theodicy to penetrate, so far as reason will permit, into the immaterial world of God's being (if He is found to exist) and strip this knowledge of all extraneous and false notions. Not opinions and passing experiences, but certainties and scientifically established truths are the aim of theodicy as a science.

Some authors object to calling theodicy a 'science,' contending that it is an integral part of the general science of metaphysics. It is true that theodicy presupposes the principles of metaphysics and applies them to the special subject-matter of 'God.' Nevertheless, the philosophical inquiry into the existence and nature of God covers a very wide field of facts and proofs which lead to a large body of demonstrated truths capable of being arranged into a general systematic body; and that is the characteristic of a science. While, then, it may be conceded that theodicy is not an independent science in its own right, it is really a 'science.' Botany, for instance, is a subdivision of the general science of biology; but it is also a true science.

The characteristic *distinction* between the science of theodicy (natural theology) and the science of dogmatic (supernatural) theology consists in the source of their respective truths. The theologian approaches the question of God and His nature from the standpoint of the authority of divine revelation and therefore presupposes God's existence as given. The philosopher begins with the principles of reason; with the aid of natural reason as his sole guide he seeks to determine whether God exists. Once the existence of God is proved, he seeks to find out what God's nature is, what His attributes are, and in what relationship creatures stand with reference to God. The philosopher prescinds from revelation as a source of information in his investigation, relying on human reason and its principles as his sole instrument in acquiring knowledge.

A Philosophical Science

When theodicy is called a 'philosophical science,' it is equivalent to saying that theodicy is a *department of philosophy,* together with logic, epistemology, ontology, cosmology, psychology, and ethics.

Philosophy is defined as the science of beings in their *ultimate* reasons, causes, and principles, acquired by the aid of human reason. The special natural sciences are concerned with the 'proximate' causes of things; philosophy, with the 'ultimate' reasons, causes, and principles. Philosophy begins where the special sciences end; it is the foundation of the natural sciences, because it tests the validity of the principles upon which these sciences rest. As such, it is the queen of the natural sciences. If the principles of philosophy are invalid, then philosophy itself and the natural sciences are all invalid.

No department of philosophy can be mastered with ease. It is always difficult to reduce things to their 'ultimate' reasons, causes, and principles. In the case of theodicy, however, the *difficulties* are greater than usual, because man finds it an arduous task to leave the sensible world and concentrate on spiritual and divine realities. This fact becomes evident when it is realized that even the best among the pagan philosophers failed to reach a conception of God which was true and clear. A Christian child, in many respects, has a sounder idea of the nature of God than the greatest philosophers of antiquity, for instance, Plato or Aristotle. These philosophers lacked the information supplied by revealed religion and were forced to depend solely on their reasoning powers. The present-day philosopher, either directly or indirectly, has absorbed from Christianity so much of the true concept of God that he need not first discard a host of mythological teachings before arriving at a reasonably sure idea of what God really is. The philosopher, of course, may not use revelation directly in his analyses and demonstrations; but he can, at least, begin with the idea of God furnished by faith and see whether this idea is rational and justifiable. In this manner he will save himself much unnecessary trouble.

Theodicy is therefore defined as the *philosophical science of God,* or *the science of God acquired by means of natural reason.*

Scope of Theodicy

The *scope* of theodicy has already been outlined in the preceding sections. The starting-point of the investigation will be the theistic idea of God, namely, the concept of a Supreme

Being who is spiritual in essence and endowed with intelligence and free-will. Theodicy does not take this theistic position for granted. It merely intends to begin with a concept of God which is generally accepted in Western civilization, instead of with some polytheistic deity found in the religion of a primitive race or of a nation long dead.

Theodicy does not assume that God exists. It must *prove God's existence beyond reasonable doubt*. The arguments for God's existence must be based on indubitable facts and self-evident principles. Mere opinions and conjectures do not suffice; solid proofs are necessary. In no other way can theodicy formulate doctrines capable of withstanding logical criticism.

The existence of God having been definitely established, the next step will be to show what *God's nature* is. Since God cannot be seen or perceived, man's knowledge of His nature can only be indirect and mediate. Still, the very nature of creatures will reveal many things about Him. If it can be proved that the universe owes its being and existence to God, creatures will of necessity mirror God's *perfections* in some degree, and man can reason from the perfection of creatures to the perfections of God. Reason can thus arrive at a true knowledge of God and His nature, even though this knowledge be very incomplete and fragmentary.

After the examination of God's nature, theodicy naturally proceeds to a discussion of His *operations*. The nature of a being is the source of its operations: as a being is, so it does. In this respect, reason can argue either from the effect to the cause or from the cause to the effect. Thus, from the destruction caused in a city by a bomb, one can legitimately draw a conclusion as to how the bomb operated; similarly, from a thorough knowledge of the construction and charge of a bomb, experts can foretell what the bomb will do when it hits a city. So, too, man can draw valid conclusions about the operations of God by studying the universe as the effect of God's creative power (if the world is the result of creation), and he can also draw valid conclusions about the operations of God from a scrutiny of God's nature.

Object of Theodicy

Every science has a 'material' and 'formal' object. The *material object* of a science is the general subject-matter which it treats. As a rule, a number of sciences occupy themselves with the same general subject-matter. For example, geology, geography, and geogony have the earth as their material object, because each of these distinct sciences treats of the earth in one way or another: geology is the science of the rock formations of the earth; geography, of the structural features of the earth; geogony, of the origin and development of the earth. Hence, the earth is the material object common to all these sciences. The *formal object* of a science is that special aspect of the common (material) object which is distinctive for a particular science, so that this science thereby differs from every other science and becomes specifically this definite science. In the example just given, the formal object of geology is the rock formations; of geography, the structural features; of geogony, the origin and development (of the earth).

As a science, theodicy also has a material and a formal object. The 'material' object of theodicy is 'God,' and this object it has in common with supernatural theology. The 'formal' object of theodicy is 'God *as known by natural human reason,'* because this characteristic distinguishes theodicy from the kindred science of supernatural theology and makes it a specifically distinct science.

The Method of Theodicy

The two methods which can be employed in scientific research are 'induction' and 'deduction.'

Induction, or analysis, is defined as a process of reasoning in which one concludes from individual cases to the existence of general laws or principles. Induction passes from the concrete to the abstract, from the complex to the simple, from the particular to the universal, from the contingent to the necessary, from the applications of a principle to the principle itself, from the phenomena to the underlying general law, from the effect to the cause. This method gives rise to the analytic, experimental, inductive sciences, and it is the primary method used by the physical sciences throughout a great part of their research into the problems of nature. Chemistry, for example, is an inductive science in its experimental work.

Deduction, or synthesis, is the process of reasoning in which one concludes from the general law or principle to a particular instance falling under the general law or principle. It proceeds from the abstract to the concrete, from the simple to the complex, from the more general to the less general, from the necessary to the contingent, from the 'logical whole' to the 'logical part,' from the principle to the applications of the principle, from the general law to the individual cases, from the cause to the effect. Sciences which employ primarily the synthetic method are called the rational or deductive sciences. Mathematics, for instance, is a deductive science because it begins with a few fundamental ideas and axioms and, without the aid of observation and experiment, gradually builds up a most profound and complicated system of truths.

If the physical sciences are called 'inductive,' it is due to the fact that their predominant method is induction. No science, however, is exclusively inductive or deductive; every science uses both induction and deduction, though in different proportions.

The science of *theodicy* uses both *induction* and *deduction.* In proving God's existence, theodicy begins with the physical universe and the manifold effects observed in it and reasons to the cause which alone can give an adequate explanation for their presence, namely, the First Cause or God. Similarly, from the beings of the universe, theodicy argues to the nature of God. So far the method employed is 'induction,' because the process of reasoning passes from the effect to the cause. From that point on, however, the philosopher uses 'deduction' to a great extent, arguing from the nature of God to His attributes and operations. The philosopher, like the scientist, employs whichever method is best under the circumstances for the establishment of truth. Both methods are legitimate procedures.

Postulates of Theodicy

All sciences rest upon certain postulates. A *postulate* is a proposition which is either self-evident or which is taken over without proof by one science from another science because it has been proved by this other science. The physicist, for instance, presupposes the validity and truth of mathematics in his own science; the principles of mathematics thus are 'postulates' of the science of physics.

Some philosophers object to the use of the term 'postulate,' as having a definite Kantian meaning. Immanuel Kant (1724–1804) understood by a 'postulate' a proposition or hypothesis which, even though unproved and unprovable, must be accepted as true. Thus, according to Kant, the existence of God, the freedom of the will, and the immortality of the human soul are indemonstrable, but belief in their truth is necessary for man so that he can intelligently perform his moral duties. Obviously, our use of the term 'postulate' is not taken in this Kantian sense, as will be seen from its definition as given above. Kant illegitimately restricted its meaning, just as he used the term 'category' in a sense radically different from 'category' as traditionally used in logic.

When a term is properly defined and is used according to this definition, no one can seriously object to it, so long as this use is historically justifiable. Scientists commonly use the term 'postulate' in our sense.

The postulates of theodicy are the *existence of the physical world* and the *trustworthiness of human reason* in its search for facts and truth. These postulates can rightly be presupposed by theodicy, because they have been definitely established in epistemology, another department of philosophy.[1]

The entire argumentation of theodicy is based on the reality of the physical world. And the instrument of argumentation is human reason. If the physical world is not objectively real, it

---

[1] See the author's *Reality and the Mind* (Milwaukee: The Bruce Publishing Co., 1936).

would be futile to conclude from the existence and nature of the physical world to the existence and nature of God as its cause. If human reason were untrustworthy in its deliverances, no amount of argumentation would be valid. The philosopher, however, need not go to the trouble of proving the existence of the physical world and of the trustworthiness of reason, when a separate department has already proved their validity. This was done in epistemology. There it was shown that the existence of the physical world and the trustworthiness of man's reasoning powers are not unwarranted assumptions and presuppositions, but are eminently rational and philosophically well grounded. They are, therefore, valid and logical *postulates of theodicy*.

The student may, at times, find theodicy taxing and difficult. However, this cursory explanation of the notion and scope of theodicy should be enough of an indication that such a study is worth every effort one may put into it.

Summary of Chapter I

In order to understand the purpose of theodicy, one must be clear as to its *notion* and *scope*.

1. *Theodicy — Natural Theology.* — Strictly speaking, the term 'theodicy' means the 'justification of God.' Gradually, however, this meaning has been broadened, so that at present it signifies the 'philosophical science of God.' That is also the signification of 'natural theology.'

2. *Theodicy as a Science.* — Since theodicy is an organized body of distinct truths regarding a special object of thought, namely regarding God, it is rightly termed a 'science.' Theodicy (natural theology) uses human reason and its principles as the sole instrument in acquiring knowledge; dogmatic (supernatural) theology approaches the question of God and His nature from the standpoint of divine revelation.

3. *A Philosophical Science.* — Theodicy is a department of philosophy, and philosophy is the science of beings in their *ultimate* reasons, causes, and principles, acquired by the aid of human reason. It is in this manner that theodicy treats of God, and it is defined

as the *philosophical science of God* or as the *science of God acquired by means of natural reason.*

4. *Scope.* — Theodicy seeks to determine the truth-value of the concept of God; whether God *exists;* what His *nature* and *perfections* are (if He exists); the extent of His *operations.*

5. *Object of Theodicy.* — The *material* object of theodicy is 'God'; the *formal* object is 'God as known by natural human reason.'

6. *Method of Theodicy.* — In investigating God's existence and nature, the philosophic method is *induction.* Arguing from God's nature to His attributes and operations, the method used is mainly that of *deduction.*

7. *Postulates of Theodicy.* — A *postulate* is a proposition which is either self-evident or which is taken over without proof by one science from another science because it has been proved by this other science. The postulates of theodicy are the existence of the physical world and the trustworthiness of human reason.

Readings

Smith, Gerard, *Natural Theology,* Introduction. — Renard, Henri, *The Philosophy of God,* Foreword and Introduction. — Brosnan, William, J., *God and Reason,* Introduction. — Joyce, George Hayward, *Principles of Natural Theology,* Part I, Chap. I.

CHAPTER II

FIRST PRINCIPLES

EVER since Descartes assumed that man consists of mind and matter as two distinct substances, it has been taken for granted in many philosophical and scientific circles that man can know only his own internal conscious states.

Theoretically, such an assumption may seem plausible. Practically, however, it is unlivable. In his daily life every philosopher and scientist is a confirmed realist; he treats the external world as existing and knows a great deal about it. The excessive cleavage between mind and body, as assumed by Descartes, does not exist. Nevertheless, the influence of Descartes's teaching still continues.

Because science has made such marvelous progress during the past century, many scientists consider 'scientific' knowledge to be the only source of truth worth bothering about. 'Metaphysics' is anathema. Some scientists, and even philosophers following the scientific trend of the times, deny or doubt the validity of anything like the First Principles of being and thought: such principles are 'metaphysical' and as such are condemned without a proper hearing. Yet the First Principles are necessary for all thinking, whether scientific or philosophical.

Before beginning with the proofs of God's existence, it will therefore be necessary to establish the *validity of the First Principles*.

First Principles

Man makes many types of judgments. The 'binding force' of these judgments is by no means the same in all cases.

Some judgments are *contingent* in character; they are true, but their truth is not necessary. Consider these judgments: 'The sky is overcast today'; 'My food is warm and tasty'; 'This man

14

wears an overcoat'; 'The boy is running.' In making such judgments we realize that the connection between the subject and predicate in each case is not necessary. The judgments express actual facts, and as such they are true; but the facts could be different, because they are 'contingent,' and then the judgments would also be different. Facts of this kind can be discovered only by *experience;* not by means of an analysis of subject and predicate.

Other judgments are *necessary* in character; they are true, and they are necessarily true. Such are, for example, the judgments: 'The whole is greater than any single one of its parts'; '2 + 2 = 4'; 'A circle is round'; 'A cube has three dimensions.' We judge such statements to be true independently of all existential conditions and all experience. They are true not only here and there, now and then, for this and that mind; they are immutably and necessarily true, everywhere, always, for every mind, without possibility of change or error.

Among the necessary judgments philosophers also place the *First Principles.* They are termed 'first' because they are the foundation of all reality and thought. The First Principles are:

The Principle of *Identity:* 'Whatever a thing is, it is'; 'Everything is identical with itself.'

The Principle of *Contradiction:* 'A thing cannot be and not be the same thing at the same time under the same respect.'

The Principle of *Excluded Middle:* 'A thing either is or is not (something).'

The Principle of *Sufficient Reason:* 'A thing must have a sufficient reason for its being and existence.'

The Principle of *Causality:* 'Whatever happens or becomes must have a cause for its happening or becoming.'

Like all necessary judgments, the truth of these First Principles does not depend upon our 'experience' for their discovery. If we understand the meaning of the subject and predicate of each statement, the truth should be evident through an *analysis* of the subject and predicate. The first three are comparatively simple; the last two are an amplification and application of the first three.

The First Principles are of extreme importance for all knowledge, for without them knowledge of whatever kind would be utterly impossible. For this reason the *self-evidence* of the First Principles will now be discussed.

The Principle of Identity

The *Principle of Identity* states: 'Whatever a thing is, it is.' It expresses the self-evident truth that a 'being, whatever it is, is identical with itself.'

The Principle of Identity is grounded on the concept of *being*. 'Being' is the noun taken from the verb 'to be,' and 'to be' means 'to exist' or to be 'capable of existence.' Obviously, whatever actually exists is 'capable of existence.' A thing, however, may not actually exist although it is 'capable of existing' and for that reason it also is a 'being'; such, for instance, would be the case of a flower which will or may bloom next spring.

The *opposite* of 'being' is *non-being*. 'Non-being' may be so either in a relative or absolute sense. A *relative non-being* is something which does not now actually exist, either because it has ceased to exist (for example, the past generation of men) or has not as yet received existence although it can exist (for example, the future generation of men); such a being, because it is 'capable of existence,' is also by that very fact a 'relative being.' *Absolute non-being* (or, *absolute nothing*) neither actually exists nor is 'capable of existence'; its very idea involves the impossibility of existing (for example, a 'one-dimensional cube,' since a 'cube' necessarily implies three dimensions).

Hence, expressed negatively, 'being' is that which is opposed to 'absolute nothing'; expressed positively, 'being' is anything which has actual or possible existence. It is thus seen that the idea of 'being' always contains a positive (actual or possible) relation to existence, while the idea of 'absolute non-being' contains no relation whatsoever to existence.

From the foregoing analysis it is evident that 'being is identical with itself,' and this fact gives rise to the *Principle of Identity* which is valid both in the realm of reality and, as a consequence, in the realm of thinking. Concretely, the principle is expressed by people in phrases like the following: 'Iron is iron'; 'East is East, and West is West'; 'Justice is justice, and injustice is injustice, no matter what people say or do.'

Many philosophers consider the Principle of Identity to be merely a tautological statement. Others deny this. Because the arguments of both sides are rather abstruse,[1] we will pass on to the Principle of Contradiction.

The Principle of Contradiction

The *Principle of Contradiction* (or *Non-contradiction,* as others prefer to call it) is based on the comparison between 'being' and 'non-being' and reads: 'A thing cannot be (something) and yet not be (it) at the same time under the same respect.'

When we compare 'being' with 'non-being,' we intuitively behold that the one is not, and cannot be, the other. We see the evident truth that 'being is not non-being' and that these concepts mutually exclude each other with *absolute necessity:* something 'that is' can never be something 'that is not.' Since 'being' and 'non-being' can never be identical, but must be universally and necessarily in opposition to each other, we express this self-evident truth in the Principle of Contradiction: 'A thing cannot both be and not be (something) at the same time under the same respect.' This principle flows immediately from the concept of 'being,' and the concept of 'being' itself is drawn from objective reality; consequently, the principle itself governs the entire realm of objective reality.

The Principle of Contradiction also governs the entire realm of *thought.* Its validity is a *pre-condition for all knowledge.* Knowledge consists essentially in judgments and inferences, and these will never be valid if the Principle of Contradiction is not valid.

The Principle of Contradiction cannot be 'demonstrated.' A *demonstration* is a mediate inference in which a conclusion is drawn consistently from true premises; and the conclusion is

---

[1] James B. Sullivan, *First Principles in Thought and Being* (Washington, D. C.: Catholic University Press, 1939), p. 51 ff.

presumed to be less known than the truth contained in the premises. The premises, however, would neither be true nor consistent, if the Principle of Contradiction were not already validly in force in the premises. 'Truth' implies that there is a difference between 'truth' and 'error,' and 'consistency' implies that there is a difference between 'consistency' and 'inconsistency.'

On the other hand, *no demonstration is needed* to establish the truth of the Principle of Contradiction; its truth is *self-evident*. A mere analysis of 'being' and 'non-being' suffices to establish its truth, since the intellect perceives intuitively that 'being' and 'non-being' are never the same thing. When something is perfectly clear in itself (as the Principle of Contradiction is), no 'demonstration' is needed to prove its truth: 'self-evidence' is the proof, and that is better than any demonstration.

Moreover, no one can sincerely deny or doubt the validity of the Principle of Contradiction without presupposing and affirming its validity in the very *denial* or *doubt*. Whoever 'denies' the truth of this principle thereby claims that his denial is the 'truth' and that the principle as advocated is an 'error.' Such an assertion, however, implies that 'truth' is not 'error' and 'error' is not 'truth'; but that assertion is obviously based on the very principle which is denied, namely, that 'A principle cannot both be true and not true at the same time under the same respect.' The same thing happens to anyone who 'doubts' the truth of this principle. In doubting its truth, he implies that his reasons contain 'truth' and not 'error,' and that means that he implies that the Principle of Contradiction is valid in his doubt.

The fact is simply that the Principle of Contradiction is so necessary as a pre-condition of all thinking and all knowledge that without it we can 'know' nothing. The failure to accept this principle makes common knowledge, science, and philosophy impossible and involves the mind in universal skepticism. Once we admit *universal skepticism*, however, we may as well quit thinking entirely, for any theory or attitude which leads logically to the absurdity of universal skepticism is doomed.

The Principle of Excluded Middle

The *Principle of Excluded Middle* is expressed in different ways by different writers: 'A thing either is or is not'; 'Everything must either be or not be'; 'Any attribute must be either affirmed or denied of any given subject'; 'Two contradictories cannot be false together'; 'One of two contradictories must be true'; 'Between affirmation and denial there is no middle course'; 'Between two contradictories a middle is excluded.' The only difference between these various statements is that some pertain more to the logical order and others more to the real order. Inasmuch as the 'logical' order of knowledge (ideas, judgments, inferences) is representative of the 'real' order (actual or possible things), both types of statements express fundamentally the same truth.

The Principle of Excluded Middle is an *immediate inference* from the Principle of Identity and the Principle of Contradiction. If it is self-evident that 'being is being' and 'non-being is non-being,' and if it is self-evident that 'A being cannot both be and not be (something),' it is also self-evident that 'A being either is or is not (something).' There is no middle thing possible between 'being' and 'non-being'; it is either the one or the other. There is no stage or state possible between 'is' and 'is not'; it either 'is' or it 'is not.'

The reason is simple. 'Being' and 'non-being' constitute a *complete division of all things.* 'Being' includes everything actual and possible, everything conceivable. 'Non-being' is the negation, or denial, of everything actual and possible, everything conceivable; it signifies absolute nothingness. The division being so complete, it is obvious that there can be no medium or third category between 'being' and 'non-being.' If something is anything at all conceivable, it is a 'being'; if it is not a 'being,' it is nothing or 'non-being.' Anything conceivable must be either the one or the other; it cannot be both, and it cannot be neither.

Even the merely *possible* is a 'being,' not absolute nothingness, because it has a positive relation to existence. In so far as the 'possible' has no actual existence, it is a 'relative non-being'; but in so far as it can receive existence, it is a 'relative being': in no case, however, is it 'absolute non-being.' When speaking of the 'possible' as a 'relative being' and a 'relative non-being,' we are not speaking of the same thing *under the same respect,* and so the Principle of Contradiction is not violated. In an 'absolute' sense, the 'possible' is always a *being* and is not a middle thing between 'being' and 'non-being,' because it is always a 'possible *being.*' It is thus seen that even the merely 'possible' does not violate the Principle of Excluded Middle.

In the realm of *knowledge* every attribute used as a predicate must be either affirmed or denied of any given subject; it cannot be both affirmed and denied under the same respect. Take, for example, the attribute 'chemical element.' Everything conceivable as a subject must either be a 'chemical element' or 'not a chemical element.' Thus, silver, oxygen, helium, gold — all are chemical elements. Water, salt, zinc, coal are compounds, not elements; protons, electrons, mesons are subelemental particles, not elements. Possible beings must be one or the other; plutonium, even before it was made by man from uranium, belonged to the class of chemical elements. No matter what attribute is applied to a subject (for instance, 'red,' 'triangle,' 'round,' 'spiritual,' 'book,' etc.), all things conceivable must either possess the attribute or not possess it. No being exists or can exist which would both possess and not possess the attribute; and no being exists or can exist which would neither possess nor not possess it: such a 'middle' would obviously violate the Principle of Contradiction, because it would both 'be' and 'not be' something simultaneously under the same respect.

To deny or doubt the validity of the Principle of Excluded Middle, whether in the realm of reality or in the realm of thought, leads to absurdity. The principle is *self-evident* and as such *true.*

The Principle of Sufficient Reason

The *Principle of Sufficient Reason* reads: 'A thing must have a sufficient reason for its being and existence.' Gottfried

W. Leibnitz[2] (1646–1716), who did much to make this principle better known, called it *determining reason* (*la raison déterminante*) rather than 'sufficient reason,' and his terminology seems to be a better phrase for expressing the meaning of the principle. German philosophers speak of the *sufficient ground* (*zureichender Grund*) in the sense of a 'sufficient basis or foundation.' 'Sufficient reason' refers more to the inquiring intellect and accounts for the *intelligibility* of a being, while 'sufficient ground' refers more to the reality of a being and accounts for its *existence*. Since, however, thought (intelligibility) follows being (nature, essence) and since only a being can have existence, the different expressions used in the formulation of the principle amount to the same thing.

The Principle of Sufficient (Determining) Reason is a necessary corollary from the Principles of Identity and Contradiction. To *deny* or *doubt* the validity of the Principle of Sufficient Reason would inevitably lead to the *absurdity* of denying or doubting the validity of the Principles of Identity and Contradiction, because it is *immediately derived* from these two self-evident principles.

'Being is being' and 'non-being is non-being' (Principle of Identity). It is impossible for a thing 'to be' and 'not to be' something at the same time under the same respect (Principle of Contradiction). Now, if a thing has not a sufficient (determining) reason for its being and existence, it both 'is' and 'is not' at the same time under the same respect. That is impossible and therefore absurd. Consider the following.

Everything, in so far as it is a 'being,' has reality. Whatever reality a 'being' has, it must have either of and by *itself* or from and by *another* being; in the first case it has the *sufficient reason* for its reality in itself, and in the second case it has it in the other. And if it has no reality, it is no 'being' at all, and this is due to the fact that it has not received reality either of itself or from another being; in both cases it is a 'non-being' because it has *no sufficient reason* for its reality. If it could

---

[2] *Théodicée*, Part I, n. 44.

have reality nonetheless, it would have to receive it from 'nothing.' But 'nothing' has no reality itself and can, therefore, never give reality to anything. Consequently, were such a reality without a sufficient reason for its being and existence, it would both 'be' and 'not be' at the same time under the same respect: it would 'be,' because that is the supposition; and it would also 'not be,' because, having no sufficient reason to account for its reality except 'nothing,' it could receive only that which 'nothing' could give, which is precisely nothing. But 'to be' and 'not to be' at the same time under the same respect is a violation of the Principle of Contradiction; and that is an absurdity. Hence, if a being has reality, it must have it either of itself or from another, *i.e.,* it must have *a sufficient reason for its being and existence.*

Since everything must have a sufficient reason for its 'being,' there must be a determining reason why a thing is what it is. This principle applies to everything present in the being — nature, properties, and qualifications. Hence, there must be a sufficient reason which explains why a man is a 'man,' why he is 'rational' (soul) and 'material' (body), why he is 'white' or 'married' or 'healthy' or 'sad.' Similarly, there must be a sufficient reason which explains why an electron is an electron and a proton a proton, why a circle is a circle and a triangle a triangle, why a horse is a horse and a rose a rose, and so forth. *We* may not always be able to assign the proximate reason for the being and existence of things, but we do know this: 'Every being has a sufficient, determining reason, either in itself or in another being, for the reality and existence which it possesses.'

The Principle of Causality

The *Principle of Causality* states: 'Whatever happens or becomes must have a cause for its happening or becoming.' The words 'whatever happens' mean 'whatever begins to be or to exist'; and the word 'becomes' means 'whatever passes from potentiality to actuality,' as when a sitting person gets up and starts to run. The word 'cause' here signifies an 'efficient cause,' and it is defined as a being which positively influences the production of something by its action. Hence, the Principle of Causality might also be formulated as follows: *Whatever passes from a state of non-existence into a state of existence must have an efficient cause for its existence.*

This latter formulation includes every kind of real production, whether absolute or relative. A real production is *absolute,* if the 'total being' passes from non-existence to existence without being produced out of the potentiality of pre-existing matter; this is 'creation.' It is *relative,* if the being is produced out of the potentiality of pre-existing matter, or if it passes from one kind of being into another kind of being; this is 'change.' In *substantial change* one substance passes over into another kind of substance, as when dead matter is assimilated and becomes living matter in a living body, for example, in an oak tree. In *accidental change* the substance remains unchanged in the process but acquires some new property or attribute, as when a person becomes sad or joyful. In either case the principle demands an *efficient cause* to account for the production of the *new reality which has come into existence.*

The *problem* revolves around realities which are or have been 'existent' but which were previously in a state of non-existence, so that they have ceased to be merely 'possible'; such a reality, whatever it may be, passes from non-existence to existence, and it is this that must be accounted for. The problem, therefore, is: Must every being passing from non-existence to existence, whether absolutely or relatively, be brought to existence *through the active influence of an adequate efficient cause?* The answer is *affirmative.*

By the very fact that a being passes from non-existence to existence, it is assumed and stated that at first it was *non-existent.* In that state it was as such only *possible,* that is to say, 'capable of existence.' In this state of possibility, 'existence' was not present in any form within the possible being; otherwise it would have been existent at the very time it was non-existent, which is impossible because contradictory. If and when this non-existent but possible being passed into a state of existence, it must have *received* existence (because it did not have existence in its own being). Now, there are only three conceivable ways in which this possible being could have received existence: either it received it from 'nothing,' or from 'itself,' or from 'some other being.'

It is impossible that it could have received existence *from 'nothing.'* If this possible being depended on 'nothing' for its existence, it could never receive the perfection of existence and would remain forever merely possible, *i.e.,* non-existent.

It is also impossible that it could have received existence *from 'itself.'* A possible being, from the standpoint of physical actuality, is *nothing;* this lies in the fact that it is only a *possible* being. As a 'possible' being it is as yet in a state of non-existence, and it becomes 'actual' by receiving existence. If it were to give itself existence, it would be necessary that it *produce itself.* A being, however, that does not as yet exist and is actually nothing, cannot act. Hence it cannot produce anything, least of all itself. Consequently, a being which passes from non-existence to existence cannot receive this existence from 'itself.'

The sufficient reason, why a possible being passes from non-existence to existence, is not found in 'nothing,' nor is it found in this possible being 'itself.' Hence, by a process of elimination, it is clear that *'some other existing being'* must give existence to it. To 'give existence,' however, means to *produce it* by the positive influence of *its action.* If it did not exert a 'positive influence of its action,' it would not *do* anything and could not *give* anything; but in that case nothing would happen to the possible being, and the latter would remain in its state of mere possibility, which is non-existence. This other being must, then, be an *existing* being itself and *give existence* to the possible being by means of a *positive productive influence.* But to produce a being, that is, to bring it from non-existence to existence, by the positive influence of its own action, is the definition of an *efficient cause.*

The truth and validity of the Principle of Causality is thus established: 'Whatever passes from non-existence to existence must have an efficient cause for its existence.'

Basic Concepts and First Principles

This analysis of the First Principles, from the Principle of Identity to the Principle of Contradiction, enables us to fix the meaning of certain basic ideas which will play an important part in subsequent discussions.

There is the idea of the *impossible*. Something is said to be 'impossible' when its concept involves a contradiction, so that it *cannot exist* under any conditions and circumstances. A 'square circle,' for example, is contradictory in its very idea, and as such it has never existed and can never exist. Then, there is the idea of the *possible* being. Something is 'possible' when it *does not exist* but is capable of existence, so that it *can exist*. A 'mountain of gold' does not exist and probably never will exist; but it is capable of existence and therefore is 'possible.' When a 'possible' being receives existence, it is no longer merely possible but 'actual.' Even as an 'actual' being, however, its existence is a 'received' or 'produced' existence, and such a being is called *contingent;* a 'contingent' being is one which *exists* but *need not exist*. Plutonium, for instance, now exists; but a few years ago it did not exist, and the time may come again when it will no longer exist. Finally, there is the *necessary* being. A being is said to be 'necessary,' when it actually *exists* and also *must exist*. A 'necessary' being has always existed in the past, exists now in the present, and will always exist in the future, because existence is a constitutive part of its nature or essence.

According to the Principle of Causality, then, neither the 'impossible' being nor the 'necessary' being can ever be the *effect* of an efficient cause. The 'impossible' is absolute nothingness, so that there is no essence to receive existence. The 'necessary' being cannot receive existence, because it must always exist; what already 'is' cannot be produced.

By contrast, a 'contingent' being and a 'possible' being have a reality in which existence is not a constitutive part (not a part of the constitution) of their nature or essence, so that their existence, if and when it happens, must be produced by an efficient cause.

Empiricism

John Locke opposed Descartes's theory that all knowledge of man is derived from innate ideas. He contended that knowledge comes solely from *experience*. But he followed Descartes when he maintained that the 'object' of man's knowledge is restricted to internal conscious states, to 'ideas.' Locke's views gave rise to empiricism.

Strict *empiricists,* like Hume, admit nothing but sense-knowledge of phenomena. For them there is no such thing as a supra-sensible, or intellectual, knowledge. 'Ideas' are but refined sense-images; consciousness is a 'bundle' or 'stream' of perceptions. Since all phenomena are but passing, changing realities, there can be no permanent and necessary knowledge in any form. Their theory of sensism precludes all knowledge which would possess a universal and necessary character. Yet it cannot be denied that we consider the *First Principles to be necessarily and absolutely true.* How account for this fact?

Hume finds their origin and explanation in the *association* of our ideas. Certain ideas or images are always experienced as occurring together; certain phenomena always appear in a regular sequence of time or in a definite contiguity in space. Thereupon we uniformly and continuously 'associate' these things in our mind. This is done in virtue of the *law of association* inherent in the mind itself, because the mind is so constituted; and this is a subjective law with a purely subjective effect. Consequently, the 'necessity' of the First Principles is not due to the reality represented in these principles, but solely to the *associative force* existing in the mind. It is a *subjective* and *psychological,* not an objective and ontological, necessity. The mind does not judge these First Principles to be necessarily true because it *sees* that they cannot be otherwise; it *cannot see* them to be otherwise because the mind in its present constitution must judge them to be true. There is nothing *intrinsically* impossible in an object having contradictory properties or in a thing coming into existence without a cause.

Here is the *argument* Hume[3] uses in order to show that the transition from non-existence to existence does not necessarily involve a 'cause.' "The separation . . . of the idea of cause from that of beginning of existence is plainly possible for the imagination; and consequently the actual separation of these objects is so far possible that it implies no contradiction or absurdity; and is therefore incapable of being refuted by any reasoning from mere ideas; without which 'tis impossible to demonstrate the necessity of a cause. . . . As all distinct ideas are separable from each other, and as the ideas of cause and effect are evidently distinct, 'twill be easy for us to conceive any object non-existent this moment and existent the next, without conjoining to it the distinct idea of a cause or productive principle."

In analyzing this argument, one must remember that all knowledge, according to Hume, is *sense-knowledge;* and when he speaks of 'ideas,' he means the vague copies of sense-impressions which exist in the *imagination.* What Hume means to say, therefore, is this: We can *imagine* something as non-existent one moment, and we can *imagine* it as existent the next moment; consequently, we can *imagine* it as coming into existence without a producing cause; and hence a productive cause is not necessary. To put it concretely: We can imagine a man as non-existent one moment and then as existent the next moment; consequently, parents and any other kind of cause are not necessary to bring this man into existence.

Imagination, and *not reason,* thus furnishes the ultimate criterion of what is real and not real, possible and not possible. Certainly, one can *imagine* something coming into existence without *imagining* its cause. That, however, does not prove that something can *actually* come into existence without a cause; it merely means that I have 'imagined' an effect with-

---

[3] Sir Lewis A. Selby-Bigge, ed., *Treatise of Human Nature* (New York: Oxford University Press), p. 79.

out 'imagining' its cause, but *reason* alone can tell me whether something can really come into existence as I 'imagine' it.

According to Hume,[4] J. S. Mill,[5] and empiricists generally (and this includes many present-day scientists), the Principle of Causality is but a mental expression of 'invariable sequence': because we observe things following each other invariably in time, we are compelled by the law of association to judge that the preceding object produces (cause) the one following (effect). And so it is with all First Principles. If we think that these principles *must* be true for all times and in all places and for all minds, we are harboring an illusion; for other minds, in other places, at other times, and under other conditions, the First Principles may not be true at all.

Empiricism fails to give an adequate account of the logical necessity existing in our judgments as expressed in the First Principles. If the theory were correct, we should perforce experience the same psychological necessity of judgment *in every case* where we observe a uniform and constant association of objects or ideas in our consciousness. This, however, patently is not the case. For instance, day follows night in an invariable sequence; however, nobody thinks that night is the 'cause' of day. Cars follow each other in invariable sequence on the highway on a Sunday afternoon, yet no one applies the Principle of Cause and Effect to them. Every time we lift our eyelids during the day, we invariably see; nevertheless, we do not judge that the lifting of the eyelids 'causes' our actual 'seeing.' On the other hand, we feel the necessity of applying the Principle of Causality in *isolated cases* that happen seldom and even only once. When a car, for example, suddenly ceases to run, we immediately look for the 'cause.' When a train leaves the track, we do not need a frequent repetition of the occurrence to establish an association of perceptions; we know that there must have been a 'cause' of the derailment, even if this was the first derailment that ever

---

[4] *An Enquiry Concerning Human Understanding,* Section VII, Part I, § 50, 52. — See also Section VII, Part II.

[5] *System of Logic,* III, 5, § 2.

happened. And so with a thousand and one other solitary occurrences. Hence, the necessity inherent in our judgment expressing the Principle of Causality (and the same line of reasoning applies to all First Principles) is not derived from the subjective influence of the association of our ideas.

The very *arguments* the empiricists use to prove the truth of their theory are not based on 'experience' but on *reasoning*. These arguments are in no way 'objects of experience' derived from sense-perception; they go far beyond the reaction of the senses. The very reasons empiricists give to impugn the validity and necessity of the First Principles *presuppose* the Principles of Contradiction and Sufficient Reason; only on the supposition that the First Principles are valid have these reasons any semblance of validity. Such a procedure, however, is illogical and inconsistent. Any theory which implicitly affirms what it explicitly denies and attempts to disprove must be false, or knowledge is impossible. Hume realized this eventually and became a skeptic.

The fact is, as we stated above, that our *intellect has an intuitive insight* into the objective validity and necessity of the First Principles.

Idealistic Monism

Georg Hegel (1770–1831) was an idealistic monist. 'Monism' is the doctrine which holds that there is but one fundamental reality or being. If this reality is matter, monism is 'materialistic'; if it is idea, it is 'idealistic.' Hegel, too, followed Descartes's basic tenet that the mind is restricted to ideas. From this, Hegel concluded that all reality is the *Absolute Idea*. Through a process of logical development the Absolute Idea becomes matter (nature) and spirit (mind).

Hegel begins by identifying all reality with the Absolute Idea of *Being*. In order to explain its development, he sacrifices the validity of the Principles of Identity, Contradiction, and Excluded Middle. Consider his words,[6] in which he denies

---

[6] *Logic,* tr. by W. Wallace (New York: Clarendon Press [Oxford University Press], 1892), Vol. 2, §§ 87, 88, 89, pp. 162, 163, 167, 169.

the distinction between 'being' and 'nothing.' "The distinction between Being and Nought is, in the first place, only implicit, and not yet actually made: they only *ought* to be distinguished. A distinction, of course, implies two things, and that one of them possesses an attribute which is not found in the other. Being, however, is an absolute absence of attributes, and so is Nought. Hence, the distinction between the two is only meant to be; it is a nominal distinction, which is at the same time no distinction. In all other cases of difference there is some common point which comprehends both things. Suppose, e.g., we speak of two different species: the genus forms a common ground for both. But in the case of mere Being and Nothing, distinction is without a bottom to stand upon: hence, there can be no distinction, both determinations being the same bottomlessness. . . . Nothing, if it is thus immediate and equal to itself, is also conversely the same as Being is. . . . In Being we have Nothing, and in Nothing Being. . . . In Becoming the Being which is one with Nothing, and the Nothing which is one with Being, are only vanishing factors; they are and they are not." Contradiction thus lies in the very heart of Being and Idea and makes the 'becoming' or development of the Absolute possible.

Hegel identifies 'being' and 'nought' because, as he contends, "Being is an absolute absence of attributes, and so is Nought." Since there is "no distinction" between the two, both are identical. In this Hegel was guilty of a gross misconception. *Being,* as we have pointed out, always possesses the attribute of a *relation to existence* inasmuch as it 'exists' (actual being) or at least 'can exist' (possible being). *Nought* (absolute nothing) has *no relation to existence* and as a consequence 'never exists' and 'cannot exist.' 'Being' thus has a *positive* content; 'nought' is purely *negative* in content, since it represents the negation of all being. From this it should be clear that the concept of 'being' is not empty of all content and as such indistinguishable from 'nought,' as Hegel maintained. Hence, Hegel bases his whole system of idealistic monism on this initial *misconception.*

Besides, when Hegel formulates his arguments, he always (though inconsistently) *implies* that the First Principles are valid. The very fact that he identifies 'being' and 'nought' because of their supposed indeterminateness and emptiness really *presupposes* the validity of the Principles of Identity and Contradiction. By denying, therefore, the Principle of Contradiction and making contradiction itself the basis of all 'becoming,' he not only cuts the ground from under his own system but destroys the foundation of all knowledge. After all, *thought* and *reality* are not the same, but the First Principles apply with equal force to both because the laws of thought are taken from the laws of reality.

Pragmatism

Pragmatism is a repudiation of absolutism and idealism and a return to empiricism. It originated with Charles S. Peirce in 1878, and its chief exponents are William James, F. C. S. Schiller, and John Dewey. It is more a *method* than a philosophical system in the strict sense of the word. Still, inasmuch as pragmatism professes certain fundamental principles, it can be classed among the philosophies.

According to pragmatists, truth is nothing permanent, necessary, universal, objective, absolute; it is relative, transient, particular, subjective, personal. Truth is 'made' by means of hypothesis and experiment, so that something is 'true' if it satisfies some human need or interest and 'false' if it does not. Good or bad *consequences* are all that count. If an idea, judgment, assumption, axiom, postulate, theory, or system of thought 'works' and satisfies our mental or emotional or social needs, it is, *so far and so long as it does this,* valuable and *true*. Truth is not an inherent property of ideas or judgments: they *become true* and are *made true* by events. Ideas, judgments, and inferences possess only a 'functional' and 'provisional' character; among such judgments are the *First Principles*. Dewey[7] denies that we have an "immediate knowledge" of

---

[7] *Logic: The Theory of Inquiry* (New York: H. Holt & Co., 1938), Chap. VIII.

their truth, and Schiller[8] ridicules the attitude of accepting the truth of certain propositions because we "feel it in our bones." Consequently, a conviction may be true at one stage of development and false at a different stage; it may be true for one class of people and false for another, depending on the intellectual and cultural conditions prevailing at a particular time and in a particular locality. Truth, therefore, is entirely *subjective.*

One can admit with the pragmatists that in the *field of science* it is necessary to 'verify' a certain opinion by hypothesis and experiment rather than accept a scientific conclusion as 'self-evident.' But when they deny the self-evidence and immediate knowledge of *all truths* whatever, even that of First Principles, they destroy the foundations of the *experimental sciences* together with that of *knowledge in general.* All science is based on the existence of truth and certitude. If contradictories can be true together, if a phenomenon can occur without a cause, and if nature is not uniform in its operation, then every form of experimentation and induction on the part of science is valueless from the start. Some truths must be *self-evident,* because they are 'implied' in every form of inference, whether that inference be deductive or inductive. They are clear to the mind through *intellectual insight,* not because we "feel it in our bones."

And pragmatists are *inconsistent.* They identify 'truth' with 'utility.' Nevertheless, they appeal to the intellect with a great array of arguments, to prove that 'truth' consists in beneficial results; in doing so, they appeal to the *objective evidence* of facts and reasons to establish their case. These arguments, however, have no value except under the supposition that the First Principles are true and valid. Their own attitude and action is their best refutation.

The First Principles are thus seen to be 'necessary' in their truth and validity. They are *not empirical,* as if their truth and

---

[8] *Logic for Use* (New York: Harcourt, Brace, 1930), p. 297.

validity can be discovered only through 'experience.' Rather, they are *analytical,* because an analysis, based on self-evidence and intellectual insight, reveals their necessary character. Once these First Principles are understood, the proofs for God's existence will also be more readily understood.

Summary of Chapter II

Since the *First Principles* govern all reality and thought, their validity must be established.

1. *First Principles.* — Some judgments are 'contingent' in character, and their truth can be discovered only by 'experience.' Other judgments are 'necessary' in character; they are necessarily true and therefore without possibility of change or error. Among these are the *First Principles.* The First Principles are the Principles of Identity, Contradiction, Excluded Middle, Sufficient Reason, and Causality.

2. *The Principle of Identity.* — 'Whatever a thing is, it is'; 'A being is identical with itself.' This principle is grounded on the concept of *being,* namely, something that 'exists' or is 'capable of existence.' The opposite of 'being' is *non-being, absolute nothing,* namely, something that 'neither exists nor is capable of existence.' Since 'being' always contains a positive (actual or possible) relation to existence, while 'absolute non-being' contains no such relation, it is clear that 'being is being' and 'non-being is non-being' (Principle of Identity).

3. *The Principle of Contradiction.* — 'A thing cannot be (something) and yet not be (it) at the same time under the same respect.' A comparison between 'being' and 'non-being' makes it self-evident that the one is not, and cannot be, the other; these two concepts mutually exclude each other with *absolute necessity,* because 'being' and 'non-being' can never be identical.

4. *The Principle of Excluded Middle.* — 'A thing either is or is not (something)'; 'Between two contradictories a middle is excluded.' There is no middle thing possible between 'being' and 'non-being,' between 'is' and 'is not'; they represent a *complete division of all things,* so that everything conceivable must be either the one or the other.

5. *The Principle of Sufficient (Determining) Reason.* — 'A thing must have a sufficient reason for its being and existence.' Whatever reality a 'being' has, it must have either of and by *itself* or from

and by *another* being; in either case it has a 'sufficient' reason to account for its being and existence. If it could have reality without receiving it either from itself or from another being, it would have to receive it from '*nothing*'; but 'nothing' has no reality and can give no reality. Consequently, were this reality without a sufficient reason either in itself or in another, it would both 'be' and 'not be' at the same time under the same respect. Hence, every being must have a *sufficient reason* for its being and existence.

6. *The Principle of Causality.* — 'Whatever passes from a state of non-existence into a state of existence must have an efficient cause for its existence.' It is assumed that a being was at first *non-existent* but *possible.* Such a non-existent being, if it reaches existence, must receive this existence either from 'nothing' or from 'itself' or from some 'other being.' It cannot receive it from '*nothing*,' because 'nothing,' having no existence, cannot give what it does not possess. It cannot receive it from *itself,* because to give existence to itself would mean to 'act' before it exists. Hence, it can receive existence only from *some other being* already in existence; but if the latter did not exert a 'positive influence of its action,' it would 'do' nothing and could not 'give' anything. Consequently, a non-existent being can receive existence only through the 'positive productive influence' of another being. Now, a being which gives existence to another through the positive influence of its action is an *efficient cause.*

7. *Basic Concepts and First Principles.* — The *impossible* is something that 'cannot exist' and therefore cannot be produced. A *possible* being 'does not exist' but 'can exist,' and as such it can be produced. A *contingent* being 'exists' but it 'need not exist'; it is, therefore, a produced being. A *necessary* being actually 'exists' and 'must exist'; since it always has been, it could not have been produced.

8. *Empiricism.* — We judge the First Principles to be necessarily and absolutely true. Hume and the empiricists place the 'necessity' of these principles in the *Law of Association* present in the mind; the principles need not be true in themselves.

This theory is *false.* We feel the necessity of looking for the cause in *isolated* events, when no repeated occurrences happen; in such instances no 'association' can form. Finally, empiricists present arguments not based on 'experience' but on 'intellectual reasoning,' and their reasons *presuppose* the validity of the Principles of Contradiction and Sufficient Reason.

9. *Idealistic Monism.* — Hegel identifies *Being* and *Nought* because, as he claims, "Being is an absolute absence of attributes" and therefore identical with 'Nought.'

'Being,' however, always possesses the attribute of a *relation to existence* (actual or possible being), while 'Nought' (absolute nothing) has *no relation to existence* and as a consequence never exists and cannot exist. Although Hegel, in his arguments, denies the Principles of Identity and Contradiction, his arguments (inconsistently, of course) *presuppose* their validity.

10. *Pragmatism.* — According to the pragmatists, truth is *subjective* and *provisional;* a principle is 'made true' and 'becomes true' by its consequences. Even the First Principles are not necessarily true in themselves.

Pragmatism *destroys* the foundation of *all knowledge and science,* if the Principles of Identity and Contradiction have no objective value. Pragmatists are also *inconsistent* in appealing to the *objective evidence* of facts and reasons to establish their case.

Readings

Garrigou-Lagrange, R., *God: His Existence and Nature,* Vol. I, Part I, Chap. II. — Renard, Henri, *The Philosophy of God,* Chap. I, Qq. 1 and 2. — Smith, Gerard, *Natural Theology,* Part I. — Driscoll, John T., *God,* Chap. I. — Aveling, Francis, *The God of Philosophy,* Chap. II.

CHAPTER III

THE POSSIBILITY OF PROOF

THE problem of God's existence is vitally important. The history of human thought shows that a wrong approach either leads to serious error or ends in a blind alley.

The validity of the First Principles having been established as rationally certain, the next step will be to inquire as to the *proper method* which must be employed in proving God's existence, provided His existence can be proved at all. Some thinkers claim that man cannot prove that God exists; others, that His existence is intuitively clear to man's mind, so that a rational proof is unnecessary. Even among those who admit that God's existence can and must be proved to the satisfaction of reason, there is a difference of view as to the proper method to be used in establishing the proof. The matter of God's existence or non-existence is too grave to be left open to serious doubt concerning the proper approach to the problem.

It will be necessary, therefore, to remove some misconceptions, before a definite attempt is made to formulate the arguments for God's existence. Some of these misconceptions result from the 'scientific attitude' so prevalent in our day; others are more 'philosophic' in nature. In either case the ground must be cleared.

Scientific Explanation

Scientists frequently state that they are concerned only with a description of *facts,* because that alone is in accord with the 'scientific temper' and the 'scientific attitude.' Science, they say, must be 'exact,' and only if science deals with facts will it be an *exact science*.

Accuracy is a necessity for any science worthy of the name. When, therefore, scientists seek to attain accuracy or 'exactness' in their findings, their endeavor is entirely praiseworthy. Hence, they seek to eliminate all prejudices and unwarranted presuppositions in their research. This, too, is praiseworthy.

However, *facts alone are not a science.* They are but the raw materials with which scientists work in order to construct a science. More is needed than facts alone. Facts must be 'correlated' and 'explained' before one can speak of having a 'science.' Relevant facts must be arranged in a definite order, and an explanation given of the operation of things, before one can speak of 'scientific knowledge.' The characteristic of science is *law,* and law is the result of the proper interpretation and explanation of facts in their relations to one another.

No real scientist is ever satisfied with a mere 'description' of facts, be these facts 'things' or 'events.' Scientists always seek to *explain why* things are as they are and events happen as they do. That is the whole purpose of *hypothesis* and its *verification* by observation and experiment. Unless they sought to find an answer to the 'How?' and 'Why?' of things and events, there would be no rhyme or reason for formulating a hypothesis and proceeding to prove or disprove its truth. True to the preconceived tenet of strict empiricism, they may speak of an 'invariable sequence of antecedents and consequents'; but in reality they look for the *causes* which will explain them as *effects.*

A cursory perusal of any scientific article or book will prove that scientists attempt to give the *causal explanation* of things and events, not merely their factual or 'phenomenal' appearance and occurrence. Most astronomers, when they discuss the 'red shift' in stellar spectra, the occurrence of a 'nova' in the heavens, the movements of stars and galaxies, and other matters, almost invariably seek to give a rational 'explanation' of the phenomena. From the data as perceived and recorded, physicists and chemists proceed to 'infer' the existence and structure of atoms, molecules, and subelemental particles, although no one has ever actually perceived such realities. How correct their 'deductions' can be was shown by the terrific explosion of the atom bomb. Medical scientists are not content with a description of the symptoms of diseases and abnormalities, but seek to determine their 'causes' so as to remove them by surgery or medication. All scientists act in this manner, because only through inference from perceived data can their science make substantial progress; and no one will deny that substantial progress in scientific knowledge has been made.

Everyone is aware, of course, that much of the so-called 'scientific knowledge' is only approximation, resting on the foundation of hypotheses and theories which still are far from complete verification. On the other hand, many hypotheses and theories have been verified in the course of time and many more will be verified in the future. The point of the whole matter is this: *inferences are a process of reasoning*. Reason, therefore, has a legitimate place in the experimental sciences, although reasoning goes beyond the bounds of factual description. After the empirical facts are all in and have been accurately recorded, science must (and actually does) attempt to find the *causal connections* which 'explain' the phenomena. Man being rational, he must use whatever powers he has, including his reason, to arrive at a complete *explanation* of things and events through their *causes*.

Scientists feel satisfied with their efforts, if they succeed in specifying the 'proximate' causes of things and events present in the physical world, and they have a perfect right to restrict their field of research in this manner. But if they are justified in the restriction of their reasoning powers for the discovery of truth, they are not justified in the *restriction of reason itself*. Since reason is an adequate instrument of true knowledge in the discovery and assignment of 'proximate' causes, why should reason not be capable of penetrating farther and of discovering the *ultimate cause or causes* of the physical world? The proper test of a power is in its actual accomplishment. If reason fails in its endeavor to determine the ultimate cause or causes of the universe, well and good; but it should not be prejudged to be incapable of doing so. After all, human reason is the same, whether it be used in the discussions of physical science or of philosophy. Philosophic knowledge is scientific knowledge, too, even though it essays to go deeper than physical science. So long as philosophy argues from the same physical world and uses the same First Principles as ordinary science does, the competency of reason must be accepted in both. To assume its competency in the natural sciences and deny its competency in philosophical science is illogical and inconsistent. Such an attitude, if accepted in principle and carried out to its inevitable consequences, would undermine the foundations of the natural sciences and lead to *universal skepticism*.

Hence, the competency of human reason in its endeavor to prove God's existence as the rational explanation of the physical world must be accepted in principle.

Deism and Agnosticism

Deism was a quasi-philosophic movement, promoted mainly by a group of thinkers in England who attacked revealed religion. *Lord Herbert of Cherbury* (1581–1648) had already defended deism, but it took the empiricism of John Locke to give it a strong impetus. Deism had no uniform system of doctrines. Chiefly, it defended a *universal natural religion*. Deists conceded that it could be proved on rational grounds that God exists and is the Creator. Many deists, however, contended that God, after creating the world, took no interest in mundane affairs. Chief among the advocates of deism were Charles Blount (1654–1693), John Toland (1670–1722), Matthew Tindal (1657–1733), and Henry St. John, Viscount Bolingbroke (1678–1751). The movement eventually gave way to outright atheism and agnosticism.

Without passing judgment on the anti-revelationist part of deism, but merely viewing it from the standpoint of theodicy (natural theology), deism must be criticized as being *too narrow and restrictive*. It is inconsistent to admit that God's existence can be proved on rational grounds and then stop short. The deists, like the theists, prove God's existence from the character of the physical world; but the physical world may reveal many things about God besides His existence, such as divine concurrence, divine providence, and the possibility of revelation. To deny their possibility or actuality is therefore totally unwarranted.

Agnosticism has a number of meanings. Literally, it means 'lack of knowledge.' However, Thomas Huxley (1825–1895) coined the word in 1869 to mean the attitude of a person who advocated the inability of the mind to know the reality represented by man's ultimate scientific, philosophic, and religious ideas. *Modern agnosticism* is a philosophic theory which affirms the constitutional inability of the human mind to know reality, so that all investigation pertains merely to the 'phenomenal.' Behind the phenomena, most agnostics assert, is an *absolute reality* of some sort, but this reality is intrinsically *unknowable*. Such is the view of Immanuel Kant (1724–1804), Sir William Hamilton (1788–1856), Henry L. Mansel (1820–1871), and Herbert Spencer (1820–1903).

Kant divided the objects of knowledge into two general classes, 'phenomena' (appearances) and 'things-in-themselves'; the former are all we know, the latter are inaccessibly hidden behind the phenomena and are absolutely unknowable. God is, therefore, unknowable, so far as human reason is concerned. *Hamilton* maintained that "all knowledge is relative"; of existence, absolutely and in itself, man can know nothing. Man cannot, therefore, acquire any real knowledge of God, because God is the Absolute, the Unconditioned, the Infinite; man's reasonings in this respect are "mere negations of thought." *Mansel* followed Hamilton's relativism, asserting that man cannot form a positive concept of God, because man is unable to obtain an 'exhaustive' concept of God in all its 'positive' contents. While Hamilton and Mansel denied man's ability to know God on rational grounds, both affirmed that faith and revelation can impart true knowledge of God and His nature. *Spencer,* too, was a relativist. Since the 'relative' always presupposes the 'absolute' as its correlative, Spencer postulated the existence of Absolute Reality; however, neither knowledge nor belief can give man any insight into the nature of this reality, because all ideas are merely 'symbolic' of reality.

Nevertheless, he often speaks of the Unknowable as the "Power manifesting itself in phenomena."

Agnosticism rests on the fallacious basis of Hume's *unwarranted empiricism*. True, if the ideas of reality are mere constructions of the mind, so that man's mind is the sole source of all knowledge, then man's efforts to know the physical world are inextricably enmeshed in the net of *subjectivism*. But if man can perceive the external world, then his reason must be able to pierce the appearances of things; in that case he can also know something of their nature and activity, and from their nature and activity draw rational inferences as to the nature and activity of their cause, because *every effect manifests the nature and activity of its cause* in some manner. Reason may not be able to know everything about God, but it should be able to know something, no matter how imperfectly. 'Imperfect' knowledge is not the same as 'indefinite' or purely 'negative' knowledge; though not complete, imperfect knowledge would still be true knowledge. When agnostics acknowledge that God (or the Absolute) 'exists,' or when they speak of God (or the Absolute) as the 'Unconditioned' and the 'Power manifesting itself in phenomena,' they express ideas which reveal *some* knowledge of the supposed 'Unknowable'; and thereby, on their own principles, they involve themselves in a contradiction.

Fideism and Traditionalism

Fideism and *traditionalism* are theories or attitudes which hold that human reason is incapable, of its own native ability, of reaching certitude regarding any truth or at least regarding truths of the philosophical and religious order; they affirm that knowledge of truth consists in an act of *faith* (hence 'fideism'), and the supreme criterion of certitude is the authority of revelation as given to man through *tradition* (hence 'traditionalism'). Like agnosticism in general, fideism and traditionalism are based on a conviction of the natural impotence of human reason in the discovery of truths referring to God's existence and nature. In order to combat agnosticism and empiricism, fideists and traditionalists sought the fundamental source of all knowledge of God in 'faith' and 'tradition,' rather than in the rational inferences of the human mind.

Among the chief exponents of fideism and traditionalism are Louis G. de Bonald (1754–1840), Félicité R. de Lamennais (1782–1854), L. Bautain (1795–1867), A Bonnetty (1798–1879), G. Ventura (1792–1861), and C. Ubaghs (1800–1875). They differed in details, but their fundamental distrust of reason was the same, and so also was their demand that an act of faith in God's revelation precede any rational discussion on His existence and nature.

It does not need much reflection to see that *faith cannot precede reason* as a source and criterion of truth in philosophical and religious matters. Revelation of any kind and faith in its pronouncements can never engender conviction in the mind unless it is first clear that God exists and that He has revealed Himself. Hence, the reasonableness and validity of revelation and the subsequent act of faith must first be established; otherwise their acceptance is a blind assent. Consequently, if our assent is to be reasonable and not blind, reason must precede faith. Only if man can prove God's existence on rational grounds, will it be possible for him to know whether revelation could have occurred at all. To assume the impotence of reason as the starting-point would involve *universal skepticism.*

Ontologism

Ontologism holds that *God* and *Divine Ideas* are the first object of our intelligence and the intuition of God the first act of our intellectual knowledge. Ontologism stems directly from Descartes's excessive dualism, in so far as he maintained that man consists of two separate substances, namely, the body as inert extension and the soul as the exclusive source of all knowledge.

N. Malebranche (1638–1715) is commonly held to be an ontologist. He maintained that man envisions all things by means of a direct intuition of God's ideas. Just as bodies have their location in space, so our ideas have their location in God. Our ideas, he says, are the divine essence itself, inasmuch as God's essence is the model of all things. It follows from this that God is always present to our intelligence and manifests to our minds the nature and existence of all we know. *V. Gioberti* (1801–1852) also maintained that our first intellectual perception is an intuition of God as creating existences. *A. Rosmini* (1797–1855) held the view that man has a direct intuition of Being in its supreme ideality, and this innate concept or intuition makes the soul intelligent. When this Ideal Being is analyzed, it is seen to pertain to God.

The doctrine of ontologism may seem strange. Two principal reasons account for it. According to these thinkers, the presence of the idea of the 'infinite' in man's mind cannot have its origin in finite beings, because the finite does not contain the infinite; the eternity, universality, and necessity which characterize many judgments, especially the First Principles, cannot be derived from finite reality (such a reality is temporal, particular, and contingent) but must originate in the mind from the Eternal, Universal, and Necessary Being or God.

In answer to the ontologists it must be stated that man has *no experience* of a direct intuition of God; if man had such an experience, he would have to be *conscious* of it at all times. Such an intuition of God would make all *doubt* or *error* concerning God's existence and nature utterly impossible; yet doubt and error in this respect can and do exist. If man knew all things in the ideas of God, man's knowledge would always be *infallibly true,* because God Himself is infinite truth. As for the reasons advanced by ontologists in defense of their position, they are based on a misconception. It is true that man has an idea of the 'infinite,' but the very word shows that it is derived from the finite ('in-finite') by removing the limitation of finiteness; hence, it must be obtained by a process of abstraction from finite beings. It is also true that our ideas and judgments frequently possess the characteristics of eternity, universality, and necessity. However, in God these attributes belong to His nature and being, while in our ideas and judgments these characteristics refer merely to their 'application to things' as a result of abstraction. Hence, these characteristics are essentially *dissimilar* to the attributes of God.

Religious Experience

Many persons appeal to *religious experience* as proof that God really exists. This experience may be either intellectual or emotional in character, and it is supposed to be 'non-inferential.' *Modernism,* for example, claims that man has a *vital experience* of God dwelling and working in him; God is present in man through 'vital immanence,' in consequence of which man is emotionally conscious of God's presence. Experience of this sort occupies considerable space in much of the religious literature of the past and present. It is claimed that many devout persons during prayer or meditation experience the presence of God in a realistic way; this is especially true in emotional crises which lead to a 'conversion.' In a similar manner, the religious experiences of 'mystics' are adduced as evidence for God's existence.

While it would be wrong to minimize the importance of religious experience in the life of individuals, its *value as evidence* is entirely too *subjective* to convince those who are not already convinced. The experience itself is incommunicable and can hardly be repeated at will. What is required is evidence of such a character that every honest inquirer can obtain it. Man being rational by nature, the evidence must be directed to his 'reason' and not merely to his emotions and intuitions. Such knowledge, therefore, must be obtained by a *process of reasoning,* by means of *inferences.* The ordinary person's inferences are often informal and spontaneous, the result of his native ability to reason; but if these inferences are valid, it should be possible to analyze them according to the laws and rules of logic, so that their validity can be tested. The philosopher, therefore, has the right to subject the ordinary person's conviction to a thorough analysis and to formulate arguments which, though more difficult to grasp, will survive the critique of reason and be placed upon a more solid foundation.

No one is as blind as he who closes his eyes and refuses to see. No logical proofs will ever be such that one is absolutely compelled to accept them. All that can be expected of any proofs for God's existence and nature is that they be logically unassailable and as such tend to bring the honest, truth-seeking mind to conviction. Not all proofs advanced possess logical unassailability; we have already pointed out some improper approaches in the foregoing sections. Another improper approach is exemplified in the 'ontological argument.'

The Ontological Proof

The ontological argument is famous in the annals of philosophy. It was first formulated by *St. Anselm* (1033–1109). He presented the argument in two slightly varying wordings,[1] but the fundamental thought is the same.

St. Anselm's proof for God's existence runs as follows. By the term 'God,' we understand the being than which nothing greater can be thought. But a being which not only exists in the mind as an object of thought, as possible, but which has also actual existence outside the mind, is greater than a being which exists in the mind only. Hence, if God did not exist actually outside the mind, He would not be that than which nothing greater can be thought. Consequently, God exists actually outside the mind, as a reality, and not merely in the mind.

The argument was neither approved nor disapproved by St. Albert the Great; it was rejected by St. Thomas Aquinas; Duns Scotus considered it valid and used it. Descartes and Leibnitz were convinced of its validity and formulated similar arguments.

The ontological argument of St. Anselm must be rejected as an *illegitimate passage from the logical order of thought to the real order of things*. All one can conclude from the argument is this: *If* an infinitely perfect Being exists, it must have the reason for its existence in itself, and consequently it

---

[1] *Proslogium*, Chaps. 2 and 3.

must exist necessarily. Hence, if one would *think* of this Infinite Being as 'real' and would not also think of it as existing of its own power and essence, one would certainly think something contradictory. But I can *think* of the Infinite Being as existing without, however, knowing whether it actually *does* exist. Whether the 'if' of the premise is verified or not is something that cannot be known from the idea alone. All the argument shows is that the idea of existence must be included *within the concept of God as such.* One must *think* the Infinite Being to have real existence, if one wants to *think* of an Infinite Being at all. But that does not *prove* the real existence of an Infinite Being, because it does not prove that a 'thing' corresponds to the 'idea' in the mind.

St. Thomas Aquinas rejects the ontological argument of St. Anselm in the following words.[2]

"Nor does it follow, as the first argument alleged, that as soon as the meaning of the word *God* is understood, it is known that God is. First, because it is not known to all, even to those who grant that there is a God, that God is that thing than which no greater can be thought of, since many of the ancients asserted that this world is God. Nor can any such conclusion be gathered from the significations which Damascene (D. Ia. I, 2.) assigns to the word *God.* Secondly because, granted that everyone understands this word *God* to signify something than which a greater cannot be thought of, it does not follow that something than which a greater cannot be thought of exists in reality. For we must needs allege a thing in the same way as we allege the signification of its name. Now from the fact that we conceive mentally that which the word *God* is intended to convey, it does not follow that God is otherwise than in the mind. And thence it does not follow that there exists in reality something than which a greater cannot be thought of. Hence this is no argument against those who assert that there is no God, since whatever be granted to exist, whether in reality or in the mind, there is nothing to

2 St. Thomas Aquinas, *Summa Contra Gentiles,* tr. by the English Dominican Fathers (New York: Benziger Bros., 1925), Bk. I, Chap. XI.

prevent a person from thinking of something greater, unless he grants that there is in reality something than which a greater cannot be thought of." Briefly, the argument of St. Thomas can be summed up as follows: The mere fact that I form an idea of a thing, and then express it in a name, does not prove that the thing, corresponding to this idea and name, actually exists; the actual existence must be proved through some other source.

Descartes proved the existence of God by the argument from effect to cause; but he also used the ontological argument, though the formulation is different from that of St. Anselm. Here is the argument:

Whoever says that something is contained in the nature or concept of a thing, thereby affirms that this something belongs in truth to that thing, is true of it. But now, the necessary existence of God is contained in the idea of God. Hence, it is true to say of God that necessary existence is in Him, in other words, that He exists.

The point of Descartes's argument lies in the phrase that we must affirm the existence of God as 'true,' that existence belongs 'in truth' to Him. This is an *equivocation*. Descartes gives the impression that 'true' and 'in truth' mean the same as 'real.' But this *need not* be so. Something can be 'true' in the logical or the real order or in both. According to Descartes's first premise, the expression 'true' is used of *concepts;* consequently, the existence of God in the 'concept' of God must assuredly be maintained. But whether this also pertains to the 'real' order of things is precisely the point in question. He slips unconsciously from the ideal to the real order, because the *conceptual* truth of the Infinite and His existence remains unshaken, even if we do not consider God to be actually existent. Only then would one be wrong in his concept of God, if one would 'know' Him to exist and then deny the necessity of His existence. But just this knowledge of God's existence is not allowed to be presupposed, but must be *proved*.

Leibnitz also used a variation of the ontological argument to prove God's existence. His argument assumes the following form:

It is possible for God to exist, since that does not involve a contradiction. But if God is possible, He must exist, for a God who is merely possible is not that which is understood by 'God.' Hence, God really exists.

Leibnitz, like St. Anselm and Descartes, is also guilty of an illegitimate passage from the ideal order to the real order. Certainly, if one *thinks* God to be the 'Infinite' and at the same time 'possible to exist,' then, in order to maintain His infinity, one would be compelled to affirm His real existence *in thought,* since a God who is merely considered as 'possible' is not as perfect as one who is considered as 'real.' In *thought,* therefore, one would have to say that the Infinite is really existent. That, however, would not yet prove that God actually exists in the *reality of things.* Hence, we have here an arbitrary and unwarranted passage from the logical order of ideas to the real order of things.

The Necessity of Proof

Many devout persons are of the opinion that it is unnecessary to *prove* God's existence; it is sufficient, they say, to *believe* in Him. One can, of course, 'believe' in God and in His existence on the authority of others, because these others are judged to be worthy of trust. However, belief always presupposes a witness. Belief in God, therefore, must always rely on the testimony of some witness who has 'proof' of God and His existence; otherwise such a belief would be unreasonable and, as such, unworthy of man as a rational being.

We have *no immediate intuition* of God's existence, as each of us knows from his own conscious experience. The testimony of certain individuals to the contrary must be discarded, because their experience is private and subjective and therefore unconvincing for humanity in general. The fact of God's existence is *not self-evident.* If it were self-evident, the fact could neither be denied nor doubted, because then the fact of God's existence would be as clear to man's mind as the truth of the First Principles and of his own existence; that God's existence has been denied or at least doubted by honest and serious thinkers, is obvious from the history of human thought. This lack of self-evidence is also manifested by the fact that philosophers and theologians through the centuries have felt the necessity of proof and formulated arguments to demonstrate the fact of God's existence.

A judgment or proposition is 'self-evident,' if its truth is revealed to the mind by an *analysis of subject and predicate.* When the concept of the predicate is contained in the concept of the subject, or the concept of the subject is contained in the concept of the predicate, then analysis will reveal that they belong together; an understanding of the one concept entails an understanding of the other, and the truth of the judgment or proposition thus becomes patently clear. Thus, if I understand what is meant by 'to be' and by 'not to be' ('being' and 'non-being'), the proposition is self-evidently true that 'A thing cannot both be and not be (something) at the same time under the same respect.' Similarly, if the judgment or proposition 'God exists' were self-evident to man's mind, an analysis of the concept 'God' and of the concept 'exists' should make it clear that 'God exists' in the *real order.* That, however, is not the case, as was seen in the discussion of the 'ontological argument'; the proposition is true in the 'logical order of thought,' but it need not be true in the 'real order of things.' Hence, we must say that the existence of God is not self-evident *to us.*

Now, if man has no immediate intuition of God and His existence and if the truth of God and His existence is not self-evident to man's mind, man can have only a *mediate and discursive knowledge* of God's existence. Hence, God's existence must be *demonstrated,* if man is to have certainty of the fact.

God's Existence Can Be Proved

Since God's existence is not self-evident, the question arises: Can it be *demonstrated?* Can God's existence be known with certainty by means of an *inferential process* of man's reasoning power? We claim that it can be demonstrated to the satisfaction of everyone capable of reasoning and willing to accept the truth.

The denial of the possibility of proving God's existence would be reasonable only on the supposition that God would *not have manifested Himself* in the universe or that man is *incapable of knowing* Him with certainty from the universe. Neither supposition can be upheld.

We have not as yet proved that the physical world needs an efficient cause to account for its existence; nor (if it does need such a cause) have we proved that God is that efficient cause. However, *if* we can prove that the world demands an efficient cause, and *if* God is that cause, then the physical world, as the 'effect' of God's causality, *should reveal something of its 'cause.'* In other words, *if* God is the cause of the universe, He *manifests* His being in some manner in the universe He caused. The reason is plain. Every effect must receive its being from the cause; and the reality of the effect must somehow proceed from the reality of the cause: no one can give what he does not have. It follows that the reality of an effect manifests in some manner the reality of the cause. Hence, if God is the cause of the universe, it is necessary that the universe manifest God in some manner. Absolutely speaking, therefore, it should be possible for man to argue from the existence of the world to the existence of God.

The only other supposition which would make such a proof impossible would be that man were *incapable of knowing God*. This incapability could be either 'constitutional' or 'factual.' It would be *constitutional* if man's reason were *by nature* incapable of rising above the merely phenomenal, so that it could draw no legitimate inferences from the physical world to a higher reality; God would indeed be the Unknown and Unknowable. In that case, however, it would be inconceivable how man could even arrive at the *idea of God*. The fact that man has such an idea shows plainly that he is not constitutionally unable to know God.

The incapability of knowing God would be *factual* if man

were by nature capable of knowing God and proving His existence, but the conditions surrounding man were such that they lend themselves with difficulty to actual *demonstration* of God's existence. The difficulty would be psychological. However, man, in virtue of his reasoning powers, is always making inferences from cause to effect and from effect to cause. Scientists continuously argue to the existence of 'proximate' causes. So why should it not be possible for man to reason to 'ultimate' causes and to the First Cause? Scientists conclude from the activities of bodies to the existence of atoms, electrons, protons, neutrons, and similar realities (although no one has ever actually 'perceived' them), and the legitimacy of their inferences is admitted. The inference from the world to God is of practically the same kind.

Everything will depend on the *nature of the inference,* whether it be convincing or not. People differ in individual talents and education. This psychological difficulty can hardly be overcome entirely. Philosophy naturally addresses itself to those interested and versed in demonstrations which are logically correct and convincing. The philosopher, therefore, must endeavor to arrange his demonstrations in such a manner that they comply with the laws of correct thinking and at the same time are clear. How far he will succeed in this endeavor depends on his ability to present the demonstrations and on the ability of the student to assimilate them. In any case, the arguments themselves must be logically flawless, or they will not be able to convince the logically minded.

Granted, therefore, the constitutional ability of man to reason from effect to cause, it must be considered *possible* for man to reason from the existing world to God.

Kant's Formalism

Immanuel Kant (1724–1804) maintained that man is *constitutionally incapable* of proving God's existence by means of his *reason* through a knowledge of the Principle of Causality. In order to understand Kant's position in this matter, it is necessary to go back to Descartes and Hume.

Descartes, as we know, postulated that all knowledge is derived solely from the mind, not from the things. Hume accepted this postulate, and from it he drew the conclusion that all experience is sense-knowledge and pertains to the particular things experienced by the senses; he drew the further conclusion that all 'principles of thought,' like the Principle of Causality, are invalid because they are not given in perception. Kant accepted Descartes's maxim that all real knowledge is derived solely from the mind, but became alarmed at Hume's extreme empiricism. Hume's view would destroy the *universal* and *necessary* character of all *scientific knowledge* and thus lead to *skepticism*. Kant, therefore, studied the entire field of human knowledge and devised his *formalism* as a safeguard for scientific (theoretical, philosophic) knowledge. His theory was as follows.

Kant made a distinction between *phenomena* (appearances) and *noumena* (things-in-themselves). The 'phenomena' are what we experience in sense-perception. The appearances or phenomena are the result partly of the physical things and partly of the mind; the manifold of physical objects existing in the universe influence the mind, and the mind responds by ordering them in 'time' and 'space.' It is a postulate of Kant that everything which is 'universal' and 'necessary' in knowledge cannot come from the things but solely from the mind. 'Time' and 'space' are universal and necessary elements in sense-perception; hence they must come from the mind and they must be *antecedently present* before sensation in the mind in order that perception be possible at all. 'Time' and 'space,' therefore, are *a priori forms* of the mind, and all impressions are clothed or molded in the 'forms' of 'time' and 'space.' 'Space' and 'time' are not attributes of reality in things; they are purely subjective in origin and character. As a result, since all phenomena are clothed by the mind in these two forms, phenomena are more in the nature of 'symbols' of objective reality. Objective reality consists of 'things-in-themselves' or 'noumena,' but these *noumena* are never known and *can never be known*.

Just as on the level of sense man's mind furnishes the forms of 'space' and 'time,' so on the level of intellectual knowledge the mind furnishes the *a priori forms of categories*. According to Kant, there are twelve types of judgments, each with its respective category. The phenomena of sense are drawn under these 'categories,' and the mind applies the 'categories' to them. These 'categories' are also antecedently present in the mind and have a purely subjective character. Whatever has a necessary and universal value in our judgments comes from the 'categories,' and so the 'categories' account for the universal and necessary validity of all principles and of all scientific and philosophic truths. Among these 'categories' or intellectual 'forms' is that of *Causality and Dependence*. The Principle of Causality, therefore, is universally and necessarily true, but *only for the intellect* in its judgments; the principle does not apply to 'things,' because we cannot know 'things-in-themselves.' Since the Principle of Causality possesses a purely mental character, it can never be applied legitimately to the universe. Hence, man cannot draw any valid conclusions from the universe to the existence of God by means of the Principle of Causality. It follows, says Kant, that man *cannot demonstrate the existence of God*.

Kant's *fundamental error* consists in his acceptance of Descartes's supposition that all knowledge originates solely in the mind, so that the 'object of knowledge' for man consists in his own internal conscious states. On this supposition man cannot contact the outside world through his mental activity, whether that activity be of the senses or of reason, and all knowledge thus becomes vitiated with complete *subjectivism*. This fact alone should have warned Kant that Descartes's initial supposition must be false.

Kant also overlooked the fact that man can establish the universality and necessity of general principles without having recourse to *a priori forms* such as he imagined existing in the so-called 'categories.' True, the senses cannot discover such general principles, because they perceive only particular things and events. However, given the things and events as they actually occur, *reason abstracts* ideas and principles which are universal and necessary in character and are independent of time and space. In perceiving things and events, man's reason soon understands that a mere sequence in time or a mere contiguity in space is insufficient to account for the happenings in nature; something more is required, namely, real *causality*. By a process of analysis, which is almost an immediate product of experience, man formulates the *Principle of Causality;* the child does this as soon as its reason is awakened. Later on, man links up the Principle of Causality with the concept of 'being' and the Principle of Contradiction; and from this comparison and *analysis* man, through a process of deduction, realizes that the Principle of Causality applies to all things universally and necessarily. To limit the application of this principle to phenomena is an unwarranted restriction and amounts practically to a denial of the Principle of Contradiction and of all possibility of true knowledge.

Hence, if man can know the objective, external world, and he can, and if the Principles of Contradiction and Causality are universally and necessarily true, and they are, it should be possible to apply these principles to the universe and its contents and then draw a legitimate conclusion to the 'cause' of the world, provided a 'cause' is necessary. In other words, since man is constitutionally capable of correct reasoning, a *demonstration of God's existence should be possible,* if God is the cause of the world in its existence and being.

The Method of Proof

We cannot demonstrate God's existence from the idea of God as the most perfect being; the ontological argument, as was shown, is invalid because it involves an illicit passage from the logical order of thought to the real order of actuality. We must, therefore, proceed in a different manner, if we expect to prove that God actually exists.

Man is a rational animal. As an 'animal,' his knowledge begins with sense-perception. As a 'rational' animal, his knowledge goes farther than sense-perception. The senses having supplied their data, *reason* becomes active and proceeds to form ideas, judgments, and inferences. By means of his reasoning, man transcends the level of sense-perception and is able to draw conclusions which reach to realities which cannot be perceived by the senses. Thus, biologists reason to the origin of living beings (for instance, when they argue about evolution), and geologists argue to the formation of earth deposits, although they are concluding to events which happened (or are supposed to have happened) in the far distant past and which they have not perceived. Unless we wish to fall into universal skepticism, we must admit the legitimacy of our reasoning processes. Reason is just as much a source of true knowledge as is the experience of sense-perception. Knowledge begins in the senses and ends in reason.

Since the proper object of man's intellect is 'material being,' it is natural for man to seek to prove God's existence from the material world by the application of the First Principles. Such arguments are called *a posteriori,* because man proceeds from the *effect* to the *cause.*

This discussion shows that the only proper approach to the problem of God's existence is an *a posteriori demonstration* of His existence.

Summary of Chapter III

The history of human thought shows that the *proper approach* to the problem of God's existence is important.

1. *Scientific Explanation.* — Facts alone do not make a science. Scientists always seek to *explain why* things are as they are and events happen as they do; they look for *causes.* Scientists are not justified in the restriction of reason itself; if they may seek the 'proximate' causes, reason must be allowed to seek the *ultimate cause* or *causes* of things and events.

2. *Deism and Agnosticism.* — *Deists* maintained that God exists and is the Creator; but that is all man can know about God. *Agnostics* affirm the constitutional inability of the human mind to know anything but the 'phenomenal.' Agnosticism rests on the fallacious basis of Hume's *unwarranted empiricism.*

3. *Fideism and Traditionalism.* — These theories maintain that

the knowledge of truth consists in an act of *faith* (hence 'fideism'), and the supreme criterion of certitude is the authority of revelation as given through *tradition* (hence 'traditionalism'). Reason must precede faith, or faith will be a blind assent and therefore unreasonable. Both theories lead eventually to *skepticism*.

4. *Ontologism.* — Ontologists held that *God* and the *Divine Ideas* are the first object of our intelligence and the intuition of God the first act of our intellectual knowledge. If the theory were true, we should be *conscious* of the intuition of God; there would be no possibility of *error* or *doubt;* man would be *infallibly certain* of truth.

5. *Religious Experience.* — Many people claim to have a direct *experience of God's presence* during prayer. Such experiences are too *subjective* and have no value as evidence.

6. *The Ontological Proof.* — This proof argues from the *idea of God* as the most perfect Being to His existence, because an existing being is more perfect than a merely possible being. The argument is invalid, because it involves an illegitimate passage from the *logical order* of thought to the *real order* of things.

7. *The Necessity of Proof.* — Since we have no immediate intuition of God's existence, and since the fact of God's existence is not self-evident, man can have only a *mediate and discursive* knowledge of God and His existence. Hence, God's existence must be *demonstrated.*

8. *The Possibility of Proof.* — If God has *manifested* Himself in the universe, and if man is *capable of knowing* Him through the universe, it must be possible to 'prove' His existence. Every effect reveals something of its cause.

9. *Kant's Formalism.* — Kant maintained that the speculative reason of man is *constitutionally incapable* of proving God's existence from the physical world. The 'world' and 'God' are noumena, not phenomena; but man can know only phenomena, and the phenomena, due to the *a priori forms,* tell us nothing of the reality of noumena. Kant's theory must be rejected. The universality and necessity of scientific knowledge can be accounted for without having recourse to antecedent mental 'forms.' By means of induction and deduction from the facts of the physical world, man arrives at a knowledge of causality; and by abstraction and analysis, he understands the *Principle of Causality.* Hence, a *demonstration* of God's existence should be *possible.*

10. *The Method of Proof.* — The only proper approach to the problem of God's existence is an *a posteriori demonstration* from effect to cause.

Readings

Brosnan, William J., *God and Reason*, pp. 19–57. — Driscoll, John T., *Christian Philosophy: God*, Chaps. I, III. — Glenn, Paul J., *Theodicy*, Chap. I. — Boedder, Bernard, *Natural Theology*, Chap. I. — Joyce, George Hayward, *Principles of Natural Theology*, Chap. II.

CHAPTER IV

CHANGE

WHATEVER sort of demonstration is used to prove God's existence, the conclusion must embody the judgment that 'God exists.' First of all, then, we must be clear about the meaning of the words 'God' and 'exists.'

What is meant by 'exist' (and 'existence')? *Negatively,* it means to be not merely an 'idea' present in some mind, nor to be merely a 'possible' thing capable of being produced by some cause. *Positively,* it means *to be actually,* just as you and I and the sun and the rivers and everything else in the physical world are 'actual' beings. Something, therefore, is said 'to exist' or 'to have existence' when it is outside the producing power of a cause and is actually present in the world of reality, so that it has 'being' of its own.

And what is meant by 'God'? We must begin with a *provisional notion* of what we understand by the term 'God.' As we proceed in our discussion, this provisional idea, if need be, may be revised and purified. Polytheists and monotheists have different ideas of 'God.' We must make a choice. As a 'provisional definition' we will begin with the concept of 'God' which is current in the Christian Western World, namely, the 'Maker and Ruler of the universe.' Whether this notion can be validated remains to be seen.

The first argument for God's existence is taken from the fact of *change.* In order to obtain a proper perspective, it will be advantageous to view the problem in the light of history.

Parmenides, Heraclitus

Parmenides (born about 544 or 540 B.C.) was one of the first thinkers to occupy himself with the problem of permanence and change, both of which seem to be a definite part of reality in nature. He became the foremost representative of the School of Elea. Parmenides was an intellectualist for whom the principles of thought and being are identical.

He began with the Principle of Identity and Contradiction: 'Being is being; non-being is non-being; both can never be identical.' From these principles he drew the conclusion: 'Whatever is, is; whatever is not, is nothing; from nothing nothing can become, because nothing has nothing to give; what already is, cannot become, because it already is what it is: hence, all becoming (change) is impossible.' It follows, he maintained, that every being remains unchangeably what it is and cannot become something else, and no possible being (since it is actually 'nothing') can ever become existent: nothing ever *becomes,* and nothing ever *ceases.* Being, since it cannot be separated from itself, is *indivisible;* and, since it is identical with itself, it is *changeless.* Being, therefore, is one, immobile, and eternal, a continuous and indivisible whole; there exists only the All-One absorbing all reality.

And yet, *multiplicity* and *change* appear everywhere in the universe. How account for them? Parmenides had a simple solution for the problem: they are nothing but the *illusions* of the senses; they do not and cannot exist, because reason assures us of the oneness and eternity of being. The final conclusion of Parmenides and his followers was that permanence alone exists and change is only apparent.

Heraclitus (535–475 B.C.) was an empiricist. As a contemporary of the Eleatics, he opposed their doctrine of unchanging being with that of continuous 'change.' Everything changes, and there is nothing permanent in the world. The one and only thing which is real is *process, perpetual flux, change.* While Parmenides found the essence of being to be an immutable reality, Heraclitus identified it with 'becoming' itself. The principle of change is 'fire.' Everything without exception is fire in some form or other, and fire is constantly undergoing transformation. Nothing becomes being, and being becomes nothing. Hence, being and non-being are identical; 'change' or 'becoming' is the only reality, and contradictories are fundamentally the same. The stability and permanence of being is the result of man's belief and as such is an *illusion*. Just as Parmenides placed his absolute credence in reason and its principles, ignoring and repudiating the testimony of the senses, so Heraclitus relied completely on the deliverances of sense-perception, ignoring and repudiating the reliability of reason and its principles.

Parmenides and Heraclitus were both right and wrong. Parmenides was right in affirming the permanence and stability of being; but he was wrong in denying the reality of change and becoming. Heraclitus was right in affirming the change and becoming of things, but he was wrong in denying the permanence and stability of being amid the change. Permanence and change are both present in nature. Things change, but something permanent remains throughout the process of change. Parmenides was in error when he considered 'permanence' to be absolute, and Heraclitus was in error when he considered 'becoming' to be absolute; in the things of this world *permanence and change are relative,* not absolute. The senses perceive the 'change' in things, but reason recognizes that change demands something that is a 'permanent subject' undergoing the change.

The solution to the vexing problem of permanence and change was given by the genius of Aristotle.

Aristotle

Aristotle (384–322 B.C.) saw the flaw in the reasoning of Parmenides and Heraclitus. The former relied solely on reason, and the latter solely on sense-perception. Man, since he is a 'rational animal,' has two sources of knowledge and truth, the senses and reason; knowledge begins in the senses, but is completed in the reason. Both sources are legitimate in their proper sphere, but they must be combined if man is to acquire real knowledge and attain to truth. Sense-perception acquaints us with the reality of change and reason acquaints us with the reality of permanence; and both are correct, because change and permanence are realities of nature, independent of the mind of man. But how can 'change' and 'permanence' of being be reconciled?

The solution which Aristotle proposed was the division of all reality into *potency* (*potentiality*) and *act* (*actuality*). Whatever exists is 'actual being.' Whatever is possible is 'potential being.'

For instance, the acorn is an 'act,' an 'actual being,' and as such it exists. The oak tree into which the acorn will eventually grow is as yet non-existent; but it is 'potentially' in the acorn, because the acorn will 'become' the oak tree later on, provided the hidden life of the acorn is awakened by heat, moisture, and soil, so that it will 'become' an oak tree through growth and development. The 'potential' oak tree thus 'becomes' eventually an 'actual' oak tree, and the acorn is thus seen to be an oak tree 'potentially,' even though the acorn as such is not yet an oak tree 'actually.' While the oak tree lives, it is an oak tree 'in act' and not 'in potency' to become an oak tree; but when it dies, it 'ceases to be' an actual tree and gradually changes through decay into chemical compounds and elements. What is said here of the acorn and oak tree applies with equal force to every living being. Change, therefore, occurs in *animate* beings throughout nature.

The distinction between 'potency' and 'act' is also found in *inanimate* beings. To take an example from modern chemistry, the elements of oxygen and hydrogen, while they exist as such in nature, are 'actually' oxygen and hydrogen; but 'potentially' they are whatever compound either will make through combining chemically with some other substance. Thus, when oxygen and hydrogen are viewed as having the possibility of combining to form water, water is 'potentially' (though not 'actually') present in oxygen and hydrogen, because these two elements are capable of 'becoming' water when combined. On the other hand, once oxygen and hydrogen have combined chemically, what is 'in act' is water. Inasmuch, however, as water can again be decomposed into oxygen and hydrogen, these elements are present 'in potency' in water.

What has been discussed so far is 'change' or 'becoming' among substances. Many changes, however, affect merely the *quantity* or *quality* of a substance, leaving the substance itself intact. Thus, during a snowstorm the quantity of snow increases, so that there is a 'quantitative change' in the amount of snow, but the snow as snow is not changed thereby; a reverse form of change occurs when the snow disappears. When the filament in a light bulb begins to glow, it undergoes a 'qualitative change,' the material of the filament remaining unchanged in the process. A similar qualitative change occurs when bodies become hot and cold, magnetized and demagnetized, pass from one color to another, and so forth. In all such cases, something becomes 'actual' which was formerly only 'potential.'

Change, or *becoming,* therefore always means the actualization of something potential; it implies the passage of a being from one state to another. Whatever 'changes,' must be *capable of receiving* some new determination and perfection through the power of a moving (efficient) cause; it must be *in potency to be* what it can *become actually,* otherwise it could never receive this actuality. *Act,* therefore, is the perfection, determination, or degree of reality present in a thing as it exists. *Potency,* or potentiality, is the aptitude of a thing to receive a perfection, a determination, or degree of reality. The being in potency always possesses within itself the germ of future actualization, even though it never becomes actualized in reality. Aristotle called this actualization (the passage of a being from a state of 'potency' to a state of 'act') *movement* and defined[1] it as "the act of a being in potency in so far as it is in potency." In every case of actualization or 'movement' there is the following sequence: Before the thing 'moves' it is in potency for both the movement (process of actualization) and the final actuality to be acquired by it; when it begins to be 'moved,' it is no longer in potency for the movement (process of actualization), but has already acquired movement as an intermediary act;

---

[1] *Physics,* III, 201a. For an elucidation of this definition, see the author's *The Domain of Being* (Milwaukee: The Bruce Publishing Co., 1939), Chap. VIII.

while 'moving' (while in the process of actualization), it still remains in potency for the final and complete actuality to be acquired at the ending-point of its movement; when the thing has acquired its final and complete act (perfection, determination, degree of being), movement ceases, and the thing comes to rest as completely actualized. Aristotle's definition of 'movement' (process of actualization) is thus seen to be very concise and correct.

Aristotle stresses the fact that all change (becoming) in nature presupposes a *subject* which persists in existence throughout the change and in which the change occurs. The subject of change, therefore, is *relatively permanent*. That this is a fact should be obvious from an analysis of any type of change which happens in nature. Whenever an organism originates or dies, matter is present as the subject of change. Whenever a chemical compound is formed or dissolved, chemical substance in some form or other is the subject in which the change takes place. In quantitative and qualitative changes, the reality gained or lost presupposes some being which gains or loses the reality, as when a person grows larger in size or becomes sick.

Aristotle's doctrine of 'potency' and 'act' thus solved the problem of permanence and change very neatly. Aristotle showed that Parmenides was right in insisting on 'permanence,' because the 'subject of change' persists during the entire process of becoming; but also that Parmenides was wrong in denying the existence of change in things, because change is too evident to be argued out of existence through an appeal to rational principles. In a similar manner, Aristotle showed that Heraclitus was right in recognizing the presence of change in the universe, but that he was wrong in his claim that nothing permanent exists and in his assertion that the principles of reason have no value. In this way Aristotle safeguarded the validity of sense-perception and of reason as legitimate sources of knowledge and avoided the error of extremism present in the doctrines of Parmenides and Heraclitus. Neither reason nor sense may be sacrificed in a theory.

Bergson

Henri Bergson (1859–1941) was the most important exponent of 'perpetual becoming' in modern times. Like Heraclitus, he was an anti-intellectualist. According to Bergson, everything is a continuous flux of becoming and change, *without any underlying subject* which becomes and changes. *Change is the whole of reality.* Everything changes, but there is no thing which changes; everything is in movement, but there is no thing which moves; everything is in a state of continuous progress, but there is no thing that progresses; everything is in a process of evolution, but there is no thing that evolves: as Bergson says,[2] "movement is reality itself, and immobility is always only apparent or relative . . . there are no *things,* there are only *actions."*

And yet Bergson speaks constantly of 'man,' 'animal,' 'plant,' 'universe,' 'matter,' and so on. This is due to his distinction between *intuition* and *intellect.* Man is characterized by 'intellect' rather than by 'intuition,' although 'intuition' is intrinsically more capable of grasping the flow of becoming. Intellect has as its function the formation of concepts, and concepts are mere 'snapshots' of reality; they represent the dynamic process of reality in static pictures. Intuition immerses itself into the very stream of life and 'feels' the rhythm of flux; it is a developed refinement of animal instinct and as such more in 'sympathy' with the process of becoming than the intellect. Intellect is concerned with 'action' and 'unorganized solids,' that is to say, with matter and its use for practical needs. Intuition reveals life and is associated with the hidden secrets of consciousness and with speculation; it comes to man in rare flashes, but it is charged with life and is the only faculty of man capable of perceiving pure duration, pure movement, creative evolution, the very inwardness of life itself.

Movement is creative evolution. This ceaseless evolutionary movement is the result of a double factor — *matter* and the

---

[2] *Creative Evolution,* tr. by Arthur Mitchell (New York: Henry Holt & Co., 1911), pp. 155, 248.

vital impulse (élan vital). From the beginning 'matter' existed, and so also did the 'vital impulse.' Movement simply began. Since life is tendency, it surges continuously upward toward different forms of life. But matter acts as an obstacle to the surge of the vital impetus and must be overcome incessantly. The vital impulse is only finite in its action, and its tendency is not directed toward any definite goal; as a result, the vital impulse, in pushing against the refractory medium of matter, gives rise to different levels of being in the course of the evolutionary process — inanimate nature, plants, animals, and men. Intellectuality and materiality are simply an "inversion of the same movement,"[3] because the upward movement or 'ascent' of the vital impulse always implies the downward movement or 'descent' of matter. Vital activity is thus "a reality which is making itself in a reality which is unmaking itself."[4]

As far as *creation* and a *Creator* are concerned, Bergson says: "Everything is obscure in the idea of creation if we think of *things* which are created and a *thing* which creates, as we habitually do, as the understanding cannot help doing. . . . God has nothing of the already made; He is unceasing life, action, freedom."[5] In other words, if we wish to speak of God at all, we must consider Him, not as a 'thing' or substance existing prior to the world, but as a part of the very *process of formation.* Reality is nothing but 'movement.' That we think of 'static things' instead of pure 'dynamic process,' is an *illusion of the intellect.*[6] Similarly, our idea of the 'nought' is an illusion: "If we analyze this idea of Nothing, we find that it is, at bottom, the idea of Everything. . . . It is therefore an idea eminently comprehensive and full, as full and comprehensive as the idea of *All,* to which it is closely akin."[7] It is a 'pseudo-idea,' as Bergson calls it. Bergson thus ends by denying the validity of the Principles of Identity and Contradiction.

---

[3] *Ibid.,* p. 206.
[4] *Ibid.,* p. 248.
[5] *Ibid.,* p. 248.
[6] *Ibid.,* p. 273.
[7] *Ibid.,* p. 296.

In evaluating Bergson's system of perpetual flux a number of *adverse observations* must be made.

Bergson's description of the entire process of world evolution is mere *conjecture*. No one, obviously, ever witnessed it; experience, therefore, is lacking. Bergson uses many arguments to make his theory plausible; but such arguments are *inferences* of the intellect, and the intellect, in his view, is deceptive and erroneous. His appeal to 'intuition' is of no value, because 'intuition' is a peculiarly Bergsonian notion which is too *subjective* in character to be submitted to objective tests of evidence; its very existence is, at best, extremely doubtful. Even if it exists, its 'flashes' are so rare and short-lived that no one can be sure of its deliverances.

Bergson's dictum that all *reality* is 'movement,' 'becoming,' 'change,' but that there are *no things* which move, become, and change, is not only strange but contrary to all science and philosophy. The world we know is a world of *things*. Things change, of course, but they are 'things' nevertheless. If we cannot trust the testimony of our senses and reason, what is the use of science and philosophy? All knowledge and all truth would be impossible if reality were nothing but process and if there were *no one to know*. Even Bergson was a permanent being, and so are his writings. St. Thomas Aquinas'[8] remarks are true and validated by the findings of exact science: "Every movement presupposes something immovable [permanent, stable]: for when a change of quality occurs, the substance remains unchanged; and when there is a change of substantial form, matter remains unmoved [unchanged]."

When Bergson discredited intellect and reason in favor of 'intuition,' he overlooked the fact that he thereby *destroyed the foundation of his entire system of knowledge and reality*. It was only through his intellect and reason that he set up the arguments and drew out the conclusions that made his theory of 'creative evolution' in any way plausible. But if we cannot

---

[8] *Summa Theologica* (New York: Benziger Bros.), I, qu. 84, art. 1, reply to obj. 3. This and subsequent passages from the *Summa Theologica* are reprinted with permission of Benziger Brothers, Inc., publishers and copyright owners.

trust reason in its normal operations, of what value are its arguments and conclusions? If intellect and reason are habitually deceptive and erroneous, giving us a distorted view of reality, then knowledge and truth are impossible for us, and *universal skepticism* is the logical outcome of such an attitude. Bergson showed this when he sacrificed the Principles of Identity and Contradiction by practically identifying Nought and All (being) for the sake of overcoming a difficulty arising from his theory of ceaseless flux. Every theory, no matter how ingenious, must collapse, once the fundamental principles of logical thinking are discarded.

Change and Causality

Every *change demands a sufficient reason*. Everything without exception demands a sufficient reason to account for what it *is* and for what it *does* and for what *happens* to it. This sufficient reason may be either inadequately or adequately sufficient. An *inadequately* sufficient reason will explain partly and proximately why a certain being exists or changes, but it will not explain the 'totality' of the occurrence. On the other hand, an *adequately* sufficient reason explains the 'totality' of a thing in all its phases, so that nothing remains to be accounted for. For example, if one were to explain the movement of a locomotive by saying that the engineer pulled the lever of the throttle, one would give an 'inadequately' sufficient reason for this movement, because one leaves out of consideration the steam in the boiler, the pipes, the pistons, the wheels, and all the other parts and activities that have a role in producing the motion of the locomotive.

In order to account for *change,* therefore, in its entirety, an 'adequate' sufficient reason will have to be given for its total being and existence, and this must be an *adequate efficient cause.*

Change implies the actualization of some potentiality. A being changes so as to obtain some *reality, determination, perfection* which it does not at present possess. In every change, therefore, something *new* is received by a being *which did not exist as such in the being before the change;* the being was merely in receptive potency (potentiality)[9] for this perfection. This change, with its perfection, is the result of an activity of some sort and, since it is *produced* by this activity, is the effect of an *adequate efficient cause.* If the efficient cause is to be the 'adequate' cause of the new perfection, it must *contain* the perfection within itself either 'formally' or 'eminently.' This new perfection is a *real being* and as such must *really* exist somewhere or somehow in its (adequate) cause; otherwise there would be a remainder and part of it without a cause to account for its existence, and the being after the change would have received more than the cause could give. It is not sufficient that the new perfection be merely *virtually* contained in the cause. If one means by 'virtually' that the perfection is present in its 'entirety' in the cause, this can only be either as a *real being* (and then it is present in the cause *formally*) or as contained in the *higher perfection* of the cause (and then it is present in the cause *eminently*). And if one means by 'virtually' that the perfection is not contained formally or eminently in the cause, but only that it can be produced by the activity of the cause in some way, then one violates the Principles of Sufficient Reason and Causality, because what a cause does not *already possess* (either as a reality or as contained in higher perfection) it *cannot give to another* — no one can give what one does not have. In the latter case, it cannot be the 'adequate' cause of the new perfection, but must be assisted by something else which contains the totality of the perfection and can supply the deficiency. It follows that the 'adequate cause' of change must contain the new perfection acquired in the change either 'formally' or 'eminently'; any other supposition would involve the *contradiction* that the perfection acquired in the change is fully accounted for and not fully accounted for, is adequately produced and not adequately produced, at the same time under the same respect.

But now, it is clear that a *being which acquires* a perfection

---

[9] For the difference between 'receptive' and 'operative' potency, see the author's *The Domain of Being, op. cit.,* p. 61.

by means of change *cannot already possess it* either 'formally' or 'eminently' (namely, in its reality or as contained in a higher perfection). If it possesses it thus already, it has it, and there is no possibility of acquiring what it already possesses. Hence, a being which is changed in order to acquire a perfection cannot be its own *adequate cause* of that perfection; otherwise it would possess the perfection (that is necessary for an adequate cause, as just pointed out) and not possess it (because it is through the change that it is supposed to 'acquire' the perfection) at the same time — a patent *contradiction*. The being, therefore, which is changed in order to acquire a new perfection cannot be the adequate cause of the perfection that it receives by means of the change.

The *new perfection* itself cannot be the adequate cause of its own existence. The new perfection is a produced reality. This reality *could not produce itself*. To produce itself would mean to act, and activity presupposes existence; how can anything act before it exists? It would both exist (because it 'produces itself,' and to do that it must exist) and not exist (because it is supposed to 'receive existence' through its productive action in the change); but to exist and not to exist at the same time is a *contradiction*.

Since a contradiction is absurd and impossible, it is evident that neither the being receiving the new perfection nor the new perfection itself can be the 'adequate cause' of the change. It follows as a necessary consequence that the 'adequate cause' of any such change must be a *being distinct* from the changing being, namely, some *external cause* producing the change. It follows furthermore that the adequate cause must be an *existing reality* capable of giving the perfection to the being which is to receive it by means of the change. It follows finally that the adequate cause must *contain* the perfection to be given in one of two ways: it must contain it either 'formally,' so that the reality of the perfection is actually present as such in the cause, or 'eminently,' so that the cause contains the perfection in a superior manner in some higher perfection. Unless all these conditions are fulfilled, one cannot account for the change and the acquired perfection in its *totality*. If any of these conditions were missing, it is evident that the changing being would receive a *plus-amount* of perfection not present in the producing cause. This 'plus-amount' would have no sufficient reason to account for its presence and as such it could not come into existence at all. In no case is it possible to have more perfection in the effect than the cause is able to give: *the more perfect simply cannot proceed from the less perfect.* If it did, the 'more,' the 'plus-amount,' would both exist and not exist: it would exist (that is the supposition); and it would not exist (because the cause cannot give what it does not have).

The Universality of Change

Change affects all things in the world; nothing is exempt, whether it be living or nonliving.

That *living beings* in this world undergo constant change is attested by all the sciences which treat of them — biology, botany, zoology, physiology. Plants, animals, and men are in a constant process of change; they grow, mature, and die. The cycle of life is characterized by activity and change from the moment of fertilization until the moment of death.

Nonliving beings are also subject to constant change. Chemistry, physics, geophysics, and astronomy are based on the fact of change among inanimate bodies. The natural sciences assure us that all bodies without exception are affected by various forces, such as heat, electricity, magnetism, light, mechanical motion, gravity, and so on. Every chemical compound, element, and subelemental particle is a storehouse of *energy*. Energy is either *potential* or *kinetic*. The former is energy at rest (position); the latter is energy in action. A constant transformation of energy takes place in the universe, so that potential energy becomes kinetic and kinetic energy becomes potential. This transformation or change occurs in the bodies, so that the bodies themselves are in a continuous process of change.

The *universe at large* consists of the same elements as are found on earth. And so it happens that the universe as a whole is also subject to ceaseless change, both in the stars and in the matter occupying interstellar space. Activity is found everywhere. And where there is activity, there is change; and change implies causality. To mention merely one fact: heat is generated all the time in the sun and stars; this heat is diffused through space uniformly and affects every particle of matter, thereby producing qualitative changes. Every kind of radiation exerts a causative influence and brings about changes of one form or another, and radiation is found everywhere in nature. Motion is universal, and motion means change. Whether the bodies be subvisible particles or astronomical galaxies, all are active in some manner. Action, however, issues into effects. As a result, the Principle of Causality reigns over the entire world.

Extra-mundane Cause of Change

It is now time to draw the threads of our argument together and formulate the conclusion.

Both permanence and change exist in the world. Substances are relatively permanent, and changes take place in them. But substances are not absolutely permanent, because one substance may change into another. Every change, whether substantial or accidental, demands an adequately sufficient reason to account for it. Change implies the actualization of some potentiality in the changing subject; it supposes that something new, some determination, some perfection is received which did not exist as such in the being before the change, so that this being was merely in 'receptive potency' for the perfection.

Since the change, with its resultant new perfection, is the product of activity, it is the effect of an efficient cause; and this cause must be 'adequately' efficient to produce the total effect. The adequate efficient cause of change must contain the new perfection either 'formally' or 'eminently' within itself, otherwise it could not give the perfection to another by means of the produced change; the reason is that the being acquiring the new perfection cannot already possess it, nor can the new perfection produce itself. Hence, the adequate efficient cause must be a being distinct from the being receiving the perfection. Change in the meaning here given affects all things in the world, living and nonliving.

Consider the implications.

Every single being in the universe is subject to change, *i.e.,* is in receptive potency for new perfections to be acquired through change. But the universe is the sum-total of all the single beings present in it. The universe as a whole, therefore, is the subject of change, *i.e.,* is in receptive potency for new perfections to be acquired through change. The actualization of a receptive potency, however, requires an adequate efficient cause to bring about the change and thereby confer the new perfection (determination) on the recipient subject. Since the adequate efficient cause must contain within itself the reality of the new perfection either formally or eminently, and since the recipient subject does not contain the new perfection either formally or eminently, the adequate cause must be a being distinct from the recipient subject. Now, the universe as a whole requires an adequate efficient cause in order to account completely for the changes which occur in the universe. Therefore the changing universe demands an adequate efficient cause, *distinct from the universe as such,* in order to account for the changes which occur in the universe.

One cannot escape this conclusion by postulating an *eternal existence* of the universe or an *infinite series* of changes in the universe. An adequate efficient cause 'outside' the universe and 'distinct' from the universe, and therefore extra-universe or *extra-mundane,* would still be indispensable.

Even if the material universe existed from eternity, so that it had no beginning in time, the conclusion would be inevitable that an *eternal* adequate efficient cause would be required. This cause would then not exist prior to the world, but it would have to 'co-exist' eternally with it. The universe, whether eternal or temporal, would need this cause in any event.

The same observation holds true in the supposition of an infinite series of changes in the universe. The nature of the changes, as the actualizations of receptive potencies acquiring new perfections, would remain the same. An infinite process of such changes does not alter their *nature* and would still require an adequate efficient cause *outside the infinite series* existing in the universe, in order to make the fact of such changes completely intelligible and possible.

Hence, whether the universe be eternal or temporal and the series of changes infinite or finite, the universe as a whole demands the existence of an *extra-mundane cause* to account completely and adequately for such changes.

Unchangeable Cause

Now, it is impossible that absolutely every being be changed by another. Eventually we must admit that there must exist a being which is not subject to change: *an unchanged and unchangeable cause of change.*

The material universe, as astronomy and astrophysics testify, is a *unitary system,* consisting of the same kinds of elements and bodies, performing the same general types of operations, obeying the same chemical and physical laws, and following the same pattern of changes. Due to this fact of unity and uniformity, the extra-mundane cause, to which these changes lead, must be a *single cause.* (non sequitur)

This extra-mundane cause of the changes in the universe must itself be either not subject to change or subject to change. If not subject to change, we have arrived at the 'unchanged cause.' If subject to change, it must itself be changed by another cause. The same question then arises regarding this 'other cause.' Is it subject to change or not? If not, we have now arrived at the 'unchanged cause.' If subject to change, it must again be changed by another cause. Now we have two such causes subject to change; a new series of changing causes has arisen. This *series* as a series demands an *outside cause*. And so the whole question comes up again. Is the series finite or infinite? No matter whether finite or infinite, the series demands an 'outside cause' as the sufficient reason and adequate cause of the change in the series. If a second and a third and a fourth series is postulated, we have a series of series, none of which is capable of accounting for the occurring changes in all of them except by an *outside cause*. We must eventually arrive at a *cause which is not subject to change,* or the changes will not be adequately accounted for. Outside of 'all' there is nothing, and nothing accounts for nothing. Hence, if 'all beings' are changed, there would be no being outside of 'all' to start the change in the others. Consequently, there must be some being which is the adequate efficient cause of change in the others, but it is *not subject to change itself;* it is at the *beginning of all change* and as such is the *unchanged cause of change* in the others. Since no other being exists which can change this unchanged cause, it is *unchangeable* as well as unchanged.

Many people are under the impression that they can escape the logic of the conclusion by pushing the problem into the vague mist of the far-distant past or by multiplying the instances indefinitely. This procedure is followed by those who think that 'eternity' or an 'infinite number' will nullify the force of the argument. What they fail to understand is that mere succession in time and multitude of numbers does not affect the *nature* of a thing. A dog, for example, will not become rational, even if he lives for an eternity; the dog would simply be a dog eternally. Similarly, a million or an infinite number of dogs will not make a dog's nature rational, any more than a million or infinite number of zeros can ever add up to a positive sum. And so it is with *change, i.e.,* with the actualization of receptive potencies. The *nature* of such change in an existing being demands a principle of change distinct from the being which is changed and must lead to a being which is not subject to change itself; all change must emanate from this being as the *Prime Changer Unchanged and Unchangeable.*

The Argument of St. Thomas

St. Thomas Aquinas (1224 [or 1225]–1274) was undoubtedly the greatest and clearest thinker of the Christian era. He gives five main proofs for God's existence. The first is the argument based on *motion.*

Motus (motion), in the mind of Aristotle and St. Thomas, implies 'change' in the sense of local motion and in the sense of accidental or substantial change. Even local motion is merely a species of 'change.' When, therefore, St. Thomas formulates his argument of 'motion,' this wider sense of the term 'motion' must always be borne in mind.

"The first and more manifest way [to prove God's existence] is the argument from motion. It is certain, and evident to our senses, that in the world some things are in motion. Now whatever is in motion is put in motion by another, for nothing can be in motion except it is in potentiality to that towards which it is in motion, whereas a thing moves inasmuch as it is in act. For motion is nothing else than the reduction of something from potentiality to actuality. But nothing can be reduced from potentiality to actuality, except by something in a state of actuality. Thus that which is actually hot, as fire, makes wood, which is potentially hot, to be actually hot, and therefore moves and changes it. Now it is not possible that the same thing should be at once in actuality and potentiality in the same respect, but only in different respects. For what is actually hot cannot simultaneously be potentially hot; but it is potentially cold. It is therefore impossible that in the same respect and in the same way a thing should be both mover and moved, *i.e.,* that it should move itself. Therefore, whatever is in motion must be put in motion by another. If that by which it is put in motion be itself put in motion, then this also must needs be put in motion by another, and that by another again. But this cannot go on to infinity, because then there would be no first mover, and consequently, no other mover; seeing that subsequent movers move only inasmuch as they are put in motion by the first mover; as the staff moves only because it is put in motion by the hand. Therefore it is necessary to arrive at a first mover, put in motion by no other; and this everyone understands to be God."[10]

It will be noted that St. Thomas, although he uses the word

---

[10] *Summa Theologica, op. cit.,* qu. 2, art. 3.

'motion,' really speaks of 'change' in the broader meaning of the term. His formulation of the argument is very concise, and it is skeletonized to such an extent that the various steps in his process of reasoning might be open to question and not be altogether convincing. Hence the more extensive formulation as given in the body of this chapter. As a consequence, this argument can also be called the argument proving the existence of a *Prime Mover*. And so it is usually designated.

Consequences

The argument as presented seems to lead to a rather vague and nondescript being, that of Prime Mover or First Changeless Changer. Yet St. Thomas says: "and this everyone understands to be God." Is St. Thomas not guilty of a tremendous 'logical leap' in this statement? We usually understand by the term 'God' something very different from a 'Prime Mover' or 'First Changeless Changer.' However, an *analysis* of what is implied in the concept of the 'Prime Mover (First Changeless Changer)' reveals much more of this being than is apparent at the first glance.

First of all, the Prime Mover can never have passed from non-existence to existence. To have done so would mean that it was once merely 'possible' and was therefore in potency (potentiality) for the act (actuality) of 'existence.' As such, existence could only be given to it by some other being actually existing. That, however, would involve a 'movement' or 'change' radically much greater than being 'moved' or 'changed' while possessing existence. Since the Prime Mover or First Changeless Changer is the 'principle of change,' it is evident that such a being could not have 'received existence' from another. Hence, the Prime Mover always had existence in virtue of its own being. It follows, therefore, that the Prime Mover (First Changeless Changer) is *eternal*.

Furthermore. The living beings in this world are in many ways subject to change, so that they pass from receptive potentiality to actuality, even in matters pertaining to their vital functions. Ultimately, this reduction from potency to act must be referred back to the Prime Mover as the first 'principle of change.' Hence, the being of the Prime Mover must contain the reality of 'life' formally or eminently and as such must be a *living being*.

Again. Among the manifestations of life in this world is the intellect and volitional life of the soul of man; and man's soul is spiritual. However, the intellect, will, and soul of man are also subject to 'change'; they are not pure actuality. These changes must find their adequate sufficient reason in the Prime Mover or First Changeless Changer. Hence, the Prime Mover must possess the perfection of *intellect, will,* and *spirituality*.

Finally. A being which is spiritual and possesses intellect and will is a 'person,' the same as man is a 'person' in the true sense of the word. Hence, the Prime Mover is also *personal*.

Now a being which is eternal, living, intellectual, volitional, spiritual, and personal is indeed, as St. Thomas observes, what "everyone understands to be God."

Therefore, *God exists*. The analysis just given is very brief. These phases of God's being will become clearer as the other proofs for His existence are unfolded in the following chapters.

Summary of Chapter IV

We begin with the *provisional notion* of 'God' as the 'Maker and Ruler of the universe.' The first proof for God's existence is taken from the fact of *change*.

1. *Parmenides, Heraclitus.* — *Parmenides* was an intellectualist for whom the principles of thought and being were identical. He denied change and maintained the *permanence* of all being in the All-One.

Heraclitus was an empiricist. He denied the permanence of being and maintained that the only reality is *process, flux, change*.

Parmenides was right in affirming the permanence of things, but wrong in denying the reality of change and becoming; Heraclitus was right in affirming the presence of change and becoming, but wrong in denying the permanence of being.

2. *Aristotle.* — Aristotle solved the problem by his division of all reality into *potency* (potentiality) and *act* (actuality). Whatever exists is 'in act'; whatever is possible is 'in potency.' What is a

'potential being' is as yet non-existent, but it is something which 'can become,' provided some efficient cause can give it existence; hence, it is not 'nothingness.'

Change, or becoming, means the actualization of something potential; when the potential being is actualized, it receives some perfection, some determination, some degree of reality. All change presupposes a subject which persists in relative permanence throughout change; the change occurs 'in the subject.'

3. Bergson. — Bergson followed the doctrine of Heraclitus that everything is a continuous flux of becoming and change, without any underlying subject: "There are no things, there are only actions." The intellect, in testifying to the existence of 'things,' is erroneous; intuition, which is always reliable, testifies to the reality of mere 'change.' 'Movement' is creative evolution and is the result of the double factor of matter and the vital impulse (élan vital), giving rise to inanimate beings, plants, animals, and man. God is a part of this evolving nature. Bergson practically identified the Nought and the All (being), thereby denying the Principles of Identity and Contradiction.

4. Change and Causality. — In order to account for 'change (becoming)' in its entirety, an 'adequate' sufficient reason will have to be given for its total being and existence, and this must be an adequate efficient cause. Since change implies the reception of a new reality (perfection, determination) which did not exist as such in the being before the change, it must be produced by the activity of an efficient cause, and the efficient cause must contain this reality either 'formally' or 'eminently.' Neither the being receiving the new perfection nor the new perfection itself can be the 'adequate cause' of the change. Hence, the efficient cause, in its reduction of receptive potency into act, must be a being distinct from the changing being.

5. The Universality of Change. — All beings in the world, whether living or nonliving, undergo change, i.e., pass from receptive potency into act in some form. Energy, potential and kinetic, is in a constant process of transformation in the elements and compounds. The universe as a whole is subject to ceaseless change.

6. Extra-mundane Cause of Change. — Every single being in the universe is in receptive potency for new perfections to be acquired through change. And since the universe is but the sum-total of all the single beings present in it, the universe is in receptive potency

for new perfections to be acquired through change. Therefore, the universe demands an adequate efficient cause, *distinct from the universe,* in order to account for the changes occurring in the universe.

Even if the universe were supposed to exist from *eternity,* or if an *infinite series* of changes were postulated, the *nature* of change would still demand and extra-mundane cause.

7. *Unchangeable Cause.* — It is impossible that absolutely every being be changed by another. This extra-mundane cause must itself be either not subject to change or subject to change. If not subject to change, we have arrived at the 'unchanged cause.' If subject to change, it must be changed by another. This 'other cause' will either be not subject to change or subject to change. We must eventually arrive at a *cause not subject to change,* or the changes will not be adequately accounted for, because outside of 'all' there is nothing. Hence, there must be an 'unchanged cause of all change' and, since no other being exists which can change this unchanged cause, it is both *unchanged* and *unchangeable.*

There exists, therefore, *a Prime Changer Unchanged and Unchangeable.*

8. *The Argument of St. Thomas.* — St. Thomas uses this same type of argument. Usually it is called the *argument from motion.* But 'motion' (motus) means 'change' in the terminology of St. Thomas and Aristotle. The argument leads to a 'Prime Mover.'

9. *Consequences.* — The Prime Mover or First Changeless Changer must be *eternal, living, intellectual, volitional, spiritual,* and *personal.* And that is what "everyone understands to be God."

Therefore, *God exists.*

Readings

Garrigou-Lagrange, R., *God: His Existence and Nature,* Vol. I, Part I, Chap. III, nn. 34–36. — Driscoll, John T., *God,* Chap. VIII. — Joyce, George Hayward, *Principles of Natural Theology,* Chap. III, Sect. 3. — Aveling, Francis, *The God of Philosophy,* Chap. VI. — St. Thomas Aquinas, *Summa Theologica,* I, qu. 2, art. 3. — Smith, Gerard, *Natural Theology,* Chap. VI. — Renard, Henri, *The Philosophy of God,* pp. 33–35.

CHAPTER V

DESIGN

THE vast majority of people are convinced of the existence of a Supreme Being above and beyond the world, no matter how imperfect their conception of this Supreme Being may be. Usually this conviction has its foundation in a contemplation of the *order* existing in the universe. Order presupposes *design*. Design presupposes an *intelligent designer*. Man's reason thus makes a spontaneous conclusion from the order of the world to an *Intelligent Supreme Being* who is the author of the order existing everywhere in nature.

The philosopher, however, cannot be satisfied with such a spontaneous conviction. He must dissect the argument and reduce it to its logical form; in doing this, he will test the validity and force of the argument.

Science should be of considerable help in pointing out order in the universe. The field of the sciences, however, is so vast that in most instances mere hints must suffice. A more extensive knowledge of the individual sciences will naturally tend to strengthen the *argument from order and design.*

Order and Design

Since this argument for God's existence has as its foundation the 'order' and 'design' present in the universe, an explanation of these terms will be necessary.

Order is the arrangement of various items into a system or whole according to some relationship existing or placed between them. This order will be *static,* if the items are ordered with regard to their entity or being; such is the order of books in a library and of cars in a parking lot. This order will be *dynamic,* if the items are ordered with respect to the performance of a unified function; for example, the parts of an automobile are arranged so that the driver can make it travel, and the organs of digestion are arranged so that they can perform the action of digesting food. The division of order into 'static' and 'dynamic' is not necessarily exclusive. Thus, there exists a 'static' order of the various parts of a machine, if the machine is considered merely as a mechanism made up of different entitative parts; but a machine also possesses a 'dynamic' order, because the parts as a system are made to perform a definite operation.

Order will also be either natural or artificial. *Natural* order, whether static or dynamic, is the result of powers operating in the nature of the items which are ordered; the order, for instance, which exists in the organization of a plant or animal body is 'natural' order. *Artificial* order is not due to the nature of the items themselves, but is put into them by an outside agent arranging these items; the arrangement of the parts of a locomotive, for example, is 'artificial,' because the machinist puts the parts together in a definite manner to produce a definite result.

Design in a strict sense is planned, intended order, namely, the arrangement of various items into a system or whole, so that this arrangement is the result of plan and intention. Wherever there is design, there is *purpose* — the purpose to achieve *a definite end through the use of definite means.* When a student sets as the purpose of his life the following of a certain professional career, his course of studies is planned and designed to enable him to reach this goal.

Not all order is 'designed'; there is also 'random' order. Order is *designed,* when all the various items are arranged so as to realize a certain purpose or aim through the use of appropriate means. In an automobile factory, for example, the purpose of producing a self-propelled vehicle effectively influences the draftsmen and mechanics in the making and assembling of all the parts which are necessary for achieving such a type of vehicle. On the other hand, order is *random,* when the effect of the cause results in some sort of actual order, although this order was never intended as the effect of this causality. Thus, the order of the cards existing in the various hands after an honest shuffle and deal is an accidental and 'random' order, because there is no effective intention of arranging the cards in this particular order. Of course, if this order is achieved through the deft manipulation of the dealer, it is 'designed' order.

Order and Chance

Chance may be defined as a mode of causal activity, not purposive in character, regarded as determining an event. Such an event, when the result of 'chance,' simply 'happens'; it is not the result of any intention or purpose on the part of the agent producing the effect.

Examples will clarify the concept of 'chance.' A strong wind blows some straw around; three pieces of straw are thrown against a fence, forming the letter 'N.' Now, it is neither the purpose of the wind nor of the three pieces of straw to form a letter of the alphabet. Hence, the effect produced is a 'chance event,' and the arrangement of the three straws is the result of 'chance.' — Two highways intersect. Two men are driving their cars, each on one of the two highways. Due to slippery roads, they collide at the intersection. Each driver, of course, intended to make his trip, and so the order of the trip was the result of a purposive action, of 'design.' However, since no mutual agreement was made by the two drivers as to the time of departure and the road to be traveled, the collision itself was not intended in any way; that they happened to meet at the intersection at the same moment was entirely due to 'chance.'

A chance event, therefore, is not the effect of a predetermining law, of a preconceived purpose, of an intelligent intention. *Regularity* is a characteristic of *law,* and a law produces uniform effects. Chance implies the absence of regularity, and for that reason it *excludes predictability* except on the basis of a *statistical average.* Insurance companies, for instance, can predict the average number of deaths or accidents which will occur in the course of a year; but they cannot specify the individuals to whom these events will occur, because many deaths and accidents are due to 'chance' and as such are not amenable to law. In many cases scientists are ignorant of the causes producing certain regularly occurring events. They perceive the *order* of events, but they do not know the cause; in such cases it would be wrong to ascribe these events to 'chance.' Chance is a factor when each individual being acts on its own, without conspiring with others to produce a definite effect as the result of their concerted action. Whenever *concerted action* on the part of many individual beings occurs, there is order among their individual actions; and this order is the effect of law, not of chance in the strict sense of the word.

Chance and Probability

Scientists, in general, leave 'purposiveness' out of consideration when treating of the phenomena of nature. Materialistic scientists do this, because purposiveness implies intelligence, and intelligence in nature is something they must exclude. Other scientists do this for the reason that purposiveness is 'unobservable' by the senses, and sense-perception is the foundation of all experience and therefore also of all science. Because of this attitude, the *origination of all phenomena through chance* is the normal scientific view of a large number of scientists.

As a consequence, the possibility and probability of natural phenomena happening through chance must be an all-important part in the scientific method. Where pure chance is concerned, the *mathematical laws of probability alone* govern everything. Those scientists, therefore, who rule out intelligence in the universe and attempt to explain all happenings on the basis of pure chance, must be *consistent* and apply nothing but these laws of probability in giving an explanation of the origin and operation of natural phenomena. Any other procedure would be an abdication of reason in favor of arbitrariness and wishful thinking.

Probability on the basis of chance follows the ratio of *geometrical progression*. A person flipping a coin has a fifty-fifty chance of calling heads or tails correctly, so that the statistical average of 'one-in-two' should always prevail in the long run.

There are only two possibilities in the case of flipping a coin ('head' or 'tail'), and the average of correctly calling the result is therefore ½ or 0.5.

When the number of items involved increases, the probability of success through chance becomes progressively less. In a game of dice each cube has six sides and six numbers, the numbers running from 1 to 6. The probability, therefore, of any number showing on top will be 'one-in-six' or ⅙. Consequently, a player calling for the number 3 has a probability of ⅙ that this number will appear. That the number 3 appears twice in succession reduces the probability to ⅟₃₆ (⅙ x ⅙, or .0277). The probability of obtaining the number 3 ten times in succession is 1/60,466,176 (0.000,000,016).

Probability decreases enormously when higher numbers are used. Pierre Lecomte Du Noüy[1] imagines a powder composed of 1000 white particles and 1000 black particles, all absolutely alike except for their color. After being thoroughly mixed in a container, the powder is allowed to run into a tube whose diameter is slightly larger than that of the particles so that one grain of powder follows another in the tube. "The probability that the 1000 white particles will be entirely separated from the 1000 black ones after being shaken is expressed by 0.489×10^{-600} or 489 preceded by 600 zeros to the right of the point; about twelve lines of zeros in an ordinary book. . . . It is evident that exponents of over 100 lose all human significance."

The *probability* of an event through pure chance is the ratio of the number of cases favorable to the event to the total number of possibilities, provided all cases are equally probable. *Theoretically*, the event could happen at any time; *practically*, it will happen according to the 'law of statistical averages' as given above, and that means that in cases where fairly large numbers of items are involved the probability of the event happening is practically nil. Speaking *scientifically*, therefore, the probability of *ordered events* happening in nature through

---

[1] *Human Destiny* (New York: Longmans, Green & Co., Inc., 1947), p. 31 f.

pure chance is *practically impossible,* especially when 100 or more items are regularly disposed in an orderly arrangement.

Order and Intelligence

According to the calculus of probability, the ordered arrangement of things and events might happen once in a while, but the same calculus of probability would make the *regular* and *constant* ordered arrangement of things and events through chance utterly impossible. And yet, such order exists.

To account for the cases of existing order where none should logically exist, scientists often speak of *anti-chance* — a term introduced by Eddington. The term means 'a factor opposed to chance,' and such a term is devoid of all sense unless this factor be specified as something concrete. As such, the term 'anti-chance' is delightfully vague, coined to hide ignorance or to supplant the intellectual urge of seeking a rationally satisfying answer to the problem. What could this so-called 'anti-chance' be?

'Anti-chance' can only mean *design due to intelligence.* If order is not due to chance, then it can only be due to intelligence designing the order by arranging the various items into a system or whole according to some definite plan. Where intelligence is absent, chance must explain everything; and where chance cannot account for an orderly arrangement, intelligence must be assumed to make up for the deficiency of chance. There is no other possibility.

Aristotle[2] was well aware of the fact that chance cannot explain the order of nature: "In general, the theory [of chance, as the dominant factor in the universe] does away with the whole order of Nature, and indeed with Nature's self. For natural things are exactly those which do move continuously, in virtue of a principle inherent in themselves, toward a determined goal; and the final development which results from any one such principle is not identical for any two species, nor yet is it any random result; but in each there is always

---

[2] *Physics,* Bk. II, Chap. VIII, 199 b 15–30 (Cambridge, Mass.: Harvard University Press, 1929).

a tendency toward an identical result, if nothing interferes with the process. A desirable result and the means to it may also be produced by chance, as for instance we say it was 'by luck' that the stranger came and ransomed the prisoners before he left, where the ransoming is done as if the man had come for that purpose, though in fact he did not. In this case the desirable result is incidental; for, as we have explained, chance is an incidental cause. But when the desirable result is effected invariably and normally, it is not an incidental or chance occurrence; and in the course of Nature the result always is achieved invariably or normally, if nothing hinders. It is absurd to suppose that there is no purpose because in Nature we can never detect the moving power in the act of deliberation. . . . That Nature is a cause, then, and a goal-directed cause, is above dispute."

Aristotle, in this passage, plainly indicates that all natural processes are for an *end* or *purpose*. In other words, there is, in his view, *finality* in nature. His entire argument in this chapter (Chap. VIII) revolves around the finality present in nature, and finality, he argues, presupposes *intelligence*. As he says:[3] "Action for an end is present in things which come to be and are by nature . . . where a series has a completion, all the preceding steps are for the sake of that. Now surely as in intelligent action, so in nature; and as in nature, so it is in each action, if nothing interferes. Now, intelligent action is for an end; therefore the nature of things also is so. Thus if a house, e.g., had been a thing made by nature, it would have been made in the same way as it is now by art; and if things made by nature were made also by art, they would come to be in the same way as by nature. Each step then in the series is for the sake of the next; and generally art partly completes what nature cannot bring to a finish, and partly imitates her. If, therefore, artificial products are for the sake of an end, so clearly also are natural products. The relation of the later to the earlier terms of the series is the same in both."

---

[3] *Loc. cit.,* 199 a (New York: Random House, 1941).

From the *relation of means to end,* both in the products of art and of nature, Aristotle concludes that the order of nature is the result, not of chance, but of *purposive intelligence.* He cites many instances to prove his point.

Scientists, unless they are also philosophers, simply refrain from considering intelligence as a factor in the order of nature. From the standpoint of 'science' such an attitude is permissible. To refrain from considering intelligence is one thing; to deny its existence is an unwarranted step outside their restricted field of research. Hence, when a scientist *denies intelligence* as a factor in the order of nature, he is guilty of the fallacy of *false exclusion.*

'Purposiveness' in nature may not readily be detectable, due to the limitations of the human mind. *Order,* however, is an *observable fact* present throughout the universe.

Order in the World of Stars

In the following discussion, relative to the order present in the universe, the philosopher relies to a great extent on the materials furnished by the scientist. The scientist operates here in his proper field. However, one must distinguish between facts and theories, data and interpretations. In the past many theories have been advanced to explain the facts. The facts remain, but the theories have often been modified or even discarded. The theories of electricity and light are such. The general philosophic system advocated by the scientist obviously has much to do with his scientific interpretation of facts, and this must be borne in mind when considering the statements of scientists.

By means of the telescope, the spectroscope, the interferometer, and other instruments, astronomers have made great strides in their knowledge of the world of stars.

The immensity of the world of stars staggers the imagination. Human words are inadequate to describe the bulk, the magnitude, and the complexity of the universe. Nevertheless, the *fact of order* throughout this vast expanse is unmistakable.

One of the most remarkable facts disclosed by spectography

is the sameness of the materials everywhere; the same kinds of *elements* built our earth and built the stars. The same kinds of *radiation* occur in our sun, in the remotest stars and galaxies, and in the entire range of interstellar space. The *structure* of the galaxies is fundamentally uniform. The same *laws* operate here on earth and in the farthest reaches of the world. Mathematicians express all this in extremely complicated formulae. Such mathematical formulae, discovered after centuries of constant toil, are proof positive that the world of stars is not only 'intelligible' but the work of an extraordinary *intelligence* which grasps everything from a photon to the unimaginable immensity of the world at large.

Astronomers become almost lyrical in their praise of the beauty, the grandeur, the magnificence, and the symmetry of the universe. They speak of the *organic unity* present throughout the universe. Witness Robert Grant Aitken:[4] "For all its gigantic dimensions, all the bewildering complexities of its structure and motions, all the endless variety of its contents, our great stellar system, our universe so far as it has come within our range of observation, is an organic whole, exhibiting an underlying structural symmetry, built up throughout of the same basic elements, and governed by the same great laws. That the mind of man has been able to reach these great generalizations and through them to attain to the power of prediction, is proof of order and rationality in the universe. It is a universe, in my belief, with thought and more than thought within it."

Order in the World of Atoms

The world of atoms is just as marvelous as the world of stars. Formerly it was thought that the atoms were solid and indivisible substances. Since the turn of the century, however, this concept has been changed completely, mainly through the research of men like J. J. Thomson, E. Rutherford, H. Mosely,

---

4 Frances Mason, ed., *The Great Design* (New York: Macmillan, 1934), p. 36.

L. LeBroglie, N. Bohr, W. Heisenberg, E. Schrödinger, M. Born, P. Dirac, and M. Planck. While much of what follows is still theory, the views of these scientists have been signally vindicated through the technique of 'atom-smashing' and the explosion of the atom bomb.

There are ninety-four, perhaps ninety-six, natural kinds of atoms or *elements*. The pattern of their construction is fundamentally the same. Each one consists of a *nucleus* and *electrons* (or, as in the case of hydrogen, of a single electron). The nucleus represents the weight or mass of the atom, and it consists of protons possessing a positive charge of electricity and of neutrons. Neutrons are electrically neutral. Electrons are particles possessing a negative charge. Both the proton and the electron have an *equal charge* of electricity, namely, 4.8025 x 10^{-10} electrostatic units, and this charge never varies. There are also other particles, such as positrons, mesons, neutrinos, etc., but they need not concern us here.

Each element has distinctive physical and chemical properties. Among them are specific gravity, melting point, boiling point, ductility, malleability, compressibility, hardness, coefficient of expansion, refractive index, density, heat of combustion, heat of formation, conductivity of electricity and heat, combining weight, and so forth. These properties are *constant* for the various elements.

Elements with similar properties occur periodically. The periodic recurrence of similar elements is termed the *Periodic Law,* and this law states that the properties of the elements are the periodic functions of their atomic number, not of their atomic weight. The periodic table is arranged according to groups and series.

As early as 1914 Rydberg called attention to the fact that the 'atomic numbers' of the group O gases can be calculated from a series of numbers now called the *Rydberg Series,* expressed in the simple formula:

$$2(1^2 + 2^2 + 2^2 + 3^2 + 3^2 + 4^2 \ldots .)$$

According to this formula we obtain these results:

Element	At. No.	Rydberg Series
Helium	2	$2(1^2) = 2$
Neon	10	$2(1^2 + 2^2) = 10$
Argon	18	$2(1^2 + 2^2 + 2^2) = 18$
Krypton	36	$2(1^2 + 2^2 + 2^2 + 3^2) = 36$
Xenon	54	$2(1^2 + 2^2 + 2^2 + 3^2 + 3^2) = 54$
Radon	86	$2(1^2 + 2^2 + 2^2 + 3^2 + 3^2 + 4^2) = 86$

We also discover a remarkable *parallelism* in the series. The first series, that of hydrogen and helium, is unique. Hydrogen is active, helium is inert. This small series of two elements epitomizes within itself all the subsequent series of the periodic table. The lithium and sodium 'short' series are parallel in nearly all respects, each containing 8 elements. The potassium and rubidium 'long' series are also parallel to each other, each consisting of 18 members, of which 10 are transitional. The caesium 'longest' series is composed of 32 elements. If the last (radioactive) series, as some scientists believe, also had originally 32 elements, the parallelism would be complete; but that is only a conjecture, although the discovery of neptunium and plutonium (and perhaps other elements mentioned more recently) tends to verify this belief at least in part. The fact of periodicity and parallelism among the groups and series of elements is undeniable.[5]

When we consider that everything in the entire universe is built up from these elements and subatomic particles, we come face to face with one of the most astounding illustrations of *orderly arrangement*. This is particularly true when we also consider the chemical combination of elements into compounds.

Chemical *compounds* are never the result of haphazard, random combinations; they are always subject to definite laws. A compound is not a mere 'mixture' of chemical substances. A true chemical compound is *homogeneous* throughout; it is a

---

[5] For a more detailed discussion of the structure of matter, see the author's *From Aether to Cosmos* (Milwaukee: The Bruce Publishing Co., 1941), Chaps. II–V.

chemically new substance with new properties, the original elements losing their chemical identity in the process of combination. A compound is a combination of elements in *definite proportions of weight or volume*. This *law of combining weights affects all matter*, whether present in the test tube or on the earth or in the remotest nebula.

Electrons, protons, and neutrons *tend* to form elemental atoms, and elemental atoms *tend* to form chemical compounds according to the inexorable law of their combining weights. This tendency is frequently called *chemical affinity*. Such is the tremendous fact of orderly arrangement governing the entire universe.

No wonder, then, that Sir Oliver Lodge wrote:[6] "I claim that the material universe with its variously designed atoms, and the way they have been used in the construction of all the objects, minerals, vegetable, and animal, that we see around us, is a sign also of gigantic Design and Purpose, and is a glorious Work of Art."

Order in the World of Plants

The *plant* is the lowest form of life on the globe. It possesses no recognizable consciousness. Nevertheless, even the unicellular plant has a structure and performs functions which are amazing in their intricacy and inherent purposiveness. It acts almost as if it had knowledge of a definite goal and consciously strove to realize it.

The fundamental unit of life is the *cell*. Just as the physicists formerly thought that the atoms were simple substances, so the biologists thought that the ultimate constituents of living beings were relatively simple parts. However, the more biological research penetrates into the structure and function of the cell, the more mysteries it discovers.

The cell is not a mere mass of matter: it is *organized*. A watch, a linotype machine, a rotary printing press, a diesel engine, when compared to the complexity and sensitivity of a

---

[6] As quoted in *The Great Design, op. cit.*, p. 231.

cell, are but clumsy contrivances. This fact becomes more obvious when consideration is given to the hundreds of thousands of *species* and hundreds of millions of *individual plants* existing on earth, all of which are different and yet are built up of single cells which are fundamentally alike as to plan. That each plant body is a *unit,* is evident; it possesses organs or structural parts distinct from one another, and the different organs have specific functions to perform, as can be observed in the roots, the stem, the leaves, the flowers, and the fruits. All parts and all functions are present not for their own sake, but for the sake of the *organism as a whole;* they are mutually dependent and conspire toward the welfare of the individual as a totality. It is the individual which counts, not so much the parts. The individual is, in all truth, more than the sum of the atoms and molecules and parts which make up its body.

Two specific functions of plant life deserve special attention: metabolism and cell division. Both functions show definitely the use of proper means to realize specific ends or purposes — *self-preservation* and the *perpetuation of the species.*

The cell is a magnificent *laboratory.* Without electric appliances and furnaces, without the aid of heat and pressure, without technical knowledge and experimentation, the cell manufactures organic compounds and by-products which man has found extremely difficult to make synthetically and which still escape, in very many instances, man's skill and ingenuity. Depending upon the part the cells play in the general economy of the total organism, each one will absorb only the kind of material needed and fabricate the type of compound required.

Nutrition, growth, and propagation[7] are the main functions of vegetative life. Although the plant has many diversified activities, they are all subservient to these three. Volumes could be, and have been, written about the wonders of plant life. These few points have been stressed so as to bring out the orderly arrangement and purposiveness existing in *all plants.*

---

[7] For illustrations of the cell division in mitosis and maturation division, see the author's *The Whole Man* (Milwaukee: The Bruce Publishing Co., 1945), Chap. II.

The plant is indeed a *whole-making and self-regulating structural unit.*

Order in the World of Animals

Like the plant, the animal is a vegetant being. It is a remarkable feature of the animal body that all vegetant life is subordinated to the building of a body specifically *ordered to sentiency.*

Every animal has a *nervous system* of some kind, because nerves are necessary for sentiency. The basic unit of the nervous system is the neuron, or nerve cell.

The nervous system in its structures and functions is without question a very complicated but orderly arrangement of means toward end, namely, a method to bring the animal in contact with its environment through knowledge and to enable it to preserve its own life and its own kind. Each sense and organ is marvelously constructed and designed for its particular function.

Consider the *eye.* Long before man invented the camera, the principles of optics embodied in the camera were already existing in the eye, only in a simpler and more efficient manner. The front of the eye must be transparent, and yet the cornea is fashioned out of the opaque connective tissue of the sclerotic coat. The convex lens of the camera is also found in the eye, made out of opaque epithelium; so as to focus the picture properly, this lens is capable of changing its convexity, something the glass lens of the camera cannot do. The iris is the diaphragm of the camera; in order to correct any aberration of light rays and to block out marginal rays, and in order to obtain a clear picture, the iris is automatically adjusted by the amount and intensity of the light rays entering the eye. Like all optical instruments, which must be blackened inside in order to quench any reflecting light from the walls, the inside of the eye is covered with a black pigment (melanin). The photo-sensitive plate of the camera is duplicated in the retina of the eye. The retina, however, is far better than the photographic plate, because the retina need not be replaced for successive pictures. The retina is constructed of cones for color vision and of rods for plain luminosity. The eye, unlike the camera, repairs its damaged parts and keeps all parts in working condition. Due to accident, disease, and heredity, the eye may be defective, but it will always be superior to the camera by the fact that it enables the individual to have *conscious perception* of images in three-dimensional views. The eye is a marvelous instrument in its order.

Practically all animals have the power of *locomotion,* and the structures are perfectly adapted to their environment in the air, on the land, and in the water. Eons before the coming of man and his inventions, levers existed in the animal body; the eyeball is moved by a muscular pulley; the heart is a force-pump; valves are used in the heart and in the veins; the poison fang of the snake is a hypodermic syringe; the cilia in the windpipe are brushes to remove mucus; electric eels have charged electric batteries; the glow-worms and fire-flies manufacture heatless light; the submarine's principle of flota-tion and submergence is utilized in the swim-bladder of the fish; the bird is the ideal heavier-than-air flying craft. If man's inventions are the result of design and purpose, these must also be such.

In commenting on the co-ordination and adaptation of that extraordinary piece of workmanship, the bird's *wing* and *feather,* Alfred Russell Wallace,[8] the eminent scientist, re-marks as follows: "Each feather 'grows,' as we say, out of the skin, each one from a small group of cells, which must be formed and nourished by the blood, and is reproduced each year to replace that which falls away at moulting time. But the same blood supplies material for every other part of the body — builds up and renews the muscles, the bones, the viscera, the skin, the nerves, the brain. What, then, is the *selective* or *directing* power which extracts from the blood at every point where required the exact constituents to form here bone-cells, there muscle-cells, there again feather-cells,

---

8 *The World of Life* (New York: Moffat, Yard, and Co., 1911), p. 318 f.

each of which possesses such totally distinct properties? And when these cells, or rather, perhaps, the complex molecules of which each kind of cell is formed, are separated at its special point, what is the *constructive* power which welds them together, as it were, in one place into solid bone, in another into the extremely light, strong, elastic material of the feather — the most unique and marvelous product of life?

"Yet again, what is the nature of the power which determines that every separate feather shall always 'grow' into its exact shape? For no two feathers of the twenty or more which form each wing, or those of the tail, or even of the thousands on the whole body, are exactly alike (except as regards the pairs on opposite sides of the body), and many of these are modified in the strangest way for special purposes. Again, what directive agency determines the distribution of the coloring matter (also conveyed by the blood) so that each feather shall take its exact share in the production of the whole pattern and coloring of the bird, which is immensely varied, yet always symmetrical as a whole, and has always a purpose, either of concealment, or recognition, or sexual attraction in its proper time and place?"

Wherever we look in the world of animals, we discover millions of examples of order, design, and purpose, but the animals themselves know nothing about them.

Order in the World of Men

Man is an epitome of the universe. In him are united the atoms and molecules and energies of the inanimate world, the power of nutrition and growth and reproduction of the vegetant cells found in plants, the sensory organs and functions present in the animal body.

Yet so completely are these three worlds integrated in man that he is a *unitary substance* in every respect. The atoms and molecules are subservient to his vegetant life, the vegetant structures and activities are subservient to his sensory life, and the sensory organs and functions are subservient to his intellectual life. In him everything is harmoniously united and becomes

one. In this connection, little more can be done than point out
a few pertinent facts.

Like every plant and animal, man originates from a single
fecundated cell. As Alexis Carrel[9] observes: "An organ builds
itself by techniques very foreign to the human mind. It is
not made of extraneous material, like a house. Neither is it a
cellular construction, a mere assemblage of cells. It is, of course,
composed of cells, as a house is of bricks. But it is born from
a cell, as if the house originated from one brick, a magic brick
that would set about manufacturing other bricks. Those bricks,
without waiting for the architect's drawings or the coming
of the bricklayers, would assemble themselves and form the
walls. They would also metamorphose into windowpanes,
roofing-slates, coal for heating, and water for the kitchen and
bathroom. An organ develops by means such as those attributed to fairies in the tales told to children in by-gone times.
It is engendered by cells which, to all appearances, have a
knowledge of the future edifice, and synthetize from substances
contained in blood plasma the building material and even the
workers."

The formation of the *human embryo* in the mother's womb
is one of the many wonders of nature. Bones, nerves, hands,
feet, eyes, ears, heart, lungs, viscera, and every other type of
structure and organ are made in the dark cavern of the womb
long before they can be used. The mother does not consciously
form the parts of the body of the child and assemble them
into the pattern possessed at birth. If the formation of the
child depended on the knowledge and conscious activity of
the parents, no child would be born or even go beyond the
first stage of life. Nonetheless, the miracle of conception and
birth happens, not once but millions and billions of times.

Among all the other things, the *hand* is formed in the
embryo at a rather early period. "The hand," says Alexis
Carrel,[10] "is a masterpiece. Simultaneously, it feels and it acts.

---

9 *Man the Unknown* (New York: Harper and Bros., 1935), p. 107 f.
10 *Ibid.*, p. 97 f.

It acts as if endowed with sight. Owing to the unique properties of its skin, its tactile nerves, its muscles, and its bones, the
hand is capable of manufacturing arms and tools. We never
would have acquired our mastery over matter without the aid
of our fingers, those five small levers, each composed of three
articulated segments, which are mounted upon the metacarpus
and the bones of the wrist. The hand adapts itself to the
roughest work as well as to the most delicate. It has wielded
with equal skill the flint knife of the primitive hunter, the
blacksmith's hammer, the woodcutter's ax, the farmer's plow,
the sword of the medieval knight, the controls of the modern
aviator, the artist's brush, the journalist's pen, the threads of
the silk-weaver. It is able to kill and to bless, to steal and to
give, to sow grain on the surface of the fields and to throw
grenades in the trenches." Similar words could be said of any
number of human organs.

Or, consider the human *brain*. The substance of the brain
consists of more than twelve thousand millions of cells, all
connected together by fibrils, so that the cells associate several
trillions of times. The entire nervous system of man centers in
the brain. The brain is the seat of consciousness. Even thought
is somehow connected with the activity of the brain. The brain
is far more complicated and intricate in its structure and operation than the whole material universe. Notwithstanding the
unimaginable number of its component parts and the immense complexity of its activity, the brain functions as an
essential unit.

From the standpoint of physical size, man is halfway between the big stars and the infinitesimal atoms; he thus
occupies the pivotal position in the universe. The crowning
achievement of man, however, lies in the field of his *intellect*
and *will*. Through these powers he surpasses the material
world and the kingdoms of plant and animal. By means of
his intellect man is able to penetrate the mysteries of nature
and interpret it. Civilization and culture, science and art,
commerce and industry, government and social service, peace
and war, good and evil — all derive their beginning and ful-

fillment from the use of man's intellect and will. Saint or sinner, man is in truth "wonderfully made."

The more the sciences advance, the more they discover of order and design. Much more could have been said than is said here, but this brief survey will suffice.

The world is, without doubt, a *universe,* a *cosmos.*

Conclusions

A system of order is the result either of chance or of intelligence. Now, the universe is a system of order. Therefore, the universe is the result either of chance or of intelligence.

Order may be, and sometimes is, the result of *chance.* However, a chance effect must conform to the probabilities inherent in chance. Statistical averages are all that can be expected in such effects, because the calculus of probability admits of nothing more uniform than a statistical average. The greater the number of items involved in the chance effect, the smaller (in geometrical progression) the probability of occurrence. Where more than one hundred items are concerned, the statistical average is so small as to be *practically impossible.* Theoretically, of course, the chance effect may occur at any time, because no opportunities are privileged. Nevertheless, chance is governed entirely by the calculus of probability and the statistical average derived therefrom. Due to this fact, a chance effect involving a large number of items can only occur here and there, now and then. As a consequence, chance can never achieve anything like *uniformity, regularity,* and *constancy* in its effects; otherwise these effects would simply not be due to 'chance.' Where there is uniformity, regularity, and constancy in an arrangement of entities or operations, there is *law;* and law is the very antithesis of chance. Hence, when law governs an event, chance is eliminated as the governing factor.

Now, *the universe,* as science testifies in each of its departments, *is governed by law.* The universe is a vast system of orderly arrangements, whether viewed in the light-year expanse of the material world at large or in the millimicron smallness of atoms and subatomic particles or in the beautifully designed kingdoms of plants, animals, and men. This order prevails not only here and there, now and then, but *everywhere* and *always.* Chance effects, of course, do occur; however, the order present everywhere of nature is uniform, regular, and constant. Order is the rule; chance effects are the exception. It follows then, that the order present in the universe cannot be explained and accounted for by 'chance.'

A system of order must be the result either of chance or of intelligence. The universe is a system of order. Since it cannot be the result of chance, it must be the result of *intelligence.*

Every atom, every element, and every chemical compound is based on an orderly arrangement of parts and activities; as such, they must be the effect of an intelligence as their proper cause. The entire universe, however, is composed of the same kinds of atoms, elements, and compounds. Hence, the same intelligence which is responsible for the orderly arrangement present in the atoms, elements, and compounds must also be responsible for the orderly arrangement of the entire universe. All plants, animals, and men are composed of fundamentally the same kinds of cells, and these cells in turn are composed of atoms, elements, and compounds taken from the inanimate world (though changed considerably in the vital processes going on in the living tissues), and all cells reveal an orderly arrangement of structures and functions. Consequently, the same intelligence which is responsible for the orderly arrangement present in the atoms, elements, and compounds must also be responsible for the orderly arrangement of the kingdoms of plants, animals, and men. In other words, since the entire universe is a *system of unity,* the order of the entire universe and of all its parts must be referred to the *self-same ordering intelligence.*

Arthur H. Compton,[11] one of the great modern scientists, recognized this principle when he wrote: "If we see in nature evidence of a plan, this will imply intelligence, for a plan or

---

[11] "A Modern Concept of God," *Man's Destiny In Eternity* (Boston: The Beacon Press, 1949), p. 8 f.

purpose is otherwise meaningless. The alternative to an intelligent plan for the world is that things have happened to be as they are through chance. . . . Here we are concerned with statistics, and the statistical probability of a world's happening to have a form similar to ours in so fantastically small that even in the billions of years that astronomers might allow for the age of our galaxy it must be considered as a highly improbable hypothesis. . . . If the simple yet prolific set of pushes and pulls to which the electrons are subject result from pure chance, then chance is more ingenious than the most clever of our scientists."

Philosophy, on the strength of the Principle of Sufficient Reason, demands intelligence as the logical explanation of order. Structures and functions always exist in order to realize a definite effect; that is their purpose — they are a *means toward a specific end.* However, only an intelligent being is capable of grasping an end to be realized and of designing the means necessary to realize the achievement of this end. Philosophy, therefore, also demands intelligence as the sufficient reason for accounting for the order of the universe.

Proof of God's Existence

Order demands intelligence, when order is uniform, regular, and constant. The order in the universe, therefore, is an intelligent order and can only be the effect of an *intelligent cause.*

It should be evident that *the universe itself does not possess intelligence.* The universe as a whole is inanimate. Intelligence, however, presupposes life, because intelligence is a form of life. The great bulk of the universe outside our earth is altogether devoid of life. All the bodies existing in the vast expanse of the world are made up of the same kinds of atoms and compounds present on the earth. The single atoms, however, lack intelligence; even if they had intelligence, they are all individual units, and it is inconceivable that they would be the cause of the general order prevailing everywhere. Plants, animals, and men have life. But the plant has no consciousness, and the animal no rational mind. Of all the beings in the world, man alone possesses a rational mind. This rational intelligence of man, however, is not due to himself; it is given with his nature, and man is not the cause of his own nature. Man is an integral part of the universe, and as such his rational intelligence must be derived from the same rational mind which ordered the entire universe; and this rational mind must be as much more powerful than man's mind as the order of the universe is greater than the order existing merely in man.

The entire universe and all its parts are *subject to the law of order*. Order has been *imposed* on them, and they *obey* the law of order in their whole being. It follows, then, that the rational intelligence which put the law of order into them *cannot be the universe itself* nor any part of the universe; otherwise it would impose the law and be subject to it, be 'orderer' and 'ordered,' at the same time under the same respect. This means that the rational mind or intelligence responsible for the order and design present in the universe is itself 'extra-universe,' *extra-mundane,* distinct in being from the universe and from all beings comprising it. And since man is an intelligent person, this rational intelligence ordering the world must also be *personal.* Now, the personal, extra-mundane designer and orderer of the universe we call God.

Therefore, *God exists.*

The Argument of St. Thomas

The proof for God's existence, based on order and design, is called by St. Thomas[12] the 'way taken from the governance of the world.' It is his fifth proof, and he formulates it as follows:

"The fifth way is taken from the governance of the world. We see that things which lack intelligence, such as natural bodies, act for an end, and this is evident from their acting always, or nearly always, in the same way, so as to obtain the best result. Hence, it is plain that not fortuitously, but designedly, do they achieve their end. Now whatever lacks intelli-

---

[12] *Summa Theologica* (New York: Benziger Bros.), I, qu. 2, art. 3.

gence cannot move toward an end, unless it be directed by some being endowed with knowledge and intelligence; as the arrow is shot to its mark by the archer. Therefore some intelligent being exists by whom all natural things are directed to their end; and this being we call God."

One cannot help but admire the brevity and penetrating logic of St. Thomas in this argument. It contains everything essential. Its brevity, however, might fail to convince the average student; and so his line of reasoning has been expanded in the foregoing sections, in the hope that the student will grasp the significance of the argument better.

We close our discussion of order and design in nature with the words of Robert A. Millikan:[13] "Wise men have always looked in amazement at the wonderful orderliness of nature and then recognized their own ignorance and finiteness and have been content to stand in silence and in reverence before Him, repeating with the psalmist: 'The fool hath said in his heart, there is no God.'"

Summary of Chapter V

Another proof for God's existence is the one based on the *order* and *design* present in the universe.

1. *Order and Design.* — 'Order' is the arrangement of various items into a system or whole according to some relationship existing or placed between them. Order may be 'static' or 'dynamic,' 'natural' or 'artificial.'

'Design' is the arrangement of various items into a system or whole, so that this arrangement is the result of plan and intention. Wherever there is design, there is purpose.

2. *Order and Chance.* — 'Chance' is a mode of causal activity, not purposive in character, regarded as determining an event. Chance implies the absence of regularity, and for that reason it excludes predictability except on the basis of a 'statistical average.'

3. *Chance and Probability.* — Where pure chance is concerned, the mathematical laws of probability alone govern everything. Probability on the basis of chance follows the ratio of 'geometrical progression.'

---

13 "My Faith" (New York: The American Weekly, Inc., 1948).

4. *Order and Intelligence.* — Where intelligence is absent, chance must explain everything; and where chance cannot account for an orderly arrangement, intelligence must be assumed to make up for the deficiency of chance.

5. *Order in the World of Stars.* — The fact of order in the universe is unmistakable. This is seen in the elements, radiation, structure of the galaxies, and the laws governing the universe. The universe is a *system*, a *unit*.

6. *Order in the World of Atoms.* — The elements, the atoms, and the subatomic particles reveal an orderly arrangement, as can be seen in the Table of Elements and in the Periodic Law. Chemical compounds are regulated by the law of combining weights, and this law affects all matter.

7. *Order in the World of Plants.* — The fundamental unit of life is the *cell*. Its activities are metabolism, growth, and reproduction. Cell division in 'mitosis' and 'maturation division' are functions directed toward self-preservation and the perpetuation of the race. The plant is a whole-making and self-regulating structural *unit*.

8. *Order in the World of Animals.* — All activities are ordered to sentiency. The *neuron* is the basic unit of the nervous system. The organs of perception are marvels of construction and function. The structures involved in locomotion are perfectly adapted to the environment in the air, on the land, and in the water.

9. *Order in the World of Men.* — The activities of the inanimate atoms, the vegetant functions of the plants, and the sensory functions of the animal are all subservient in man to his intellectual life. Man is a *unitary substance* in every respect. The crowning achievement of man lies in the field of his intellect and will.

10. *Conclusions.* — Chance cannot achieve anything like *uniformity, regularity,* and *constancy* in its effects. The universe, however, is governed by *law,* and as a result there is everywhere uniformity, regularity, and constancy. Hence, the universe, as a system of order, must be the result, not of chance, but of *intelligence,* and this intelligence must be *one* for the entire universe. This conclusion is borne out by common sense, by science, and by philosophy.

11. *Proof of God's Existence.* — The universe itself does not possess intelligence. The entire universe is *subject to the law of order.* Hence, the intelligence responsible for the order in the universe cannot be identified with the universe, but must be *extra-mundane.* Since man is a 'person,' the rational intelligence ordering the world

must also be *personal*. This personal, extra-mundane designer and orderer of the universe we call God. Therefore, *God exists*.

12. *The Argument of St. Thomas.* — The fifth proof of St. Thomas is the argument based on order and design. It is essentially the same as the argument developed in this chapter.

Readings

Driscoll, John T., *God*, Chap. IX. — Joyce, George Hayward, *Principles of Natural Theology*, Part I, Chap. IV. — Boedder, Bernard, *Natural Theology*, Book I, Chap. II. — Aveling, Francis, *The God of Philosophy*, Chap. IX. — *The Great Design*, ed. by Frances Mason. — Carrel, Alexis, *Man the Unknown*. — Smith, Gerard, *Natural Theology*, Chap. IX. — Renard, Henri, *The Philosophy of God*, pp. 45–48.

Chapter VI

CONTINGENCY AND CAUSALITY

MOST people are convinced of God's existence through a contemplation of 'order and design' in the universe, because order demands intelligence, and intelligence is not found in inanimate things themselves. Many scientists accuse such persons of *anthropomorphism,* that is to say, of attributing human activities to nonhuman beings; because man has an intelligent purpose in ordering things, therefore also the order manifest in the world must have an intelligent cause. The principle, however, underlying order is a logical principle, one demanded by reason as the rational explanation of order; otherwise 'chance' must be accepted as the sole explanation of order, and chance is totally inadequate as a rational explanation. Hence, the proof from 'order' leads to the existence of God.

Another argument, more philosophical in character, is based on the *contingency* of the beings present in the universe. The argument from *causality* is closely related to that of contingency. These will now receive consideration.

Necessity and Contingency

For a clear presentation of the argument, the terms involved must be defined.

Necessity is that state in virtue of which something cannot be otherwise than it is. Something, therefore, is said to be *necessary* if it *must be* what it is; or, to put it negatively, something is necessary if it *cannot not be* what it is.

A distinction is made between moral, physical, logical, and ontological necessity. *Moral* necessity is the 'obligation' which a moral law imposes on the will; such is, for instance, the obligation to respect human life as required by the law 'Thou shalt not kill.' *Physical* necessity is the necessity imposed on a thing according to the law of physical nature; thus, the movements of the planets around the sun are physically necessary. *Logical* necessity is the necessity resulting from the force of a law of logic; it is, for example, a law of logic that contradictories can neither be true nor false together. *Ontological* necessity is the necessity which arises in a thing because of its 'being,' 'essence,' 'nature'; because a being is an 'organism,' it necessarily possesses 'life.' Something, therefore, may be necessary in any of these given meanings. Here we are concerned solely with 'ontological' necessity.

A further distinction is made in 'ontological' necessity. In the order of its being a thing may be either 'hypothetically' or 'absolutely' necessary. Something is said to be *hypothetically* necessary when its existence is dependent on a cause, but which, once the condition of its existence is given, must be (cannot not be) a definite reality; man need not, for example, always exist but, if he exists, he must be an 'animal' while he exists. Something is *absolutely* necessary when it exists in such a manner that it *must exist,* independent of any condition; such a being *cannot not* exist, because its non-existence would imply a contradiction.

Since non-existence would be a contradiction in an absolutely necessary being, it is evident that it *cannot receive existence* from another being; that means that it is *uncaused* and must exist always. Such a being can have the sufficient reason for its existence in itself only, so that it exists entirely of itself and by reason of its *nature* or *essence.* Existence belonging to the constitution of its essence, the absolutely necessary being includes existence in its very concept and definition, at least implicitly. To exclude actual existence from the concept of the necessary being, or to consider actual existence as something superadded to its essence, would deny absolute necessity itself, because then this being would have the sufficient reason for its existence in itself and not have it in itself at the same time and under the same respect. In the absolutely necessary being, therefore, essence and existence must actually be identical; otherwise it would necessarily exist and not necessarily exist, and that would be a contradiction.

Contingency is that state in virtue of which something can be otherwise than it is in its being or existence or both. A *contingent* being is a being which is what it is, but could be different; if it actually exists, it exists in such a manner that its non-existence would involve no contradiction because existence does not belong to the constitution of its essence.

'Contingency' is the contradictory of 'necessity,' and a 'contingent being' is the contradictory of a 'necessary being.' A contingent being is essentially *non-necessary:* if it does not exist, it can receive existence; and if it exists, it can lose its existence (or at least be thought of as non-existent), without a contradiction being expressed or implied. It follows that a contingent being has not the sufficient reason for its existence in itself and by reason of its nature or essence; if it had, it would be a necessary being and would exist through absolute necessity.

Since the contingent being has not the sufficient reason for its existence in itself, it can have this sufficient reason only *in another.* The necessary being's existence is uncaused, and as a consequence the contingent being's existence must be *caused.* Just as 'absolutely necessary' and 'contingent' are contradictory terms and cannot be true together, so 'uncaused existence' and 'caused existence' are contradictory terms and cannot be true together.

Contingency and the World

Having explained the meaning of a 'contingent being,' we must now turn our attention to the different types of being present in the universe and establish the *fact of their contingency.* The first point to consider is the *mode of the physical world at large.*

Astronomers and astrophysicists assure us most emphatically that the *mode of the universe* never remains the same; it has undergone a great change in the past, is changing continuously in the present, and will continue to do so for eons to come. Not only do 'new stars' explode into brilliance, but all the stars slowly alter their physical and chemical form without cessation, as can be observed in the emission of various kinds of radiation, particularly of light and heat. The vast galaxies, according to all evidence, are in a constant evolution of structure, as would be expected if this is an expanding universe. Motion exists everywhere, and motion means physical change.

Our *earth* is a typical planet-star. That it is presently undergoing an incessant process of form and structure, is an observable fact. The evidence accumulated by the science of geology points in a fairly conclusive fashion to the fact that the earth was a molten body in the far-distant past and has gradually cooled off through radiation; the oceans flowed together; the continents rose; the mountain ranges upheaved their massiveness; extensive deposits of rocks covered the globe. And all this happened in calculable time. What occurred on the earth presumably also took place in similar fashion on planets such as Mars and Venus and other stars, and all celestial bodies are headed toward a similar fate.

Since the mode or structure of the universe at large is continuously changing now, the conclusion is justified that it has changed in the past and will change in the future. The process may take millions or billions of years, but the time element is of no particular significance. The fact of change in the structure of the universe is positive proof that it *does not exist necessarily;* if this structure were a 'necessary being,' it would have to remain as it always has been. The *mode* of the universe, therefore, is *contingent.*

Contingency and Organisms

So far as we know, the earth is the only planet which contains organisms. Plants, animals, and men comprise the three kingdoms of living beings. If it should ever be established that life also exists on some other planet or star, it would still remain a fact that *organisms are contingent beings.*

Organic life cannot exist on the incandescent stars; the heat is far too intense to sustain it. Even on this earth organisms did not always exist, because the earth, as geologists point out, was formerly in a stage of incandescence; this is shown by the sequence of the rock deposits, because the oldest formations are layers of igneous rocks.

In any case, the idea of 'kingdoms' of plants, animals, and men is an abstraction. In reality, nothing exists but *individual* plants, animals, and men. That every one of them is a 'contingent being,' is obvious. Each one has had its *origin in time*. The life span of every organism is relatively short, and then it dies and *ceases to exist*.

Anything, however, which has a beginning and an end to its existence cannot be an absolutely necessary being, because a necessary being must be whatever it is and remain such at all times. Organisms, therefore, are non-necessary and, as a consequence, *contingent*.

Contingency and Atoms

Wherever there is *composition* there is *contingency*. Protons, electrons, and neutrons may exist in a 'free state' or in 'conjunction.' At one time they may exist in the one state and at another time in the other. Elements, of course, are being continuously formed and dissolved, both in the laboratory and in nature; they are, therefore, manifestly contingent. Atoms and elements do not remain the same at all times, because they are in a constant process of change, whether viewed individually or as constituents of chemical compounds; they, too, must be classified among the contingent beings. Even the subatomic particles undergo change in many ways, because their behavior is different when in the 'free state' and when in conjunction with others in an element or compound; one cannot say, therefore, that they 'must be' forever what they are at any particular point of time. For the scientist who is convinced that matter and energy are interchangeable the conclusion must be inevitable that subatomic particles, elements, and compounds are by their very nature unstable in their entity. Whether one agrees or disagrees with this view, that fact of *change* and *composition* in all bodies constituting the universe is proof positive that individual bodies are not absolutely necessary.

Subatomic particles, atoms, elements, and compounds, no matter what their size or number, are therefore *contingent beings*.

Contingency and Matter

While many persons, particularly materialistic scientists, are willing enough to admit that individual bodies and their component particles change continuously, they maintain that *matter* is eternal and therefore necessary. If matter is actually eternal, without a beginning and a passage from non-existence to existence, it has its existence in virtue of its essence; such a being is not hypothetically but absolutely necessary so that it *must be whatever it is*.

Now matter does not exist in the abstract but *in the concrete*. Matter exists in specific forms, namely, concretely as subatomic particles, elements, chemical compounds, plants, animals, men, stars, galaxies, and interstellar material. They change, and *matter changes* in and with them. Because of this constant change, matter cannot be said to be 'necessarily what it is.'

If matter were necessary and eternal, then it would necessarily and eternally be and remain the same, because it would be absolutely independent of every other being in its essence and existence. Regarding a state of *rest* or a state of *motion,* it would have to exist at rest or in motion, whichever is *first*. Both states cannot be present at the same time under the same respect, because that would be a contradiction, and contradictories cannot be true together. If matter existed from eternity in motion, then *motion is necessary,* because motion would be given with the essence of matter; motion would simply be a mode of the existence of this essence and as necessary as the essence of matter itself. If a state of rest is considered as being present at first, then *rest is necessary and essential to matter*. Scientists are more inclined to the viewpoint that all matter is in motion. However, motion is always definite with regard to *velocity* and *direction;* there is no such thing as 'indeterminate' motion. Consequently, if matter were in motion eternally, it would necessarily have a motion which is definite with regard to velocity and direction, and this motion *could never change*. Now, motion changes continuously, both as to velocity and direction. Therefore, motion is not essential to matter. But neither is rest, since there is real motion in the world. Consequently, the essence of matter is not necessary, but must be *contingent*.

Materialists put forth the claim that matter is eternal. In this claim they contradict the best *evidence of science*. Thermodynamics assures us that the amount of energy available for useful work is diminishing; various forms of energy are converted into heat, and heat is being dissipated into space. Since heat can do work only when passing from a higher to a lower level, it is 'unidirectional' in its activity, with the result that the universe is caught in an *irreversible process*. This means that the universe is gradually running down and is slowly proceeding toward energy-death. The end of activity in the universe may be immeasurably far away in the future, but it is unavoidable and final because the supply of energy in the stars is not unlimited. The supply of energy being limited, the conclusion is evident that sometime in the past there was a *beginning to the universe as presently constituted:* where there is an end there must be a beginning. But if there is a beginning to the activity of the universe, there must also be a beginning to the matter of which the universe is composed. Hence, the universe and its matter is contingent in its existence. Scientists have discovered various clues which enable them to calculate the *age of the universe*. The radioactive elements, such as uranium, thorium, and actinium, have a stable and unvarying rate of disintegration, and no known force is capable of inaugurating, accelerating, retarding, or stopping this process. The amount of radioactive elements is relatively small, and there is no indication whatsoever of the formation of a further supply. The entire supply, for example, of uranium on earth must therefore have had its beginning at *one specific time* in the past; it could not have existed from eternity, otherwise it would now, according to the established rate of disintegration, be already converted into radio-lead. Geophysicists calculate that the origin of radioactive elements occurred about two billion years ago. Astronomers, judging from the rate at which radiation takes place in the stars, also arrive at the figure of approximately two billion years for the beginning of the universe. Similarly, the cosmogonists, in their study of the velocity of the receding galaxies, calculate that the beginning of the expansion of the universe occurred about two billion years ago. All these clues indicate that the universe will come to an end definitely fixed in time and for the same reasons had a beginning definitely fixed in time. If these calculations are basically sound, the universe, together with its matter, *cannot have existed from eternity but must have had a beginning in time.* Even if one assumed (and this is a gratuitous assumption, without any foundation in fact) that a previous world existed, out of which the present world was somehow formed, one would have no rational explanation of the *collocation of matter* so as to account for the *orginal formation* of the present world. After all, the only universe we know is the present one, and it is the origin of this universe which must be accounted for. The pertinent facts of our present universe, however, all lead to the conclusion that it began in time. And since matter in the concrete is identical with the present universe, matter too must have had a beginning. But if matter had a beginning, it cannot be eternal and it must be *contingent.*

The same conclusion is reached on purely *rational grounds.* An absolutely necessary being is such that its non-existence would imply a contradiction. Hence, *it cannot be thought of as non-existent without a contradiction.*

I can take any single molecule, atom, or subatomic particle (for example, any electron or proton in the ink of my pen) and think of it as ceasing to exist, without any contradiction in the thought. I see no 'necessity' in its existence; the rest of the world could and would exist without its presence. If it were possible to annihilate it, the universe would suffer no perceptible loss thereby; its non-existence would involve no contradiction. And that holds true of every single molecule, atom, or subatomic particle existing as an individual reality in the world; each one is no more absolutely necessary in its existence than the one present in the ink of my pen. Now, the universe as a totality consists entirely of such individual molecules, atoms, and subatomic particles. Hence, if the individual entities can be non-existent without a contradiction being implied, their totality (the universe) can also be non-existent without a contradiction being implied. Consequently, the totality of all material beings is not absolutely necessary. The *universe,* and all the *matter* composing it, is non-necessary and therefore *contingent.*

Proof for God's Existence

A contingent being is the contradictory of an absolutely necessary being. The necessary being owes its existence to itself in such a manner that it has existence in virtue of its own essence. The necessary being *must be what it is,* both as regards its essence and existence; hence, it must be unproduced, independent of every other being. Non-existence would imply a contradiction in the very idea of the necessary being.

The contingent being, on the other hand, since it is the contradictory of the necessary being, cannot owe its existence to itself in such a manner that it has existence in virtue of its own essence; its essence is such that it can exist or not exist. The contingent being *need not be what it is,* both as regards its essence and existence; if it has a definite essence and existence, it is not due to the contingent being itself. The contingent being, unlike the necessary being, must be produced, because its existence is dependent on some other being. The non-existence of the contingent being does not imply a contradiction in its very idea.

Therefore, the contingent being does not contain the sufficient reason for its essence and existence in itself. Of itself, the contingent being is nothing. Whatever it is and has it owes, not to itself, but to some other being. Consequently, if a contingent being has determinateness of essence and has actual existence, it must have *received* everything from *some other being* distinct from itself.

This 'other being' must also be either *contingent* or *not contingent;* this division is one of contradictories and as such exclusive. If it is *not contingent,* then we have arrived at an absolutely necessary being whose non-existence implies a contradiction in terms; and this being has the sufficient reason for its total essence and existence in itself and is absolutely independent of every other being in all that it is and has. If *contingent,* it will not have the sufficient reason for its essence and existence in itself but in some other being. Then this 'other being' must again be either contingent or not contingent; and this process of elimination will have to continue until we eventually arrive at the *absolutely necessary being* which has the sufficient reason of its own essence and existence in itself and also the sufficient reason of the essence and existence of the contingent beings throughout the universe.

To postulate an *infinite number* of contingent beings will not save the situation for those who do not admit the existence of an absolutely necessary being outside the present universe. This entire infinite series, since it is contingent in every member, would not have the sufficient reason for its existence in itself, and so the *entire series* and all its members could not exist. The mere multiplication of numbers explains nothing and does not account for their existence, if every single member of the series is a contingent being: an infinite number of blind persons will not give sight to a single one of them. Now, contingent beings actually exist, as we know from experience, and the present universe is contingent. Therefore, an *absolutely necessary being exists* outside the present universe, and the universe and everything in it depends on this necessary being for its essence and existence.

This being is absolutely necessary and therefore unconditioned and eternal. Its existence is due solely to its own essence. Since this being cannot have received its essence and existence from any other being, it is essentially and existentially *self-*

sufficient and *self-existent.* Philosophers express this idea by the term *ens a se,* namely, a being which is what it is and exists 'of and by itself.' The expression *ens a se* does not mean that it 'produced' itself, because such an interpretation of the phrase would contain a contradiction. The absolutely necessary being can never have 'received' existence, neither from itself nor from another, but has always existed and will always exist; otherwise it would be 'contingent.' To 'produce itself' would involve the further contradiction that such a being would exist and not exist at the same time under the same respect: it would not exist, because the supposition is that existence was produced and given to the being; it would exist, because the being must already exist in order to produce anything. The fact is simply that the existence of the *ens a se,* of the absolutely necessary being, can never have been produced at all; existence belongs to the very *constitution of the essence* of the absolutely necessary being, so that this essence cannot be conceived except as existing. The necessity of such a being is so unconditioned and absolute that the completely sufficient reason for its essence and existence is found solely in itself, not in another. For this reason it is said to be 'self-sufficient' and 'self-existent' or *'ens a se.'*

This absolutely necessary being or *ens a se* we call 'God.' *God, therefore, exists;* and He is the one and only sufficient reason to account adequately for the essence and existence of all the contingent beings present in the universe.

God exists, and He is eternally what He is.

The Argument of St. Thomas

St. Thomas[1] gives his formulation of the argument from contingency or, as he expresses it, possibility and necessity as follows:

"The third way is taken from possibility and necessity, and runs thus. We find in nature things that are possible to be and not to be, since they are found to be generated, and to corrupt, and consequently they are possible to be and not to be. But it

---

[1] *Summa Theologica* (New York: Benziger Bros.), I, qu. 2, art. 3.

is impossible for these always to exist, for that which is possible not to be at some time is not. Therefore, if everything is possible not to be, then at one time there could have been nothing in existence. Now if this were true, even now there would be nothing in existence, because that which does not exist only begins to exist by something already existing. Therefore, if at one time nothing was in existence, it would have been impossible for anything to have begun to exist; and thus even now nothing would be in existence — which is absurd. Therefore, not all beings are merely possible, but there must exist something the existence of which is necessary. But every necessary thing either has its necessity caused by another, or not. Now it is impossible to go on to infinity in necessary things which have their necessity caused by another, as have been already proved in regard to efficient causes. Therefore we cannot but postulate the existence of some being having of itself its own necessity, and not receiving it from another, but rather causing in others their necessity. This all men speak of as God."

A few comments will be in order regarding the formulation of the argument on the part of St. Thomas. He speaks of 'possibility and necessity.' It should be clear from the context that what he calls 'possibility' is identical with 'contingency.' A 'possible' being is evidently only contingent, not absolutely necessary. A 'contingent' being, by the very fact that it is not absolutely necessary, must receive its existence from another; hence, there must have been a time when it was non-existent and merely 'possible.'

The terms 'generate' and 'corrupt' will be misleading, unless one knows the meaning of these words in the technical philosophic language of Aristotle, St. Thomas, and scholastics generally. In their language 'generation' means the formation of a material body through the union of matter and form; and 'corruption' means the dissolution of such a being through the separation of matter and form. It makes no difference whether this body be inanimate or animate. Thus, the origin of a chemical compound and of a living being (for example, of a plant or animal), would be termed 'generation'; similarly, their dissolution would be termed 'corruption.' With us, 'generation' is commonly restricted in meaning to the origin of a living body, and 'corruption' has a distinctly moral connotation. The context shows that St. Thomas used these terms in their technical aristotelian meaning.

The Principle of Causality

A *cause* is anything which assists in the production of a thing through some positive influence. There are four kinds of causes: material, formal, final, and efficient. The problem of God's existence revolves around the *Principle of Efficient Causality* which reads: That which begins to exist demands a cause (an efficient cause) for its beginning; that is to say, it demands an existing being to bring it from non-existence to existence.

The *validity* of this principle has been established before (Chap. II). Here a few summarizing remarks must suffice. A being which does not actually exist but is capable of existence is a 'possible being.' In order that a possible being actually exist, it must pass from non-existence to existence. Now, there must be a sufficient reason to account for the possible being's passage from non-existence to existence. This reason cannot be *nothing,* because 'nothing' can produce nothing; it possesses no activity which would enable it to bring a possible being from non-existence to existence. Mere *possibility* cannot be the sufficient reason, since 'possibility' is actually nothingness, so far as existence is concerned, and as such cannot be the reason why a possible being should receive existence; otherwise all possible beings would become existent, and that is obviously not true. A non-existent, though possible, being *cannot produce itself;* because to 'produce' means to act and 'acting' demands existence, and so the possible being would have to exist in order to make itself exist, which is absurd. Hence, whatever begins to exist (passes from non-existence to existence) demands another being, an *efficient cause,* for its existence.

As will be seen from the preceding paragraph, the Principle of Efficient Causality is an *analytical* principle, *i.e.,* it's truth is established by means of an analysis of the terms; anyone who knows what the terms mean must recognize the validity of the principle both in the order of thought and in the order of reality. The principle, taken alone, does not prove that anything has ever passed from non-existence to existence; observation proves that.

The Fact of Causality

Observation proves that many things pass from non-existence to existence throughout nature. We behold *new things and realities* coming into existence which were non-existent before. The facts are innumerable. Here are a few.

Geophysics acquaints us with many realities that come into existence: hurricanes and ordinary storms are produced through the clash of air masses; volcanoes erupt violently and then quiet down; earthquakes throw up vast mountain ranges and level entire cities; heat and cold, wind and rain erode the soil; rivers rise and carry silt through hundreds of miles of flowage; lakes and pools emerge and then disappear; oceans roll tempestuously against the shores of continents, taking away and depositing land through their powerful action.

Physics tells us of the activity of various forces: electricity drives buses and streetcars, machines and appliances of a million and one kinds; magnetism generates electric currents in powerhouses and lifts tons of metal; light from the sun and stars illuminates the earth and the world; gravitation draws together the smallest particles of matter and the systems of galaxies; mechanical force makes walls crumble under the impact of cannon shells and splits a tree through the fall of an axe.

Chemistry shows the causality of things in their reactions: the elements are formed through the combination of various subatomic particles; chemical compounds are made and unmade through the interaction of different elements constantly uniting and dissolving; atoms are ionized through the addition and subtraction of electrons; radioactive substances disintegrate at a definite rate according to their own inherent laws, forming new substances in the process.

Biology deals with the activities of life and organisms: the assimilation of nutritive material in the plant, animal, and man; the vital processes going on continuously in the organic body; the growth of the organism through the purposive action of mitosis; the marvelous structure and function of asexual and sexual reproduction.

Psychology describes the functions of the mind; the organs and wonderful activities of sense-perception; the formation of ideas, judgments, and inferences on the part of the intellect; the eminently useful actions performed under the stimulus of instinct and free will; the direction of individual and societal life through moral principle and action.

These and a billion other facts are witness to the influence of efficient causes in leading realities from potentiality to actuality, from possibility to reality, from non-existence to existence. New atoms, new elements, new compounds, new plants, new animals, new men, new stars, new solar systems — they continuously appear in nature through the positive influence of producing agencies. Whenever a new reality of any kind makes its appearance, it is the result of *efficient causality,* and without efficient causality nothing new can appear. The chain of causality reaches back into the past in an *unbroken series,* one reality producing another in uninterrupted sequence. There are, of course, *many series* of such causal relationships in the world, but they are all *interrelated* and *interdependent.* In the universe there is no complete isolation.

Finite or Infinite Series of Causes

Concretely, causality means the active production of a new being or reality by bringing it into existence from a state of possibility. This production, as was pointed out before, demands the active influence of an efficient cause. Cause and effect are merely two aspects of one and the same action: in so far as this action pertains to the producing agent, we speak of a 'cause'; in so far as this action pertains to the produced thing or reality, we speak of an 'effect.' *Cause and effect* are, therefore, *correlative terms* and mutually include each other whenever there is a question of actual production of any kind.

Obviously, something might be a cause without itself being an effect, as when it produces another thing or reality but is not itself produced; and something might be an effect without itself being a cause, as when it is produced by another but does not itself produce some other thing or reality. Every *effect,* however, *must have a cause* for bringing it from non-existence to existence. Whenever an effect is produced by a cause, and this cause is produced by a second, and this second cause is produced by a third, and so on, there is a *series of causes and effects.* Nature abounds in many such series which reach into the far-distant past.

Now, the *series* of causes and effects in the universe is *either finite and limited* in number or *infinite and unlimited.* In either case efficient causality inevitably leads to a *First Uncaused Cause.*

If this series is *finite* and *limited,* it can be counted out, because the number of effects would be finite and limited. This means that the series has *an end in the past,* no matter how far into the past the series may go. But if the series has an end in the past, there must be a *first* cause in the beginning of the series which started the chain of production. And this first cause could not itself be produced (caused), because it is the 'first' in the series and nothing can precede the 'first.' If it were itself caused, it would have to be produced by another being, since it cannot cause its own existence; then this 'other being' would be the 'first' in the series. Hence, that cause alone is the 'first' which alone is at the end of the series and is not preceded by another cause. It follows, then, that the first cause of a finite and limited series must be a cause but *not an effect;* that is to say, it must be *uncaused,* it must exist in virtue of its own essence, it cannot have passed from non-existence to existence, it must have the sufficient reason for its existence in itself and not in another. If this were not so, the 'first' cause could never have been brought from non-existence to existence, and there could be no effects following it. However, effects do actually occur, as we know from experience. Consequently, if the series of causes and effects is finite and limited, this finite and limited series demands an uncaused cause as the 'first.' Under this supposition, therefore, there exists a *First Uncaused Cause*.

If this series is *infinite* and *unlimited* (and atheists usually assume this, so as to eliminate the existence of a First Uncaused Cause), the conclusion is the same. There are certain properties which apply to the single parts of a whole, but not to the whole as a totality (e.g., those pertaining to the hand or foot, and so forth, of man); others, which apply to the whole as a totality, but not to the single parts comprising the whole (e.g., those pertaining to an army, a family, a society, and so forth). There are other properties which apply both to the whole and to all its parts, because they are 'essential' to the whole and to the parts together. In a series of men who descended in a direct line from one another, each one is a man, and the totality is a totality of men, no matter whether the line of descent be finite or infinite, because each member of the series is 'essentially' a man. And the same is true of a *series of causes and effects*. It is essential to an effect to have a cause; and every 'caused cause' is thus 'essentially' an effect demanding an other being as its cause; *i.e.*, it must have been produced *by another*. This property is essential to each member of the series of 'caused causes,' whether the series be finite or infinite in number. Hence, the *total series*, even though *infinite*, is always and will always remain a *caused* or *produced totality*. Here, too, the entire produced series either produced itself or was produced by some other cause outside the series of produced causes; there is no other possibility. It is self-evident that the series, even though supposed to be infinite, could not produce itself, because in that case it would exist and not exist at the same time. Hence, *a cause outside the entire series of caused causes* is required as the adequate sufficient reason for the production and existence of this series. If this extra-serial cause were itself produced by another cause, a second series, either finite or infinite, would be started, and the argumentation given above would apply to this series as well. Consequently, even an infinite series of causes and effects eventually requires an uncaused cause, that is, a *cause or being unproduced and existing of itself.*

It follows with necessity, then, that there must be a *First Uncaused Cause* to which every causal series of the universe must be referred as its ultimate producing cause. This First Uncaused Cause, because it is unproduced, is essentially and existentially self-sufficient and self-existent, an *ens a se.*

Infinite Series Impossible

In the foregoing section it was *assumed* that an infinite series of causes and effects in the universe could possibly exist. We will now examine this *possibility* itself. Can an infinite series of causes and effects actually exist?

Where there is a 'series' of discrete entities, such as causes or effects obviously are, there is 'number.' By *number* we understand a *collection* or *aggregate measured by a unit.* An infinite series of causes and effects thus implies an *infinite number* of causes and effects arranged in a sequence so as to form a 'series.'

In speaking of an 'infinite number,' it is necessary to distinguish between a 'potentially infinite number' and an 'actually infinite number.' A *potentially* infinite number is a number which is finite and limited in itself, but is capable of being increased indefinitely, without limit. An *actually* infinite number is an existing number greater than which none can be conceived. It is, therefore, *incapable of increase,* because the increased number would evidently be greater than if the increase had not occurred; and it *cannot be exhausted* by successive subtractions, because a number that can be exhausted in this way is manifestly limited and as such finite. An actually infinite number is thus seen to be *positively without limit in its sum of units.* This latter, the 'actually infinite number,' is in question when we speak of an 'infinite series' of causes and effects; and we contend:

An actually infinite number is impossible.

Such a number involves a *contradiction in terms.* Every number begins with the unit 1; this is followed by 2, 3, 4, 5, and so forth, until the infinite number is reached. Half of this supposedly 'infinite' number consists of odd numbers (1, 3, 5, 7, 9, etc.) and half of even numbers (2, 4, 6, 8, 10, etc.); the sum of these two series (odds plus evens) forms the infinite number. Is the odd series infinite? Obviously not; it is only half as large as the original infinite number. If it were 'infinite,' it would be equal to a number double its size, and the original number would be equal to a number half its size; that would be a contradiction. The odd series, therefore, is finite and limited. For the same reason, the even series must be finite and limited. Both series, singly and individually, being finite and limited, each can be exhausted by subtraction of individual units or groups of units. However, the odds plus even form the original 'infinite' number. Since both can be exhausted, their sum can be exhausted. Their sum, however, is the original 'infinite' number. Consequently, the original 'infinite' number can be exhausted. If it can be exhausted, it is not infinite, but finite. Hence, the 'infinite' number is a 'finite' number — a contradiction in terms.

An actually infinite number is thus seen to be absurd. The fundamental reason for this contradiction should be evident: since any number, even a supposedly infinite number, is nothing but the sum of units or groups of units, *each of which is finite in itself,* the total collection or aggregate of such units must itself be finite. Like a 'square circle,' an 'infinite number' is simply a mental fiction, an *ens rationis,* a logical or conceptual being, which can never become or be actual.

And so it is clear that we can indeed speak of an 'infinite series' of efficient causes, but such a series can never actually exist. Even omnipotence could not make an infinite series of efficient causes actually exist, not because of lack of power, but because there is, under such conditions, nothing to make or posit without introducing a contradiction into omnipotence itself.

When, therefore, atheistic materialists, compelled by their philosophic doctrine of materialism, appeal to an 'infinite series' of efficient causes, they can do so only upon denial of reason. No series of efficient causes can exist except it be a *finite and limited series,* and such a series logically demands a First Uncaused Cause.

Circle of Causes Impossible

Some thinkers, in order to evade the logical necessity of admitting a First Uncaused Cause, have had recourse to a *circle of efficient causes.* A circle of produced causes, however, is as *self-contradictory* as an 'infinite series.'

The circle of causes and effects operates as follows. The cause A produces the effect B; B produces C; and so forth. Eventually X produces Y; and Y produces Z. Now Z, in turn, produces A; and then the process continues. As the result of this process of production, a *circle* of producing and produced causes is brought about, and the circle goes around and around without coming to an end and to a 'first cause.' The circle of efficient causes is illustrated in the subjoined diagram:

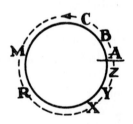

This idea of a circle of causes and effects is not even ingenious. The *contradiction* involved in such a circle is apparent. A would have *to exist and not exist* at the same time under the same respect, and that is absurd. A, in order to produce B, must exist, otherwise it could not act in the production of B; but at the same A would not exist until Z produces it. Now A, since it does not exist until Z produces it, cannot produce B, and B cannot produce C; consequently, X does not exist and cannot produce Y, nor can Y produce Z. Since Z cannot be produced by the non-existent Y, Z does not exist and cannot produce A. Consequently, under the conditions as envisioned, the *entire circle is non-existent;* nothing exists. On the other hand, if *A* does actually exist, *Z* is too late to produce it and bring it to existence. But then, what produced *A,* if *A* is not a First Uncaused Cause? A circle of produced causes reminds one of the possibility of a man becoming the father of his great-great-great-grandfather. The whole idea is simply contradictory.

Proof for God's Existence

The *proof* for God's existence, taken from the fact of *efficient causality* in the universe, can be briefly stated.

The universe is replete with instances of efficient causality. Real effects exist. They demand efficient causes. Real effects are not brought from non-existence to existence by themselves, but by other beings through their productive action as causes. Such an efficient cause is itself either produced or not produced. If not produced, it is uncaused, and we have arrived at the Uncaused Cause. If produced, it was produced by some other efficient cause. Then this 'other' efficient cause must either be produced or not produced. We will face this alternative until we arrive at an unproduced being or commit ourselves to a circle of producing causes or have recourse to an infinite series of efficient causes. However, the circle involves a contradiction, and an infinite series does not eliminate a 'first uncaused cause.' Consequently, the fact of efficient causality in the universe leads irrevocably to a *First Uncaused Cause.* And this First Uncaused Cause, the beginning of all efficient causality, we call 'God.'

Therefore, *God exists.*

The Proof of St. Thomas

St. Thomas,[2] with his usual brevity and clarity, formulates the argument from efficient causality in few and simple words:

"The second way is from the nature of the efficient cause. In the world of sense we find there is an order of efficient causes. There is no case known (neither is it, indeed, possible) in

---

[2] *Ibid.*

which a thing is found to be an efficient cause of itself; for so it would be prior to itself, which is impossible. Now in efficient causes it is not possible to go on to infinity, because in all efficient causes following in order, the first is the cause of the intermediate cause, and the intermediate is the cause of the ultimate cause, whether the intermediate cause be several or one only. Now to take away the cause is to take away the effect. Therefore, if there be no first cause among efficient causes, there will be no ultimate, nor any intermediate cause. But if in efficient causes it is possible to go on to infinity, there will be no first efficient cause, neither will there be an ultimate effect, nor any intermediate efficient causes; all of which is plainly false. Therefore it is necessary to admit a first efficient cause, to which everyone gives the name of God."

Corollaries

As in the argument based on 'change,' these proofs from contingency and efficient causality seem to lead to a being which is rather drab and impersonal. But that is only apparently so.

All these proofs for God's existence have their foundation in the phenomena observed in the *same universe,* and these phenomena pertain to the *same objects.* The same objects change, are contingent, and are the subjects of efficient causality. The same objects of the same universe show order. Hence, these proofs must all be referred to the *selfsame being* as regards change, order, contingency, and causality; it would be illogical to refer change to one being, order to another, contingency to another, and causality to another. Since the universe is *one,* though viewed in different aspects, all the phenomena of this one universe must be referred to *one single being* responsible for them.

Now, this one single being is changeless, intelligent, necessary, and the first cause. *Intelligence* of the highest degree is manifested in the order of the universe, and this intelligence must be at least as understanding as that of man. Therefore, if man, with his intellect, is a 'person,' it is evident that the

Changeless Changer, the Absolutely Necessary Being, and the First Causeless Cause is also *personal*. There is nothing drab about a 'person,' and this Supreme Being is obviously much more than man. When, therefore, St. Thomas ends each of his proofs with some simple phrase like "This is God," he states the exact truth.

Notwithstanding the intensity of man's study of nature, he has been able to glimpse only an infinitesimal fraction of the beings in the universe. However, what he has been able to observe and understand reveals an *immense intelligence and power* extending all the way from the minuteness of subvisible atoms to the light-year vastness of billions of stars. All the potentialities which underlie every change of every body in the world, all the mathematical intricacies governing the ordered movements of innumerable interrelated beings, all the mysteries of essence and existence due to the contingency of things, all the inconceivable multiplicity of causal activities spread throughout the length and breadth and height of the universe — all owe their origin and being to the one, personal, Supreme Being who is eternal, changeless, absolutely self-sufficient and self-existent.

These are a few of the implications residing in the proofs for God's existence developed so far. Little by little our knowledge of God is taking shape.

Summary of Chapter VI

The following proofs for God's existence are based on the fact of *contingency* and *efficient causality*.

1. *Necessity and Contingency.* — *Necessity* is that state in virtue of which something cannot be otherwise than it is. A *necessary being* is one which must be what it is. Necessity may be either moral, physical, logical, or ontological. *Ontological* necessity is the necessity which arises in a thing because of its 'being,' 'essence,' 'nature.' Ontological necessity may be either 'hypothetical' or 'absolute.' Something is *absolutely* necessary when it *must exist,* independent of any condition; non-existence would imply a contradiction.

Contingency is that state in virtue of which something can be otherwise than it is in its being or existence or both. A *contingent being* is a being which is what it is but could be different; if it actually exists, its non-existence would not imply a contradiction. 'Contingency' is the contradictory of 'necessity.' A contingent being is essentially non-necessary.

2. *Contingency and the World.* — The *mode* of the physical world at large is contingent, because it is subject to continuous change and never remains the same.

3. *Contingency and Organisms.* — Organisms are contingent. They did not always exist. Each has a beginning, grows, and dies.

4. *Contingency and Atoms.* — Atoms, elements, and compounds are in a constant process of formation, change, and dissolution. Their change and composition imply contingency.

5. *Contingency and Matter.* — Materialists maintain that *matter is eternal.* Now matter does not exist in the abstract but in the *concrete,* namely, in actual bodies; since bodies change, matter changes with them, and matter must therefore be contingent. If matter were eternal and necessary, it would eternally and necessarily have to be in a state of rest or motion, whichever is first; but matter is now at rest and now in motion.

On purely *rational* grounds matter must be said to be contingent. A 'necessary' being cannot *be thought of* as non-existent without a contradiction. Now, any single molecule, atom, or subatomic particle can be thought of as ceasing to exist, without any contradiction in the thought. Since the universe is but the sum of such realities, it also can be thought of as non-existent without contradiction. Hence, the universe, and all the matter composing it, is contingent.

6. *Proof for God's Existence.* — The necessary being has the sufficient reason for its existence in itself; the contingent being, since it is the contradictory of the necessary being, cannot have the sufficient reason for its existence in itself but in some *other being.* This 'other being' must also be either *contingent* or *not contingent.* If not contingent, we have arrived at the absolutely necessary being; if contingent, it will be dependent on some other being. The process of elimination will continue until we arrive at the absolutely necessary being, unless we postulate an infinite number of contingent beings, one dependent on the other. But an *infinite number* of contingent beings also demands an absolutely necessary being as the sufficient reason for its existence, because the *entire series* is contingent and as such requires an absolutely necessary being as the sufficient reason for its existence. Hence, there must exist a

being which is absolutely necessary. This being is essentially and existentially *self-sufficient* and *self-existent,* an *ens a se.* This being we call *God.* Therefore, God exists.

7. *The Argument of St. Thomas.* — It is substantially the same as the argument just proposed.

8. *The Principle of Causality.* — The Principle of Efficient Causality reads: That which begins to exist demands an efficient cause to bring it from non-existence to existence. The *validity* of this principle has been established in Chapter II.

9. *The Fact of Causality.* — Geophysics, physics, chemistry, biology, and psychology show that *new things* and *realities* come into existence which were non-existent before. These new things and realities are the result of efficient causality.

10. *Finite or Infinite Series of Causes.* — Causes and effects in the universe appear in various *series.* Now, such a series is either finite or infinite. If *finite,* the number of causes is limited and has an end in the past. Since the series has an end, there must be a *first* cause in the beginning of the series which started the chain of production. This first cause is uncaused, because it is the 'first,' and so we arrive at a First Uncaused Cause. If the series is postulated as *infinite,* the entire series is a caused or *produced totality* and as such demands a cause outside the entire series to be the sufficient reason for the existence of the produced series. This cause is, therefore, unproduced and exists of itself. Hence, there must exist a *First Uncaused Cause* which is essentially and existentially self-sufficient and self-existent, an *ens a se.*

11. *Infinite Series Impossible.* — Where there is a series of discrete entities, there is *number;* an infinite series of causes and effects means an *actually infinite number* of causes and effects. Now, an actually infinite number is impossible because *contradictory.* Numbers are odd and even in a series; half are odd and half are even. Both the odd series and the even series are limited, because each is only half the total series; since each is limited, each can be exhausted. But the sum of the odds and evens constitutes the total series; therefore, the total series can also be exhausted and must be limited and finite. The 'infinite' series is thus seen to be actually 'finite,' and that is a contradiction. Consequently, an 'infinite series' is *impossible.*

12. *Circle of Causes Impossible.* — A *circle of produced causes* is as self-contradictory as an 'infinite series.' In such a circle *A*

produces *B, B* produces *C,* and so forth; eventually *X* produces *Y, Y* produces *Z; Z* in turn, produces *A,* and so the circle is completed without the necessity of an 'uncaused cause.' The *result* of such a circle would be as follows: *A* must exist, in order to make *B* and *Z* existent; but *A* cannot exist until produced by *Z.* Therefore, *A* will both *exist* and *not exist* at the same time, and that is a contradiction.

13. *Proof for God's Existence.* — Every efficient cause is itself either produced or not produced. If *not produced,* we have the 'uncaused cause.' If *produced,* it was produced by some other cause, and this other cause will either be produced or unproduced. Eventually, we must arrive at an 'uncaused cause' or have recourse to a 'causal circle' or an 'infinite regress.' Since a 'causal circle' and an 'infinite regress' are impossible, there must exist a *First Uncaused Cause;* and this is *God.*

14. *The Proof of St. Thomas.* — It is the same as the one given above, only in brief form.

15. *Corollaries.* — All these proofs are drawn from the *same objects* of the *same universe.* Hence, these proofs must be referred to the *selfsame being.* This one being is changeless, intelligent, necessary, and the first cause. This Supreme Being is also *personal,* endowed with immense intelligence and power; He is eternal, absolutely self-sufficient and self-existent.

Readings

Driscoll, John T., *Christian Philosophy: God,* Chaps. VI, VII. — Joyce, George Hayward, *Principles of Natural Theology,* Chap. III. — Boedder, Bernard, *Natural Theology,* Bk. I, Chap. II. — Brosnan, William J., *God and Reason,* pp. 58–76, 187. — Aveling, Francis, *The God of Philosophy,* Chaps. V, VII. — Garrigou-Lagrange, R., *God: His Existence and Nature,* Vol. I, pp. 289–302. — Smith, Gerard, *Natural Theology,* Chap. VII. — Renard, Henri, *The Philosophy of God,* pp. 35–40.

Chapter VII

LIFE AND PERFECTION

CONTINGENCY and causality are facts present throughout all nature. Nothing escapes them. Because of their universal presence, as we have seen, the things of this world demand a necessarily existing and uncaused (eternal) Supreme Being as the sufficient reason for their being and existence. An infinite regress involves a contradiction, and a contradiction involves an intrinsic impossibility. Both contingency and causality thus lead to a Supreme Being who is and must be self-sufficient and self-existent, the *ens a se,* the uncaused cause of the physical world.

From a philosophical standpoint the arguments from contingency and causality are the most cogent of all arguments. They are based on the self-evident principle that everything must have a *sufficient reason for what it is.* Whatever has not the sufficient reason for its being and existence in itself must have it in another. Such are the things in the universe, and such is the universe itself: they need an extra-mundane being as the sufficient reason for everything they have and are, and without this Absolute Being they could neither exist nor be what they are. This Absolute Being is God.

There are other arguments which prove God's existence. However, in order to possess full cogency, they must eventually be based on contingency and causality. The arguments taken from the *origin of life* and the *grades of perfection* in the physical world are of this kind. These will now be presented.

The Problem of Life

None but the most confirmed materialist will deny that a *radical difference* exists between *living* and *nonliving* beings. The materialist, of course, asserts that the only kind of activity which is present in both living and nonliving beings is the ordinary chemical and physical activity found everywhere in nature; a living being is simply a complicated chemical and physical system of material energy.

Observation and experiment, however, reveal a radical difference, both in *structure* and in *function,* between living and nonliving beings.

Every living being known to exist on earth (and we know of no other place in the universe where life is indubitably present) is an 'organism.' Biologically, an *organism* is an individual constituted to carry on the activities of life by means of parts and organs more or less separate in function but mutually dependent. There is more to an organism than the mere summation of all the parts present.

One of the most remarkable phenomena of the organism is its all-pervasive *unity of being,* manifested by the marvelous *co-adaptation of structure and activity.* The entire organism consists of *cells.* Each cell possesses an intricately complicated structure. Every cell has functions which are the same as those of every other cell, namely, assimilation and dissimilation, growth and division. And yet, cells also possess individual and specific peculiarities, so that cells differ greatly among themselves. In multicellular organisms the cells group themselves into various kinds of *tissues* and *organs;* and these tissues and organs perform activities distinctively their own, over and above the general functions of the cells as the biological units of life. Again, cells, tissues, and organs group themselves into the higher unity of the organism as an *individual being functioning as a whole.*

The supreme law which governs the structure and functions of cells, tissues, and organs is the *need,* the *exigency,* of the type of organism of which they are the subsidiary parts. What kind of food material, for instance, shall be digested and assimilated depends entirely on the nature of the organism; the same kind of grass will be transformed into the flesh of a cow, a horse, a sheep, or an elephant, according to the needs of the animal that eats it. The entire body is built according to the requirements of the organism, all parts *being mutually depend-ent* and *harmoniously interrelated.*

Every organism manifests an unmistakable morphological and physiological *unity, individuality,* and *totality.* The organ-ism is primary; the structures and functions are secondary. The organism exists for itself; the structures and functions exist for the organism. The organism acts *as a whole;* the structures and functions are *subservient parts* of the whole.

If we now turn our attention to the *manner of operation,* we find that it is radically different in living and nonliving matter.

Action in inorganic substances is always *transient* (or transi-tive) in character. 'Transient' action is the action in virtue of which one being influences and changes another being. The energies of light, heat, electricity, magnetism, physical impact, gravity, etc., are such that the goal of their influence lies 'outside' their efficient causality; they tend to change other bodies. On the other hand, the inherent tendency of vital activity within an organism is the *organism's own develop-ment and perfection.* All vital action originates in the organ-ism, remains in the organism, and has as its natural goal the well-being of the organism itself. Hence, organic action is rightly termed *immanent.* No matter how much the vegetative, sensory, and rational process may differ among themselves, they are characterized by 'immanence.' Immanence or spontaneity of vital action proceeds from the *inner constitution* of the organism which reacts *as a whole* to outside agencies. Life is essentially self-perfection through self-development.

Organisms, of course, consist ultimately of elements and compounds; but these elements and compounds now act no longer in a merely 'transient' fashion, as they do in the ordi-nary circumstances of nature, but partake of the 'immanence' of the organism. In the organism, atoms and molecules form *organic compounds* as the result of the *natural tendencies* operating within the organic body. The inorganic elements have no natural tendency within themselves to produce such compounds. Outside the organism the elements combine ac-cording to the general laws of affinity, and as such they always tend to form rigid combinations with a stable equilibrium. The proteins and other organic compounds, however, are extremely complex and in an unstable colloidal state. That the *principle* operating in the formation of organic compounds is different from that operating in the formation of inorganic compounds, can be seen after the *death* of organisms. They decay, and the organic compounds dissolve, reverting again to the status of ordinary inorganic compounds and elements. If organisms and organic compounds were not the effects of some *higher principle utilizing them,* no sufficient reason can be assigned why they should not continue indefinitely in existence, even after 'death.'

Every organism is characterized by *inherent natural purposiveness.* This purposiveness follows a double course — the realization of the well-being of the individual and the preservation of the species.

That the realization of the *well-being of the individual* dominates the entire life history of an organism, should be evident. It manifests itself in the entire process of *metabolism* and *cell-division.* The purposiveness of the organism's *embryonic development* is particularly noteworthy. Here only one fact will be mentioned. If it should happen, as it occasionally does, that the first two embryonic cells are split apart, the two cells do not develop into two half-organisms, but each cell develops into a complete individual of that particular type; the entire structural plan is simply doubled and carried separately to completion. It is as if one were to cut a machine in half, and each half-machine would then proceed to shape itself into an exact duplicate of the original machine. This 'prospective potentiality' of the germ cell is one of the most remarkable features of the embryonic organism.

The *preservation of the species* is another fundamental natural end or goal inherent in the organism. The method of reproduction varies with the different kinds of organic beings; but reproduction itself is universal and is eminently purposive. There is perhaps no greater marvel in the world, viewed from a purely organic standpoint, than the wonderful arrangement of structure and function for the purpose in view.

Action flows from a principle of action. Since the 'immanent' action of organisms is beyond the natural capabilities of ordinary inorganic matter and its physico-chemical forces, vital action must flow from a *vital principle*. Without a distinct vital principle, co-equal with matter, the phenomena of life cannot receive adequate explanation.

That vital activity is far superior to nonliving activity becomes increasingly evident in the higher forms of life. Animals and men manifest *consciousness* — the brute in sense-perception, and man in his sensory and rational activities.

Over and above the ordinary activities of cells, compounds, and atoms present in the animal body, the animal possesses *conscious perception:* it sees, hears, tastes, smells, feels, imagines, remembers, and desires. Such activities are far beyond the capabilities of inanimate beings and must therefore proceed from a totally different principle of activity. In man, the activities of forming abstract ideas, judgments, and inferences, and the ability to strive after spiritual ideals, completely transcend the material reality of aggregations of elements and chemical compounds; they are *rational* and *spiritual* in nature and as such must of necessity proceed from a spiritual vital principle and essence.

Whatever we may think about the ultimate nature of living beings, this much is clear: the *immanent* activity of all living beings is radically and essentially *superior to the transient activity* of nonliving substances.

Abiogenesis

Since vital activity is far superior to nonvital activity, how do we explain the *origin of life?* A thoroughgoing materialist, of course, has no choice but to claim that all life has derived its origin from nonliving matter; his theory of the origin of life is 'abiogenesis.'

Abiogenesis means literally 'origin from nonlife.' The term is used to designate the theory that living beings ultimately came into existence through a development on the part of the forces indigenous to nonliving matter. Another term for abiogenesis is *spontaneous generation*. What have science and philosophy to say about the fact or possibility of abiogenesis?

Up to the end of the seventeenth century even scientifically minded men believed that certain low types of animals were generated 'spontaneously,' *i.e.,* abiogenetically. Worms were supposed to develop out of putrid flesh; frogs, it was thought, were produced from the mud of pools through the action of the sun's rays; insects, and even rats and mice, were believed to originate without the generative action of living beings. At present, no scientist dares defend spontaneous generation on *scientific* grounds.

In 1668 Francesco Redi made a number of experiments and disproved the popular contention that maggots were produced spontaneously in meat. From that point on, one case of supposed abiogenesis after another fell before the investigations of determined scientists. The epoch-making experiments of *Louis Pasteur,* begun in 1860, exploded the theory of spontaneous generation beyond recovery. The genius of Pasteur, through a lifetime period of rigid and exact experimentation, established beyond the shadow of a doubt that germs can originate only from pre-existing germs. In 1905, John Butler Burke claimed that radioactive substances acting on gelatin media produced 'bacterialike' cells, containing a nucleus, and that these cells grew and finally subdivided. But Sir William Ramsay, the famous investigator of radium, proved conclusively that the phenomenon was nothing more than a chemical, lifeless process. All observations and experiments of science show that *life derives its origin only from life*. Hence, so far as science is concerned, spontaneous generation (abiogenesis) never occurs.

The Origin of Life

While science, therefore, has disproved the fact of abiogenesis as occurring at the present time and under conditions similar to the present, there still remains the problem of the *origin of life in general*. Must there be an 'origin' to life at all?

It is the unanimous verdict of geologists that living beings did not always exist on our globe. There were long ages in the early period of the development of the earth, when it was in a fiery-molten state. No organism, as we know it, could possibly have existed under such circumstances. Nor did it exist, as the rocks of the 'azoic' ('lifeless') period definitely show. Life appeared eventually. It had a beginning, an *origin,* in time. Since life did not always exist on the earth, how did it originate?

Helmholtz, Van Tiegham, Lord Kelvin, Arrhenius, and others sought to avoid the problem by advancing the theory that life might have originated on earth through life-germs carried by *meteorites* from some other stellar body; or, the germs might possibly have *floated across* the intervening space and landed on the earth. This arbitrary assumption merely defers the question without offering a genuine solution. How did life originate on these stars? They, too, were at one time in a fiery-molten state and as such incapable of sustaining organisms. Meteorites melt through friction on contact with the earth's atmosphere, and the heat would kill all germs. Nor could the germs float through interstellar space; the absence of heat and moisture in interstellar space would freeze the germs and desiccate them, so that they could not live. Becquerel placed germs in a vacuum with a temperature of liquid air, thus approximately reproducing the conditions of interstellar space, and exposed the germs to ultraviolet rays present so abundantly in space. The result was the death of all germs. Scientists rightly concluded that all life-germs would have died in transit to the earth. This theory is hardly worthy of serious consideration, but it reveals the desperate extremity in which the defenders of abiogenesis had been placed.

When, therefore, certain scientists and philosophers maintain that the origin of life *must* have occurred by means of abiogenesis in the *bygone ages* of the earth, their assertion no longer rests on scientific grounds. Abiogenesis is then advanced as a *postulate* of science and philosophy.

From what has been discovered by science concerning the fact of abiogenesis, it is clear that abiogenesis is not a self-evident postulate; every bit of scientific evidence is against its actual occurrence. W. Branca[1] was fully aware of this when he wrote: "Whoever accepts spontaneous generation here on earth thereby believes that two diametrically opposed Laws of Nature have equal value. The first states: Life can originate only through Life. The second states: Life originates also or at least has originated in the past out of nonlife. The first law is proved by billions of facts, and it is true without any doubt. The second, however, has until the present never been proved by a single fact. Both Laws of Nature contradict each other diametrically." These words of an eminent scientist show conclusively that abiogenesis is *not a scientific postulate*.

Science is based on observation and experiment. Since the origin of life in general lies beyond the scope of observation and experiment, the solution of the problem exceeds the competence of the scientist. The problem is strictly a philosophical one. When, therefore, a scientist attempts a solution of this problem, he ceases to be a scientist and becomes a philosopher. Obviously, then, if abiogenesis is advanced as a 'postulate,' this can only mean that it is a *philosophical postulate*. In no case can abiogenesis be said to be a self-evident truth. It can be considered a 'philosophical postulate' if it is the *only* rational and logical explanation of the origin of life. Certainly, if a Supreme Being does not exist, life must have originated in virtue of the forces inherent in matter, because there would be no other way in which it could originate. Is the existence of a Supreme Being inconsistent with reason and logic? If not, then abiogenesis is *not the only* rational and logical explanation of the first origin of life in the universe. What do reason and logic say and demand?

God, the Ultimate Cause of Life

The Principles of Sufficient Reason and Causality are the indispensable foundation of all science and all philosophy. Reason and logic demand, according to the Principle of Sufficient Reason, that nothing can exist and be what it is

---

[1] *Der Stand unserer Kenntnisse vom fossilen Menschen* (1910), p. 91.

except that there be an adequate reason which accounts for its existence and being; without such an adequate reason, either in itself or in another, it would simply be nothing. Reason and logic demand, if the reality in question has passed from non-existence to existence, that there be a cause for this passage and that there be a *proper proportion between cause and effect* to bring about this passage. The effect can never be actually greater than what is contained in the cause; otherwise a part of the effect would be without an adequate cause and as such could never come into existence. It is against all reason and logic to suppose that the more perfect can receive its adequate explanation in the less perfect; a more perfect reality can produce a less perfect reality, but the reverse is a contradiction and therefore impossible.

Now, the activities and phenomena of organic life *exceed the inherent causality of inorganic substances.*

A living being, since its activity is 'immanent,' is superior to nonliving matter. It is true, of course, that organisms consist of material elements in their structure and utilize material forces in their vital functions. But that is only a part of the total picture of life. One cannot, by the wildest flight of fancy, conceive of sensory and intellectual *knowledge, consciousness,* and *appetitive behavior* as phenomena directly resulting from the actions and reactions of atom complexes considered strictly as such. Even the *colloidal state* of protoplasmic material and the formation of *organic compounds* cannot be adequately accounted for on the basis of ordinary chemical affinity between elements. The inherent natural *purposiveness* of organisms, as manifested in *metabolism, cell-division,* and *reproduction,* in virtue of which they plan and build for future use, is a qualitative factor far beyond the capabilities of mere atoms and their aggregates. Above all, the *dynamic unity* of the organism as a whole, with complete subordination and co-adaptation of all structures and functions for the *well-being of the individual* and the *preservation of the species,* is something so unique that it cannot receive its ultimate explanation in the grouping of billions of inanimate and unintelligent atoms. The simplest forms of plant and animal life, bacteria and protozoa, are so superior to inorganic elements and compounds that even confirmed materialists admit that they belong to *different levels of being.*

Unless we wish to make the gratuitous assumption (contrary to all observed facts) that all matter without exception is 'living,' the arrival of the organism on earth and in the universe involves the appearance of something *totally new and superior,* namely, life in all its manifold forms and manifestations. Life, since it is intrinsically superior to matter and material forces, must be accounted for by some *cause outside the totality of matter and of the material universe;* and since the cause must be at least equal in perfection to the effect produced, it must itself be *endowed with life:* no being can give what it does not possess.

That the intricate structure and inherently purposive function of even the unicellular organism (not to mention the higher organic forms of plant, animal, and man) could be the result of *chance* and *without intelligent planning* would indeed be a miracle; chance is no cause of permanent order. Not only must the first organism have arisen through the chance concurrence of billions of unintelligent atoms; it must have arisen completely furnished with cytoplasm, nucleus, chromosomes, and genes, and with the *perfect mechanism of reproduction.* Unless this were so, no reproduction could have occurred in the first organism, and there would be no offspring, no second generation; life would have become extinct immediately, and there would be no life today. Reproduction has a purpose for the *future,* but it is of no particular advantage to the reproducing organism itself. Such a purpose for the future necessitates the use of specific means for a specific end, and that implies *intelligence.* This intelligence, however, resides neither in the speck of protoplasm called 'organized matter' nor in the inorganic elements.

Besides, *man* is an organism and an integral part of the organic world, and any argument about the general origin of life must include the *rational life* of man. Man's psychic, rational life of intellect and will cannot be reduced to the material forces of inorganic nature. These activities are immaterial, simple, and *spiritual* and can proceed only from an immaterial, simple, and spiritual vital principle or 'soul.'[2] As such the soul of man is neither composed of matter nor intrinsically dependent on matter, while every other being in the universe is. The soul's very essence requires a spiritual cause to give it existence.

Life thus demands a *living, intelligent cause outside of matter and the material universe.* This living, intelligent, extramundane cause we call 'God.'

God, therefore, exists.

God and Evolution

Very many scientists, especially biologists, accept the theory of 'evolution.' The theory is even advocated by many who are theists. What is to be said about the combination of *theism* and *evolution?*

Among the prevalent theories of evolution two deserve special consideration: 'organic' and 'emergent' evolution.

Organic evolution is the theory according to which the various species and types of animals and plants derive their origin, not through distinct and separate creative acts of God, but through development from other pre-existing species and types, all differences being accounted for by modifications acquired in successive generations according to purely natural laws. Organic evolution thus presupposes the existence of living beings, and it begins to operate only after organisms are already present on earth. Strictly speaking, therefore, the theory of organic evolution does not attempt to solve the problem of the 'origin' of organisms in general.

So far as the *scientific* side of organic evolution is concerned, it must be borne in mind that the theory revolves around the question whether the *fact* of evolution has occurred or not occurred. What may have occurred in the past ages is obviously

---

[2] See the author's *The Whole Man* (Milwaukee: The Bruce Publishing Co., 1945), Chap. XX.

beyond the ken of scientific observation and experiment. The evolutionary theory is at best only a *conclusion,* and this conclusion is usually the result of a doubtfully valid argumentation.

The evidence for organic evolution rests upon the facts, observed in the fossil remains found in the strata of the earth, that there has been a gradual change from simpler to more diversified forms in plants and animals in succeeding geologic periods and that all plants and animals are patterned according to a more or less similar plan of structure. From these facts scientists conclude that all plants and animals are related to one another through *genetic descent.*

The general argument for evolution then runs somewhat as follows: 'If evolution occurred, we must find a gradual transition from the simpler to the more complicated structures of organisms in the fossils of the earth, together with a definite homological plan for all plants and animals; but that is precisely what we find in nature; therefore, evolution took place.' Cast into this form, the conditional syllogism lacks logical force, because it contains the *Fallacy of False Consequent.* 'Accepting the consequent' will always be a fallacious argument, unless the cause given in the antecedent is the *only* cause which could produce this particular effect. Here, the result contained in the consequent could be the effect of either one of two causes: creation or evolution. The argument as given does not eliminate creation. Hence, the mere fact that the consequent is true does not establish evolution as the cause; evolution *may* have occurred and be the cause, but it *need not* be, because everything could be the result of creation just as well.

If the conditional syllogism is reversed, the argument is even less cogent. The argument would then have to be formulated as follows: 'If we find a gradual transition from the simpler to the more complicated structures in the fossils of the earth, together with a definite homological plan for all plants and animals, then all this must have happened through evolution; but that is what we find; therefore, evolution is the cause.' Now the argument contains the *Fallacy of Begging the Question.* The antecedent (condition) *presupposes* the very thing it is attempting to prove, namely, that 'evolution' is the *only* possible cause of the change. It omits 'creation' as a possible cause of the effect.

Even if one accepted evolution, and even if evolution were established as a fact, the *transition* from plants to animals cannot be adequately explained on the basis of natural powers alone. The *psychic* simply cannot be produced by the non-psychic, without violating the Principle of Sufficient Reason; and the *spiritual life of man* cannot derive its origin from the nonspiritual life of the animal, because these forms of life are entirely incommensurate and the higher would be produced by the lower. Without the *intervention of God* in some way, the organic processes cannot be conceived as passing from the less perfect to the more perfect, because that would entail the contradiction of an insufficient cause; and animal life is certainly of a higher order than plant life, and human life of a higher order than animal and plant life combined. We cannot sacrifice the principles of sound reason in science any more than we can deny the facts of science; both are the foundation of all our knowledge.

Emergent evolution, as propounded by C. Lloyd Morgan, S. Alexander, and others, is much broader in scope than organic evolution. In general, the theory maintains that nature is the product of evolution in such a manner that entirely new and unpredictable properties originate through synthesis and thereby form new and higher levels of reality in a continuously ascending process of development. *Nature as a whole* is thus conceived as having 'evolved' in the course of time. The new properties or 'novelties' (as Morgan terms them) are not the mere resultants obtained by addition or subtraction from among previously existing properties; rather, these 'novelties' have no counterpart in the lower levels: they simply *emerge* with specific characters not discoverable in the former (lower) levels of being. It is thus that *life* and later *mind* have had their first origin; Alexander even has 'deity' emerge as the product of evolution.

The 'stuff' out of which nature evolved was at first something homogeneous, undifferentiated, indeterminate. Alexander calls it *Space-Time;* it is pure space and pure time, without limit and without beginning, the stuff of substances and of all existents, because all things evolve or 'emerge' out of it in the course of the ages. Space-Time possesses a blind, aimlessly driving *nisus* or impetus (where this 'nisus' comes from, Alexander does not properly explain) which is responsible for the continued upward advance of evolution. And so all things 'emerge' — first matter, then the material universe, then life in plants, then mind in animals and man, and finally 'deity.'

Alexander's *deity* is in no sense a 'person' who, as the uncaused cause of reality, exists prior to the universe: on the contrary, his 'god' is a finite product of evolution. As he puts it:[3] "When we think of God as that to which all things owe their existence, we are reversing the order of fact and are regarding the universe of Space-Time, which does create all things, in the light of its highest empirical quality, which is not first but last in the order of generation." Deity is thus a creature of Space-Time, the outcome of the pre-existing finites of the world, finite in perfection, a superior quality of the evolving universe, and as such simply one of the 'emergents' which develop in virtue of the 'nisus' present from the beginning. It will, in all probability, be eventually superseded by some higher quality. Alexander makes the remarkable statement[4] that his so-called deity is both theistic and pantheistic, but "that if a choice must be made it is theistic." This, of course, is nothing but a confusion of words; Alexander's deity, as the context of his exposition clearly reveals, is merely a part of the universe and therefore *pantheistic*.

Only a few words need be said about this theory. No adequate explanation is given concerning the *origin* of this kind

---

[3] *Space, Time, and Deity* (New York: Macmillan, 1920), Vol. II, p. 399.
[4] *Ibid.*, p. 394.

of universe. It is said to be 'eternal,' but that is a statement which cannot be accepted, because this universe is so weak in being that it cannot be conceived as having the sufficient reason for its existence in itself. From the start, this Space-Time universe is altogether *indeterminate* and *undifferentiated;* all determinateness of being and differentiation 'emerges' in the course of time under the impulse of the *nisus* present from the start. The presence of this 'nisus' is assumed; and such a *gratuitous assumption* may rightly be gratuitously denied, because no proof is or can be given for its supposed presence. Besides, the *emergence* of such new and unpredictable properties has no foundation except in theory; it involves a definite violation of the Principles of Sufficient Reason and Causality, and if we must renounce the principles of reason to make a theory possible or plausible we do not need emergent evolution to 'explain' the rise of the new qualities. When 'novelties' occur as effects which are not precontained in the being of their causes, the plus-amount is unaccounted for and really proceeds from 'nothing' (and 'nothing' is no adequate explanation for anything) unless one accounts for the deficiency of the universe as a proper cause by an appeal to an adequate cause *outside the given universe.* That, of course, Alexander's theory does not do; it is, therefore, inadequate and must be rejected as irrational.

Morgan's 'emergent evolution' is of a different kind. He is a theist and expressly refers the efficacy of this evolution to God. He states:[5] "In surveying the evolution of terrestrial life . and mind there seems to have been advance through ascending modes of mentality to that highest example which is distinctive of man as rational and self-conscious. Now it is my belief that this evolutionary ascent of mind in living creatures is due to the Creative and Directive Power of God. But that does not imply that any such phrase as 'the ascent of mind' is applicable to God, as *Spiritus Creator.* The Divine Mind or Spirit is Eternal and nowise limited by the trammels of space and

---

[5] Frances Mason, ed., "The Ascent of Mind," *The Great Design* (New York: Macmillan, 1933), pp. 115, 132.

time. . . . What I find in evolution is *one great scheme from bottom to top, from first to last*. What I also believe is that this advance throughout nature is a revelation of Divine Agency. And since mind at its best is the highest term in the course of evolutionary ascent, it may well be said that the evolution of mind reveals the agency of Mind. But it is, as I believe, Mind or Spirit infinite and timeless. . . . Spiritus Creator as eternal and omnipresent is not the outcome of evolution, but that of which evolution is the progressive revelation."

As will be noted, Morgan's concept of emergent evolution is very different from that of Alexander. He finds in evolution "one great scheme" which points to an eternal Mind and Creator who arranged the scheme. Whatever we may think of emergent evolution as a general scientific and philosophic explanation of 'life' and 'mind,' the theory, as envisioned by Morgan, is conceived as a 'purposive evolution.'

God and Purposive Evolution

Viewed from a purely *philosophic* standpoint (leaving Revelation out of consideration), one must say that *purposive evolution is possible,* at least in its general outlines.

Evolution itself, obviously, is not impossible; it must, however, be a 'purposive evolution,' if the Principles of Sufficient Reason and Causality are to be safeguarded. Since purposiveness implies an intelligent foresight into the future, and since intelligent foresight cannot be ascribed to the forces of nature, the only possible alternative is the assumption that *the Supreme Intelligence endowed nature with a purpose* and with the necessary principles of action to realize this purpose through evolution. The required intelligence would reside not in nature itself but in the Author of Nature; and it would then make little difference whether evolution were gradual or emergent in character.

Life could not originate in the *first organism* through an absolute emergence, solely from matter and its indigenous forces, because vital activity and the vital principle (soul) are by their very nature *superior to matter and material forces.* In some manner, the causality of God was necessary for the production of the first organism. Nevertheless, a direct creation was not absolutely necessary. The vital principle of the plant and animal is essentially *material* in nature, being intrinsically dependent on matter in its being and existence. All that would strictly be required for the appearance of organic life is the original *fiat* of God ordering and disposing matter and material agencies in a purposive fashion, so that at a given time and place the first organic principle or soul, the conditions being favorable, would 'emerge' or *be educed* out of the hidden potentialities of matter. Life would thus 'emerge' spontaneously, but in virtue of an *inherent tendency* placed in bodies from the beginning by the Creator. God would be the primary cause of the origination of life, with the agency of bodies as a secondary and instrumental cause. We do not say that this is the actual way the origin of life occurred; but we do think that such an origin of organic life is *possible.*

Even man's body, speaking again from a purely philosophic standpoint, *could* have been prepared from an animal body through 'purposive evolution.' Man's *soul,* however, is a *spiritual entity* endowed with a spiritual life and as such completely transcends matter and material conditions. Since matter and material energies do not possess spirituality in any form, because materiality and immateriality are contradictory, they cannot produce or give rise to a spiritual being. Plants and animals are organisms, material systems; plant and animal souls are material in essence, completely immersed in matter and intrinsically dependent on matter. Consequently, neither the matter nor the soul of plants and animals could give rise to the existence of the human soul. Therefore, whether we view the human soul as originating by means of an *absolute emergence* from lifeless matter directly, or through a *generative process* on the part of plants or animals, or through the *transmutation* of a plant or animal soul into a human soul, the effect, not being contained in the cause, would totally exceed the capabilities of such a cause. A spiritual being must be produced by a spiritual cause; any other supposition would violate the Principles of Sufficient Reason and Causality. Hence, the origin of the human soul, since it is spiritual, must be attributed to a cause existing outside the ensemble of the material universe. Emergent evolution, therefore, must be excluded in the case of the spiritual soul of man. *Only God can produce the spiritual human soul, and that directly.*

One may say, therefore, that 'emergent evolution' as a general theory is, absolutely speaking, a 'possible' explanation of the origin of life on the globe (a 'working hypothesis' in the scientific sense), provided one accepts the First Cause (God) as having placed a *purposive direction* into the material beings and their activities. Without such a 'purposive direction' it is inconceivable how the unintelligent beings and blind forces of nature could conspire to form a universal, all-embracing scheme or plan; only *chance* would be left as an explanation, and chance can never account for the permanent orderliness of nature, especially in the organic world. In no case, however, can the origin of the spiritual soul of man receive an adequate explanation on the basis of emergent evolution, organic evolution, or any other form of evolution.

We will conclude this discussion with a quotation from Sir J. Arthur Thomson,[6] the great naturalist: "As we must agree with the Aristotelian dictum that in a continuous process there can be nothing in the end which was not also present in kind in the beginning, we are led from our own mind, and the story of its enfranchisement, back and back to the Supreme Mind 'without whom there was nothing made that was made.' Facing everyday things in the World of Life, around which our scientific fingers will not meet, what can we do but repeat what is carved on the lintel of the Biology Buildings of one of the youngest and strongest of American Universities: 'Open Thou mine eyes that I may behold wondrous things out of The Law.' "

---

6 "The Wonder of Life," *The Great Design, op. cit.,* p. 324.

Notion of Perfection

The discussion on life and evolution, with its emphasis on the unity found in the organic realm and in the universe at large, leads to the argument for God's existence based on the *grades of perfection or being* found everywhere in the world. Before proposing the argument, however, it will be necessary to explain the notion of 'perfection' as used in this context.

By *perfection* we mean any *reality* or *real entity* which is present in any kind of being. Perfection or reality may be *potential* or *actual:* it is 'actual' if it exists; it is 'potential' if it does not exist but is capable of being brought into existence. For example, since you exist, you are an 'actual' being or perfection while you exist; all human beings which could exist in the past and will exist in the future are 'potential' beings or perfections.

Perfection or reality, whether actual or potential, is either 'mixed' or 'simple.' A *mixed* perfection is one which in its very concept implies limitation and imperfection. Examples of mixed perfections are 'heat,' 'health,' 'plant,' 'brute,' 'man,' because each of these beings involves materiality and materiality implies some sort of limitation and imperfection. A *simple* perfection does not include in its concept a limitation or imperfection (though it does not exclude it either); for example, 'wisdom,' 'goodness,' 'being,' 'life,' because they could exist without limitation or imperfection in a spiritual being.

Some perfections (realities) are 'accidental' and others 'essential.' They are *essential,* if they refer to the essences or natures of beings; for example, 'animal,' 'rational,' 'humanity,' 'being,' 'substance.' They are *accidental,* if they do not belong to the essence or nature as such, but are connected with the essence or nature as a superadded modification and determination; 'color,' 'weight,' 'age,' 'temperature,' 'activity' are accidental perfections or realities which modify and determine an essence, but they are not a part of the essence itself.

Again, perfections (realities) will be either 'predicamental' or 'transcendental.' They are *predicamental* when they represent generic concepts; for example, 'animal,' 'body,' 'plant.' They are *transcendental* when they are found in, or can be applied to, all beings; of this kind are 'one,' 'being,' 'good,' 'true,' since they 'transcend' all categories or special types of being.

Grades of Perfection

In scrutinizing the beings in the universe, we find considerable diversity. They possess being (reality, perfection); but this being (reality, perfection) is distributed among the classes and individuals in varying grades, so that one can rightly speak of a *gradation of perfection*.

True, there are no varying grades of being (reality, perfection) in the essence or nature of the individuals of a certain species: a plant is always a plant; an animal, an animal; and a man, a man. Essences or natures, taken by themselves, do not admit of a 'more' or 'less,' as if one plant were more of a plant than another, or one animal more of an animal than another, or one man more of a man than another. But grades of being (reality, perfection) vary, when *one kind of being is compared to another*. Thus, in the *inanimate* world, an electron, proton, neutron, etc., possesses less perfection in isolation than when combined into an atom or chemical compound; in the atom or compound these subatomic particles possess their own individual perfection and also partake of the perfection of the atom or compound as a totality in combination. The *organic* world possesses a higher grade of reality than the inorganic world, because 'life' or 'immanent' activity is of a higher order of being than the 'transient' activity found in subatomic particles, atoms, and chemical compounds taken by themselves. Among organic beings the *animal* has a higher grade of being than the *plant,* because it possesses the vegetative life of the plant and sensory life characteristic of animal life. *Man* has a higher grade of being than the plant and animal, because in man we observe the rational life of a human being in addition to sensory and vegetative life.

Each individual nature in the world is the result of *com-*

position. Such a being is a composition of *essential* and *accidental* grades of being, because accidental modifications and determinations are found in all; such are, for example, the accidental perfections of age, weight, extension, magnitude, temperature, and activity of all kinds. The accidental perfections are real and actual; but they change continuously, while the essence or nature remains the same. Composition is present even in the *essences* or *natures* themselves; in organisms, for instance, there is a composition of matter and the life principle, and a similar situation obtains in subatomic particles, atoms, and compounds. No being in the universe realizes its being completely at once, but does so in successive stages and in *partial actualizations.* The reason for this universal composition lies in the fact that all these beings are a combination of *actuality* and *potentiality* in many ways, and the two are really distinct. Man, for example, has the potentiality of learning, but this potentiality does not become actualized except in successive stages and then never completely. That is why there are various *degrees of perfection* (grades of being) in the same individual and among individuals relative to one another. As a consequence, the same individual may become more (less) learned, wise, good, strong, healthy, and so forth, in the course of time; and that applies also to different individuals and classes of being when compared with one another. As a further consequence, it is clear that all beings in the universe are 'perfectible,' and *perfectibility* is definitely a matter of 'more' and 'less,' of 'higher' and 'lower,' in degrees of reality and perfection; perfectibility is the direct result of the potentiality in all beings present in the universe.

Limitation of Perfection

It should be evident that the grades of being (reality, perfection), as a matter of observable fact, are limited. And *limitation implies imperfection.*

The very *number* of beings in the universe is limited. There is more matter in the stars than in interstellar space; there could, then, be more perfection in the universe, even if the universe were considered to be endless in extent in all directions. For the same reason, the higher grades of being present in atoms and compounds could be greater than they actually are. The species and varieties of plants and brutes could be larger in number, and there could be more individuals in each species and variety. The number of human beings in the past, present, and future could be greater than it actually has been, is, or will be. Wherever we see beings, there could be more of them. Limitation in number involves limitation of perfection in an *absolute* sense.

The *relative perfection* of the grades of being is also limited. There exists, without doubt, a wonderful harmony in the gradation of beings in the universe, from subatomic particles to atoms to chemical compounds to plants to animals to men. None of these beings are unlimited in being (reality, perfection); the very fact of a 'gradation' presupposes limitation in the various types of beings forming this ascending scale. The *composition* existing in each type and individual is a sign of limitation of perfection. *Potentiality* and *perfectibility* are evidence of this limitation.

Where there is limitation there is *imperfection*. The reason is clear; limitation means that there could be 'more' and 'higher' perfection; but it is not present, it is lacking. This does not imply that things are not what they are supposed to be. Absolutely speaking, however, each individual being could possess more reality, essential and accidental, than it actually possesses, and that means that it is an *imperfect* being through and through. All beings in the universe, by the mere fact that they are 'composite' beings, consist of two or more grades of being united together; and every composite being is a 'one-made-of-many.' That alone is an imperfection, because such a being would be more perfect in its entity if it consisted of 'one' grade of being possessing the perfections of the 'many.' Man, for instance, would be more perfect (and less imperfect) if his knowledge were complete at birth rather than acquired piecemeal in the course of the years.

Potentiality definitely involves imperfection of being. Potentiality means the power to do or acquire something. Such a power is a sign that the perfection of the actuality to be done or to be acquired is absent and as yet missing. Potentiality is possibility. In comparison with actuality, possibility is a very imperfect sort of being, because it is a relative nonentity capable of becoming an entity through the activity of some efficient cause giving it existence. Non-existence, however, is imperfect, relative to existence. Every form of potentiality, therefore, is an imperfection, and all beings in the universe possess a large number of such potentialities. The act of playing a musical instrument, for instance, is obviously more perfect in itself than the mere possibility of playing it; but no musician actually plays an instrument all the time. All activities are the actualization of some potentiality existing in a being. Such activities come and go, depending on the nature of the being in which they occur. Sometimes activities are present, sometimes they are absent; but a being in act is more perfect than a being not in act.

Wherever we look in nature, we observe a hierarchy of being with relative perfection and relative imperfection. Limitation of essential and accidental perfection is found everywhere. Nowhere do we see absolute perfection. All things possess *being,* but they possess it in imperfect degrees. Not to possess being in fullest measure implies *limitation* and consequent *imperfection.*

God and Perfection

The argument for God's existence, based on the *limited grades of perfection* found in the beings of the universe, is somewhat abstruse and demands close attention.

First step. Whenever a large number of beings possess *perfection arranged in a graded scale,* these beings are not themselves the sufficient reason for these perfections. As a matter of plain fact, no being in the universe is the sufficient reason of its own being and its existence. Every being, of course, is what it is; but that it is what it is, is not the result of its own doing or making. Each of us has simply *received* our being, and it was not up to us in any way to decide what we shall be or not be; that is true of man and of every other being. When, therefore, we observe a *gradation of reality* among the beings of the universe, starting from the subatomic particle and reaching from the inorganic world through the organic world up to the spiritual life of man, this gradation of reality (perfection) cannot be attributed to the individuals in the series nor to the series as such. Not to the *individuals* in the series. No single beings are responsible for what they are themselves; much less for what the other beings are. The hydrogen atom on earth has nothing to do with the hydrogen atoms in the sun and other stars; the calcium in my body is not the sufficient reason for the existence of the calcium present in the gases of interstellar space. Each element and compound exists as an individual being, but it is not the reason or cause why the other elements and compounds also exist. Not to the *series as such*. By far the greatest portion of this graded series is devoid of intelligence and does not know that such a gradation of reality exists. And man, who alone knows of the existence of the series, certainly had nothing to do with bringing the realities into existence and with arranging them into a series of graded perfections. Since no single individual and no group of individual beings in the series is the sufficient reason for the series, the entire series has not the sufficient reason for its existence and arrangement *in itself*. It could be different from what it actually is. Hence, the entire series and each individual in it must have the sufficient reason for this gradation *outside the series*. Now, this series of graded perfections comprises the entire universe. Hence, the sufficient reason for the gradation of reality must reside *outside the universe*.

Second step. *Diverse perfections combined into a unity* do not combine of their own accord; a causal agency is required to bring about their unification in a being. "Every composite is posterior to its component parts, and is dependent on them. . . . Every composite has a cause, for things in themselves different cannot unite unless something causes them to unite."[7] The very

---

fact that such perfections (realities) are 'diverse' implies that they are multiple in character. Multiplicity, however, is the opposite of unity. Strictly speaking, therefore, diverse and multiple perfections should, of their very nature, never combine to form a unitary being. If they do so nevertheless, the sufficient reason for their union cannot lie in these realities themselves, because what is 'multiple' is of its own nature and being not 'one.' All creatures, however, are 'one' in their being, but they are also 'composite' — made up of a diversity and multiplicity of realities, namely, essential and accidental perfections of various kinds. One may object and say that there exists an *inherent tendency* in things which urges these diverse and multiple realities (perfections) to form a unified nature. That, of course, is true. But it is also true that this 'inherent tendency' must have a sufficient reason to account for its presence. Beings, however, are *subject* to this tendency and as such cannot themselves account for its presence. Since the entire universe consists of composite beings with diverse and multiple realities, it necessarily presupposes an efficient cause *outside itself* in order to explain how the 'many' become 'one.'

Third step. *Limitation of perfection* also demands an efficient cause outside the universe. The *number* of beings in the universe is not infinite, but limited; and that means that the amount of reality (perfection) in the universe is limited. Why is this amount as large as it is and yet definitely limited? Why are there just so many subatomic particles in the universe? Why are there just so many natural elements, not more and not less, although they could be more or less? Why are there more of one kind than of another? Why are some elements active and others inert? Why are some naturally radioactive and not all? Why do certain elements tend to combine with others to form compounds, while others show no such tendency? Why the difference in freezing point and boiling point, ductility, heat conductivity, and all other qualities? Whence the limitation of plants to vegetative functions and of animals to vegetative and sensory functions, while man has these and rational functions? Whence the limitation of perfection in the structures

of plants, animals, and men? Whence the limitation of perfection in their powers and capabilities? No being is altogether
perfect in its nature; every one is limited and imperfect along
many lines. It is manifest that every individual and every type
of being is what it is and has what it has, not through its own
choice and doing, but because it 'received' its being as limited
and imperfect. This limitation demands a sufficient reason. The
explanation does not lie in the things themselves. Consequently,
the sufficient reason for the limited perfection (relative imperfection) of all beings in the universe must be sought in some
outside intelligence planning their number and nature. In other
words, *an efficient cause outside the universe,* immensely intelligent and powerful, gave all things in the universe their being
and existence and decided how much perfection they shall
receive and how many of all the possible beings of a certain
class shall obtain existence. Any other explanation is illogical.

Last step. *Transcendental perfections are simple perfections.*
Such are 'being,' 'one,' 'true,' 'good.' They apply to all things.
Everything, whether material or spiritual, whether a substance
or an accident, is a 'being.' Everything is undivided in itself
and distinct from other beings; it is 'one.' Everything, since it
is a being, can be known by an intellect and is therefore 'true.'
Everything has suitability and can be desired, because being is
always desirable; hence, it is 'good.' These attributes 'transcend'
('go beyond') all categories and classes; that is why they are
termed *transcendental.* In themselves these attributes are *simple,*
because they can be found in pure spirits. The simple, transcendental attributes are present in all beings *in varying degrees.*
That such attributes are present in creatures in varying degrees
and not in their absolute perfection demands a sufficient reason
and an *adequate cause.* Since, however, the simple, transcendental attributes are found in all beings in the universe and in
the universe as a whole, there must be *one cause* responsible for
them all. Similar things are related, and that means that eventually they have the *same cause.* All perfections (realities)
found in the universe must, therefore, be present in this one

same cause, either formally or eminently; otherwise they could not be given by this cause.

Conclusion. There must exist outside the universe *a cause possessing unlimited perfection (reality)*, responsible for all the limited perfection (reality) present in varying degrees in the beings of the universe. The perfection of this cause must be 'unlimited,' because limitation of perfection demands a cause for this limitation. Hence, if the cause of the universe were itself limited in perfection, another cause would be required. Since an infinite regress is impossible, we must ultimately arrive at an *uncaused cause possessing unlimited perfection.* This uncaused cause possessing unlimited perfection we call 'God.'

Therefore, *God exists.*

The Argument of St. Thomas

St. Thomas made no argument for God's existence based on the *origin of life.* The reason for this omission is apparently very simple. Up to the time when Louis Pasteur startled the scientific and philosophic world with his revealing experiments on the origin of subvisible organisms, it was the common belief that spontaneous generation (abiogenesis) occurred among certain classes of lower animals and plants. Since biology, as an exact science, was unknown in his day, St. Thomas also entertained this common belief. In order to ascribe an adequate cause for the fact of spontaneous generation, he referred the origin of life in these instances to the action of the sun's rays and to the causality of the intelligences who moved the celestial spheres. We are better informed in these matters than St. Thomas could be expected to be in his time. Astronomy tells us that there are no 'celestial spheres,' and biology has proved that living beings do not derive their origin from nonliving matter. Had St. Thomas possessed the more accurate knowledge which we have, he undoubtedly would have used the 'origin of life' as a proof for God's existence.

He did, however, make an argument for God's existence by

using the fact of the *grades of perfection* universally found in nature. Here is his formulation:[8]

"The fourth way is taken from the gradation to be found in things. Among beings there are some more and less good, true, noble, and the like. But 'more' or 'less' are predicated of different things, according as they resemble in their different ways something which is the maximum, as a thing is said to be hotter according as it more nearly resembles that which is hottest; so that there is something which is truest, something best, something noblest, and, consequently, something which is uttermost being; for those things that are greatest in truth are greatest in being, as it is written in *Metaph. II.* Now the maximum in any genus is the cause of all in that genus; as fire, which is the maximum of heat, is the cause of all hot things. Therefore there must also be something which is to all beings the cause of their being, goodness, and every other perfection; and this we call God."

This proof, as given above, calls for some comment. As formulated by St. Thomas, the objection has been made that it is rather *Platonic* in trend and involves an *illicit transition* from the ideal to the real order. The brevity of the phrasing is probably responsible for this serious objection. St. Thomas was by no means so inept in philosophizing that he would have been guilty of such a flagrant error. However, in order to avoid this accusation, the presentation of the argument in the preceding sections is based on the Principles of Sufficient Reason and Causality.

Furthermore, St. Thomas has been ridiculed for his 'bad physics' in stating that "fire, which is the maximum of heat, is the cause of all hot things." St. Thomas, of course, knew nothing of modern physics or chemistry. Everybody in his age followed Aristotle's division of the terrestrial elements into 'earth, water, air, and fire.' Among these four elements (we know now that none of these realities is an 'element' in the strict sense of the word) fire was considered to be the pure

---

[8] *Summa Theologica* (New York: Benziger Bros.), I, qu. 2, art. 3.

principle of heat; and it was only natural that St. Thomas would refer all hot things to this fire as to their real cause. The illustration he used here was unfortunate, in view of our more accurate information; but his error is certainly pardonable and does not affect the validity of his argument as a whole. All in all, his argument is basically sound, especially when linked up with the Principles of Sufficient Reason and Causality so as to keep it within the realm of the 'real order' of beings.

Inferences

Since God is the ultimate adequate cause of the origin of life in the world, *He must possess life.* And since the immaterial soul of man is endowed with spiritual life, God's life must also be *spiritual.*

Beings which possess a nature characterized by 'limitation' and 'composition' cannot have the sufficient reason for this limitation and composition in themselves. If they themselves had to impose limitation and composition upon their nature, they would have to do this before they assumed their nature, and so they would exist before they actually existed. Hence, the sufficient reason for the limitation and composition of their nature must be found ultimately in God. God cannot have limitation and composition in His nature, otherwise another cause would have to impose limitation and composition upon *His* nature. There can, however, be no cause prior to the First Cause. Consequently, God must be without limitation and composition in His nature and perfection. As a result, God cannot be an organism; nor can He have materiality in His nature. For the same reason, His nature *cannot have potentiality.* God's being, therefore, must be pure actuality, *pure act.* Having no materiality is His nature, God must be a *pure spirit.* And since there can be no limitation to His perfection, He must be a spirit of unlimited perfection. It follows that God is *Pure Act* and a *Pure Spirit of unlimited perfection.*

Summarizing the results of the foregoing proofs for God's existence, we find that God is the unchangeable author of all change, the intelligent planner of the universe, the necessarily existing eternal being, the being which has the sufficient reason of existence in Himself (*ens a se*), the uncaused cause, spirit, unlimitedly perfect, pure act. He is in all truth the *Supreme Being*.

Summary of Chapter VII

Here we treat of the *origin of life* and of the *grades of perfection* as proofs for God's existence.

1. *The Problem of Life.* — Observation and experiment reveal a radical difference, both in *structure* and *function,* between living and nonliving beings. The organism acts as an individual being functioning as a 'whole.' Vital activity is 'immanent' action, while inorganic action is 'transient.' Every organism is characterized by 'inherent natural purposiveness,' striving for the well-being of the individual and the preservation of the species. In particular, sense-perception, consciousness, and the rational activities present in man are far superior to nonliving activity and require a vital principle or 'soul.'

2. *Abiogenesis.* — Abiogenesis (spontaneous generation) is the theory that living beings ultimately came into existence through a development on the part of the forces indigenous to nonliving matter. Science has proved that *life derives its origin only from life.* Abiogenesis has never been observed and never occurs.

3. *The Origin of Life.* — Life originated in time and had a beginning. Abiogenesis can only be a 'postulate' of science (or, rather, of philosophy), if it is the *only* rational explanation of the origin of life. That would be the case if God does not exist.

4. *God, the Ultimate Cause of Life.* — Logic and reason demand that there be a proper proportion between cause and effect. Now, the activities of organic life *exceed the causality of inorganic substances.* The arrival of the organism involves the appearance of something totally new and superior. Hence, it must be accounted for by some cause *outside* the totality of *matter* and of the material universe. This extra-mundane cause must possess *life.* And since man has a rational, spiritual life, the origin of life demands a *living, intelligent, extra-mundane cause.* This cause we call *God*.

5. *God and Evolution.* — *Organic evolution* is the theory which maintains that the types and species of all plants and animals derive their origin through development from other pre-existing species

and types, all differences being accounted for by modifications acquired in successive generations according to purely natural laws. The argument for evolution is valid only if it can be proved to be the *only possible* cause; it leaves 'creation' out of consideration, but does not eliminate creation. *Without the intervention of God,* the organic processes cannot be conceived as passing from the less perfect to the more perfect (e.g., from plant to animal, and from animal to man), because that would entail the contradiction of an insufficient cause.

Emergent evolution maintains that nature is the product of evolution in such a manner that entirely new and unpredictable properties originate through synthesis and thereby form new and higher levels of reality in a continuously ascending process of development. It is thus that life and mind have had their first origin. Such an emergence demands a *nisus* or *impetus* toward more perfect levels of being; this nisus, however, cannot be accounted for except on the supposition that a *cause outside the universe* has put it there. It would then be a 'purposive evolution.'

6. *God and Purposive Evolution.* — Evolution, if it ever occurred, must be *purposive,* if the Principles of Sufficient Reason and Causality are to be safeguarded. Since 'purpose' implies the use of specific means toward a specific end to be realized in the future, only the Supreme Intelligence could endow nature with such a purpose. Even then the *spiritual* soul of man, being intrinsically independent of matter, must have been produced by God directly.

7. *Notion of Perfection.* — By *perfection* here we mean any reality or real entity which is present in any kind of being, whether this being be 'actual' or 'potential.' Perfection may be either 'mixed' or 'simple,' 'essential' or 'accidental,' 'predicamental' or 'transcendental.'

8. *Grades of Perfection.* — The plant is superior to the inorganic being; the animal superior to the plant; man superior to the animal: there thus exists a *gradation of perfection* in the universe. Each individual nature is the result of *composition* between essential and accidental perfection, between actuality and potentiality, resulting in a 'more' or 'less' of reality (perfection).

9. *Limitation of Perfection.* — As a matter of observable fact, the grades of being (reality, perfection) are all *limited,* and limitation implies *imperfection.* Potentiality and perfectibility are evidence of this limitation in all beings.

10. *God and Perfection.* — Perfections are arranged in a graded

scale; the sufficient reason for this gradation resides neither in the individuals nor in the series. Hence, it must be found in a reason or cause outside the series (the universe). Diverse perfections combined into a unity require a causal agency outside themselves to bring about their unification in a being. Limitation of being does not find its sufficient reason in the beings subject to limitation; it must be sought in some outside intelligence. Transcendental perfections are 'simple' perfections; their varying degrees demand an adequate cause outside the beings possessing them. Hence, there must exist outside the universe of graded perfections *a cause possessing unlimited perfection*. Its perfection must be 'unlimited,' because there can be no cause capable of limiting the perfection of the Uncaused Cause. This Uncaused Cause possessing unlimited perfection we call 'God.' Therefore, *God exists*.

11. *The Argument of St. Thomas.* — St. Thomas made no argument for God's existence based on the 'origin of life,' because he believed in spontaneous generation as a fact of nature. He did, however, make an argument proving God's existence from the fact of the 'grades of perfection.'

12. *Inferences.* — God must possess *life;* and since man has a spiritual life in his immaterial soul, God must also have *spiritual life*. Since limitation and composition of reality demand a cause, there can be no limitation and composition in God the Uncaused Cause. Hence, God cannot be an organism, nor can He have materiality in His nature; He must, therefore, be a *pure spirit*. For the same reason, there can be no potentiality in God's nature; He must be *pure act*. Since to be without limitation means to be 'unlimited,' God must be a pure spirit or *act with unlimited reality* or perfection.

Readings

Joyce, George Hayward, *Principles of Natural Theology,* Chap. III (pp. 105–115), Chap. IV (pp. 145–152). — Aveling, Francis, *The God of Philosophy,* Chaps. VIII, X. — Heydon, J. K., *The God of Reason,* Chap. VI. — *The Great Design,* ed. by Frances Mason. — Garrigou-Lagrange, R., *God: His Existence and Nature,* Vol. I, n. 39, pp. 302–345. — Smith, Gerard, *Natural Theology,* Chap. VIII. — Renard, Henri, *The Philosophy of God,* pp. 40–45.

Chapter VIII

OPPOSING VIEWS

EXCEPT for the ontological argument of St. Anselm, medieval philosophers had no doubts about the general validity of the traditional proofs. Many moderns accuse them of being prejudiced through their Christian faith. That their faith influenced them may be admitted as undoubtedly true; but that they were prejudiced, in the sense that their faith led them into false reasoning, is an entirely different matter. It is up to the individual to judge whether the reasoning process proving God's existence is convincing or not. Accusation is not proof.

René Descartes is the one mostly responsible for the confusion which exists in modern thought. He revived St. Anselm's ontological argument, and the result was no happier in his hands than in the hands of St. Anselm. Mainly, however, Descartes was responsible for the excessive dualism of matter and mind in man, as found in much of modern philosophy, thereby opening the door to the empiricism of Hume. *Empiricism* still is strong in the English-speaking world, especially among a certain group of scientists. It gave rise to *agnosticism,* so prevalent in the past century. Nowadays neither philosophers nor scientists of the secularistic type are quite so dogmatic in their assertions; but the empiricistic and agnostic trend still taints their thinking to a great extent. Much of their opposition to the traditional proofs for God's existence stems from the objections made by Kant.

It is well-nigh impossible to consider all the opposing views advanced in modern thought. The main ones will alone be considered.

Objections of Transcendentalism

Immanuel Kant (1724–1804), although he has lost a great deal of prestige as an infallible authority, still ranks highly among many modern philosophers. Most of these thinkers are acquainted with the arguments for God's existence only in the version given by Kant. Thus A. E. Taylor[1] remarks in typical fashion: "Kant's great achievement lies in having demonstrated that the whole force of the 'proofs' [for God's existence] depends upon the famous ontological argument, best known in modern philosophy in the form adopted by Descartes in the Fifth Meditation." We must, therefore, turn our attention to *Kant's objections.*

Kant apparently knew nothing about St. Thomas and the 'Five Ways,' because he admits of but three possible proofs. He says:[2] "There are only three modes of proving the existence of a Deity, on the grounds of speculative reason. All the paths conducting to this end begin either from determinate experience and the peculiar constitution of the world of sense, and rise, according to the law of causality, from it to the highest cause existing apart from the world — or from a purely indeterminate experience, that is, some empirical existence — or abstraction is made of all experience, and the existence of a supreme cause is concluded from *à priori* conceptions alone. The first is the *physico-theological* argument, the second the *cosmological,* and the third the *ontological.* More there are not and more there cannot be." He then proceeds to show why these arguments are invalid.

As regards the *ontological* argument, Kant holds that it involves an illegitimate transition from possibility to existence. St. Thomas pointed out long before Kant that it is impossible to draw a valid conclusion from the ideal to the real order of things, and for this reason he rejected the 'ontological argument' of St. Anselm. It was the revival of this argument on the part of Descartes which prompted Kant to examine it anew. Kant's rejection coincides with what most scholastic philoso-

---

[1] *Elements of Metaphysics,* 5 ed. (London: Methuen, 1920), p. 400.

[2] *Critique of Pure Reason,* tr. J. M. D. Meiklejohn (New York: Macmillan, 1900), p. 331.

phers have always maintained, and so nothing further will be said about it.

As regards the *cosmological* argument (we call it the 'argument from contingency'), Kant[3] states that it is framed as follows: "If something exists, an absolutely necessary being must likewise exist. Now I, at least, exist. Consequently, there exists an absolutely necessary being. The minor contains an experience, the major reasons from a general experience to the existence of a necessary being. Thus this argument really begins at experience, and is not completely *à priori*, or ontological. . . . The proof proceeds thus: — A necessary being can be determined in only one way, that is, it can be determined by only one of all possible opposed predicates; consequently, it must be *completely* determined in and by its conception. But there is only a single conception of a thing possible, which completely determines the thing *à priori:* that is, the conception of the *ens realissimum*. It follows that the conception of the *ens realissimum* is the only conception, by and in which we can cogitate a necessary being. Consequently a supreme being necessarily exists." It is in this manner that Kant formulates the argument from contingency or, as he calls it, the 'cosmological argument.'

Kant advances *two main reasons* for the rejection of the argument from the contingent to the necessary.

The *first* reason is that the argument from contingency is ultimately nothing but the *ontological* argument in disguise. Kant[4] proceeds to prove his claim. "That it may possess a secure foundation, it bases its conclusion upon experience, and thus appears to be completely distinct from the ontological argument, which places its confidence entirely in pure *à priori* conceptions. But this experience merely aids reason in making one step — to the existence of a necessary being. What the properties of this being are, cannot be learned from experience;

---

[3] *Ibid.*, pp. 338–339.
[4] *Ibid.*, pp. 339–340.

and therefore reason abandons it altogether, and pursues its inquiry in the sphere of pure conceptions, for the purpose of discovering what the properties of an absolutely necessary being ought to be, that is, what among all possible things contain the conditions (requisita) of absolute necessity. Reason believes that it has discovered these requisites in the conception of an *ens realissimum* — and in it alone, and hence concludes: The *ens realissimum* is an absolutely necessary being. But it is evident that reason has here presupposed that the conception of an *ens realissimum* is perfectly adequate to the conception of a being of absolute necessity, that is, that we may infer the existence of the latter from the former — a proposition which formed the basis of the ontological argument, and which is now employed in the support of the cosmological argument, contrary to the wish and professions of its inventors. For the existence of an absolutely necessary being is given in conceptions alone. But if I say — the conception of the *ens realissimum* is a conception of this kind, and in fact the only conception which is adequate to our idea of a necessary being, I am obliged to admit that the latter may be inferred from the former. Thus it is properly the ontological argument which figures in the cosmological and constitutes the whole strength of the latter; while the spurious basis of experience has been of no further use than to conduct us to the conception of absolute necessity, being utterly insufficient to demonstrate the presence of this attribute in any determinate existence or thing." Put into simple words, Kant's objection amounts to this: We go from the experience of existing and 'contingent' things to the idea of a 'necessary being,' and from this *idea* we argue to the *existence* of the necessary being; and that is the ontological argument.

Kant's *second* reason consists in denying that the *Principle of Causality* is universally applicable to all finite realities. He maintains[5] that the argument from contingency possesses a large number of unproved assumptions, one of which is "the

---

[5] *Ibid.*, p. 341.

transcendental principle, everything that is contingent must have a cause — a principle without significance, except in the sensuous world. For the purely intellectual conception of the contingent cannot produce any synthetical proposition, like that of causality, which is itself without significance or distinguishing characteristic except in the phenomenal world. But in the present case it is employed to help us beyond the limits of its sphere." To understand Kant's objection here, one must realize that ideas like 'causality,' 'existence,' 'contingency,' and 'necessity' are, according to his theory of knowledge, nothing more than *categories of the mind,* in the mind prior to all experience, *subjective forms or constructs* whose sole function it is to *regulate* the data of sense experience (the 'phenomena') in our thinking, and as such have *no objective value* in the world of realities outside the self. Hence, the Principle of Causality cannot lead to God, because God is a 'thing-in-itself,' a 'noumenon,' which remains forever unknown and unknowable to man.

As regards the *physico-theological* argument (we term it the 'argument from order and design'), Kant respects it more than the other two, but he claims that it, too, is but the 'ontological' argument in disguise. He says[6] this in the following quotation: "After elevating ourselves to admiration of the magnitude of the power, wisdom, and other attributes of the author of the world, and finding we can advance no further, we leave the argument on empirical grounds, and proceed to infer the contingency of the world from the order and conformity to aims that are observable in it. From this contingency we infer, by the help of transcendental conceptions alone, the existence of something absolutely necessary; and, still advancing, proceed from the conception of the absolute necessity of the first cause to the completely determined or determining conception thereof — the conception of an all-embracing reality. Thus, the physico-theological, failing in its undertaking, recurs in its embarrassment to the cosmological argument; and, as this is

---

[6] *Ibid.,* p. 352.

merely the ontological argument in disguise, it executes its design solely by the aid of pure reason, although it at first professed to have no connection with this faculty, and to base its entire procedure upon experience alone."

Kant, of course, has much more to say about these arguments. The above, however, contains the gist of his thoughts.

Refutation of Transcendentalism

Kant was neither an atheist nor a pantheist. He defended the theistic position in his *Critique of the Practical Reason* while he repudiated the traditional arguments for God's existence in his *Critique of Pure Reason*. What prompted him to adopt this peculiar position? His attitude is explained by the trend of modern philosophy as inaugurated by Descartes and carried forward by Hume.

Both Hume and Kant accepted without question the (apparently evident) dictum of Descartes that *all knowledge originates solely in the mind;* knowledge is altogether a subjective product; the mind can know nothing but its own conscious states; the mind cannot go beyond itself and know what the objective world is 'in itself.' Hume, in accepting this basic tenet of Descartes, reduced all knowledge to sense-perception and the mind to a 'bundle of perceptions.' As a final result, Hume rejected the validity of reason and denied the necessary character of all rational and scientific principles; he ended as a *skeptic.*

Kant became alarmed at the outcome of Hume's philosophy and attempted to place science (and philosophy) upon a firm foundation. In seeking to do this, Kant made the *initial mistake* (fatal in the long run) of accepting Descartes's and Hume's original *assumption* that all knowledge originates *solely in the mind* and that the mind can know only its own conscious states. He thought he could nevertheless avoid Hume's final conclusion of skepticism. He agreed with Hume that knowledge must be grounded in 'experience'; but, he maintained, the *necessary character of science* (and philosophy) must also be safeguarded. To do this he devised his own system of knowledge.

Kant made the distinction between the *noumenon* ('thing-in-itself') and the *phenomenon* ('appearance'). The 'noumenon' (for example, the external world as it actually is) is absolutely unknowable, because it is a reality which exists outside the mind. All man can perceive and know is the 'phenomenon' (for example, the 'appearances' of things as perceived by the mind), because the phenomenon is an elaboration of the mind. On the sense level, all phenomena appear in 'time' and 'space'; and this happens because 'time' and 'space' are not attributes of objective reality at all, but are purely subjective 'forms' into which all the intuitions of sense are cast. These *forms* are the conditions of knowledge and make knowledge possible. It is a postulate of Kant's system that *nothing which is necessary and universal can have its origin in experience,* because experience treats only of the particular, contingent, transitory. It follows, then, that such 'forms' must be present in the mind *prior to all experience* as subjective elements of the mind making knowledge possible; and since 'space' and 'time' are the necessary and universal attributes of all appearances (phenomena), 'space' and 'time' are *a priori forms* of sensibility. After the intuitions of sense are cast into the 'forms' of 'space' and 'time,' they are drawn under the influence of the pure understanding and cast into the *a priori* forms of the understanding, namely, the *categories*. These latter have the same relation to intellectual knowledge that 'space' and 'time' have to sense-knowledge: they are the 'conditions' which make intellectual knowledge possible; but they, like the sense forms of 'space' and 'time,' are purely subjective elements and tell us nothing of what the reality of the 'things-in-themselves' (noumena) is like. Since the 'categories,' of which there are twelve, possess the character of universality and necessity, they are not the result of experience but are *a priori* and present in the mind prior to all experience. These twelve 'categories' are: unity, plurality, totality; reality, negation, limitation; subsistence and inherence, causality and dependence, reciprocity (active and passive); possibility and impossibility, existence and non-existence, necessity and contingency. Every judgment, therefore, which is based on any of these relations contains the *a posteriori* element of experience and the *a priori* element of a 'category'; the multiplicity of sense intuitions is thus unified in intellectual judgments by means of the 'categories.' It is in this manner that *scientific* judgments are formed and obtain a necessary and universal value. Finally, in the field of reasoning, we encounter three *a priori* 'forms,' namely, the *ideas*. These are: the psychological 'idea' of the *soul,* the cosmological 'idea' of *matter* (the totality of phenomena), and the theological 'idea' of *God*. These 'ideas,' like the 'categories' and 'space' and 'time,' are subjective elements of the mind, and their sole function is to regulate our thinking and to bring greater unity into the manifold of intellectual experience. As such, therefore, these 'ideas' *do not refer to any objects existing outside the mind,* because they exist in the mind as mere 'forms' and must be present prior to all experience: they make reasoning possible, but they do not lead to extra-mental reality.

We now see why Kant insisted that the 'cosmological' and 'physico-theological' arguments for God's existence involve the fallacy of the 'ontological' argument. They assuredly do — *according to Kant's system of knowledge*. None of the 'forms' apply to the 'things-in-themselves.' Neither the twelve 'categories' nor the three 'ideas' have any value beyond the world of sense, the 'phenomena.' If we attempt to use them in an endeavor to prove that the 'world' or 'God' actually exists *outside the mind,* we are guilty of the fallacy of an illegitimate transition from the ideal to the real order, and that is fundamentally what the 'ontological' argument attempted to do.

The question then arises: *Is Kant's system of knowledge true?*

Today practically nobody accepts Kant's system in its entirety. It is too *arbitrary* and *subjective*. If Kant's system were true, all our knowledge is nothing but a grand *illusion:* we think we know something of the world and the things in it, but actually we do not; it is a subjective construct, elaborately executed, but without any reference to objective reality. We live in a dreamworld. The mind is imprisoned in a cell of its own making, from which there is no possibility of escape. Of what value is such a knowledge? Since we *cannot help* but think that our knowledge tells us something of the things outside the mind, this knowledge is *essentially false*. The outcome is the very *skepticism* which Kant attempted to avoid, because we must naturally mistrust a power which irresistibly leads to error and misunderstanding. But in that case — of what use is Kant's system? His system is certainly not the result of 'experience'; it is the result of 'reasoning,' and all reasoning, according to Kant, is based on *a priori forms* which have subjective value only. Kant's system may satisfy Kant, but that would be no guarantee that it is true in itself; it is essentially a *noumenon* of which we could know nothing.

Kant's system is inconsistent with the *principles of reason*. In repudiating the arguments for God's existence, Kant criticizes the use of the Principle of Causality as applied to contingency and order. It is illegitimate, he says, to apply this principle to anything but "the sensuous world," *i.e.,* to phenomena, because phenomena are all man can experience. Since 'contingency,' 'causality,' and 'existence' are mere empty *a priori forms,* or *categories* innately present in the mind, according to Kant's theory of knowledge, one can understand how he could make such a remarkable statement. Kant, however, overlooked the fact that man, besides having sensuous powers, also has *rational* powers. Man is a 'rational animal,' and his rational knowledge has as much validity as his sensory knowledge. Now, rational knowledge is acquired through the application of *reason* and *rational principles* to the data acquired through sense-knowledge. To deny this is to deny the validity of intellectual knowledge. In that case, however, the foundation of Kant's own system is invalid, because it is essentially a system of intellectual knowledge which he proposes. To deny the validity of intellectual knowledge always leads to *skepticism.* Furthermore, the *Principle of Causality* is but an extension of the Principle of Sufficient Reason, as the latter is an extension of the Principle of Contradiction (see Chap. II). If the sufficient reason of a thing cannot be found in the thing itself, it must be found in another; and if the sufficient reason for the existence of a thing cannot be found in the thing itself, then this thing is 'contingent,' and the sufficient reason for its existence must eventually be found in a being which is not contingent but 'necessary.' That, however, is equivalent to saying that its existence is 'caused' by this other; otherwise it would both exist (for that is the supposition) and not exist (because there is no sufficient reason for its existence). Hence, the Principle of Causality, like the Principles of Contradiction and Sufficient Reason, must have *universal application* both in the realm of thought and of being, or man's rational knowledge is intrinsically illusory.

Even from the standpoint of Kant's own transcendentalism, there must be a sufficient reason to explain the existence in man's mind of all the 'forms' which he claims are present there prior to all experience. Man himself certainly is not responsible for the presence of these 'forms'; they are there without his doing. Man's mind, however, did not always exist, neither individually nor collectively. Therefore, man's mind and its entire apparatus of knowledge is 'contingent' and must have been *brought from non-existence to existence,* or there would be no sufficient reason why they exist in this particular manner or why they exist at all. The Principle of Sufficient Reason thus demands that *some other being* gave them existence, *i.e.,* is their *cause.* And since the entire question here hinges on the existence of 'intellectual life' in man, this efficient cause must be a being possessing intellectual life, otherwise the sufficient reason for the existence of man's intellectual life would be lacking, and then man's intellectual life could not exist at all. Consequently, since nothing can be in an 'effect' which is not in its 'cause,' the cause of man's intellectual life must also be endowed with intellectual life. This cause we call 'God.'

The same criticism applies to Kant's objection to the argument from *order* and *design*. As in the argument from 'contingency,' Kant claims that the 'school' (scholastic philosophers) argues from the world of phenomena to the 'pure conception' or 'idea' of God and then *deduces* the existence of God from this 'pure conception' or 'idea'; in this manner, he says, scholastics are guilty of a surreptitious 'ontological' inference. To put it mildly, Kant labors under a misapprehension. Neither St. Thomas nor the scholastics in general argue in this fashion. All anyone has to do is to examine the arguments for God's existence as formulated by them. It is to their everlasting credit that St. Anselm's ontological argument has always been repudiated as an illegitimate transition from the ideal to the real order of things. Certainly, they conclude from the existence and properties of the visible universe to an extra-mundane God; but they do this by applying the rational Principles of Sufficient Reason and Causality to the *data furnished by the visible universe*. If this procedure is illogical, well and good; but that is something very different from Kant's accusation of introducing an 'ontological' line of reasoning into their arguments, as was done by St. Anselm, Descartes, Leibnitz, and others. That a 'transcendent inference' from phenomena to noumena is permissible, can be seen by Kant's own system (although, from the standpoint of his own premises, Kant was guilty of gross inconsistency), because Kant concludes to a *world of noumena* as existing beyond and outside his own mind. He accepts this 'world of noumena' on the basis of the Principles of Sufficient Reason and Causality, because otherwise he could not account for the 'sensations' which give rise to empirical knowledge; and yet he claims that the 'noumena' are unknown and unknowable. But if Kant can argue to the existence of an unperceived and unperceivable 'world,' why should it be illogical to argue to the existence of a Being beyond the world, if the rational principles employed demand such a conclusion?

All in all, Kant's transcendentalism and the resultant objections to the arguments for the existence of God are unfounded in fact and illogical in principle.

Objections of Materialism

Kant's transcendentalism, since it reduced everything to a form of knowledge, was at bottom idealistic. He thus followed the mental side of Descartes's excessive dualism of mind and body in man. Others followed the bodily side of Descartes's dualism and reduced everything to matter. Materialism was the result.

Materialism is the philosophic system of thought which considers *matter to be the only reality* and attempts to explain everything in the universe as the result of the *conditions and activities of matter*. As a consequence, materialists deny the existence of every kind of spiritual or even truly psychical reality, including God. To be consistent, materialists are, or at least should be, atheists. If they speak of 'God' at all (and some do), they interpret the word in the sense of 'world-force' or 'world-energy.'

Materialism, as a philosophy, is as old as Greek thought. The first efforts toward philosophic explanation were more or less materialistic; one must not overlook the fact, however, that the polytheistic religion of ancient Greece was not of a kind to appeal to earnest thinkers. *Systematic materialism* began with *Democritus,* who taught that everything results from the combination and division of atoms which are infinite in number and separated by empty spaces. *Epicurus* was a thoroughgoing materialist. Bodies alone exist, and they are ultimately composed of unchangeable atoms falling downward through space. Since space is infinite, an infinite number of atoms also exists. Some deviate from their original direction of motion, and so collisions occur and combinations are made. Atoms themselves are not qualitatively different; their difference consists merely in size, weight, and shape. Man's soul is simply a kind of vapor diffused through the body. *Lucretius* gave poetic expression to materialism. While Epicurus sought to explain the origin and order of the present world through chance, Lucretius was somewhat more philosophical; he maintained that the world is nothing more than one of the infinitely numerous possibilities in atomic arrangement, and the present arrangement was as possible as any other. Soul and mind are material in nature, consisting of the smallest, roundest, and most mobile types of atoms. The materialism of these earlier philosophers was, as will be noted, rather crude.

The victory of Christianity over paganism put an end to ancient materialism. The reign of Christian thought lasted through sixteen centuries. The rise of the Renaissance, together with the general waning of faith in Europe, gradually developed into a materialistic attitude in some intellectual quarters. Descartes's splitting up of the human person into a thinking mind (soul) and quantitative extension (body), both practically independent of each other, led many thinkers either to idealism or to materialism.

The *Age of Materialism* began in France with Julian O. de la Mettrie (1709–1751), Baron Paul H. d'Holbach (1723–1789), and Piérre J. G. Cabanis (1757–1808). The latter not only identified man's mind with his nervous system but frankly asserted that thought is only a secretion of the brain. In Germany Karl Vogt (1817–1895), Jakob Moleschott (1822–1893), Ludwig Büchner (1824–1899), and Ernest Haeckel (1834–1919) were ardent defenders of materialism. English materialism stemmed from the empiricism of John Locke (1632–1704) and David Hume (1711–1776); the chief advocates were John Tyndall (1820–1893), Thomas H. Huxley (1825–1895), and Herbert Spencer (1820–1903). Spencer, the most important philosopher of this group, claimed to be a mere agnostic; in reality, however, he was a materialist. There were, of course, many lesser lights in all countries who followed the tenets of materialism.

The marvelous success of the *natural sciences* provided the materialists with a great opportunity to defend their thesis that every event in nature receives its full and adequate explanation in the configurations of matter and its activities. Nature, according to the general teaching of scientists, is a 'closed system of causation'; each natural phenomenon is based on another as its cause, and the *chain of natural causes* is a determined series complete in itself. The materialists seized upon this idea. Since this chain is a series of 'material' causes, there is no place in it for a free-will and a spiritual soul, because they would break the chain of 'natural events.' By postulating the *eternity of matter,* materialists obviated the necessity of a 'beginning' in the world and its causal events, and so the idea of God was eliminated. When R. Mayer (1814–1878), J. P. Joule (1818–1889), and Herman L. F. von Helmholtz (1821–1894) formulated the scientific *Law of the Conservation of Energy,* materialists were convinced that they now possessed a definite proof of the non-existence of a spiritual soul. The law, they argued, proves that energy can neither be created nor destroyed. Kinetic energy may be transformed into potential energy, and potential energy into kinetic; but the sum-total remains always the same, because the world is a 'closed system.' If a spiritual soul existed, it would produce energy and pour it into the events, thus increasing the sum of energy present in the closed system; and every external stimulus influencing the soul would produce sensations which are not a form of energy in a physical sense, and thereby the sum of energy in the closed system of the world would be decreased. However, the Law of the Conservation of Energy precludes any increase or decrease in the sum-total of energy present in the universe. Therefore, they concluded, the soul of man as a spiritual entity does not exist. It is material, or it does not exist at all. In this manner materialists utilized the findings of the natural sciences to support their theory.

The upsurge of *evolutionism* in consequence of Charles R. Darwin's (1809–1882) epoch-making *Origin of Species* gave a new impetus to materialism. The question of teleology (purposiveness) in nature, especially in the plant and animal kingdoms, had always been an awkward problem for materialists. Darwin's theory of organic evolution, however, disposed of 'design' completely; everything was the result of 'fortuitous variations' effected in the course of natural events, so that a 'Designer' was superfluous. Natural evolution accounted for everything through pure mechanism. The theory pleased the materialists immensely. It was a simple matter to expand the evolutionary concept to embrace the entire universe. Given an infinity of time to work in, the mechanical operations of the atoms could make every conceivable combination, including the present form of the universe in all its complexity. Hence, an extra-mundane God was no longer required in order to explain the origin and development of the world. Science thus accounts for inanimate and animate nature, and nature is a completely *material system*. The materialists, without question, had achieved a very advantageous position and boldly proclaimed their doctrine.

That materialism in our times has many adherents among the educated and uneducated, is an obvious fact. However, a reaction has set in, especially among the scientists themselves. Having examined the foundations of the sciences more closely, scientists and philosophers have become increasingly aware that materialism does not contain the full solution for the problems which agitate man's mind.

Refutation of Materialism

Materialism is the very opposite of idealism. Idealism attempts to reduce all material reality to the knowledge state of the conscious subject. Materialism does the reverse. It attempts to reduce everything that is 'psychical' to the 'physical.' Both views are extremes and are wrong.

Materialism is an *oversimplification*. It is right, of course, in stressing the material realities present in nature. It is wrong in *denying the psychical realities*. In man, for instance, we observe both the physical and the psychical. The body of man is physical in its composition, composed as it is of the ordinary chemical elements found everywhere in nature. Materialists claim that 'nothing but' chemical elements and their material activities are present in the human body. It is in this 'nothing-but' that materialists are guilty of the *Fallacy of False Exclusion*. Organic compounds are the result of natural activities in man's body (and also in plants and brutes), but nowhere in nature do the ordinary elements form such compounds when left to themselves. These compounds conspire to develop various tissues and organs in the organic structure of the body, something they never do otherwise. There is a unity of structure and function in the body which transcends the capabilities of the atoms and elements in their ordinary status. In other words, *life* is an *immanent* activity totally different from that of the atoms as the physicist and chemist know them. Life, too, is an integral part of nature and must be explained; and this explanation is not forthcoming on the basis of an out-and-out materialistic interpretation of nature.

Then, there is the *psychic* factor which materialism simply denies. A mere denial is easy; but it does not prove the non-existence of the psychical. Even the materialist cannot deny the fact of *sensation*. He tries to explain it as a complicated form of atomic motion of some kind. That atomic motion is present in sensation, is true enough. Such motion, however, by no means explains the fact of conscious perception. *Conscious perception* is something 'over and above' the motion of atomic and subatomic particles accompanying the act of sensation. Here again we encounter the 'nothing-but' fallacy. Certainly, every act of sensation is a bodily function involving movements of parts consisting of elements, atoms, and subatomic particles; but that is only a part of the phenomenon. While these movements occur, man actually 'sees,' 'hears,' 'smells,' 'tastes,' and 'feels' objects; and he is 'conscious' of perceiving these objects. Perception and consciousness, however, though they are accompanied by material movement, cannot be said to be 'nothing but' material movements. They represent a 'psychical factor' of life distinct from the merely material. This fact becomes evident when a living body is compared with a dead body; both possess the same organs and material components, yet the former is capable of perception and the latter is not.

The same observations must be made concerning the *intellectual activity* of man. To deny that intellectual activity exists is both futile and foolish. It is experienced by each one of us. We all use 'ideas,' 'judgments,' and 'inferences.' But they are in no sense 'material' like electrons, atoms, elements, and their respective activities. Every material reality can be measured quantitatively. What quantitative measure of length and weight can be applied to an 'idea' or a 'judgment' or a 'process of reasoning'? They have no size, color, or temperature. They are realities, assuredly, and as such their existence and presence as a part of the universe cannot be denied; but all material standards used in chemistry and physics fail to apply to them. Similarly, man's mind is capable of thinking about things that have *no material existence as yet*. Our ideas, in the view of materialists, are 'nothing but' refined sense-images. Sense-images, however, are the product of stimuli which proceed from objects at a specified time from a specified place. The *future* is thus barred to the senses, because future events cannot send stimuli to the sense organs existing in the present; otherwise a non-existent cause would produce an actual effect. Nevertheless, we have ideas of the future, and the scientists predict future happenings in many instances.

G. T. Ladd,[7] recognizing these facts, did not hesitate to write: "With no mere figure of speech we are compelled to say, every mind thus *transcends* completely, not only the powers of the cerebral mechanism by springing into another order of phenomena, but also the very existence, as it were, of that mechanism by passing into regions of space, time, causality, and ideality, of various kinds, where the terms that apply to the existence and activity of the cerebral centers have absolutely no meaning whatever. For example, the human mind anticipates the future and predicts, on a basis of experience in the past, the occurrences which *will* be but are not now. Into this future, which is itself the product of its own imagining and thinking, it projects its own continued and yet characteristically altered existence, as well as the continued similar existence of things. But the existence of the brain, and of its particular forms of nerve commotion, is never other than a purely here-and-now existence. This physical existence is, therefore, transcended in an absolute way by every such activity of the mind."

[7] *Philosophy of Mind* (New York: Charles Scribner's Sons, 1895), pp. 400, 401.

Man is without doubt a material organism. However, besides the physical component of his nature there is also a *psychical* component. Both are real. For materialists to accept only the 'physical' and to deny the very existence of the 'psychical,' is an unpardonable error.

Materialists have referred to the *Law of the Conservation of Energy* as a positive proof of the non-existence of spiritual reality, such as the human soul and God. However, even this law has been dethroned; it no longer holds absolute sway over the domain of matter. Modern physicists are convinced that matter can be, and actually is, transformed into energy, and energy into matter. The law has therefore been altered to read The Law of the Conservation of Energy and Matter. It may be disputed whether the theory of the transformation of matter and energy is a correct interpretation of the facts in the case. This much, however, is clear; the law is empirical and subject to change. Consequently, when the materialists appealed to it as a proof of the non-existence of the human soul and of God, they appealed to a law which had only 'provisional value' and was not as sound as they imagined it was. Besides, it is very questionable whether *thinking* (accepting 'thinking' in the strict sense of an activity of the spiritual soul) is accompanied by any expenditure of physical energy. That ordinary vital activities, such as occur in the human body, involve energy, can be admitted; this energy would come from the elements and atoms composing the bodily tissues and organs. The activities of the spiritual soul, however, should neither increase nor decrease the sum-total of energy, because the soul is not material. All experiments made show that 'thinking' apparently does not involve the expenditure of energy. Consider the words of Alexis Carrel:[8] "Intellectual work, strange to say, does not increase metabolism. It seems to require no energy, or to consume a quantity of it too small to be detected by our present techniques. It is, indeed, an astonishing fact

---

[8] *Man, the Unknown,* 27 ed. (New York: Harper and Bros., 1935), p. 81. See also T. V. Moore, *Cognitive Psychology* (Philadelphia: Lippincott, 1939), pp. 540, 541.

that human thought, which has transformed the surface of the earth, destroyed and built nations, discovered new universes in the immensity of siderial spaces, is elaborated without demanding a measurable amount of energy. The highest efforts of our intelligence have incomparably less effect on metabolism than the contraction of the biceps when this muscle lifts a weight of a few grams. The ambition of Caesar, the meditation of Newton, the inspiration of Beethoven, the passionate contemplation of Pasteur, did not modify the chemical exchanges of these great men as much as a few bacteria or a slight stimulation of the thyroid gland would easily have done." Provided these scientific findings are substantiated, they show that thinking, precisely as such, is not a material process but an immaterial operation. Whatever minute metabolic changes might occur, could be attributed to the cerebral activity which normally accompanies all acts of thinking. It is thus seen that the Law of the Conservation of Energy does not militate in any way against the existence of the soul or of God.

The materialist's appeal to the universe as a *closed system of causation* fares no better. No scientist has ever proved through observation and experiment that the entire universe is such a 'closed system.' The inductive method of science does not reach that far. This claim is a *conclusion,* but it is not subject to an actual proof. At best, the claim has merely 'empirical value' and is 'provisional' in its very nature. The principle of the 'closed system' is true in a limited and well-defined sphere; but to extend it to the universe at large goes far beyond the premises of scientific induction. Even if admitted to be valid for the whole world, it would apply only to *material causes,* not to spiritual causes, such as the soul and especially God.

Materialists postulate the *eternity of matter* and the *infinity of time* in their theory. Neither the eternity of matter nor the infinity of time-moments is in accord with the findings of science. Einstein's 'curved space' and the theory of an 'expanding universe' imply a limited space, and a limited space implies a limited number of particles; hence, there can be no such thing as an infinite number of possible combinations for the particles of matter to form the universe. It is fairly well established, too, that the present world, as we know it, has existed for only a *limited time,* not from eternity. The calculations differ, as is to be expected, but practically all scientists agree that the indications point to the fact that the duration of the universe can be measured in a number of billions of years.[9] Billions of years are, of course, a long period of time, but such a period is definitely limited. When materialists, therefore, set up the postulate that matter is eternal, they do so for the sake of their theory, because they wish to eliminate God as the author of the universe; in doing so, however, they run counter to the findings of science and the principles of philosophy, and that is fatal to any theory.

Scientists begin their research with the universe as given. The *origin of the universe* lies beyond the scope of scientific investigation. Very properly, then, scientists may omit God from their discussions. When, therefore, they refer to God, they no longer speak as scientists but as philosophers and lose their status as experts in a particular field of science. This should always be borne in mind.

The better scientists, as a class, are not in sympathy with materialism. To them the world is an *intelligible and rational universe,* with an order and harmony that can be expressed in precise mathematical formulae. No wonder, then, that most of them are *theists.*

Neither idealistic transcendentalism nor mechanistic materialism can satisfy the inquiring mind anxious on discovering the truth. Both are extremes, and extremes are always a one-sided distortion of truth. Honest thinking invariably leads to God.

Summary of Chapter VIII

Kant's *transcendentalism* and the teachings of *materialism* are, in the main, the views which oppose the traditional proofs for God's existence.

---

[9] Sir Edmund Whittaker, *Space and Spirit* (Hinsdale, Ill.: Henry Regnery Co., 1948), p. 112 ff.

1. *Objections of Transcendentalism.* — Kant says that there are only three proofs for God's existence, and all three are invalid; the ontological, physico-theological, and cosmological.

He rejects the *ontological* proof as an illegitimate transition from the ideal to the real order. We do the same.

He rejects the *cosmological* proof, because in it we go from the experience of existing and contingent things to the 'idea' of a necessary being, and from this 'idea' we argue to the existence of the necessary being; and this is the ontological argument in disguise. The Principle of Causality is valid in the world of 'phenomena,' not in the world of noumenal reality.

He rejects the *physico-theological* proof (order and design), because we pass from the empirical order, with the help of transcendental conceptions alone, to the existence of something absolutely necessary, and from this 'idea' deduce God's existence; this, too, he says, is nothing but the ontological argument.

2. *Refutation of Transcendentalism.* — Kant made the initial mistake of accepting Descartes's and Hume's *assumption* that all knowledge originates *solely* in the mind and that the mind can know only its own conscious states. To safeguard the necessary character of science, he made the distinction between *phenomena* (which are known through experience) and *noumena* (which cannot be known). All phenomena are necessarily clothed in 'space' and 'time' and these are *a priori forms* of sensibility. On the intellectual level there are twelve such 'forms,' called *categories*. On the level of reasoning there are three 'forms' or *ideas,* namely, the soul, the world, and God. Since these 'forms' make knowledge 'necessary,' they exist prior to all experience and are, therefore, not the result of experience; they are subjective and make necessary knowledge possible. It follows, then, that all arguments for God's existence are deduced from the 'idea' of God, and such arguments are therefore 'ontological.'

Kant's theory is *arbitrary* and *subjective.* Since we cannot help but think that our knowledge tells us something of the things outside the mind, our knowledge would be *essentially false* and end in skepticism. It is contrary to the *principles of reason,* because one cannot deny the objective validity of the Principles of Sufficient Reason and Causality without destroying the validity and trustworthiness of reason itself.

3. *Objections of Materialism.* — Materialism is the philosophic sys-

tem of thought which considers matter to be the only reality and attempts to explain everything in the universe as the result of the conditions and activities of matter.

Modern materialism bases its contention on the findings of the *natural sciences* and especially on *evolution*. It postulates the eternity of matter.

4. *Refutation of Materialism.* — It is an *oversimplification*. By denying the existence of psychical realities, it is guilty of the Fallacy of False Exclusion. Conscious perception and intellectual activities are as real as physical bodies, but are *psychical* in nature and transcend the capabilities of matter and material activity. The *laws of science* are empirical and provisional, not absolute. The materialistic *postulate* of the eternity of matter and the infinity of time is not in accord with modern science; science is reasonably certain that the universe is *limited* in extent and had a definite *origin in time*.

Neither idealistic transcendentalism nor mechanistic materialism, therefore, disprove the arguments for the existence of God.

Readings

Garrigou-Lagrange, R., *God: His Existence and Attributes,* Vol. I, pp. 121–126, 136 ff., 368 f. — Taylor, A. E., *Does God Exist?* — Whittaker, Sir Edmund, *Space and Spirit.* — Smith, Gerard, *Natural Theology,* Chap. III.

Part II

The Nature of God

Chapter IX

GOD'S ESSENCE

THE proofs for God's existence rest on a twofold foundation: experience and reason. Experience provides the data taken from the universe as supplied by common sense and scientific research. Reason provides the First Principles and applies them to the data of experience. In this way the mind is led inevitably to the conclusion that a personal Supreme Being, or God, exists.

One cannot refuse to accept the data of experience without denying the validity of common sense and science; and one cannot refuse to accept the First Principles without denying the validity of reason. Such a refusal means the denial of the fundamental sources of all human knowledge and, when consistently followed, must end in skepticism, the bankruptcy of the mind.

The individual proofs for God's existence must not be taken in isolation. Since all are derived from an analysis of the *selfsame, one universe,* they refer to the *selfsame, one cause.* This selfsame, one cause is the First Cause, absolutely uncaused, changeless, self-sufficient, self-existent, a spirit of unlimited perfection, pure act without potentiality and composition of any kind. This being we call *God.*

Having proved God's existence, it will now be necessary for us to investigate God's *essence* and *attributes* more in detail. Some attributes of God are 'absolute,' in the sense that they pertain to His essence as such; some are 'relative,' in the sense that they have a relation to things other than God. Both kinds of attributes must be considered, because they reveal to us the perfections of God and thus increase our knowledge of 'what God is.'

Man's Knowledge of God

We have no intuitive knowledge of God, because we cannot perceive Him directly. The proper object of man's intellect is the 'sensible,' namely, material beings. Material beings stimulate man's senses in various ways and give rise to sense-images, which represent material beings in a concrete manner. From these images man's intellect forms (not by means of a 'conversion' of any sort, but through a process of 'abstraction') its 'ideas' of the material things. Once such ideas are formed, the intellect proceeds to build up a system of knowledge, partly by analysis and partly by discursive reasoning. Ultimately, of course, all human knowledge is based on the data of the senses, according to the axiom: 'nothing is in the intellect which was not beforehand somehow in the senses.'

Because of the fact that all man's knowledge has its beginning in sense-perceptions, *agnostics* contend that man cannot know the nature of God in any way. At most, they say, man can arrive at the judgment that there exists some kind of *ultimate ground for the reality of the universe,* but that is as far as man's mind can go; the ultimate ground itself ('God,' if we wish to call it that) is absolutely *unknowable,* because man's mind simply cannot transcend the material world. Oddly enough, in making this statement, agnostics do the very thing they say cannot be done: they transcend material reality, because they make a statement the content of which is not found in material reality. Agnostics overlook the fact that man is not only an 'animal' but is also 'rational.' It is man's rationality which enables him to apply rational principles to the data of sense and by their help to draw *conclusions to non-sensible reality.* The agnostics do this continuously, as anyone reading their articles and books can see for himself.

Much of the knowledge acquired through the *physical sciences* is the result of discursive reasoning, not of direct observation. No physicist has ever seen, for instance, an atom, an electron, a proton, a neutron, or a chain reaction; yet he does not on that account doubt their existence and nature. No chemist has ever observed the actual process of electrolysis or, for that matter, of chemical combinations in general; nevertheless he is firmly convinced that they occur. No biologist has ever perceived with his senses the growth and metabolism of plants and animals; but he accepts them as established facts. Why are scientists certain of these things? Because they form the only conclusion consonant with observed facts. Reason, not observation, certifies their existence and nature. Without the validity of man's reasoning power, science would be nothing but guesswork.

The same principle guarantees the validity of man's conclusion as to the existence of God and His nature. True, our knowledge of God is only *indirect* and *discursive;* but indirect, discursive knowledge is valid and genuine, so long as it is logical. Science has no privileged position in this matter. If indirect, discursive knowledge is valid and genuine for science, it is also valid and genuine for philosophy. Hence, if the scientist can draw valid conclusions concerning the nature of physical realities, the philosopher can also draw valid conclusions concerning the nature of spiritual realities, provided the facts demand such conclusions.

The scientific and philosophic principle underlying all such conclusions is the *Principle of Causality.* No effect can possess any reality except in so far as it receives this reality from its cause, and no cause can give to its effect any reality which it does not itself possess. From the nature of the effect, therefore, we can legitimately draw a valid conclusion as to the nature of the producing cause: as the effect, so the cause; and as the cause, so the effect. To deny the validity of this line of reasoning is to deny the validity of all common sense and science and philosophy.

The application of the principles of reason to the data of the material world leads the mind to the existence of a Supreme Being behind and beyond the world. And it does much more than this. It reveals at the same time a great deal about what this Supreme Being is. *That a reality is,* refers to its existence; *what it is,* refers to its essence or nature. The proofs given in the first part of the book not only tell us that God exists; they also tell us very much about His essence. The reason is clear: the nature of the effect reveals something about the nature of the cause. Since God is the cause of the universe, the nature of the universe must declare, to some extent, the nature of God.

Ways of Knowing God

The 'sensible' is the proper object of man's knowledge. As a consequence, the 'sensible' alone can be known by man directly and intuitively. Any reality that is immaterial can only be known indirectly and discursively. God is an immaterial being. It follows that man cannot attain to a knowledge of God except by leaning upon knowledge of material reality. This fact is the result of the constitution of man, because man is not a pure spirit but a 'rational animal.' Since man is limited and relatively imperfect (when compared to a 'pure spirit'), his knowledge of God is necessarily also limited and relatively imperfect. How, then, does man arrive at a true knowledge of God?

Man acquires and also expresses his knowledge of God *in three ways.*

First, the *way of affirmation.* There are many perfections which are styled 'pure perfections,' namely, such as contain no imperfection in their concept and reality; for example, 'being,' 'good,' 'life,' 'person,' 'substance,' 'intelligence.' Although these perfections are also found in creatures, they need not be restricted to creatures. To be an 'organism' or 'body,' for instance, is a perfection, but it is restricted to a material being and cannot be applied to a pure spirit; such a perfection is termed a 'mixed perfection.' God is not a material being, and therefore any perfection based strictly on materiality cannot be attributed to Him. 'Pure perfections,' however, not being based strictly on materiality are found in all their purity in spiritual beings. Hence, *pure perfections can be affirmatively predicated of God.* Nevertheless, such 'pure perfections,' when predicated of God, must be affirmed of Him in such a way that all creatural imperfection is definitely excluded. The 'way of affirmation' must therefore be combined with the 'way of negation.'

Second, the *way of negation.* St. Thomas calls this 'the way of removal—*via remotionis.'* Joseph Rickaby renders St. Thomas' expression into English by the term 'negative differentiation.' The meaning is the same. The 'way of negation' consists in denying of God every sort of imperfection and in attributing to Him the corresponding perfections in such a manner that they apply to Him alone. Even 'pure perfections' are found in creatures, but they are always limited. This limitation must be removed, when such a perfection is affirmed of God; otherwise there would be no essential difference between God and creature. Thus, all creatural being, whether material or spiritual substances, are by their very nature 'limited' in perfection; they are substances of limited perfection. There can be, however, no limitation in the perfection of God's substance; and so we must remove ('negate') this limitation of perfection by saying that 'God is a substance of unlimited (or infinite) perfection.'

Strictly speaking, the 'way of negation' expresses what God *is not* rather than what He *is.* As St. Thomas[1] puts it:

"Now in treating of the divine essence the principal method to be followed is that of remotion. For the divine essence by its immensity surpasses every form to which our intellect reaches; and thus we cannot apprehend it by knowing what it is. But we have some knowledge thereof by knowing *what it is not:* and we shall approach all the nearer to a knowledge thereof according as we shall be enabled to remove by our intellect a greater number of things therefrom. For the more completely we see how a thing differs from others, the more perfectly we know it: since each thing has in itself its own being distinct from all other things. Wherefore when we know the definition of a thing, first we place it in a genus, whereby we know in general what it is, and afterwards we add

---

[1] *Summa Contra Gentiles,* tr. by English Dominican Fathers (New York: Benziger Bros., 1925), Bk. I, Chap. XIV.

differences, so as to mark its distinction from other things: and thus we arrive at the complete knowledge of a thing's essence.

"Since, however, we are unable in treating of the divine essence to take *what* as a genus, nor can we express its distinction from other things by affirmative differences, we must needs express it by negative differences. Now just as in affirmative differences one restricts another, and brings us the nearer to a complete description of the thing, according as it makes it to differ from more things, so one negative difference is restricted by another that marks a distinction from more things. Thus, if we say that God is not an accident, we thereby distinguish Him from all accidents; then if we add that He is not a body, we shall distinguish Him also from certain substances, and thus in gradation He will be differentiated by suchlike negations from all beside Himself: and then when He is known as distinct from all things, we shall arrive at a proper consideration of Him. It will not, however, be perfect, because we shall not know *what* He is in Himself."

We observe the 'way of negation' in many expressions used to designate the perfections peculiar to God alone; for instance, in expressions like '*un*changeable,' '*un*caused,' '*in*finite,' '*im*mense,' '*un*limited,' '*in*effable.' Perfections expressed in this negative manner plainly show their creatural origin. The original notions are derived from the sensible world, with all the limited perfection characteristic of this world. Obviously, a 'limited perfection,' when viewed from the standpoint of God, is a relative 'imperfection.' This 'imperfection' must be removed when applied to God, and this is done by the 'way of negation.'

Third, the *way of eminence*. Just as all imperfections must be denied of God, so all pure perfections must be ascribed to God in a superlative degree, without any kind of limitation. In other words, all pure perfections in God, as we shall see later, are without limit, infinite. This is usually done by ascribing to God a pure perfection and then raising the perfection to the highest degree conceivable by 'way of eminence.' It is thus that we speak of God as being 'infinitely good,' 'infinitely wise,' 'omniscient,' 'omnipresent,' and so forth. God is really good in Himself, but so are creatures; in order, then, to distinguish the goodness of God from the goodness of creatures, we say that God is 'infinitely good,' 'good without limit,' because that is what God's goodness is and that applies to God alone. Similarly, knowledge is found both in God and in creatures; but knowledge in creatures is essentially limited, while in God it is essentially unlimited, and so we say that God is 'omniscient' and thereby distinguish His positive perfection of knowledge from the positive perfection of the knowledge present in creatures.

Analogical Knowledge of God

Many perfections are, in a sense, *common* to God and to creatures; for instance, the perfections of 'substantiality' and 'intelligence' are present in God and man. Evidently, however, such perfections differ in manner and in degree when attributed to God and man (and to creatures in general).

A term may be applied to a number of things either in a univocal, equivocal, or analogical sense. It will be applied *univocally,* when the sense of the term is identical in all the realities to which it is applied; the term 'man,' since the meaning is identical in all human beings, is used univocally of all men. An *equivocal* term is applied to a number of realities in entirely different meanings; such is the use of the term 'coach' as applied to a vehicle and to an athletic director. An *analogous* term applies to unlike, but related, things, so that it is used in a meaning that is partly the same and partly different. There is always some relation between such things, entitling the mind to designate them by the same term; hence, the term is not equivocal. Due to the partial unlikeness in the things, however, the term is not used in a strictly univocal sense; hence, the term is not univocal either. An analogous term designates related things in such a manner that it applies primarily to one thing and secondarily to other things.

In what sense do we use the terms signifying perfections

common to God and creatures, when they are applied to God and creatures? In a univocal sense? equivocal sense? analogical sense? Practically all Christian philosophers claim that such terms are used in an *analogical* sense, and we subscribe to this thesis.

For one thing, pure perfections common to God and creatures are *not* ascribed to them in an *equivocal* sense. For example, the term 'existing being' is applied to God and to every being in the universe; each one is said to be an 'existing being.' Is this term ('existing being') applied to God and to the creatures in the universe in entirely different meanings, as the term 'coach' is used of a vehicle and of an athletic director or the term 'pitcher' is used of a vessel and of a person throwing a ball at a batter? Evidently not. What is meant by an 'existing being'? Anything which is not 'nothing,' not a 'non-being.' God is assuredly not 'nothing'; and He is assuredly not a 'non-being.' God actually exists, and the creatures in the universe actually exist. God and the creatures in the universe must, therefore, be 'existing beings' in the true sense of the word. Consequently, the term 'existing being' does not apply to God and the creatures in the universe in an equivocal sense, as if the term had entirely different meanings in its application to them.

Nevertheless, terms which apply to creatures are *not* applied to God in an absolutely univocal sense, as if there were no real difference in their meanings. In God all perfections are underived, uncaused, and unlimited; while in creatures all perfections are derived, caused, and limited. God is the source and origin of all perfections found in creatures; creatures, however, are in no sense the source and origin of God's perfections. God 'gives' perfections to creatures as their 'cause'; creatures 'receive' these perfections from God, and their whole being is an 'effect' produced by God. God's perfections are identical with His essence and are therefore essentially infinite (as will be shown later); the perfections of creatures are not identical with their essence and are essentially finite.

As a consequence, the terms designating the perfections of God and the creatures are not absolutely identical in meaning and are not, therefore, absolutely 'univocal.' When we, for instance, say that 'God is wise' and that 'man is wise,' the term 'wisdom,' though not equivocal in its use, is not absolutely univocal; God's wisdom is essentially infinite and eternal, while man's wisdom is essentially finite and temporal.

The conclusion is evident. Since the terms referring to the perfections common to God and creatures are neither absolutely identical nor absolutely equivocal in meaning, but are used in a sense which is partly the same and partly different, they are rightly said to be *analogous* terms. The use of these terms is not purely 'metaphorical.' The analogy underlying the application of the same terms to God and creatures is an *analogy of intrinsic attribution based on the fact of causality* (or, as many prefer to call it, an analogy of 'proper proportionality'). As such, therefore, all pure perfections are present in God 'primarily,' because He is the essential source of these perfections in Himself and in creatures; they are present in creatures 'secondarily,' because ultimately they have their essential source in God who gave them to the creatures. Hence, pure perfections are attributed to God in a 'primary meaning' and to creatures in a 'secondary meaning,' because all creatural perfections are utterly dependent in their being and existence on the causality of God.

It is thus seen that the terms used to designate pure perfections common to God and creatures have a meaning which is partly the same and partly different; that is to say, they are *analogous* terms — not univocal and not equivocal.

So far as man's knowledge of God is concerned, it is *neither intuitive nor comprehensive.* Man in his natural life never knows God as He is in Himself, for the simple reason that He cannot see God directly. Intuitionists and ontologists have put forth the claim that man has a direct knowledge of God through intuition; that their view is erroneous is evidenced by the fact that all man's terms of God show an unmistakable derivation from creatural conditions. Man's knowledge of God, being indirect and analogical while he lives here on earth, will always be incomplete and fragmentary; as such, it can never be comprehensive. God exists 'in light inaccessible.' For man, therefore, as a creatural being limited in mental power, God must always be *incomprehensible* and *ineffable*. All man's concepts of God contain a core of impenetrable darkness, and this darkness can never be completely dispelled.

The indirect, discursive, and analogical character of man's knowledge of God and His perfections must always be borne in mind in the subsequent discussions of His essence and attributes.

Notion of Essence and Attribute

Essence in general is defined as *that through which a being is just what it is* (*id quo res est id quod est*). What for instance, is the essence of man? That which makes him to be simply and positively a 'man,' and not a brute or a plant or an inanimate object or anything else. 'Animality' and 'rationality' are found in every individual 'man' and distinguish him from every other being. 'Rational animal,' therefore, is the essence of man.

Every being present in the natural order of the universe consists of essentials and nonessentials; altogether, the concrete realities existing in a being form a complex whole. And for all this complex whole of reality or entity there must be a common source and fountainhead of being and operation. This source or ultimate principle in the thing, from which it derives whatever it possesses in the line of 'being' in any form, is appropriately designated the thing's *essence* (Lat., *esse*, to be; *essentia*, being).

The 'essence' of a thing is sometimes called *nature*. Out of the essence as out of a matrix all being of a thing is, so to say, born (Lat., *nasci*, to be born; *natus*, born; *natura*, nature, that which is given by birth); the elements of a thing, which constitute its being, have existence only in so far as they flow (are born) from the essence. Specifically, 'nature' is an essence considered as the ultimate principle of operation in a being. 'Essence' is more static, and 'nature' more dynamic, in its meaning; in reality, of course, both mean fundamentally the same thing, viewed from different standpoints.

A distinction is made between 'physical' essence and 'metaphysical' essence. The distinction is important.

A *physical essence* is an essence in so far as it is, or can be, something in the order of reality, independent of the consideration of the mind contemplating it. The term 'physical,' as used here, must not be interpreted in the sense of 'material,' although that is the sense in which the term is frequently used. 'Physical' here means the same as 'natural,' 'pertaining to the nature of a thing' (Gr., φυσικός, natural; from φύσις, nature, constitution of a thing); as such, therefore, a 'physical essence' may be either material or spiritual. Thus, when 'man' is defined as 'an organism composed of a (material) body and a (spiritual) soul,' the definition gives the 'physical essence' of man, because that is what makes man to be man in the order of reality; 'body' and 'soul' are the actual, physical constituents which exist as such in man, independent of the mind that thinks of man. The 'physical essence' of an angel is its simple substantial entity, excluding all accidental reality modifying the substance. As it will be noted, the 'physical essence' of a thing is understood to be the complex of all the fundamental elements without which this thing cannot exist.

A *metaphysical essence* is an essence consisting of all those elements which are necessary for the *concept* of the thing and without which this thing cannot be conceived. The 'metaphysical essence' of a being consists of two elements, distinct in concept (meaning), one of which is conceived as being 'common' and the other as 'differentiative.' Because of the 'common element,' the thing in question agrees with two or more other beings; and because of the 'differentiative (differentiating) element,' it differs from all beings which are not itself. The definition of 'man' as 'a rational animal' expresses his metaphysical essence: 'animal' expresses the constitutive element which man has in common with other sentient organisms (for instance, with dogs, cats, horses, and so on), while 'rational' expresses the constitutive element which distinguishes man from every other type of animal (for he alone possesses 'rationality'). Hence, a 'metaphysical essence' is the sum of the various grades of being which constitute a thing in the concept of the mind; we do not consider an object as it exists concretely in the world of reality, but according to the manner in which it is conceived by the mind in its thinking.[2]

While, therefore, the 'physical essence' of a thing is the complex of all the fundamental elements without which this thing cannot *exist,* its 'metaphysical essence' is the sum-total of the various grades of being without which it cannot be *thought.*

An *attribute* is defined as *that which follows by natural necessity upon a fully constituted essence.* Given the essence, the attribute is also given. The attribute always characterizes the essence, since it flows necessarily from the essence. Another term for 'attribute,' practically synonymous with it, is *property.* As the word indicates (Lat., *proprium,* one's own), a 'property' belongs to an essence in such a manner that it is 'proper to' this essence. Thus, the 'power of speech' is an attribute or property of man as a rational animal: only an 'animal' can have organs capable of emitting articulated sounds; and only a 'rational' being has ideas which can be communicated to others by means of speech.

Attributes reveal the underlying essence. They lie closer to the surface of things than does the essence. Hence, man in his knowledge recognizes the attributes sooner than he does the essence. Since the attributes flow necessarily from the fully constituted essence, there exists an intrinsic connection between the attributes and the essence, and so the mind of man naturally goes from a knowledge of the attributes to a knowledge of the essence itself. Oftentimes man is incapable of defining an essence by means of proximate genus and specific difference;

---

[2] See also the author's *Science of Correct Thinking,* rev. ed. (Milwaukee: The Bruce Publishing Co., 1950), pp. 83–86.

in that case a descriptive definition by means of attributes is the only way of arriving at a knowledge of the essence. Such a form of knowledge will be *imperfect,* but it will be *true.*

When speaking of God, we understand by the *divine attributes* all those perfections which flow necessarily from the divine essence and which are found in no other being but God. First, though, we must try to discover the metaphysical and physical essence of God, before making a detailed investigation of God's attributes. Ordinarily, this procedure should be reversed; inasmuch, however, as the proofs for God's existence have revealed many of His attributes, this procedure is logical.

God's Metaphysical Essence

By the *metaphysical essence of God* we understand God's essence, not as it 'exists' objectively in itself, but as it is *known by the human mind,* namely, God's essence in so far as man's mind can signify it by a definition or quasi-definition which embraces the element (or elements) common to it and to all other beings and the element differentiating it from all other beings. A strict definition, of course, would be by proximate genus and specific difference; God, however, does not properly belong to any genus, and therefore a strict definition of God is impossible. A *quasi-definition,* however, is possible, for a description, containing a common and a differentiating element, can be made.

It is not a question here of giving a quasi-definition of the essence of God as it exists objectively in itself; that would be a definition of the 'physical essence' of God rather than of his 'metaphysical essence.' It is a question of what *man in his way of thinking must consider to be the most fundamental element in God's being,* the one from which all other elements and attributes are ultimately derived. It is, therefore, that reality in God's being which, for man's thought, must be considered to be the root-principle of all the realities which can be predicated of God; or, in other words, the primary and foremost characteristic by which man recognizes God as God. Some one perfection of God's being must, to man's mind and his way of thinking, be regarded as *primary* among His perfections, so that it is the *root* that gives rise to all His other perfections and distinguishes Him from any and every type of being which is not God. Because of the imperfection of his intellect, and because his concepts of God are acquired through various considerations of creatural things, man has many different concepts pertaining to God; among these concepts, some refer to perfections which are absolute and some to perfections which are derivative. That *perfection which is conceived by man as being the most basic* to an understanding of God is what is meant by the 'metaphysical essence' of God. Even if man disavows any division in God, he cannot avoid making mental distinctions in the concepts about God. Hence, the need of discovering which of these concepts represents God's 'metaphysical essence.'

All authors agree that in God's metaphysical essence the element or item which is *common* to Him and creatures is 'being'; and by the term 'being' is here meant 'existing being,' not being which is merely possible. There is, however, considerable dispute about the element or item which *differentiates* God from every other being.

A number of *theories* have been advanced regarding this differentiating element in God's metaphysical essence.

Duns Scotus and many *scotists* maintain that the primary differentiating element in God's essence is *infinity*. Infinity may be either extensive or intensive. 'Extensive' infinity means the possession of all possible perfections, viewed from a quantitative standpoint. 'Intensive' infinity means the possession of divine perfections in an infinite degree. Some scotists, and also Palmieri and others, claim that 'radical infinity' constitutes God's metaphysical essence, and by 'radical infinity' they understand the exigency of God's being for both extensive and intensive infinity. Very recently, A. Antweiler has come out in defense of 'infinity' as the metaphysical essence of God. Other defenders are: Van de Woestyne, Belmond, and Minges.

Ockham and the *nominalists,* and also Descartes and Leibnitz, claimed that the divine essence is but the *sum of all His perfections:* hence, no single fundamental perfection can be mentioned which would logically explain the rest.

Another theory has been advocated by *some thomists,* among whom are John of St. Thomas, Gonet, and Billuart. According to their view, the primary difference which distinguishes God from all other beings lies in *intelligence* or in the subsistent act of divine *intellection.* These authors feel that the metaphysical essence of God must be sought and found in His highest attribute; but this is the divine intellection, not radical but actual, viewed from the standpoint of supreme actuality which is *per se* subsistent. Some, however, defend the 'exigency' for knowledge, rather than actual intelligence, as the fundamental differentiating note of the divine essence.

Relatively few authors have favored the view that the primary distinguishing mark of God's essence is divine *love* and *life:* God is love, and God is life.

Some modern *voluntarists,* such as Secrétan, Lequier, and Boutroux, look upon God's *absolute liberty* as the most characteristic item which differentiates God from all other beings. God, being a pure spirit of the highest order, consists only in what He does; and for that 'absolute liberty' is necessary.

Many modern scholastics defend the thesis that the primary differentiating element in the metaphysical essence of God is His *aseity* (*aseitas*), namely, that God is *a se,* the being who exists of and by Himself, the self-existent being. This is the thesis of J. Hontheim, B. Boedder, J. Donat, and others.

F. Suarez and most modern scholastic philosophers place the primary characteristic of God's metaphysical essence in His *self-subsistence.* Among prominent thomists who hold this view are Capreolus, Bañez, Gotti, Contenson, Ledesma, Del Prado, and Garrigou-Lagrange. Among nonthomists, besides Suarez, authors like Molina, Vasquez, Torres, G. H. Joyce, J. Hellin deserve mention. God is 'subsistent being,' and by that term is understood 'being subsisting independently of any potentiality, absolute reality, reality excluding all non-actuality.' A being is said to be 'subsistent' when it is an existing substance, complete and autonomous; it is said to be 'self-subsistent' when it owes its subsistence to its own self and its own constitution, and not to any kind of supporting cause. Creatural substances possess subsistence, but their subsistence is derived ultimately from the causality of God. God's subsistence is underived, unconditional, absolute, necessary, uncaused; and for this reason God *is* self-subsistent being, while all other beings can only be said to *have* subsistence. 'Self-subsistent being,' these thinkers contend, constitutes God's metaphysical essence.

Evaluation of Theories

As was stated at the beginning of the last section, by the 'metaphysical essence of God' is understood God's essence in so far as it can be expressed in a definition or quasi-definition which embraces the element (or elements) *common* to it and to all other beings and the element *differentiating* it from all beings which are not God. The element which is 'common' to God and all things is 'existent being'; about this there is practically universal agreement among scholastics. The difficulty arises in determining the 'differentiating element' and the problem of determining it has led to the formation of a number of divergent theories. These theories must now be evaluated.

The first theory to be examined is the scotistic theory of *infinity*. If the term 'infinity' is taken primarily in its literal meaning of 'without limits,' then the term has a negative connotation. The negative, however, always presupposes something positive. God's being is absolute and supreme actuality. Hence, negative infinity, in God, presupposes positive infinity; and so negative infinity cannot be the primary and constitutive element which differentiates God's essence from all other beings: this differentiating element must be something positive. If the term 'infinity' is taken in a positive sense, it can mean either the aggregate of all perfections ('extensive' infinity) or the supreme degree of God's perfections ('intensive' infinity) or the exigency of God's being for both extensive and intensive infinity ('radical' infinity). Now, none of these three possibilities is satisfactory as the primary differentiating element.

Taken as 'extensive infinity,' the term signifies the sum-total of God's perfections as they exist in reality, and in this sense the term means what is commonly understood to be God's 'physical' essence; the problem would still be unsolved as to which of these divine perfections is the root-perfection which, for man's mind, explains all the other divine perfections. Taken as 'intensive infinity,' the term signifies primarily the 'degree' of perfection, and as such expresses the 'mode' in which these perfections exist in God's essence; all divine perfections have the 'mode' of infinity, and therefore this 'mode' offers no explanation to man's mind of how the various perfections are derived from the essence. Taken as 'radical infinity,' the term still characterizes the 'mode' or 'way' in which God's essence exists rather than the essence itself. According to man's thinking, man conceives God's essence *to be* before he conceives it *to be infinite*. 'Infinity,' whether extensive or intensive or radical, is conceived as being more in the nature of a 'property' of the divine essence and its perfections than a characterization of the essence itself. If 'radical infinity' is interpreted as meaning 'being through essence' or 'subsistent being,' then there is only a verbal distinction between this view and the Suaresian view.

The *nominalist theory* must be rejected. The metaphysical essence of God must be expressed in a manner that gives the differentiating element which distinguishes God from all other beings and at the same time gives the root of all the perfections existing in God. The nominalist theory fails to do this. The *sum-total of God's perfections* is merely a confused expression of all the reality which exists in God, but it does not express the root of all perfections existing in God. 'Omniperfection' expresses God's being as it exists objectively in the order of things; and thus the nominalist conception expresses God's physical essence, not His metaphysical essence.

The theory which places God's metaphysical essence in *intellectuality* or *actual intellection* must also be adjudged inadmissible. If this term is used in the sense of 'actual' comprehension

and understanding, it should be obvious that it is not the metaphysical essence of God. 'Actual intellection' is conceived as an
'operation,' and an operation always presupposes a person who
performs the operation; hence, 'actual intellection' flows from
the essence, but only as something secondary to it, just as the
exercise of a power is secondary to the power itself. If this term
is used in the sense of 'radical' comprehension and understanding, it signifies the intellect of God; but the intellect itself is
conceived as a vital power resulting from the spirituality of the
essence, and as such is not primary but secondary. In no case
can intelligence be considered to be the root and foundation
of all the perfections existing in God: what is itself conceived
as derived from something else cannot be conceived to be the
root-perfection from which all other divine perfections are ultimately derived. There must be something in God more ultimate than intelligence, whether actual or radical.

For a similar reason, the theory must be rejected that *life* or
love is the metaphysical essence from which all other perfections in God are deducible. True, God is life, and God is love.
But 'life' and 'love' are not conceived as being the ultimate perfections of God's nature. 'Love' is definitely conceived as an act
of the divine will, and the will is dependent on the intellect for
the object which it loves; hence, 'love' is not conceived as the
primary source of divine perfections and as the distinguishing
characteristic of the divine essence. Even 'life' is not conceived
as primary. In the case of God's 'life,' it is a manifestation of
God's spiritual substance; hence, spirituality and substantiality
would be more ultimate, from the standpoint of man's knowledge, than 'life.' We must therefore conclude that 'life' and
'love' are not the metaphysical essence of God.

Neither is *liberty* the characteristic feature which is the distinguishing mark of the divine essence. 'Liberty' is a mode of
the will's action and presupposes the will itself; it also presupposes spirituality and substantiality in God's nature. How, then,
can it be conceived by man as being the source, the root-perfec-

tion, from which all divine perfections are logically deduced? In the logical order of thought, the intellect is prior to liberty, because we cannot think of liberty except as following the judgment of the intellect; liberty without consciousness is inconceivable, and consciousness in God is conceived by man as being a function of the divine intellect. Consequently, the theory of the voluntarists that God's metaphysical essence consists in God's will and its absolute liberty is totally inadequate.

The view that *aseity* constitutes the metaphysical essence of God is held by many prominent philosophers. According to this theory, the fact that God is *ens a se, self-existent being,* is the fundamental perfection of God's essence from which all other perfections are deduced and the ultimate characteristic differentiating His essence from all beings which are not God. Because of the prominence of the philosophers who support this theory, their view deserves careful consideration.

The term 'aseity' may be taken negatively or positively. If taken *negatively,* the term implies that God does not owe His existence 'to another' as the contingent creatural beings do; and this negative sense of *ens a se,* or self-existent being, we can hardly accept as an expression of the metaphysical essence of God. A negative element is always grounded in some positive element, and so we would be forced to seek this positive reality in God by asking the further question: 'What is the reality in the divine essence which precludes the possibility of God being from another and necessarily being an *ens a se?'*

As George Hayward Joyce[3] rightly observes: "The objection to regarding this attribute as God's metaphysical essence is that it does not really express what we conceive as an internal constitutive principle of the Divine nature. The real significance of the notion *Ens a se* is to deny that God is, like creatures, caused by another. He is conceived as self-existent in the sense of 'unoriginated.' Undoubtedly this is the first aspect under which we conceive God, as we reason from the existence of

---

[3] *Principles of Natural Theology,* p. 297.

contingent things to that of a necessary Being. But it still remains for us to ask what is the internal constitutive, in virtue of which He is unoriginated and needs no cause. And to reply to this question we must fall back on our concept of Him as subsistent existence — as the Being whose existence is His nature."

If the term 'aseity' is taken in its *positive* meaning, the meaning seems to be identical with *self-subsistence*. The words are different but the meaning is the same. This being the case (as a close examination of the arguments advanced by these authors reveals), we feel that the metaphysical essence of God lies in 'self-subsistence.'

God, the Self-Subsistent Being

The metaphysical essence of God must be expressed in a definition or quasi-definition which contains the element common to other beings and also the primary differentiating element which distinguishes Him from all other beings. This is what is understood by 'metaphysical essence,' in so far as man's knowledge of God is concerned. Now, the expression 'self-subsistent being' contains both this 'common' element and this 'primary differentiating' element; as such, therefore, the expression 'self-subsistent being' is a definition, or rather a quasi-definition, of God's metaphysical essence.

That the expression contains the element which is *common* to God and all other creatures, is clear from the fact that both God and creatures are 'beings'; the term 'being' applies to all possible and actually existing things, and it also applies to God. That God is conceived as the 'self-subsistent' being, certainly differentiates Him from all other beings, whether they be possible or actually existing. And this *differentiating* element is undoubtedly 'primary.' This latter point will now have to be proved.

In order that the 'differentiating' element in a metaphysical essence be truly *primary* the following conditions must be fulfilled: the primary differentiating element must be something real and positive; it must be characteristic; it must be a reality which is not derived from a prior intrinsic perfection; and it must be a reality from which all other necessary attributes (realities, perfections) are deducible and receive their logical explanation. Each of the conditions will have to be shown to be required, in order that the differentiating element can be said to be 'primary.'

The primary differentiating element of a metaphysical essence must be *real;* when it is a question of realities, as is the case here, only something that is 'real' can bring about a 'real' differentiation. It must be something *positive;* if it were 'negative,' it would ultimately have to be grounded in something 'positive,' and then this positive reality would have to be conceived as prior to this differentiating element. It must be something *intrinsic;* otherwise it would not characterize the essence itself, but something else. It must be *necessary;* God is a necessary being, and anything belonging to His essence must also be necessary. It must be *characteristic;* if it were not something 'exclusive' and 'proper,' it would not distinguish God's essence from that of every other being and would thus fail in its 'differentiating' function. It must be a reality which is *not derived* from a prior intrinsic perfection; if it were so derived, it would be secondary, not primary, and this other prior intrinsic perfection would be the primary differentiating element. It must be a reality from which all other attributes (realities, perfections) are *deducible* and receive their *logical explanation;* it would not be the characteristic mark of the divine essence, distinguishing God from all other beings, if it were not the 'primary' attribute from which all other attributes are deducible and thus were not the radical principle explaining the presence in God of His other perfections.

The term *'self-subsistent being' fulfills these conditions* adequately, so far as man can know God's essence at all. A 'self-subsistent being,' as was stated before, means a being which exists as a complete, autonomous substance and owes its existence to no other reality but to its own essence; to be 'self-subsistent,' therefore, is equivalent in meaning 'to exist in virtue of the being's own essence,' so that 'essence' and 'existence' are identical.

That the *conditions* required for the 'primary differentiating element' are verified in the 'self-subsistent being,' can be shown as follows:

The 'self-subsistent being' is evidently something *real,* something *positive,* and something *intrinsic* to the nature of God. It is, furthermore, a reality which is a *necessary* constituent of God's essence, because it is God's essence or nature itself; if God were not a reality 'self-subsistent in virtue of His essence,' He would have received His existence from some other being and would not be an *ens a se.* 'Self-subsistence' is also a *characteristic,* or exclusive and proper mark, of God; no other being can be said to possess the perfection of 'self-subsistence,' because all other beings are contingent and as such have received existence from God. The 'self-subsistence' of God's essence is *not derived* from any other prior intrinsic perfection, because no such perfection can be found; the only other perfections, which could come into consideration, would be 'aseity' or 'infinity,' and these perfections really have their foundation in the self-subsistence of God, since the only intrinsic reason why God can be said to be 'of Himself' and 'infinite' is the fact that He subsists in virtue of His essence (as will be shown later in detail). That the other divine perfections have their *ultimate foundation* in the self-subsistence of the divine essence, will become increasingly clear as we proceed in the discussion of the attributes of God; let it suffice to repeat the remark of St. Thomas:[4] "Although existence does not include life and wisdom, because that which participates in existence need not participate in every mode of existence; nevertheless God's existence includes in itself life and wisdom, because nothing of the perfection of being can be wanting to Him who is subsisting being itself."

It is for these reasons that very many scholastic philosophers prefer the view that the 'primary differentiating element' in

---

[4] *Summa Theologica* (New York: Benziger Bros.), Ia, qu. 4, art. 2.

God's metaphysical essence is His *self-subsistence*. In this they follow in the footsteps of the greatest of all Christian philosophers, St. Thomas,[5] who says: "The fact that the being of God is self-subsisting, not received in any other, and is thus called infinite, shows Him to be distinguished from all other beings, and all others to be apart from Him." In the Book of Exodus (3:13, 14) it is related that, when the Lord told Moses to lead the Israelites out of Egypt, Moses asked Him, "If they should say to me, 'What is his name?' What shall I say to them?" And the Lord answered him: "Thus shalt thou say to them, 'He Who Is,' hath sent me to you." St. Thomas[6] gives three reasons why he considered *'He Who Is'* as most properly applied to God:

"First, because of its signification. For it does not signify form, but simply existence itself. Hence since the existence of God is His essence itself, which can be said of no other (qu. 3, art. 4), it is clear that among other names this one specially denominates God, for everything is denominated by its essence.

"Secondly, on account of its universality. For all other names are either less universal, or, if convertible with it, add something above it at least in idea; hence in a certain way they inform and determine it. Now our intellect cannot know the essence of God itself in this life, as it is in itself, but whatever mode it applies in determining what it understands about God, it falls short of the mode of what God is in Himself. Therefore the less determinate the names are, and the more universal and absolute they are, the more properly are they applied to God. . . . Now by any other name some mode of substance is determined, whereas this name *'He Who Is'* determines no mode of being, but is indeterminate to all; and therefore it denominates the *infinite ocean of substance.*

"Thirdly, from its consignification, for it signifies present existence; and this above all properly applies to God, whose existence knows not past or future."

---

[5] *Ibid.*, qu. 7, art. 1.
[6] *Ibid.*, qu. 13, art. 11.

The name *'He Who Is'* can hardly mean anything else but the *self-subsistent being,* and St. Thomas considers it to be the one name most properly applicable to God.

All things considered, therefore, we think we are justified in favoring the theory that 'self-subsistent being' is the quasi-definition which best expresses the metaphysical essence of God as conceived by man. Our next choice would be *ens a se* or *radical infinity.* However, if these terms are interpreted in a positive manner, they signify practically the same thing as what is expressed by the term 'self-subsistent being.' Hence, the latter term seems preferable, because it contains the element common to God and creatures and the differentiating element which is most fundamental in God's essence and which distinguishes Him primarily from every other being; and that is precisely what the 'metaphysical essence of God,' viewed from the standpoint of man's imperfect and limited knowledge, is supposed to do.

God's Physical Essence

The *physical essence* of a thing is defined as the essence of a thing in so far as it exists in the actual order, independent of all mental consideration and distinction. Taken concretely, the physical essence of a thing is its *total reality, not including accidents and properties.* 'Accidents' ('accidental realities') are excluded because they are superadded to the essence and are not a part of the essence itself. 'Properties' are excluded because, although they flow necessarily from the essence as fully constituted, they are not constitutive of the essence itself.

As applied to God, His physical essence consists in His *omniperfection,* namely, in the sum-total of all His perfections. The proof is simple.

In the concrete, the 'physical essence' of a thing is its total reality, taking this reality as distinct from all its accidents and properties (in the sense given above); that is what is understood by the term 'physical essence,' and that is its definition. Now, in God there are no 'accidents' and no 'properties' (in the sense given above); otherwise there would be a composition in

God between His essence and these accidents and properties. Composition, however, is impossible in the being which is pure actuality (as was shown in the proofs for God's existence), because composition would presuppose a being prior in existence to God, so as to bring together the composing realities; but there can be no being prior in existence to God who is the First Being. Hence, since there are no accidents and properties in God's essence, the absolute omniperfection of God is His total reality. Consequently, *God's absolute omniperfection is His physical essence.*

The *difference* between God's physical and metaphysical essence should be evident. His 'physical essence' is His reality as it exists in the objective order of things, irrespective of man's mode of thinking. His 'metaphysical essence' is, from the standpoint of man's mode of thinking, the quasi-definition which enables him to grasp intellectually and then express God's essence in such a way that this quasi-definition contains the element 'common' to God and all other beings and also the element which 'primarily differentiates' God from all other beings. Man's knowledge of God is derived from creatural reality and as such is only indirect and analogous; yet this knowledge is true and genuine, even though it is incomplete and fragmentary. This fact is, naturally, reflected in the attempt to determine God's physical and metaphysical essence.

It was stated that God's physical essence consists in 'omniperfection.' Just what are God's perfections or attributes? The following chapters should give an answer to this question.

Summary of Chapter IX

This chapter treats of *man's way of knowing God* and of God's *metaphysical* and *physical essence.*

1. *Man's Knowledge of God.* — Much of the knowledge acquired through the *physical sciences* is the result of discursive reasoning, not of direct observation. In a similar manner, man applies rational principles to the data of experience and draws conclusions as to the nature of God.

2. *Ways of Knowing God.* — Man acquires and expresses his knowledge of God in three ways: the way of *affirmation,* the way of *negation,* and the way of *eminence.*

3. *Analogical Knowledge of God.* — The terms man uses to express his knowledge of God are neither univocal nor equivocal, but *analogous.*

4. *Notion of Essence and Attribute.* — 'Essence' in general is that through which a being is just what it is. Essence, considered as the ultimate principle of operation in a being, is called 'nature.' *Physical* essence is an essence in so far as it is, or can be, something in the order of reality, independent of the consideration of the mind contemplating it. *Metaphysical* essence is an essence consisting of all those elements necessary for the concept of the thing; its definition or quasi-definition contains a 'common' and a 'differentiative' element. An *attribute* is that which follows by natural necessity upon a fully constituted essence. The *divine attributes* are all those perfections of God which flow necessarily from the divine essence.

5. *God's Metaphysical Essence.* — By this we understand God's essence in so far as man's mind can signify it by a definition or quasi-definition which contains the element (or elements) 'common' to it and to all other beings and the element 'differentiating' it from all other beings; it is that perfection which is conceived by man as being the most basic.

The element *common* to God and to other things is 'being.' A number of theories have been advanced regarding the element *differentiating* God from all other beings:

Some authors have considered this differentiating element to be *infinity* (either extensive or intensive or radical). Others, *the sum of all perfections* in God. Others, divine *intelligence* (radical or actual). Others, God's *love* and *life.* Others, absolute *liberty.* Others, *aseity.* Suarez and very many modern scholastics place the primary characteristic of God's metaphysical essence in His *self-subsistence.*

6. *Evaluation of Theories.* — 'Infinity' is a mode of the divine perfections rather than of the essence itself. The 'sum-total of all perfections' represents God's physical essence, not His metaphysical essence. 'Intelligence' is not primary, because it presupposes the substance of God. 'Love' presupposes will; and 'life' presupposes spirituality and substantiality. 'Liberty' presupposes will and intellect. 'Aseity,' taken negatively, presupposes some positive perfection in which it is grounded; taken positively, it seems to be identical

in meaning with 'self-subsistence.' We consider 'self-subsistence' to be the differentiating element in God's metaphysical essence.

7. *God, the Self-Subsistent Being.* — When we say that 'God is the self-subsistent being,' we give a quasi-definition which contains an element *common* to Him and to all things ('being') and an element which *differentiates* Him from all other things ('self-subsistent'). In order that the differentiating element be the truly distinguishing mark in God's metaphysical essence, it must fulfill certain *conditions:* it must be something real, positive, intrinsic, necessary, characteristic, not derived from a prior intrinsic perfection, and a perfection from which all other perfections are deducible. 'Self-subsistence' verifies all these conditions. Consequently, 'self-subsistent being' represents God's metaphysical essence.

8. *God's Physical Essence.* — Taken concretely, the *physical* essence of a thing is its total reality, not including accidents and properties. In God, the physical essence is His *omniperfection,* namely, the sum-total of all His perfections in an absolute sense.

Readings

Garrigou-Lagrange, R., *God: His Existence and Nature,* Vol. II, p. 3 ff. — Joyce, George Hayward, *Principles of Natural Theology,* Chaps. VIII, IX. — Boedder, Bernard, *Natural Theology,* Bk. II, Chap. VII. — Brosnan, William, *God Infinite and Reason,* pp. 35–48. — Glenn, Paul J., *Theodicy,* Bk. II, Chap. I. — Smith, Gerard, *Natural Theology,* Chap. XI. — Renard, Henri, *The Philosophy of God,* pp. 65–75.

Chapter X

SIMPLICITY, INFINITY, UNICITY

MAN knows God piecemeal. The process is similar to photographing an object from different angles: each photograph represents the same object in a particular aspect, though none represents the object in its entirety; and all the photographs must be assembled and viewed together, in order to obtain a fairly complete view of the object. It is thus that man speaks of the various *attributes* and *perfections* of God: they are man's way of conceiving God's reality, although this reality, as will be seen, is fundamentally one and not multiple. Hence, we really know God Himself, but in our characteristically human manner — by means of diverse concepts.

Some attributes of God pertain to His being or *essence,* and some pertain to His *operations.* These attributes are *absolute,* in the sense that they are present in God irrespective of any creatural beings. Other attributes are *relative,* in the sense that they have reference to the existence of beings other than God Himself.

First, then, we must treat of the *absolute* or *essential* attributes of God. And among the various essential attributes, the ones first to receive attention are *simplicity, infinity,* and *unicity.*

Notion of Simplicity

A thing is said to be 'simple' when it is not a 'compound,' that is to say, when it is devoid of composition. A 'compound' is a unit made up of a number of parts; in other words, a 'compound' is one and undivided in such a manner that it can be resolved into a number of components called its parts. Hence, a 'compound' is actually undivided (and therefore a unit) but divisible. On the other hand, a thing is said to be 'simple' when it is neither divided nor divisible.

Simplicity is thus the opposite of 'composition,' and it is defined as *the absence of composition in the reality of a being.* This definition is negative in form but positive in content. The reason for this negative form of the definition lies in the derivation of the concept of 'simplicity.' All the things man perceives in this world are affected by composition in some way. Hence, man arrives at the notion of 'simplicity' by denying composition. Since, however, it is some 'reality' which is said to be devoid of composition, the definition is positive in content. Composition may be of various kinds; and simplicity, correspondingly, may also be of various *kinds.*

Where there is composition, there are components or parts united into some sort of totality. And where there are components or parts, a distinction can be made between them. There will, then, be as many kinds of distinction as there are kinds of composition. What are these different kinds of distinction?

The *two main kinds of distinction* are 'real' and 'logical,' inasmuch as they signify the absence of a real or logical identity between things or concepts.

Real distinction is the absence of sameness between *things different in their reality,* independent of the consideration of the mind. The entity of the one is not the entity of the other, even though they be components or parts of the same totality. Thus, the leaves and branches and fruits of a tree are 'really distinct' among themselves, although they are parts of the same tree; and the foundation and walls and fixtures are 'really distinct' with respect to each other, even though they belong to the house as a whole.

Besides a real distinction, we have also a 'logical' distinction.

Our experience shows us that the universe consists of a multitude of beings. They are different entities, and as such they are distinct in thought and thing; there is a real distinction between them. It is equally true, however, that we often have different concepts of things that are really one in nature; they differ in thought, but not in the thing.

Such a distinction is called a *logical* or *mental distinction,* and it is defined as *the absence of sameness between concepts of the same reality.* In making this distinction between concepts of the same thing, there is either a reason in the thing itself for making it, or the reason for making it is only in the mind. Correspondingly, we have a 'virtual' or a 'purely mental' distinction.

A purely mental distinction (*distinctio rationis ratiocinantis*) is the distinction we make between concepts of one and the same reality, *without a foundation in the object* itself (*ratio ratiocinans*). The content of the different concepts is identical, and so the meaning is the same; the difference between them lies merely in the difference of the manner of their representation or expression. Such a distinction exists between terms and ideas which are 'synonymous' in meaning; for example, 'lance' and 'spear,' 'water' and 'H2O,' 'twelve' and 'dozen,' 'century' and 'one hundred years.' It also exists between a definition and the thing defined; for example, 'man' and 'rational animal,' 'brute' and 'sentient organism,' 'clock' and 'mechanism for measuring time.'

A virtual distinction (*distinctio virtualis, distinctio rationis ratiocinatae, distinctio rationis cum fundamento in re*) is the distinction which exists between concepts of one and the same reality, *with a foundation in the object* itself for making the distinction. The mind is induced to make the distinction because of the nature of the object itself. The object is by nature complex, and the limited power of the human mind is incapable of expressing the entire reality of the object in one adequate concept and so expresses it in a number of concepts, each of which expresses a phase or aspect of the one reality. The concepts are, therefore, not identical in meaning, when compared to one another, but they all refer to the one same reality taken as it is in itself. This distinction will become clearer when we consider the two kinds of virtual distinctions, based upon the two kinds of 'foundations' which are possible: they are the virtual distinction with a 'perfect' foundation and the virtual distinction with an 'imperfect' foundation in the thing.

The foundation of the virtual distinction is *perfect*, when the concepts are so distinct in comparison to each other (although they apply to the same reality) that they are *objectively different in content;* each has a definition objectively different from that of the other. When the mind forms objectively different concepts of the same reality, and these concepts have as their foundation the fact that they can be separately realized in different kinds of being (though in this individual kind of being under consideration they stand for one and the same reality only), then the distinction between such concepts is a 'virtual' distinction with a 'perfect foundation' in the nature of the thing itself. A case in point is the distinction made between the concepts of the soul in man, when we speak of it as a 'vegetant' soul, a 'sentient' soul, and a 'rational' soul. A plant demands a vegetant soul for its vegetant functions; a brute demands a sentient soul for its sensory functions; man demands a rational soul for his rational functions. Since man has the triple vital functions of vegetancy, sentiency, and rationality, we are justified in speaking of a vegetant and sentient and rational soul in man. As a matter of fact, however, there are not three souls in man but only one soul performing these three kinds of functions. Since, though, we have the foundation or reason in the nature of the human soul itself for making this threefold distinction, the distinction between a vegetant, sentient, and rational soul in man is a 'virtual distinction with a perfect foundation.'

A *virtual* distinction with an *imperfect foundation* in the thing is one in which the different concepts of the one reality are distinct in such a manner that they are not mutually exclusive but rather *include each other implicitly.* Because each includes the other implicitly, they can never be realized separately in different kinds of beings. The reason for the distinction between such concepts lies in the object itself, and thus there is a 'foundation in the thing'; but it is not as adequate a foundation as that of the virtual distinction with a perfect foundation. Consider the concept of 'being' and its inferiors. In man, for instance, there is no complete and perfect difference between the concepts of 'being' and 'substance,' 'being' and 'body,' 'being' and 'life,' 'being' and 'sentiency,' 'being' and 'rationality.' The concept 'being' means everything that is 'not nothing'; consequently, 'being' includes within itself implicitly also 'substance,' 'body,' 'life,' 'sentiency,' and 'rationality.' Similarly, each of these various concepts includes within itself implicitly the concept of 'being,' because their reality is but a form of being. Hence, the distinction between the concept of 'being' and the concept of any particular kind of being is a 'virtual' distinction with an 'imperfect foundation in the thing.'

Since distinctions presuppose a plurality of things or concepts, it must be obvious that 'composition' also implies distinctions. Everything will depend upon the type of composition; but every type of composition consists in some manner of a plurality of things or concepts united into a whole, a totality. The very fact that a compound consists of components or parts shows that it is made up of a plurality of *things or concepts which are distinct among themselves.* Hence, composition follows distinction very closely.

Following the lines of distinctions in so far as they affect compounds, *composition* may be either *real or logical (mental), substantial or accidental.*

Simplicity being the absence of composition, the denial of composition in a being implies the affirmation of simplicity in that being. Since a simple being is undivided in itself and indivisible (in the order in which it is said to be 'simple'), the two main kinds of 'simplicity' are 'absolute' and 'relative.'

Simplicity is *absolute,* when the being *excludes all parts* of whatever nature, be they real or conceptual. An absolutely simple being, therefore, is not only actually undivided but also potentially indivisible. A 'composite being' is actually undivided, because it is a unit, a whole, a totality; but it is potentially divisible, because it consists of (real or conceptual) parts which make it to be a compound and into which it can be divided. An 'absolutely simple being,' because it is devoid of all parts, is incapable of being divided.

Simplicity is *relative*, when the being excludes parts of one kind but has parts of another kind. Hence, the 'relatively simple being' is indivisible in one respect but divisible in another. The fewer parts such a being has, the more simplicity it possesses. Man, for instance, has a composite nature, consisting of body (matter) and soul (form). Man's body is a compound, because the substance of the body is made up of a number of different integral parts (head, trunk, arms, legs, etc.); man's soul, however, is simple, because it does not consist of substantially different parts. However, a composition exists between man's substantially simple soul and many types of accidents (acts of thinking and willing). Similarly, besides this 'physical' composition, there also exists a 'metaphysical' composition in man between his essence and existence, his genus (animality) and specific difference (rationality), his nature and individuality, and his nature and personality. Man thus possesses 'relative simplicity' in the simple substance of his spiritual soul; but in many other respects he is a 'composite being.' In no case, however, can he or any other creatural being be said to be 'absolutely simple.'

After this general exposition of the notion of 'simplicity' and allied concepts, we are now in a better position to understand the problem of God's simplicity.

The Problem of God's Simplicity

The question of God's simplicity presents the following problem for solution: Is God's being composite or simple? If 'composite,' what sort of composition exists in His being? If 'simple,' is His simplicity absolute or only relative?

Where there is composition, there must be *parts* distinct from one another. Parts which are 'really' distinct effect a physical composition in a being; parts which are 'virtually' distinct with a 'perfect foundation in the thing' effect a metaphysical composition in a being; parts which are 'virtually' distinct with an 'imperfect foundation in the thing' are not parts in the strict

sense of the term, and their union effects a logical composition
(a composition improperly so called). Hence, if God is a composite being, He must consist of parts which are either really
distinct or virtually distinct with a perfect foundation.

Reversely, if God is a simple being, He must be either 'absolutely' or 'relatively' simple. If only 'relatively' simple, He
would be simple in some aspect of His being but composite in
some way or other. If 'absolutely' simple, His Being would be
devoid of all parts, so that composition in the proper sense of
the term would be totally absent.

We claim that *God is absolutely simple.*

The *opponents* to the doctrine of the absolute simplicity of
God's being naturally teach that some form of composition
exists in God, so that He consists of parts which are distinct.
Among these opponents the following may be mentioned:

The *stoics* maintained that God is something *material,* because the material alone is real. The stoics had a number of
appellations for the Deity, such as 'fire,' 'ether,' 'air'; they even
called the Deity 'soul,' 'mind,' 'reason,' 'providence,' 'destiny.'
Their fundamental doctrine, however, was materialistic and
pantheistic.

The *spinozists* (followers of Spinoza) held that there exists
but a single substance, God. But this single substance consists
of many attributes, of which two are known to us, namely, 'extension' and 'thought.' Spinozism is pantheistic; God has
evolved into the physical world ('extension') and the conscious
world of man's mind ('thought'). God is identified with the
corporeal and spiritual worlds, and thus God is a composite
being.

Most pagan religions are *polytheistic* and *anthropomorphis-
tic.* Their gods and goddesses are at best beings which possess
a human nature with superhuman powers and affections.

Modern *pantheists* either identify God with the visible world
as such or consider Him to be the 'soul' of the universe. He
may be looked upon as spiritual in nature or only as a world-
force. Many modern pantheists consider the beginning of

things to have been the Absolute, which then evolved into the present world; this Absolute (as with Hegel, Fichte, etc.) is nothing more than 'being-in-general,' or 'indeterminate being.' The idealistic philosophy of the Absolute is now no longer in vogue. Its place has been taken by the secularistic philosophy of *evolutionism* and *finitism*. God is a man-made deity, fashioned in the image of man, the result of evolution and finite in all respects. This 'finite, evolving' God is replete with potentialities, continuously being perfected; composition is definitely a characteristic of His essence, if He is judged to exist at all. For many of these moderns 'God' is nothing more than an ideal, the personification of the human desire for assistance in time of trouble and distress, not an objective Supreme Being existing independent of man's mind. That such views are hardly more than a veiled atheism, is evident.

We are not interested in a sublimated human god, manmade as a friend or protector to satisfy some human need and emotion, but the God of Reason whose existence as an extramundane Supreme Being has been proved by the application of incontrovertible rational principles to the data of our experience of the physical world. These objective proofs not only establish God's existence but also show that He is *absolutely simple*.

Proof of God's Absolute Simplicity

As was pointed out in Chapter VII, every composite being consists of parts which are distinct. The union of these parts into a whole forms the undividedness of a composite being. Hence, the parts are *potential* to the whole; the composite being becomes *actualized* into the whole or unit only through the unification of the parts, so that the existence of the composite being is *contingent* upon this unification. The composite being is posterior to its component parts and thus, by its very nature, was originally merely *in potentiality* to their union; as such, it cannot have passed from this state of 'potentiality' to the state of 'actuality' except under the influence of another being already in act. In other words, parts, in themselves distinct and different, cannot of their own accord unite to form a composite being; they necessarily demand *a pre-existing cause* to bring them together and make them unite into a whole.

Now, God exists, and He is first, necessary, and uncaused. It is contradictory to suppose that something should exist *prior* to the first being. It is contradictory to suppose that the necessary being should be *contingent* upon the action of a prior being bringing the component parts of His being together. It is contradictory to suppose that the uncaused being should require a *cause.* But all this would be necessary under the supposition that God is a composite being consisting of parts. Hence, God is not, and cannot be, a composite being consisting of parts. Consequently, there are *no parts of any kind in God,* since the argument applies to any and all parts.

A being, however, which is devoid of any and all parts is absolutely simple. *God, therefore, is absolutely simple.*

The proof just given applies to any kind of composition in God's being. A number of *corollaries* follow as a necessary consequence.

God is a *substance.*

Ever since Hume attempted to show that the notion of 'substance' is but a chimera of the human mind, it has become customary for many modern philosophers and scientists of the empiricistic school to deny the existence of anything like a 'substance.' Notwithstanding the prevalence of this view, it is easy to show that the notion of 'substance' is valid. Everything that exists must be either something which exists in itself and does not exist in another as in a subject of inhesion or something which does not exist in itself but exists in another as in a subject of inhesion; in the first case it is called a 'substance,' and in the second case an 'accident.' Everything must be either the one or the other, because there is no middle ground between contradictory ideas. Therefore, everything will be either a substance or an accident. Not everything, however, can be an 'accident,' because every accident demands a subject (substance) in which it exists. It is impossible for an 'accident' to exist without a subject of inhesion; an accident without a 'substance' to inhere in would be like motion without a moving body. If nothing existed but 'accidents,' they would exist without a subject in which they inhere, and thus, by definition, all accidents would in the very nature of things become automatically 'substances.' Hence, substance there must be. And a substance, by the very fact that it is the subject in which the accidents inhere, must be *prior in nature* (in the order of dependence) to the accident (or accidents) it supports.

Now God exists in and for Himself, because He is the first and uncaused being. Therefore, God does not exist in another as in a subject in which He must inhere. God, therefore, is a *substance*.

God is a spiritual substance, a *spirit*. His essence contains *no matter* of any kind. If matter were a part or component of God's substance, 'composition' would be necessary. A material substance always consists of physical and extended parts, of which one is not the other. Hence, though actually undivided, such a material reality is potentially divisible. An absolutely simple being, however, is not only actually undivided but potentially indivisible; hence, it cannot consist of matter. Now, a substance which does not contain matter in its nature is a spiritual substance, a spirit. God, therefore, being devoid of all parts and composition, is a *spirit*. As a result, He is neither a purely material being, such as an inanimate metal, nor a being which is partly spirit and partly matter, such as man. As a further result, since matter is no part of His nature, He cannot be dependent on matter in His existence and operations. But a substance which is neither composed of matter nor dependent in its existence and operations on matter is a 'pure spirit.' Consequently, God is a *pure spirit*.

There can be *no accidents* in God's spiritual nature. Accidents are determinations and modifications of the substance in which they inhere; as such they are actualizations of the potentialities of the supporting substance as the subject in which they inhere. The combination of substance and accidents in a being always presupposes *potentiality,* because the existing substance is in potency toward the reality which the accidents confer upon it. Whenever, therefore, there is a combination of accidents with a substance, there is a resultant *composition*. In God's essence, however, all composition and potentiality must be excluded, since He is the first, uncaused, and necessary being. Hence, His spiritual substance cannot be perfected by accidents supervening upon His essence; whatever reality the accidents could possibly confer must be present in God's substance from the very beginning. Consequently, God is a pure spirit without accidents, absolute spiritual substantiality.

Just as there can be no 'physical' composition in God, so *metaphysical composition* must be absent. Instances of metaphysical composition in existing beings are: the union of essence and existence, of genus and specific difference, of nature and individuality, of nature and personality. In order that a creature exist in the actual order of things, such a union is required. In every instance mentioned, the first of the dual members is in potentiality toward the determination or perfection contained in the second: the essence is determined by existence; the genus is determined by the specific difference; a nature is determined by individuality; a (rational) nature is determined by personality. Where there is a union of metaphysical parts, there is metaphysical composition; and where there is composition, another being is required to bring them together. Since God is the first, uncaused, and necessary being, no other being can be conceived as being prior to Him. Hence, in God there can be no metaphysical composition, because he cannot be dependent on anything or anybody. All perfection, determination, and actualization which would or could result from a metaphysical composition must be His always without such a composition.

Since God is 'absolutely simple,' whatever is in God is *absolutely one reality*. Hence, God *is* His existence, His essence; God *is* mercy, justice, knowledge, love, and so forth.

Notion of Infinite Perfection

Before discussing whether or not 'infinite perfection' should be predicated of God, we will have to know the meaning of 'perfect' and 'infinite.'

In general, *perfection* means reality or actuality. A thing possesses perfection in so far as it possesses reality or actuality. In particular, a being is said to be 'perfect' when it possesses all the reality (actuality) it is supposed to have in order to be *the kind of thing* it should be. A being would be 'imperfect' if, and in so far as, it lacks something required by its respective type of being. As such, 'perfection' is independent of the place a thing occupies in the general scale of being, so that a rose can be as perfect in its own line of being as a horse is in its line of being.

However, because of the *types of being* in the general scale of being among themselves, the amount of reality present in these various types forms a graduated series, so that one type of being possesses more reality (perfection) than another. Thus, a rose is more perfect than gold, a horse more perfect than a rose or gold, and man more perfect than a horse or a rose or gold. Perfection, therefore, differs.

Perfection is either 'relative' or 'absolute.' Perfection is said to be *relative* when it pertains to a certain *type of being.* The perfection pertaining to gold or a rose or a horse or a man or any particular type of being is thus seen to be 'relative,' namely, relative to the type or nature of the being in question. Perfection is *absolute* when it pertains, not to a certain type of being, but to *every line of being without restriction.* 'Relative' perfection, since its concept is restricted to a particular type of being, is always 'limited' in its meaning and application. Does 'absolute' perfection, then, involve the further concept of 'infinite'? Just what is the meaning of 'infinite' and 'infinity'?

Infinite, as the word indicates (Lat., *in,* not, non-; *finis,* end, limit, boundary), is that which is without limits or bounds. The form of the term is negative, but the content is positive; it means a reality or actuality which is limitless or boundless. Originally, the term had a quantitative signification, inasmuch as it was applied to extension or magnitude. Gradually, however, the term was also applied to qualities and perfection (reality) in general. *Finiteness* means being with limitation.

Infinity is either 'potential' or 'actual.' A being is said to be *potentially infinite,* or to possess *potential infinity,* if its reality can be increased without limit. Such a being, therefore, is always actually finite and always in potency to a further increase of reality, without ever reaching the ultimate limit of an increase in its reality. It would be more accurate to call such a being 'indefinite' rather than 'infinite.' A being is *actually infinite,* or possesses *actual infinity,* if its reality exists without limitation. Actual infinity will be either 'relative' or 'absolute.' A thing possesses *relative* actual infinity if it is actually infinite in a certain line of being only; for instance, in the line of substance or quantity or quality or some other reality, but not in them all. It possesses *absolute* actual infinity if it is actually unlimited (infinite) in every line of being. A being, therefore, which possesses absolute actual infinity is so unlimited in its being or reality that a greater or better being cannot exist nor be conceived in thought; it is an existing being possessing an absolute *plenitude of reality.*

When the concepts of 'perfection' and 'infinity' are combined, *infinity of perfection* is perfection which is actually and absolutely without limit. Infinity of perfection is either 'extensive' or 'intensive' or 'radical.' It is *extensive* when an essence possesses all perfections possible. It is *intensive* when an essence has the supreme degree of all perfections possible. It is *radical* when an essence is intrinsically determined in such a manner that the essence demands both extensive and intensive infinity of perfection.

The Problem of God's Infinity

'Absolute perfection' in an existing being means the same thing as 'actual infinity of perfection.' An absolutely or infinitely perfect being is a being that possesses a *limitless plenitude of reality* in every conceivable manner, and that without imperfection of any kind.

It is clear that the 'infinite' cannot be the result of a summa-

tion of finite realities. Finite reality, by the very fact that it is
'finite,' implies limitation, and a mere summation does not
remove this limitation in the single realities. No matter how
large the number may be, each and every one of these realities
is and remains limited; and since the total sum consists of the
single units which comprise the sum, the total sum must always
be and remain limited in its perfection. Such a sum would
always be merely 'potentially infinite' by its very nature, because
another unit could always be added to it. The 'potentially infinite,' however, since it is 'actually finite,' can never equate the
'actually infinite.' If God, then, is infinitely perfect, His essence
cannot be a summative totality of finite perfections.

In making the claim that God is infinitely perfect, we must
prove that He contains within His essence the *plenitude of
reality without limitation*. It must, therefore, be inexhaustible.
If His perfections could be exhausted by continued subtraction,
it would evidently be limited and finite. It would not be actually infinite extensively and intensively.

Opponents are the *pantheists,* who believe that the world is
an evolution of God (such as B. Spinoza, G. Hegel, J. Fichte,
F. Schelling, and their followers); the *materialists,* who deny
the existence of anything spiritual (such as T. Hobbes, J. Moleschott, L. Büchner, E. Haeckel, and others); the *positivists,*
who claim that man's knowledge cannot reach beyond the
phenomenal (such as J. Stuart Mill, H. Spencer, and a host of
scientists); the *finitists,* who maintain that God is always in a
process of 'becoming' (such as F. C. S. Schiller, W. James,
H. G. Wells, H. A. Overstreet, A. C. McGiffert, M. Calkins,
and many moderns).

Proof of God's Infinity

We claim that God is *infinitely perfect* and that this truth
can be known and demonstrated to the satisfaction of an unprej-
udiced and truth-seeking mind.

The first argument is *indirect*.

No finite being can be an *ens a se,* so that it is a self-subsistent being. An *ens a se* has its existence in virtue of its essence,

since it has no 'cause' for its existence. Hence, if a finite being could be an *ens a se,* a self-subsistent being, it would also have its existence in virtue of its essence. But then all the *possible* beings of the *same class* would also have to have their existence in virtue of their essence and consequently also *actually exist: a like essence* would then entail a *like existence.* But this is evidently not a fact, since there are many more beings of a particular class which are merely possible than those which actually exist. For example, many more human beings 'could' exist than actually 'do' exist; and this is true of all classes of beings. Consequently, no finite being can be an *ens a se,* a self-subsistent being. God, however, as was shown in the arguments for His existence, is truly an *ens a se,* a self-subsistent being. Therefore, no finite being can be God, and God cannot be a finite being.

An actually existing being that is not a 'finite' being is of necessity an 'infinite' being: 'finite' and 'infinite' are contradictory concepts, with no middle ground between them, and every being must be one or the other. Hence, since God is not finite, He is the Infinite Being and as such must possess all reality and perfection (for 'reality' and 'perfection' are identical) infinitely.

The second argument is *direct.*

'Being' is everything that is not nothing; it therefore includes *all* reality and perfection without restriction, limitation, curtailment. Nothing can be thought of that would be a perfection and would not be contained in 'being': there can be no more reality, and no reality could be added. Absolutely everything without exception is included in the concept of 'being' as such. Essence, existence, beauty, power, goodness, mercy, justice, wisdom, individuality, personality, substance, and so forth, are simply so many forms of 'being,' because they are forms of reality or perfection. Not only this or that reality, or this or that degree of reality, belongs to 'being'; absolutely every conceivable kind of reality and every conceivable degree of reality are included in the concept of 'being,' and that both extensively and intensively. Since, therefore, the concept of 'being' includes every conceivable kind and degree of reality (perfection) both extensively and intensively, 'infinite perfection' is *intrinsically possible of realization,* so long as the perfection itself is not limited for some reason.

A *limitation* of perfection exists (1) either because the reality itself as such is a limited perfection (e.g., 'whiteness,' 'materiality'); or (2) because the subject of the reality has only a limited passive capacity for receiving it (e.g., man's capacity for receiving knowledge is limited, since the intellect itself is limited); or (3) because the one giving the reality cannot, or does not want to, give more than a limited amount (e.g., everything man does and gives is limited in perfection).

So far as the *first* source of limitation is concerned, it would not apply to God's essence and perfection; in His case it is only a question of 'pure' perfections, not 'mixed' perfections, because He is, as was shown, *absolutely simple.*

The *second* and *third* source of limitation can be taken together, because in both sources a limited amount of perfection is *received.* In this case God either limited Himself or another being limited Him in the reception of reality. Neither alternative is possible. God cannot have received a limited (finite) amount of reality *from another.* Under that supposition He would have received essence and existence from a being other than Himself; God, however, since He is *ens a se* and consequently self-subsistent, did not receive His reality from another being. Neither could the limitation come *from Himself.* If God imposed a limitation of perfection upon Himself, this would mean that He either had infinite perfection first and limited it later, or that He was at first in potency toward an infinite and finite amount and then (voluntarily or involuntarily) gave Himself only a finite amount. The first of these two alternatives is impossible; because, if He had infinite perfection first, He had to have the perfection of 'necessity' in His being and so could not discard any amount of reality (perfection). The second of these alternatives is also impossible; because potency is excluded in the 'absolutely simple being' and, if He were first in potency toward a finite or infinite amount, He could never have passed from potency to actuality except through the agency of another being (and that cannot occur in the being who is first, uncaused, and necessary). It follows then, that a *limitation of perfection is excluded* in God's essence and existence.

Consequently, since the concept of 'being' as such includes infinite perfection in God, the Supreme Being, and since no cause can be assigned for any limitation of being (perfection, reality) in God, God must be infinitely perfect.

Hence, *God is infinitely perfect.*

A formidable *objection* has been raised against the 'infinite perfection' of God. It runs somewhat as follows:

Besides the essence of God there exist many other essences and beings, namely, the *physical world* and everything in it. These essences and beings, and therefore also their perfections, are not present in God. Consequently, their perfections are missing in the essence and being of God, and He is not infinitely perfect.

The *answer* to this objection is not difficult. The infinite being must certainly possess all the perfections found in the beings present in the universe. However, it is not necessary for Him to possess them according to their individual existence; it suffices, if He possesses these perfections according to their worth or value virtually and eminently. These things do not and cannot possess any perfection greater than His nor independent of Him; whatever they possess in the line of reality and perfection, they have *received* from Him. So long as God does *not lose* any perfection of His own thereby, one cannot say that these things possess perfections which He does not possess. Their existence merely multiplies the number of beings possessing perfection, but the *perfection itself* does not thereby become any greater. A teacher imparting knowledge to his pupils does not lose his own knowledge, nor do the pupils have a more perfect knowledge than the teacher, nor does the addition of the knowledge of all the pupils to that of the teacher make the knowledge as a whole greater or more perfect. The knowledge has the same amount of perfection, whether communicated or not; the number of knowing individuals has been increased, but not the perfection of the knowledge itself. The objection is thus seen to be invalid.

A somewhat *similar objection,* though different in form, is also made against God's infinity. The beings in this world possess a certain amount of real perfection. Let us suppose that God's perfection is infinite. Then the addition of the perfections of the creatures to the perfection of God gives an amount of perfection which is *greater than infinite.* But that is impossible. Now, one cannot deny the existence of creatural perfections. One must, therefore, deny the infinity of God's perfection.

The *answer* to this objection is about the same as that to the foregoing objection. By adding the perfections of creatures to the perfection of God one does not increase 'perfection as such,' since perfections are predicated of God and creatures only in an analogical sense; one merely increases the number of those possessing perfection. The number of creatures is only *finite,* though it is potentially infinite; adding God as another number to the number of creatures does not increase this number to such an extent that its magnitude would be 'actually infinite.'

God is a substance, absolutely simple, possessing infinite perfection (reality), devoid of all potentiality and composition. God, in other words, is *pure act (actuality).*

The Unicity of God

Unicity is *singleness* or *uniqueness,* the absence of plurality. The phrase 'unicity of God,' therefore, is equivalent to the assertion that there is and can be *only one God.*

Unicity may be 'imperfect' and 'perfect.' Unicity is *imperfect* when no one other being of the same kind actually exists, but another being of the same kind is possible. Thus, when the first human being came into existence, he at that time possessed 'unicity,' because he was the only human being in actual existence; this unicity, however, was 'imperfect,' since other human beings were possible. Unicity is *perfect* when no other being of the same kind actually exists, and another being of the same kind is impossible; such a being is truly 'unique.'

Of *God* we assert that He possesses *perfect unicity,* so that no other God is even possible. There is, and can be, but one God.

Opponents to the doctrine of the unicity of God are the *polytheists,* who admit a plurality of gods, and the *manichaeans,* who assumed the existence of two supreme principles, one good and one evil.

That there is *only one God* follows naturally and necessarily from the *infinity* of God's essence.

If a plurality of Divine Beings existed (or, for that matter, *could* exist), they would either be alike or not alike. If they are *not alike,* they are different; if different, then one must have some perfection which the other does not possess. In that case, however, the latter lacks some perfection and by that very fact would not be infinitely perfect; the former alone would have supreme perfection and be God. If they are *alike,* there can be no difference between them. In order to simplify the argument, let us assume that there are two infinite beings in existence. Both are infinitely perfect, according to the supposition. However, the one's infinite perfection is exclusively His own, because He is a self-subsistent being, an *ens a se;* as a result, His perfections are not present in the second infinite being, and the second lacks the perfection of the first and is not infinitely perfect at all. But the same situation applies to the second infinitely perfect being. The second's infinite perfections are also exclusively His own and are not present in the first; therefore, the first lacks the perfections of the second and is not infinitely perfect either. Hence, if both are alike, they would be infinitely and not infinitely perfect at the same time under the same respect. That, however, would be impossible because *contradictory.* Consequently, a plurality (or even duality) of infinitely perfect Supreme Beings is impossible.

Again. If two infinitely perfect Beings could exist at the same time, either they would be mutually dependent upon each other; or one would be dependent, while the other is independent; or both would be independent of each other. They cannot be *mutually dependent* upon each other; because under that supposition neither would be infinitely perfect, since both would lack the perfection of being 'independent' of the other. One cannot be *dependent* on the other, while the other is *independent;* because under that supposition the 'dependent' being would not be infinitely perfect, since such a being is obviously less perfect than an 'independent' being. They cannot be *mutually independent* of each other; because under that supposition neither would be infinitely perfect, since each would lack the perfection of having the other dependent on himself. These two supposedly infinite beings must exist, if they exist at all, in one of these three ways. But all three ways destroy the infinity of perfection either in both or in one of the two. The only way in which the infinitely perfect Being can exist is to be *independent* of every other being and have every other being *dependent;* in that case, however, the independent Being alone is infinitely perfect. Hence, no two infinitely perfect beings can exist at the same time. But God exists and is infinitely perfect. Therefore, there can be no other infinitely perfect being besides God; He alone is and can be God. Consequently, a duality or plurality of deities is impossible.

Unicity, therefore, is an *attribute of God.*

Distinctions in God

The absolute simplicity and infinite perfection of God preclude 'composition' in His Being. Where composition does not exist, division is impossible; division presupposes parts of some sort, and in the absolutely simple Being there can be no parts.

Then what about *distinctions* in God? Are they also precluded? Or are they admissible? If these distinctions are based on 'actual' composition, they are manifestly inadmissible in God, because in the absolutely simple and infinitely perfect being there can be no actual composition. The question therefore arises: Does every distinction involve actual composition?

If so, all distinctions are inadmissible; if not, those which involve no actual composition should be admissible. Are there distinctions of this latter kind?

There can be no question about the fact that man's concepts of God *differ*. Man's concept of God's essence is different from that of His goodness or power and so forth, so that man makes a distinction between God's *essence* and His *perfections*. Man's concept of God's mercy is different from that of His justice, of God's power is different from that of His wisdom, and so on, so that he makes a distinction between the *attributes or perfections among themselves*. What is the nature of such distinctions?

Gilbert de la Porrée (died 1154) maintained that the distinction between God and His divinity (essence) and between God's essence and attributes is a *real distinction,* based on a difference of realities in God. This doctrine must be *rejected,* because God is absolutely simple and infinitely perfect. A real distinction implies real composition, which is excluded in God's being.

Eunomius the Arian and the *nominalists* of the Middle Ages (Gregory of Rimini, Gabriel Biel, and William of Ockham, as many claim) asserted that all the names and attributes ascribed by man to God are *synonymous,* so that the distinctions man makes between God's essence and attributes are 'purely logical and mental,' without any sort of foundation in God's being. This view must also be *rejected* as inadequate. When we speak of God's mercy and justice, intellect and will, power and wisdom, and so forth, we do not use synonymous terms. These terms do not represent the same objective concept; each term has a different thought-content, and for that reason each has a different definition. We admit that the *objective reality meant* by these different concepts and terms is identically the same reality in the divine substance, because of God's absolute simplicity. But we contend (and an analysis of the concepts and terms shows this to be true) that each concept *explicitly* signifies something different from that signified by the other concepts, although each one *implicitly* contains the other. Hence, these terms and their corresponding concepts are *not synonymous* like 'lance' and 'spear,' or 'twelve' and 'a dozen.'

The distinction between essence and attributes and between the attributes themselves thus is neither a real distinction nor a purely logical (mental) distinction. By way of elimination, then, the distinction must be a *virtual distinction* (*distinctio rationis ratiocinatae*), with a foundation in God Himself for the distinctions.

The foundation in God's being for the distinctions *cannot be a perfect foundation*. If the foundation were 'perfect,' the essence and attributes could be *realized separately* in other beings, even though in God they are only one reality. That, however, is impossible. The essence and attributes of God are 'infinite perfections,' and infinite perfections can never be realized separately in other beings; they are realizable solely in God, because God alone is infinite. Whenever the foundation for distinction is 'perfect,' so that the items in question are 'realizable separately,' they are combined by means of a 'metaphysical composition' in the being possessing them. In God, however, metaphysical composition is also excluded, due to His absolute simplicity. Consequently, the distinction man makes in God cannot be a 'virtual distinction with a *perfect* foundation.'

But a *foundation is present* in God. It consists in the infinite wealth of reality in God's being. Man's finite intellect is incapable of exhausting and expressing this infinite wealth of reality in a single concept. As a result, man is compelled to form *successively* a number of *varying attributive notions* of God; in this manner the limited intellect of man seeks to express God's infinite being. And so the foundation for man's distinct concepts of God and His perfections lies in *God's infinite perfection itself*.

This foundation in God, however, is not perfect. On the contrary, it is necessarily an *imperfect foundation,* because the divine attributes are not distinct parts in God but an inseparable identity. So far as their reality is concerned, God's essence and attributes are all *identical* with each other: God is one reality, absolutely simple and infinitely perfect. That is why the distinction man makes in God between His essence and attributes and between the attributes themselves can only be a 'virtual distinction with an imperfect foundation.'

It follows, therefore, that the distinctions formed by man about the Divinity are *virtual distinctions with an imperfect foundation in the thing.* Such distinctions are valid and alone admissible.

It is evident, of course, that a knowledge of God, expressed in distinct concepts and terms, is very inadequate. The inadequacy, however, results from the constitutional limitation of man's intellect, which must grasp piecemeal what it cannot grasp all at once. No finite intellect can fully grasp the plenitude of the Infinite.

To sum up: God is an absolutely simple, spiritual substance, devoid of all composition and potentiality; God is infinitely perfect in every respect; God is unique so that a duality or plurality of divine beings is impossible. The distinct concepts man forms of God's being are 'virtually distinct, based on an imperfect foundation,' and they introduce no composition in God's nature and perfections.

Summary of Chapter X

God's *simplicity, infinite perfection,* and *unicity* are the attributes treated in this chapter.

1. *Notion of Simplicity.* — Simplicity is the opposite of composition, the absence of composition in the reality of a being. Composition is either real or logical, depending on the distinction between the components or parts. *Real* distinction is the absence of sameness between things different in their reality. *Logical* or *mental* distinction is the absence of sameness between concepts of the same reality; it is either 'purely mental' or 'virtual,' and the virtual distinction has either a 'perfect' or 'imperfect' foundation in the thing.

Composition may be either 'real' or 'logical (mental),' 'substantial' or 'accidental.'

Simplicity is either 'absolute' or 'relative.'

2. *The Problem of God's Simplicity.* — We claim that God is

absolutely simple, so that composition in the proper sense of the term is totally absent from His Being.

3. *Proof of God's Absolute Simplicity.* — Every composite being consists of parts which are distinct. The parts are 'potential' to the whole; the composite being becomes 'actualized' into a whole through the unification of the parts. Parts of themselves distinct and different cannot unite of their own accord to form a composite being, but demand a *pre-existing cause* to make them unite. Now, God exists, and He is first, necessary, and uncaused. Hence, if He consisted of parts united to form His being, a being prior in existence to Himself would be required to bring the parts together and lead Him from potentiality to actuality. Since God is the first, necessary, and uncaused being, this is impossible. Hence, there can be no parts in God. *God,* therefore, is *absolutely simple* in His being.

Corollaries: God is a substance, a pure spirit; in God there are no accidents; God is absolutely one reality.

4. *Notion of Infinite Perfection.* — In general, *perfection* means reality or actuality; in particular, it means the reality a being should have in order to be the kind of being it is supposed to be. Perfection is 'relative' when it pertains to a certain type of reality; 'absolute,' when it pertains to every line of reality without restriction.

Infinite is defined as being without bounds or limit; it means boundless, endless, limitless. Infinity is said to be 'potential' if the reality is always finite and in potency to a further increase of reality; it is 'actual' if the reality exists without any limitation. Actual infinity is 'relative' if the reality is actually infinite in a certain line of being only; it is 'absolute' if unlimited in every line of being.

Infinite perfection is perfection which is actually and absolutely without limit; and it is either 'extensive' or 'intensive' or 'radical' infinity of perfection.

5. *The Problem of God's Infinity.* — God is infinitely perfect; He contains within His essence the plenitude of reality without limitation and imperfection.

6. *Proof of God's Infinity.* — *Indirect* argument. No finite being is an *ens a se;* God is an *ens a se;* therefore, God is no finite being. But, if a being is not finite, it must be infinite (because 'finite' and 'infinite' are contradictory ideas); now, God is not finite; therefore, God is infinite.

Direct argument. 'Being' is everything that is not nothing; it therefore includes all reality without limitation. 'Infinite perfection' is, consequently, intrinsically possible, so long as the perfection is not limited for some reason. A *limitation* of perfection, however, can exist only for a threefold reason: (1) either because the perfection as such is a limited perfection; or (2) because the subject has only a limited capacity for receiving it; or (3) because the one giving the reality cannot, or does not want to, give more than a limited amount. None of these alternatives apply in the case of God, because He is the first, necessary, and uncaused being. Therefore, God is *infinitely perfect.*

7. *Unicity of God.* — *Unicity* means 'singleness' or 'uniqueness.' God possesses perfect unicity, so that no other God is even possible.

If a duality (or plurality) of Divine Beings existed or could exist, they would either be alike or not alike. If *not alike,* one would lack a perfection which the other possessed, and so would not be infinitely perfect. If *alike,* the perfections of each, being exclusively his own, would not be present in the other; hence, neither would be really infinitely perfect. Yet God is infinitely perfect. Therefore, plurality (or even duality) of Supreme Beings is impossible.

Again. 'Independence' is a perfection; 'dependence,' an imperfection. If two (or more) infinitely perfect Beings could exist simultaneously, either they would be mutually dependent; or one would be independent and the other dependent; or both would be mutually independent. If both are *mutually dependent,* neither is infinitely perfect. If one is *independent* and the other *dependent,* only the first would be infinitely perfect; the dependent would be limited and finite. If both are *mutually independent,* neither is infinitely perfect, because it would be more perfect to be independent and have the other one dependent. But God exists and is infinitely perfect. Therefore, there can be no infinitely perfect being besides God. Consequently, a duality or plurality of Gods is impossible. *Unicity,* therefore, is an *attribute of God.*

8. *Distinctions in God.* — Man has distinct concepts concerning the essence and attributes of God. A *real* distinction cannot be admitted, because they presuppose a real composition. A *purely logical (mental)* distinction cannot be admitted, because man's concepts of God are not synonymous. A *virtual* distinction with a *perfect foundation* cannot be admitted, because such a distinction implies a metaphysical composition. The distinction, therefore, is a

'virtual distinction with an *imperfect foundation.*' The concepts are 'explicitly' distinct, but each 'implicitly' includes the reality contained in the others, because God is one absolutely simple reality and man can grasp God's plenitude of reality only piecemeal and in distinct concepts.

Readings

Boedder, Bernard, *Natural Theology,* Bk. I, Chap. III. — Joyce, George Hayward, *Principles of Natural Theology,* 2 ed., Chap. X. — Brosnan, William J., *God Infinite and Reason,* pp. 49–92. — Garrigou-Lagrange, R., *God: His Existence and His Nature,* Vol. II, pp. 42–50. — Aveling, Francis, *The God of Philosophy,* Chap. XV. — Glenn, Paul J., *Theodicy,* pp. 112–129. — Mercier, D. Card., *A Manual of Modern Scholastic Philosophy,* Vol. II, pp. 65–79, 88–90. — Smith, Gerard, *Natural Theology,* Chap. XII. — Renard, Henri, *The Philosophy of God,* pp. 77–85, 86–88.

CHAPTER XI

IMMUTABILITY, ETERNITY, IMMENSITY

WHEN speaking of man's knowledge of God, St. Thomas Aquinas seems to be inconsistent. In one place[1] he says: "Because we cannot know what God is, but rather what He is not, we have no means for considering how God is, but rather how He is not." Soon after that, however, he[2] states: "Hitherto we have considered God as He is in Himself." It is hardly conceivable that so acute a thinker would contradict himself in such a short space. Then how reconcile the two statements?

When St. Thomas remarked that "we cannot know what God is, but rather what He is not," he meant to say that man in this life has no 'intuitive' knowledge of God as He exists in Himself. Man derives his knowledge of God from creatural beings, and their imperfections and limitations must be denied of the essence of God; hence, man's knowledge of God is acquired by 'way of negation,' rather than 'directly.' Since man does not know God infinitely, he does not really 'comprehend' God as He is in Himself. Nevertheless, man can reach God through his knowledge, even though only indirectly. Negation always presupposes and implies affirmation. By denying composition and potentiality in God, man affirms His simplicity; by denying limitation in God, man affirms His infinity; by denying multiplicity in God, man affirms His unicity. We "consider God as He is in Himself," even though our knowledge is imperfect and inadequate. Thus, the inconsistency in St. Thomas is more apparent than real.

Man's knowledge of God's *immutability, eternity,* and *immensity* is of a similar character. These attributes will now be discussed. The falsity of *pantheism* will then become clear.

---

[1] *Summa Theologica* (New York: Benziger Bros.), Ia, qu. 3.
[2] *Ibid.,* qu. 12.

Notion of Immutability

As the word indicates, 'immutability' is the negation of 'mutability.' In order, then, to understand the meaning of 'immutability,' we must begin with the concept of 'mutability.'

Mutability means capability of change (mutation). A thing is said to 'change' when it passes from one state into another state. Every change involves two things: a subject which acquires or loses something, and a reality which is acquired or lost by the subject.

Change is 'extrinsic' or 'intrinsic.' Change is *extrinsic* when it is the result of an extrinsic denomination. An illustration will clarify this rather abstruse definition. I see, for example, a tree, and then I walk away and no longer see the tree; the tree has changed from a 'seen' tree to a tree 'no longer seen.' The tree has obviously not undergone a real change in its own being by passing from the state of an 'unseen' tree to the state of a 'seen' tree and then from the state of a 'seen' tree to that of a tree 'no longer seen.' Whatever real change occurred took place in me and not in the tree, because the act of sight affected my being but not the tree; I acquired and lost some reality (the 'act of sight'), but nothing happened to the being of the tree thereby. Since no reality was acquired or lost by the being of the tree in its change of status ('seen' and 'no longer seen'), such a change is termed 'extrinsic'; the knowledge relation affects the knower in a real fashion, but not the object known.

Change is *intrinsic* when some reality is either acquired or lost in the passage of the subject from one state to another. Intrinsic change is either a change 'properly so called' or 'improperly so called.' When the change is of such a nature that the entire being of the subject either passes from non-existence to existence (creation) or from existence to non-existence (annihilation), the change is *improperly so called,* because the subject undergoing this change does not remain throughout the change. In 'creation' the subject was not in existence before it was created, and in 'annihilation' the subject ceases to exist after it is annihilated. When, however, an existing subject undergoes change, so that it acquires or loses some reality while remaining in existence, the change is an intrinsic change *properly so called*. Thus, when a piece of iron changes from hot to cold or from cold to hot, such a change is 'intrinsic' and it is 'properly so called,' because the piece of iron has actually acquired or lost the quality of heat. A change 'properly so called' is also styled an intrinsic change in the 'strict sense' of the term, while a change 'improperly so called' is styled an intrinsic change in a 'wider sense.'

An intrinsic change in the strict sense of the term (or an 'intrinsic change properly so called') may be either 'physical' or 'moral' or 'intellectual' in nature. A *physical* intrinsic change in the strict sense consists in the acquisition or loss of a substantial or accidental reality. When, for example, nonliving matter is converted into living matter by a plant, animal, or man, its substance is changed, and such a change is a *substantial* physical change; but when a piece of iron is heated, it undergoes an *accidental* physical change, because the substance of iron remains the same in the (accidental, qualitative) change. A change is *moral,* when there is a passage from one resolution of the will to another. It is *intellectual,* when there is a change from one judgment to another.

When these notions are applied to God, it is obvious that an 'extrinsic' change occurs in relation to Him: He is known and not known, loved and hated, and so forth; but in all such cases, the change really occurs in the creatures, not in God Himself. Intrinsic change in the 'wider sense' of creation or annihilation, does not apply to God; as the 'first being' He cannot be created, and as the 'necessary being' He cannot be annihilated. The question here is that of *intrinsic change in the strict sense,* namely, of a 'physical' or 'moral' or 'intellectual' change in the true meaning of the terms.

Proof of God's Immutability

The opponents of the immutability of God are the polytheists and the pantheists.

As *theists* we maintain that God is in no way changeable. *God is immutable.* Not only does He not change as a matter of fact, but He is *incapable* of intrinsic change.

First, a *general* proof of God's immutability.

An *intrinsic* change is the passage of a subject from one state to another state, the subject thereby acquiring or losing some reality. If a reality is 'acquired,' the subject does not already possess it; if the subject possessed it already, it could not 'acquire' it by means of the passage from one state to another. It follows, therefore, that the changing subject does not possess it already and 'acquires' the absent and missing reality by means of the change. Hence, if God could 'acquire' some reality, He would, of necessity, have to receive it, either *from Himself* or *from some other being.* Now, He could not receive it from Himself, because in that case He would already possess it, since no one can give what he does not have; but if He already possesses the reality in question, He cannot 'acquire' it, not even from Himself. Neither can He receive it from some other being. This follows from the fact that God is the first being, as was shown in the proof of His existence, and the first being is the necessary being, because He exists in virtue of His essence. Hence, whatever God is, He is necessarily whatever He is. If, then, God would not have a certain reality, He would 'necessarily' lack this reality and could never 'acquire' it from another being. God, therefore, cannot 'acquire' any reality through passing from one state into another state.

Nor can God 'lose' reality. When reality is lost, the subject possesses it already and then loses it in the change. Now, if God could lose reality, this loss of reality would have to be due either *to His own action* or *to the action of some other being.* Neither case is admissible. God is the necessary being; He is necessarily whatever He is. But if He could lose some reality He possesses, whether through His own action or the action of some other being, He would not be 'necessarily' what He is. God, therefore, cannot lose reality by passing from one state to another state.

The same consequence follows from the *infinite perfection* of God. If He could 'acquire' reality by means of change, He would not be infinitely perfect *before* the change; He would certainly be more perfect if He did not acquire it but possessed it already. And for the same reason He cannot 'lose' reality in any manner. All reality being a form of perfection, God would be less perfect *after* giving up some reality than He was when He possessed it. Besides, to be capable of acquiring or losing reality involves passivity and potentiality; a being, however, with passivity and potentiality is not infinitely perfect.

Again, the *absolute simplicity* of God's essence makes it impossible for Him to 'acquire' or 'lose' reality through change. Because of this absolute simplicity, everything in God's essence is one single reality; composition of any and every kind is excluded. However, if any reality could be acquired by God through change, there would be an addition to His being, and that would entail a composition between His absolutely simple being and the new reality; but composition is excluded in an absolutely simple being. Similarly, God cannot lose any reality through change. Since His being is an absolutely simple essence, the loss of any reality at all would mean the loss of His entire essence, and that would be equivalent to annihilation; God, however, cannot lose His essence and cease to exist, because the necessary being cannot cease to exist.

It is evident, therefore, that change is impossible in God, and He must, consequently, be *immutable*.

Second, a *specific* proof of God's immutability, in so far as the single types of intrinsic change are impossible.

God is *physically* unchangeable. Whatever is capable of change cannot be infinite in perfection, because it can be augmented in its being by the acquisition of some new reality or be decreased in its being by the loss of some reality it possesses. God, however, is absolutely infinite in His being. Therefore, He cannot change by passing from one state to another through the acquisition or loss of physical reality. Besides, every changeable being has potentiality, since it is capable of receiving what it does not possess and of losing what it possesses. God, however, is pure actuality and, therefore, without potentiality.

God is *morally* unchangeable. If God ever changed morally, so that He would begin to will something He did not will before, we would have to conclude that He either made no decision before regarding this matter and then began to exercise His will regarding it or that He changed the decision made before. Neither alternative, however, is possible. In either case God would acquire the reality of a decision, and this reality would be something new in God's being, since it was not there before. God, however, since He is infinitely perfect, cannot acquire such a reality, because every reality is a perfection for the one possessing it.

God is *intellectually* unchangeable. God could undergo intellectual change in one of two ways, either by acquiring knowledge of something He did not know before, or by losing knowledge already possessed. In the first case He would pass from a state of ignorance into a state of knowledge, and in the second case from a state of knowledge into a state of ignorance. Ignorance, however, is an imperfection, and God would be more perfect if He had this knowledge and retained it always. Now God is infinitely perfect. Hence, ignorance, whether antecedent or subsequent, must be excluded from Him. God, therefore, can neither acquire nor lose knowledge, and intellectual change is thus impossible in God.

It follows that God is *immutable* in every respect.

Not only is God immutable; *He alone is immutable.* Every creatural being is subject to change. All creatures, as a matter of observable fact, undergo change in one form or another. All are contingent and potential. All are composites of substance and accidental determinations, and they realize their being successively through passage from potentiality to actuality. The entire world is in a continuous process of 'becoming,' so that some form of reality is always being acquired and lost through change; this is true of all inanimate and animate beings, of all material and spiritual beings. Consequently, since all beings

outside of God undergo change or are at least capable of undergoing change, God alone is immutable.

Extrinsic change does not involve mutability in God Himself, in the sense that there is *real* change in Him. He is more
the 'object' of the change, rather than the 'subject' which undergoes real change. Creatures like men, for instance, at first do
not know God and then know Him. God, of course, can be
said to change from 'not being known' to 'being known.' The
subject undergoing the 'real' change in this process of acquiring
knowledge is, obviously, the creature; the creature really
acquires the act of knowledge and thus passes from the state
of ignorance to a state of knowledge. In the creature, therefore,
a 'real' change takes place, because he actually receives a new
reality when he knows God. God, however, since He is merely
the 'object' of this knowledge and not the 'subject,' does not
undergo real change by passing from 'not being known' to
'being known'; He is merely the 'term of extrinsic denomination,' as philosophers call it, because the real change, while 'intrinsic' in the knowing subject, is altogether 'extrinsic' in the
object known. God's being is not affected in any way by the
real change which takes place in the creatural mind. While,
then, the word 'extrinsic change' is applied to God in such a
case, it must be understood to mean that God does not undergo a real change in His being. Hence, notwithstanding this
'extrinsic change,' God remains absolutely what He was before.
It is clear, therefore, that an 'extrinsic change' does not imply
mutability in God's being.

Notion of Eternity

Eternity is duration in existence which is essentially without
beginning and end and which is essentially without real succession and intrinsic change. As such, therefore, eternity is a type
of duration and must be viewed in the light of the meaning of
duration. *Duration* is the permanence of a being in its existence.
Existence, as was noted before, is the actuality of a being in so
far as the being is outside any causes it may have; in other

words, a being is existent when it is neither 'nothing' nor merely 'possible.'

Duration is either 'divine' or 'creatural.' *Divine* duration is proper to God and is necessarily infinite and immutable, because God Himself is infinite and immutable in every respect. Divine duration goes under the special name of 'eternity,' and its definition has been given in the preceding paragraph. *Creatural* duration is proper to all beings outside God; it is the type of duration characteristic of creatural beings. Such beings are 'capable' of having a beginning and (or) end in their actual existence, even though, as a matter of fact, they have been produced from eternity and would last forever.

Creatural duration is either 'successive' or 'permanent.' It is *successive* when one part of the duration continuously follows the other; the being having successive duration is in a continuous process of change, whether this change be local motion or qualitative alteration or quantitative increase or decrease. Thus, the flow of an electric current (not the electrons as such) is successive in nature. Creatural duration is *permanent* when the being remains constant and intact in its existence. For instance, the electrons, even though in a continuous state of agitation, are practically the same at all times, considered as entities.

Permanent creatural duration is mainly of two types, depending on whether a being is by nature corruptible or incorruptible. A being which is by nature 'corruptible' can be dissolved into its component parts at some time or other, although it is endowed with a relatively permanent existence as a composite being; its duration is by nature not everlasting but *temporal*. For example, a plant or animal or man is a composite being possessing a relatively permanent duration in existence as a plant or animal or man, but this duration is 'temporal' in character; its existence began in time and will end in time, so that its duration is not everlasting. On the other hand, a being which is by nature 'incorruptible' does not consist of component parts, so that it cannot be dissolved into component parts; as a result it possesses a permanent duration which is by nature *everlasting*. Beings which are 'simple (non-composite)' in their constitution are by nature incorruptible; in other words, this type of duration is proper to spirits or spiritual entities. The only kind of spiritual being known to man here on earth is man's immaterial soul; angels, too, are spirits, but they are outside the purview of man's natural knowledge. This kind of everlasting duration is termed *eviternity*, and it is defined as the everlasting duration of a naturally incorruptible being in its existence. Such a being is said to be 'eviternal.'

The *difference* between God's eternity and all other types of duration is clear. It differs from *creatural* duration: creatural duration can have a beginning and an end; God's eternity, on the other hand, is an absolutely necessary existence, incapable of having a beginning or end. It differs from *eviternity:* such a duration, though permanent and by nature everlasting, is in itself capable of having a beginning and, absolutely speaking, an end, and it is also capable of intrinsic change in its accidental determinations. All this is impossible in the duration of God's existence, due to His immutability and infinity. It differs from the *temporal* permanence of corruptible composite being, because God is incorruptible in His being and so is His eternal duration. It differs from the *successive* duration of time: such a duration changes from moment to moment, so that there results a past, a present, and a future; God's existence, however, is always a 'present' without past and future, without succession and change, everlastingly immutable.

The definition which *Boethius* (480–525) gave of eternity has been famous through the centuries. It reads: *Aeternitas est interminabilis vitae tota simul et perfecta possessio: Eternity is the simultaneously complete and perfect possession of interminable life.* Eternity is 'life'; the eternal Being must be a living being, and 'life' designates both being and operation, so that the eternal Being possesses vital being and operation. Eternity is the 'possession' of life; the term expresses the full and absolute enjoyment of life on the part of God. Eternity is the possession of 'interminable' life; the eternal duration of

God's existence excludes the possibility of a beginning or end in His life. Eternity is the possession of interminable life, and this possession is 'simultaneously complete'; this means that God's life is without succession or change in its being and operation. Eternity is the 'perfect' possession of interminable life; this expression signifies that the eternal Being possesses life so as to include absolute perfection and exclude every imperfection. A comparison between the definition given by Boethius and the one given at the head of this section will show that both are identical in meaning.

Proof of God's Eternity

Eternity is understood to be a duration in existence which is essentially without beginning and end and which is essentially without real succession and intrinsic change. This statement represents the definition of 'eternity.' The question now is whether the definition applies to God. It does.

God exists. His existence is absolutely necessary like His essence, since God's existence is in reality identical with His essence; and God's essence is absolutely necessary. To say that the absolutely necessary essence could 'not exist,' is a contradiction. Hence, God's duration in existence must be without beginning and end, and that in virtue of His essence; in other words, God's existence is essentially without beginning and end, because He is the 'necessary being.'

That God's duration in existence is essentially without real succession and intrinsic change, follows from His absolute immutability. Where there is 'real succession' and 'intrinsic change,' there can be no immutability.

Hence, God is essentially *eternal*.

God *alone* is eternal.

Every creatural being is contingent in its essence and existence; not a single one can be said to be a strictly 'necessary' being. As such, it is dependent in its essence and existence on God, the necessary being. Even though a creatural being had received its existence from eternity, it would have been pos-

sible for the being to have received existence in time and it
is also possible for its existence to end. In any case, its existence
had a beginning, even under the supposition that God created
it from eternity. A necessary being, however, is absolutely incapable of having a beginning and (or) end in its existence.
Furthermore, every creatural being is subject to change either
in its substance or in the accidental determination of its substance, because every creatural being possesses potentiality in
some form or other. Hence, no creatural being can be essentially
eternal. God, however, is essentially eternal.

Therefore, *God alone is eternal.*

From the fact that God alone is essentially eternal, it is
manifest in what manner we make statements of God which
imply temporality. Strictly speaking, there can be no 'past'
or 'future' in God's duration. *Past* and *future* are terms which
imply the succession peculiar to time, where one moment
follows after the other. Creatural beings exist in time; and
'past' and 'future' apply to their essence and existence, but
not to God. God's existence is absolutely eternal, so that He
lives in an absolute present; His duration is an *eternal 'now'*
without 'past' or 'future,' and He co-exists eternally with the
successive and continuously changing duration of creatural
beings. It is plain, then, that any expressions involving temporality can be used of God and His activity only in a *metaphorical*
sense or, as the technical language of philosophy puts it, by
means of an *extrinsic denomination* derived from the creatural
beings existing in time. Thus, we say that God 'has created'
the world (as if it were a past act) and 'will reward' the
just (as if it were a future act); such acts, however, are really
one with His immutable essence and exist from all eternity
in an everlasting present.

Notion of Immensity

Immensity is taken here as that intrinsic attribute of God
in virtue of which He is necessarily present wherever any
being exists which is not God.

This attribute is *eternal,* because it is really identical with God's eternal essence and is independent of whether creatural things exist or do not exist. Even if no creatural beings existed, the attribute of God's immensity would be intrinsic to Him and would require that He be present to all creatural beings as soon as they began to exist. This attribute is *infinite,* and as such it is not delimited or measured by place and space. It demands that God be present to all beings in place and space, if and as long as these beings exist, even if they could be infinite in number and space itself could be infinite in extent; if their number is increased indefinitely, God would be present to them without any intrinsic change on His part. This attribute is *intrinsic* to God, not a mere extrinsic denomination derived from existing creatural beings. It is a character of the divine essence, so that He would be immense in His essence, irrespective of the actual existence of beings other than Himself. The necessity of His presence is not to be conceived as a 'potentiality' of some sort, but as the fullness of the divine being requiring His presence in every being. This attribute is *absolute,* because it is unconditioned by creatural existence or non-existence. On the part of God the existence of creatural beings does not introduce a 'real relation,' but only a 'logical relation,' between God and such beings; nothing is added to God's being by the fact of creatural existence, because He is essentially immutable and infinitely perfect.

Some authors have tried to construe the nature of God's immensity as *its reference to absolute space,* in the sense that immensity is the presence of God in absolute space. 'Absolute space' is taken here in contradistinction to 'real' or 'filled space'; absolute space is considered to be infinite in extent, whether it be empty or filled. For those who are convinced that the universe is limited in extent, 'absolute space' is conceived as the space extending beyond the boundaries of the existing universe (or universes). Such an interpretation of God's immensity, however, is inadmissible. Absolute space is the same as 'imaginary space,' and the immensity of God would also be nothing more than a fiction of the mind.

Others have sought to explain God's immensity as the *relation of His presence to extended things*. This explanation must also be rejected. The reason is obvious. The existence of extended realities is altogether finite and temporal. Hence, if God's immensity were nothing more than the relation of His presence to extended things, it would of necessity begin to exist and cease to exist with the existence of extended beings. However, God's immensity is independent of the actual existence of extended reality, because it is eternal and actually identical with His divine essence, as will be shown.

There is a difference between God's immensity and 'omnipresence' or, as it is often termed, 'ubiquity.' By *omnipresence* or *ubiquity* one understands the relation of God's presence to the beings which actually exist and to the real space which they occupy. Omnipresence is a consequence of God's immensity; because He is immense by nature, He must be actually present in all beings which exist. The *relation* of God's presence to existing creatural beings is 'real' on the part of creatures, because their very reality is dependent on God's presence; on the part of God, however, this relation is only 'logical,' because creatural beings cannot exert real influence on God's being. Since omnipresence implies the existence of creatural beings, and since this existence is entirely temporal in character, omnipresence is an attribute of God which is *relative* and *temporal*. The immensity of God, on the contrary, is prior to the existence of creatural beings and is an eternal and infinite perfection.

Proof of God's Immensity

The *opponents* among theists who have discussed the problem are relatively few. *Aristotle* was of the opinion that God would be contaminated by beings of a lower nature, if He were present among them. According to his view, the entire universe above the moon consisted of celestial spheres, and these spheres were composed of incorruptible matter. To safeguard God's purity of being, Aristotle placed Him in the periphery of the ultimate celestial sphere, in which place He alone resides in eternal repose and self-contemplation. The theory of celestial spheres is now obsolete and discredited, due to the information supplied by astronomy and astrophysics. *Vorstius* (a Calvinist) and *Augustinus Steuchus Eugubinus* (a Catholic) maintained that God is omnipresent in all creatures through His power and knowledge, but He is not omnipresent through His essence and substance.

The *polytheists,* due to the decidedly anthropomorphic idea of their divinities, looked upon the gods and goddesses as very limited in essence and operation. As a result of this limitation, the divinities possessed neither immensity nor omnipresence.

The *pantheists,* since they identify God and the universe of reality, naturally admit the omnipresence of God, in the sense of God's absolute immanence (identity) in the world; God 'is' the world. That the immensity of God is an attribute of the Supreme Being transcendently distinct from the world of creatures, is something which they do not and cannot consistently admit. Christian philosophers, of course, are theists and as such opposed to the fundamental tenets of pantheism.

We claim that *God possesses the attribute of immensity.* Some authors contend that a stringent proof of God's immensity and omnipresence cannot be furnished by reason without the aid of divine revelation. The proof, as formulated by D. Card. Mercier,[3] is subjoined, and we think it is sound and valid. He says:

"The infinite Being comprises every absolutely pure perfection; immensity is an absolutely pure perfection; therefore the infinite Being is immense.

"*Proof of the minor premiss:* To be endowed with an absolutely pure perfection means to possess a perfection which excludes all imperfection that can detract from it. Now the presence of a thing somewhere, inasmuch as it is something positive, is a perfection; immensity is just this same perfection without the other impairing elements that are mixed with it

---

[3] *Manual of Modern Scholastic Philosophy* (New York: Herder Book Co., 1917), Vol. II, 'Natural Theology,' n. 52, pp. 82, 83.

when realized in creatures. In the case of a creature, presence involves imperfection for the double reason that it is a mode of being which depends on the creature itself, and that, as it is circumscribed or in some other way restricted, it is essentially subject to limitation. The immensity, however, of God is identical with His substantial being; that being has no extended parts but is indivisible reality unlimited in every line, and excluding by its very essence every limit, no matter what may be the number and size of the worlds to which His action extends. "Therefore immensity is an absolutely simple perfection." The conclusion is evident: *God is immense.*

The *omnipresence* or *ubiquity* of God, in relation to all existing creatural beings, follows as a necessary consequence from His absolute immensity. Immensity signifies the exigency on the part of God's being to be present to every existing creatural being. Consequently, God must be present to all creatural existences as soon as they come into being, no matter what their size or number. And since God's immensity is identical with His essence, like all His other attributes, it is neither an accidental determination nor a mode of His substance; as a result, God's omnipresence does not in any way involve a change in God's being when He becomes present to a newly existing creatural being. As a further consequence, omnipresence is peculiar to *God alone, so that God alone is omnipresent.*

God's presence in creatural things is a presence of His *essence,* so that the total substance of God is in all things and in all real places; since God is absolutely simple, wherever God is said to be present, He must be there with His total essence or not at all. It is also a presence of *knowledge;* knowledge is a perfection, and consequently God must have complete knowledge of all the beings to which He is present. It is also a presence of *power,* because all creatural beings (as will be shown later on) are dependent on God in their being and operation. All this follows from the very nature of immensity and omnipresence.

If 'place' indicates 'where' a being is, the presence in a place is its *whereness* or *ubication* (Lat., *ubi,* where). Presence in a place may be either 'circumscriptive' or 'definitive' or 'repletive.'

A *circumscriptive* presence is the presence of an extended corporeal substance, so that it has parts outside parts quantitatively extended in the place which it occupies; all bodies fill extended space with their own extended reality. A *definitive* presence is the presence of a spatially unextended substance in such a manner that it can exercise its activity only within certain limits of space. Such is the presence of spiritual creatures in the universe; and such, too, is the presence of man's immaterial soul within the limits of his body. Spiritual beings, since they are simple entities, have no parts outside parts in their substance, and thus they do not have a circumscriptive presence in space; but their activity is limited to certain restricted areas of space, so that they are 'localized' and are not present everywhere. A *repletive* presence is the presence of a spatially unextended ('spiritual') substance in all places and spaces, past, present, and future; such a being is naturally 'everywhere.'

God's omnipresence in the universe (or universes) is not 'circumscriptive.' He is not circumscribed by a particular place or space; His infinitely perfect being cannot be restricted and limited. Nor is His omnipresence 'definitive,' in the sense that His activity and presence is localized like that of an ordinary spirit or immaterial substance; because that, too, would imply restriction and limitation. God's omnipresence is *repletive.* He is 'everywhere,' totally and compenetratingly. This 'repletive presence' is what is meant by 'omnipresence' or 'ubiquity,' and the infinite perfection which is its foundation is 'immensity.'

Pantheism

Opposed to theism, expounded so far, is the doctrine of pantheism. In general, pantheism (Gr., πᾶν, all, everything; Θεός, God) teaches the *identity of the Deity with the beings of this world.* In the course of the centuries pantheism has appeared in many diverse forms. The varieties of pantheism are too numerous to be discussed in detail. Yet, a brief outline of the main types of pantheism will not be amiss.

The *two main divisions* are *partial* (imperfect) and *total* (perfect) pantheism.

Partial pantheism maintains that God is not the totality of world-beings, but only a *part of the world.* This type of pantheism is always realistic, never idealistic.

Chief among the proponents of partial (imperfect) pantheism were the *stoics.* The school was founded by Zeno of Cittium (350–258 B.C.) and lasted for centuries. The material is the only reality; God Himself is but a finer sort of matter. God is conceived as the 'soul' of the universe. The reality of God and the world is at bottom identical, with only a relative difference existing between God (reality, regarded as a whole) and the world (reality, regarded in its various aspects). In medieval times, partial pantheism was revived by Amaury (Amalric) of Bène, who taught that God is the formal principle of all things, and David of Dinant, who held that God is universal matter; both lived in the twelfth and thirteenth century. In recent times Oscar Külpe expressed the view that God is the world-soul. Some modern pantheists identify God with world-energy or something similar. Generally speaking, partial pantheism was never very popular among philosophers; if they defended pantheism at all, it was a form of total pantheism.

Total pantheism (also called 'perfect' pantheism) maintains that *all reality is but one.* Because of this oneness of being, Deity is totally identified with this 'one being.' Total pantheism is either 'realistic' or 'idealistic.'

Total *realistic* pantheism holds that the reality which is identified with God is a *physical entity* (not a mere product of mind or thought). This type appears in a variety of forms.

One form of realistic pantheism teaches that there exists but a *single physical reality,* and it is absolutely permanent and unchangeable; multiplicity and change are but an illusion.

Among the early Greek philosophers who belonged to this group are those of the School of Elia, namely, Xenophanes (570 B.C.), Parmenides (540 B.C.), Zeno of Elia (490 B.C.), and Melissus. Most prominent in this group was Parmenides. He claimed that all 'becoming' was utterly impossible; hence, only the All-One exists, indivisible and immobile (see Chap. IV). In opposition to this doctrine is the pantheistic teaching that the only physical reality which exists is 'pure motion' and 'change.' Heraclitus (530 B.C.), among the ancients, best represents this type of pantheism (see Chap. IV). The principle of change is the divine, all-controlling 'fire,' and it is called by Heraclitus 'Zeus,' 'Deity,' 'Logos,' 'Justice.' His system is thus a system of dynamic monism. The origin of the world is explained as a transformation of primal fire.

Another form of realistic pantheism is that of the *evolution of the Deity* into the world. This evolution may be either 'transient' or 'immanent.'

Transient realistic pantheism is also called *emanationism.* Its general doctrine consists in the tenet that all beings in the world 'emanate' or flow from the divine substance, so that they originate, not by means of God's causal action, but through a transformation of God's substance. The *gnostics* of the second century of the Christian era, particularly Valentinus, taught the origin of numberless 'aeons' through emanation from God. Plotinus (A.D. 205–270) and the *neo-platonists* defended a system of emanations. According to Plotinus, God is the One, the Good, the primal reality which is undifferentiated. Goodness gives rise to emanation; and emanation gives rise to the multiplicity of things, as a kind of overflow of the One. Mind is the first reality to emanate from God; then comes the world-soul; then plastic forces (forms, individual souls); and finally matter. Matter is the ultimate degradation of the One, because it is the source of multiplicity and evil. In medieval times John Scotus Eriugena (about 810–877) defended a transient, emanatistic pantheism.

Total *immanent* pantheism applies the principle of *evolution* to God and maintains that the divine reality has evolved into the present world. World-beings, therefore, are *modifications* of the divine reality, produced through a 'real' evolution of the divine entity. The philosophy of *India,* as laid down many centuries before Christianity in the Veda and the Upanishads, taught that originally there was but a single permanent reality, namely, 'Brahman' (God), which then evolved into the things of the world. A modern version of Indian pantheism is found in *theosophy.* Perhaps the best-known system of immanent evolutionistic pantheism is the one propounded by *B. Spinoza* (1632–1677). Spinoza began his system with an arbitrary definition of 'substance,' allowing but a single substance to exist, namely, God. This substance consists of infinite attributes of which two only are known to man, 'extension' and 'thought'; these attributes are the same reality as God Himself, and for that reason are not really distinct among themselves. Besides these attributes, infinite 'modes' exist in God; and of all these modes man knows but the particular thoughts present in his own mind and the particular extensions constituting the various bodies found in the world. These modes, however, like the attributes, are not really distinct but are merely different aspects of one and the same substance of God. God thus evolves into 'nature' and 'spirit,' so that "God is a thinking thing" and "God is an extended thing." However, when Spinoza attempts to derive 'mind' and 'matter' ('spirit' and 'nature') from the infinite substance as the finite determinations of God's being, he explains the evolution of differentiation and multiplicity in a way which makes them unreal. At any rate, Spinoza's God is an impersonal substance.

Total *idealistic* pantheism proclaims as its fundamental tenet the principle that all being is actually *thought-being,* so that things have existence only in a mind and only in so far as they are thought. Hence, everything is derived from 'mind' and is essentially 'mental.' The main proponents of idealistic pantheism are the German philosophers J. H. Fichte (1762–1814), F. W. J. Schelling (1775–1854), and G. W. Hegel (1770–1831). Theirs is the pantheistic philosophy of the *Absolute,* and each of these thinkers sought, in his own way, to harmonize the 'phenomenal (appearance)' and 'noumenal (thing-in-itself)' of Kant's idealism by starting with a being which would be the unifying ground of these Kantian opposites.

The human mind invariably seeks a *principle of unification* for the multiplicity and diversity observed among the beings of the world. However, instead of finding this principle of unification in the efficient causality of a personal God, these thinkers placed it in the very being of God, and thereby they fell into the error of pantheism. Pantheism, as the materialist Ernest Haeckel once said, is nothing but "polite atheism."

Refutation of Pantheism

In view of what has already been established concerning God's existence and nature, it is clear that any type of pantheism, identifying Him either partially or totally with the things of the world, is erroneous. All that is required here is to point out how pantheism contradicts these established truths.

Partial pantheism must be *rejected*.

Any theory that makes God a part of the world is erroneous. To be a part of anything means *composition,* and composition in this case would mean that the result is a 'composite being.' Now, the composite being, considered as a totality (whole), is more perfect than the parts which constitute the totality (whole). Hence God would be less perfect as a part than the totality (whole) of which He is the part. God, however, is infinitely perfect, and therefore He cannot be a part of the world.

Total pantheism must also be *rejected*.

According to the teaching of total pantheism, God is identified with the totality of the world, not merely with a part of it. Whether this pantheism be 'realistic' or 'idealistic,' it cannot be accepted.

Realistic total pantheism is erroneous. The origin of the world is explained either as an 'emanation' or as an 'evolution' of the divine substance. In either explanation God is identical with the world and the world with God. If this were so, the world would of necessity be a *single being,* because God Himself is one, undivided and indivisible. Such a view of the world, however, contradicts both experience and reason.

Idealistic total pantheism is also erroneous. Idealistic pantheists of modern times claim that the beings of the world are but 'modes' or modifications of the divine substance through a process of necessary evolution; and these modes are only 'thought-modes' or thought-modifications of God's evolving being. This system is an egregious error. Creatural beings are not 'modes' of any substantial being. As William J. Brosnan[4] rightly observes: "They are complete substances in themselves, really distinct from God numerically and essentially, and really distinct from one another numerically and, in numberless cases, specifically and also generically. What is more, unless we wish to admit that our cognitive faculties are utterly and absolutely untrustworthy, we must admit that we ourselves and the rest of the creatures in the world are not mere thought-modifications of any being, but have an existence in the physical world, an existence, namely, really distinct from, and outside of, the intellect or thought of any being, even God. To insist that the world is a mere illusion of God's intellect or of our intellects is intellectual suicide. To attempt to live practically in accord with such a theory is impossible. Even the Idealists themselves admit this."

The great *fallacy* underlying the system of idealistic immanent pantheism, especially of the Hegelian type, lies in the failure to distinguish between the *ontological* concept of God as the *ens a se* (ὁ ὤν) and the *logical* concept of *universal being* (τὸ ὄν). A comparison of the two concepts will bring out their radical difference. The concept of God is that of a *concrete* being; the concept of universal being is *abstract.* The absolute being of 'God' has the fullest 'comprehension,' because He com-

---

[4] *God Infinite and Reason* (New York: America Press, 1928), p. 220.

prises within Himself the *plenitude of being* in an infinite manner; but the concept of God is the smallest in 'extension,' because He is *only one in number.* The reverse is true of the abstract, logical entity of the concept of 'universal being.' From the standpoint of its 'comprehension,' it is the most meager of all concepts, because it consists of the single item of *being in general* and as such is next to 'nothing'; from the standpoint of its 'extension,' it is the widest of all concepts, since it can be predicated of every sort of *actual and possible being,* of substances and accidents and modes. Furthermore, 'God' and 'universal being' differ altogether in regard to the manner of their *origin.* The concept of 'God' is the result of reasoning, acquired through the process of applying the principles of reason to the data of experience. On the other hand, the concept of 'universal being' is formed through the logical process of abstraction, by ignoring the manifold differences existing in the actual realities. Again, 'God' and 'universal being' differ completely in their *mode of existence.* 'God' exists as an individual being, independent of any creatural mind. 'Universal being' exists formally only in the abstracting mind and as such has only a mental existence; in actuality, individual beings alone exist, and 'universal being' does not exist as a real being anywhere in nature. Finally, 'God' and 'universal being' are totally different in their *properties.* Both are simple; but this 'simplicity' is predicated of them in radically diverse meanings. 'God' is said to be 'simple' in the sense that He is infinitely perfect; He possesses ontological indivisibility in the fullness of His Being. 'Universal being,' however, is said to be 'simple' only because of its indeterminateness, logical incompositeness, and poverty of content.

From all this it is clear that pantheism, no matter in what guise it appears, cannot stand the test of logical analysis. When examined carefully and objectively, pantheism always manifests itself as a system of flagrant contradictions. Any system of thought, however, which is inherently contradictory, must be rejected as erroneous.

God Is Personal

The term 'person' must not be confused with the term 'personality.' In ordinary parlance, 'personality' means the combination of all those mental, moral, and emotional traits, natural and acquired, which distinguish one human being from another. Philosophically, a *person* is defined as an individual, complete, subsistent, intellectual substance. Originally, the notion of 'person' has been acquired by man through a study of his own being in comparison with lower beings. Then, finding that God, too, is an individual, complete, subsistent, intellectual substance, but in an infinite degree, man applies the concept of 'person' analogically to God.

God is personal.

God is a *substance.* He certainly exists in Himself and by Himself, so that He does not need another being as a subject in which He must inhere in order to exist. This follows necessarily from the fact that He is the first being and that He is infinitely perfect. It is certainly more perfect to exist independently of another being than to need another as a subject of inhesion.

God is an *individual* substance. Obviously, if God is unique, so that a plurality of Deities is excluded, He is an individual substance. A pantheistic deity does not possess individuality, but a theistic God certainly does.

God is a *complete,* individual substance. God is in no sense a part-substance like the human soul conjoined with matter to form 'man.' God is neither a part of the world at large nor of any being in the world. If God were not a 'complete' substance, He would not be infinitely perfect.

God is a *subsistent,* individual, complete substance. Something is said to be 'subsistent' when it is self-contained and autonomous (*sui juris*) in its existence, nature, and operations. Since God is the first being, the uncaused cause, and infinite substance, He must also be 'subsistent.'

God is an *intellectual,* individual, complete, subsistent substance. It is manifestly a greater perfection for a being to have an intellect than not to have it. Hence, since God is infinitely perfect, he must be an intellectual being. Besides, God is the author of the order, harmony, and rationality observed in the arrangements present in the world.

God, therefore, is truly personal. The world at large is not personal, because it is lifeless and lacks an intellect. Hence, God is *distinct from the world,* even though *immanently present* to every being.

Summary of Chapter XI

In this chapter God's *immutability, eternity,* and *immensity* are considered. *Pantheism* is refuted.

1. *Notion of Immutability.* — The opposite of 'immutability' is *mutability,* and mutability means capability of change. 'Change' is the passage of a being from one state into another state. Change may be 'extrinsic' or 'intrinsic.' With reference to God's immutability, intrinsic change in the strict sense of 'physical,' 'moral,' or 'intellectual' change must be denied of God.

2. *Proof of God's Immutability.* — Intrinsic change means the acquisition or loss of some reality. If God could change intrinsically, He would have to *acquire* reality either from Himself or from another. Neither supposition is admissible. Nor can God *lose* reality. God is the first and necessary being and as such cannot acquire or lose any reality. Intrinsic change is also contrary to God's infinite perfection and absolute simplicity. Specifically, God cannot undergo physical, moral, or intellectual change.

God *alone* is immutable. All creatural beings are contingent and potential and undergo change, so that they are constantly acquiring and losing reality in many ways.

3. *Notion of Eternity.* — Eternity is a form of duration; *eternity* is defined as a duration in existence which is essentially without beginning and end and which is essentially without real succession and intrinsic change. Duration is either divine or creatural; either successive or permanent; either temporal or everlasting. The everlasting duration of spiritual entities is termed 'eviternity.'

Boethius has defined eternity as "the simultaneously-complete and perfect possession of interminable life."

4. *Proof of God's Eternity.* — That God's duration is eternal, follows from the fact of His necessity and immutability of being.

God *alone* is eternal, because He alone is necessary; all creatural beings are 'contingent' in their existence and dependent on God for their being.

5. *Notion of Immensity.* — Immensity means that God must be necessarily present wherever any being exists which is not God. Immensity is an infinite, intrinsic, and absolute attribute of God, unconditioned by creatural existence or non-existence. *Omnipresence* or *ubiquity* is the relation of God's presence to the beings which actually exist and to the real space which they occupy. Omnipresence is the result of God's immensity.

6. *Proof of God's Immensity.* — The presence of a thing 'somewhere' is something positive and therefore a perfection. Immensity is this perfection without the limitation and imperfection found in creatures. Consequently, immensity is a pure perfection and as such must be an attribute of the infinitely perfect essence of God.

God *alone* possesses immensity, because no creatural being has the exigency to be present everywhere and in everything. God's presence is a presence of His essence, knowledge, and power. His presence is neither 'circumscriptive' nor merely 'definitive,' but *repletive.*

7. *Pantheism.* — Opposed to theism, *pantheism* teaches the identity of the Deity with the beings of this world. Pantheism is *partial,* when it identifies God with a part of the world; *total,* when it identifies God with the totality of the world. Total pantheism may be either 'realistic' or 'idealistic.'

8. *Refutation of Pantheism.* — *Partial* pantheism must be rejected. God cannot be the 'world-soul,' because such a supposition contradicts God's infinite perfection, simplicity, and immutability. Nor can He be 'universal matter,' because matter is essentially passive, potential, and changeable.

Total pantheism must also be rejected. In the *realistic* interpretation of total pantheism, the world would of necessity be a single being, because God Himself is one, undivided and indivisible. Such a view of the world, however, contradicts both experience and reason. In the *idealistic* interpretation, the beings of the world are 'thought-modes' of the Absolute's (God's) necessarily evolving being. This doctrine is contrary to fact, because man and other beings are complete substances in themselves, really distinct from God and among themselves. Idealistic pantheism would make our power of knowledge utterly untrustworthy, and so universal skepti-

cism would be inevitable. The *fallacy* underlying idealistic pantheism lies in its failure to distinguish between the 'ontological' concept of God as the *ens a se* and the 'logical' concept of *universal
being*.

9. *God Is Personal.* — Philosophically, a *person* is an individual,
complete, subsistent, intellectual substance. This definition is verified
in God. Therefore, God is a personal being.

Readings

Boedder, Bernard, *Natural Theology*, Bk. II, Chaps. I, II, III. —
Brosnan, William J., *God Infinite and Reason*, pp. 93 ff., 123 ff., 131 ff.
— Aveling, Francis, *The God of Philosophy*, Chap. XVI. — Mercier,
D. Card., *Manual of Modern Scholastic Philosophy*, Vol. II, 'Natural
Theology,' Part II, Chap. II. — St. Thomas Aquinas, *Summa Theologica*,
Ia, qq. 9, 10. — Smith, Gerard, *Natural Theology*, Chap. XII. — Renard,
Henri, *The Philosophy of God*, pp. 89–101.

Chapter XII

GOD'S INTELLECT AND WILL

THE attributes discussed in the two preceding chapters are 'essential' attributes, in the sense that they pertain directly, according to our human way of thinking, to the essence of God.

Next in line are the *internal operational* attributes of God. God's essence is not an inert, inactive reality, but one that is absolutely active and operative.

In God, since He is pure actuality and infinite perfection, everything is identical with His absolute essence. Man cannot conceive this complete identity. Man's ideas are derived from finite beings, and they are always finite in their comprehension of perfection. When applied to God, all limitation must be denied. Hence, even though we predicate 'operations' of God, we must always bear in mind that such operations are not something superadded to God's essence but are identical with His absolute being.

The operational attributes proper to God's essence, considered absolutely in itself, are *vital spiritual activities,* mainly those of *intellection* and *volition.* These will now be discussed.

Nature of God's Intellection

It is clear that God *cannot be a material entity.* A material entity consists of matter; and matter consists of two or more parts in a side-by-side position, existing in such a manner that normally they are spread out in space but form a unified reality. Whenever matter exists, there is a resultant *composition* of the material parts into a whole. In God, however, there can be no composition of any kind, because He is the first being and pure actuality. God, therefore, is not a material entity. As a consequence, He is an immaterial or spiritual entity.

Every spiritual being is a *living being*. Life is 'immanent' action, and immanent action is either vegetative or sensory or spiritual. Vegetative and sensory action, however, are essentially organic, and whatever is organic is material. God, since He is immaterial, is not organic; consequently, his life cannot be vegetative and sensory. Hence, the life proper to God must be spiritual, characterized by intellection and volition.

Intellection, in general, has subjective and objective elements. The *subjective* element is the *act* (operation) of the knower, namely, thought or knowledge itself in virtue of which the thinking subject actually 'knows.' The *objective* element is the *formal principle* which immediately and proximately orders the subject's power of thinking to elicit the act of thinking.

So far as the *act of knowledge* is concerned, the divine activity of knowing is evidently very different from that of man. In man, the act of knowing is 'really distinct' from man's nature. This fact is manifest beyond doubt, because man's act of knowing comes and goes while his nature remains. Man's act of knowledge, therefore, is always an 'accidental determination' of his intellect, so that his intellect passes from the potentiality of knowing to the actuality of knowing. In God such a passage from potentiality to actuality cannot occur; He is all essence and actuality. While, therefore, man makes a distinction in God between His essence and intellection, this is only in accordance with the limited conception of God's nature characteristic of man's thought. This conception views divine intellection as an *operational attribute* proper to God's essence. It is necessary, however, to guard against certain false notions; otherwise the limitations of man's intellection will be predicated of God's intellection.

In God there are no 'accidents' of any kind, because there is no composition. Therefore, God's intellection is *identical with His substance*. For the same reason God's intellection may not be conceived as any sort of 'process' which unfolds gradually in the course of His existence. It must be absolutely *self-subsistent* and *immutable;* consequently, through a single,

comprehensive act of knowledge God must exhaust the knowable, without change in Himself and without the necessity of
progressive learning. And since God's intellection is identical
with His essence, it is absolutely *simple* and infinitely *perfect,*
complete *understanding,* so that He need not reason from
premises to conclusions nor make distinctions nor combine
subjects and predicates into judgments; God's knowledge is an
infinitely penetrative insight into all things which can be
known, and this knowledge must be absolutely *true* and *infallible.* Similarly, infinite perfection precludes in God's intellectual act the possibility of dependence on creatures. If God
in His intellectual act were dependent in any manner on creatural beings, His very essence would be dependent because of
the identity between His intellection and essence; that, however, is impossible in the self-subsistent being. Hence, God's
intellection is unconditionally *independent,* even with respect
to man's free acts.

The Object of God's Knowledge

All human thoughts are contingent realities, because they
are not eternal in their existence but begin to be and cease to
be at definite moments in time. As such, human thoughts
demand specific causes which determine them both in their
origination and in their character as representations of determinate objects. This cause of human thought is termed, in
technical language, its *formal principle* (*principium formale*),
and it is defined as that by means of which the intellect is
determined or ordered to elicit the knowing act.

In man, the *formal principle* of thought contains a double
element, one 'external' and one 'internal.' The *external* formal
principle of knowledge is the *known object* itself, in so far as
it impresses itself upon the intellect and through this impression prompts the intellect to elicit the act of knowledge, thereby
making the mind pass from the potentiality of knowing to
the actuality of knowing. Unless such an object presents itself
to the intellect, the intellect simply cannot know anything
about it. However, the mere presence of an object is insufficient

for the eliciting of the act of knowledge; the intellect is not completely passive in the process of knowledge. In the presence of the object the intellect actively abstracts a 'representation' of the object. This representative or cognitional image is the *internal* formal principle of knowledge in the knowing subject and is called the *intelligible species;* by its means the intellect is proximately determined to elicit the act of knowledge.

In the case of human intellectual knowledge, the intelligible species is a contingent reality and an accidental perfection super-added to the reality of the intellect. God, of course, cannot be the subject of an accidental perfection superadded to His essence, for He is pure actuality. The divine intellect is identical with the divine essence and substance, and as such it is in no sense a 'power' or 'potency' which requires the help of an intelligible species, distinct from itself, to actualize itself. In God nothing is prior to His self-subsistent essence, and nothing is distinct from His essence. Hence, if we wish to speak of an 'internal formal principle' of God's knowledge, we must use the term 'intelligible species' in a wider and less proper sense than in the case of human knowledge. Taken in this *wider* and *less proper meaning,* we can say with St. Thomas[1] that "the intelligible species does not differ from the substance of the divine intellect, as it differs in our intellect when it understands actually; but the intelligible species itself is the divine intellect itself, and thus God understands Himself through Himself." And God's intellect being identical with His essence, one must also say that His essence is the 'internal formal principle' ('intelligible species') of His infinite act of knowledge. It follows, then, that God Himself is the *primary object* of His knowledge, because His knowledge is the same as His essence. All other things are *secondary objects* of His knowledge, inasmuch as He is the source of their being and they are imitations in some way of His essence. God, therefore, knows Himself and all other things in the infinitely perfect perception of His own being. As St. Thomas[2] puts it: "God sees Himself

---

[1] *Summa Theologica* (New York: Benziger Bros.), Ia, qu. 14, art. 2.
[2] *Ibid.,* art. 5.

in Himself, because He sees Himself through His essence; and He sees other things not in themselves, but in Himself; inasmuch as His essence contains the similitude of things other than Himself."

First, then, God knows *Himself*. And He knows Himself through an infinitely perfect act of self-contemplation. Intellectual knowledge always implies that the knower knows that he knows; this, in turn, implies that the knower knows himself in the act of knowing. God, therefore, must know Himself. And since the act of knowledge is identical with God's infinite essence, it follows necessarily that God knows Himself in an infinitely perfect manner. This means that God's self-knowledge is absolutely *comprehensive,* because the act of divine knowledge is co-extensive with the divine object present to His intellect. If God did not know Himself comprehensively, He would be lacking in a most important phase of knowledge and would not be infinitely perfect. But God is infinitely perfect. Therefore, He must have a comprehensive knowledge of Himself as the primary object of His intellect.

The objective of all knowledge is *truth,* and truth is the conformity between thing and knowing subject. Since God's intellect and essence are absolutely the same reality, the conformity between His intellect and His essence is absolute in every respect. Hence, God does not 'possess' truth; *God is Truth.*

Second, God knows *all things distinct from Himself*. This conclusion is a necessary consequence of His infinite perfection. If it is a perfection for man to know things other than himself, this perfection must also be present in God. And since everything in God is infinite, this perfection must also be infinite. Hence, God must know all things distinct from Himself in an infinitely perfect manner, comprehensively. Anything short of absolute comprehension would be a limitation and imperfection. This means that God's knowledge of things is not 'abstract' and through 'universals,' as in the case of human knowledge, but 'distinct' and 'adequate' and 'without confusion.' God knows man, therefore, better than man knows himself; He knows man and every other being down to the smallest and most intimate detail of reality. Furthermore, God not only knows every *operation* of creatural beings throughout their existence, but also every operation which they can possibly perform. Everything in the past and present and future is thus open to His view, and this knowledge of God is, like His essence, *eternal.*

From all this it should be clear that *creatural reality does not determine God's knowledge,* because it does not induce His intellect to pass from potentiality into actuality. Creatural reality is merely the *term* of God's knowledge, because by the 'term of knowledge' we understand the 'object of knowledge,' namely, that which is known to the knowing subject; and creatural reality, obviously, is known to God, otherwise it could not even exist.

Hence, God knows *all beings* both extensively and intensively with complete comprehension.

Some modern authors, especially the *pantheists,* have denied knowledge in the Absolute, on the grounds that every act of knowledge involves two distinct realities, the *knower* and the *object known.* Hence, they say, the God of theism would of necessity be a divided reality ('knower' and 'thing known') and as such could not be infinitely perfect. Furthermore, they claim, by the very act of knowledge God would be 'limited,' since every knowing subject is 'limited' by the object it knows. Consequently, God would be infinite (unlimited) and finite (limited) at the same time; and that is a contradiction. The objection is futile. Certainly, a creatural mind is distinct as knower from the object known when it knows objects distinct from itself; and it is 'limited' by such objects, because the act of knowledge is something acquired and as such is superadded as a new reality to the 'power' of knowing. If the knowledge present in God were like that of man or of any other creatural being, division and limitation would be carried over into His essence. But God's knowledge is not like that. His knowledge is identical with His essence. Hence, in knowing Himself there is a perfect identity between God as the 'knower' and as the 'object known'; and because of that fact He is not 'limited' in any way by the object of knowledge. Unlike man who merely *has* knowledge of himself and other beings, God *is* His own knowledge; that is merely another way of stating that *God is Himself,* and such a statement contains no contradiction whatever. At most, there is but a *logical distinction* between God as the 'knower' and the 'object known.'

Practically all the difficulties which the moderns advance against the knowledge of God are based on a confusion of creatural knowledge and divine knowledge. They draw a complete *parallel* between the two and argue to their *parity.* It is unfortunate that these thinkers cannot rise above the essential imperfection inherent in human knowledge to the essential perfection of divine knowledge. Basically, they labor under the misconception of an 'anthropomorphic God,' and then they are guilty of the inconsistency of accusing the theists of 'anthropomorphism.'

Kinds of Divine Knowledge

Everything in God is fundamentally and ultimately a single reality. Man cannot conceive God in a single, comprehensive idea; if he could, he would be God Himself. Man must make distinctions, even though he knows that God's essence is absolutely one, because that is the only way man can form ideas of God's being. In a similar fashion, man forms distinct ideas of God's intellect and knowledge, although he is aware that there is no multiplicity in God. Hence, man distinguishes various *kinds of knowledge* in God's intellect.

Viewed from the standpoint of the *objects themselves,* God's knowledge is either that of 'simple intelligence' or of 'vision'; many authors add to these 'intermediate knowledge.' God's knowledge of *simple intelligence* has as its object those things that are merely possible. Such things have never existed, they do not exist, and they will never exist, because they never leave the realm of mere possibility; but they could, absolutely speaking, exist, provided God had decided to give them existence. God's knowledge of *vision* pertains to objects which at some time, either in the past or present or future, have existence. Such realities, no matter at what point of time (past, present, or future) they have actual existence, are intuitively seen by God as they actually exist when they exist. Many scholastic philosophers posit a knowledge in God which is midway between simple intelligence and vision; it is termed *intermediate knowledge* (*scientia media*) and pertains to conditionally future events dependent on the free will of man. These events will never happen, because the conditions for their happening will never be actually realized; but they would happen by the free choice of man, if these conditions would be actually realized. Hence, such events refer to things which a man *would* do through free choice under certain unfulfilled conditions; since these hypothetical conditions are never fulfilled, the events will never actually occur. The 'conditionally future events' are also called *futuribles* (*futuribilia*). The defenders of 'intermediate knowledge' maintain that this type of knowledge has a midway position between 'simple intelligence' and 'vision.' It agrees with 'simple intelligence' in that it deals with events and things which will never actually exist; it differs from it in that these events and things 'would' actually exist if certain conditions were fulfilled. For example, if Napoleon had not lost the Battle of Waterloo, Europe would (or would not) have fallen under his sway. It also agrees with 'vision' in this that it deals with (conditional) existing events and things; it differs from it in this that these events and things never will exist *de facto* but would come into existence if certain conditions would have been fulfilled. In the case of the Battle of Waterloo, Napoleon did not win it, and so the fate of Europe, as a consequence of Napoleon's hypothetical victory, remains unknown to us but known to God.

Viewed from the standpoint of the *manner* of God's knowledge of beings, this knowledge is either 'abstractive' or 'intuitive.' God's *abstractive* knowledge deals with events and things which never exist; His *intuitive* knowledge, with events and things which actually exist at one time or another.

Viewed from the standpoint of *prospective use,* God's knowledge is either 'speculative' or 'practical' or 'speculative-practical.' *Speculative* knowledge looks solely to the truth involved in knowing. Thus, God's knowledge of Himself is speculative. *Practical* knowledge refers to the use of knowledge for the making of something, when the intention of making is present. The knowledge which God has of the things he intends to create is a 'practical' knowledge. *Speculative-practical* knowledge is the knowledge required to make something, but the intention to make it is absent. For instance, God has the knowledge required for the creation of the purely possible beings; however, since He does not intend to create them and give them actual existence, this knowledge, though 'practical' in itself, remains 'speculative,' so that it is a 'speculative-practical' knowledge.

Viewed from the standpoint of God's *attitude* toward things, His knowledge is knowledge either of 'approbation' or 'simple cognition.' God's knowledge of *approbation* pertains to the good. God approves of all morally or (and) physically good things which have existed in the past, or exist in the present, or will exist in the future. *Simple cognition* in God pertains to all morally or (and) physically evil things; these He does not approve. Whatever is a moral or (and) physical evil is a defect, a privation, of a good, and as such it is a lack of being, something which is negative. God, of course, knows of the actual or possible existence of such an evil, because He perceives the defect in the good being, but He does not and cannot approve of the privation of what ought to be present. Every crime is thus known by God through the knowledge of 'simple cognition' without 'approbation' on His part.

It should be carefully noted that these various kinds of knowledge in God represent *no real distinctions* in God. Because of the limitation of his mind, man must form different concepts of God's intellect and speak of these kinds of knowledge *as if* they were diverse forms of knowledge. As has been said before, however, God is one single, infinitely perfect essence and exhausts all knowable truth regarding Himself and all things distinct from Himself.

The problem of the *scientia media* (intermediate knowledge) has agitated the minds of eminent scholastic philosophers for centuries. It might seem that here is the logical place to discuss the problem of 'intermediate knowledge.' Inasmuch, however, as the divine will-act plays a prominent part in the controversy, the discussion will be postponed until later.

Existence of God's Knowledge

In giving the proof of the existence of intellectual knowledge in God, one can make use of a general argument or of a special argument concerning the various kinds of objects.

The *general* argument.

Knowledge is a *perfection,* because it is a vital activity, and vital activity is a perfection for a living being. Animals belong to a higher level of being than plants and minerals precisely in virtue of their knowledge. Man is more perfect than animals and plants and minerals because of his rationality, his intellectual knowledge. Therefore, God must have knowledge. God being the cause of the intellect and intellectual knowledge present in man, he must also have an intellect and intellectual knowledge. Since God is infinitely perfect and absolutely simple, His intellect and its thinking must be infinitely perfect and absolutely simple. Because of His infinity, He must exhaust intensively and extensively everything knowable. Now, the knowable is the truth, and every kind of being is something that is knowable and in so far true. Therefore, everything that is a being must be known by God. But if God knows every kind of being, He must also know the privations affecting these beings, be they moral or physical. Consequently, nothing whatsoever is excluded from the knowledge of God, and *God knows absolutely everything.*

Everything is a 'being' which does not involve a contradiction, since only a contradiction is strictly a non-being, as it is also a non-truth. Now, whatever is *possible or actual* is really no contradiction; and this includes everything which is necessarily or freely possible, everything necessarily or freely actual (in the past or present or future), and everything conditionally future. These realities involve no contradiction and as such are 'knowable.' Hence, all these objects must be known to the infinitely perfect intellect of God. Consequently, *everything without exception* must be encompassed in an infinite manner in the act of God's knowledge.

The *special* argument.

That God has infinite knowledge of *Himself,* has already been shown; it follows necessarily from the fact that His essence and knowledge are identical. The problem here, then, is to prove that His knowledge also extends to all beings other than Himself.

God knows *possible realities.*

Whatever is possible can exist. But a thing can exist only because God can give it being and existence. Such a being, if it received being and existence, would be an *effect* whose perfections must be precontained in their cause, God. God, in giving them being and existence, cannot communicate to them a *part* of His own essence, because that would be contrary to His infinite perfection and immutability. Hence, in giving them being and existence, God can only give them a perfection *similar* to His own. He could never make anything dissimilar to His perfections; because the only thing dissimilar to Himself is nonentity ('absolute nothing') and God cannot make nonentity. Hence, things are possible only in so far as they imitate God's own perfections. However, since God knows His own essence, He also knows the *imitability* of His essence; otherwise He would lack this great perfection of self-knowledge. But He can only then know His own imitability if He knows the things that can imitate His perfections. The things, however, which can imitate God and His perfections in their own being and existence, are precisely the things that are 'possible.' Consequently, *God knows all possible realities.*

God knows *actual realities.*

At some time or other, in the past or present or future,

actual realities really exist. When they exist, they exist in the presence of God, because of the perfection of His *immensity* and *omnipresence.* Since God is present to them when they exist, He must certainly know them, otherwise His knowledge would be defective; and since His knowledge is eternal and immutable (being identical with His eternal and immutable essence), God must know them from eternity. It follows, then, that from all eternity God knows whatever realities will be actual in the course of time. Consequently, *God knows all actual realities.*

God knows all *future free acts* which actually occur.

The future free acts are acts which a free agent (for example, man) actually performs at some time as the result of a free decision of the will; they will actually occur at some moment in the future. Due to His *immensity* and *omnipresence,* God must be present to these free acts, and these free acts must happen in God's presence, when they actually occur. Hence, God must know them at the very *moment* when they really happen. Now, this knowledge of the future free acts is absolutely eternal and immutable, since it is identical with God's essence. His essence being eternal and as such prior to the temporal occurrence of these future free acts, His knowledge must also be eternal and prior to them. Consequently, God knows future free acts before they actually take place.

Furthermore, God being infinitely perfect in every way, His knowledge must also be infinitely perfect. In order that God's knowledge be infinitely perfect, it is necessary that He know everything which is *objectively true.* Now, all future free acts are objectively true; they will actually occur, and this is a truth which can be expressed in a true judgment. For instance, I am writing these words at the present moment, and this writing is the result of a free decision on my part; last night it would have been impossible for me to say whether I would be writing at this moment or not, because I myself did not know at that time what I would freely decide to do at this moment. However, now that I am writing, the 'fact' of my writing at this moment is an objective truth which can be expressed in the judgment that 'I am writing.' And since I am writing at this moment, the true judgment that 'I am writing' expresses a fact which God must have known from all eternity; He knew from all eternity that I *would* write at this moment, because He knows *now* that I am writing, and what God knows now He knows eternally. Hence, since God's knowledge is infinitely perfect, and since an infinitely perfect knowledge must know all truth, *God knows all future free acts* which actually occur.

It will be noticed that this thesis closely resembles the foregoing one. The difference lies in the fact that the acts under consideration are the result of a here-and-now free decision. The foregoing thesis dealt with actual realities in general.

God knows all *conditionally free acts* which will not occur.

'Conditionally free acts' are those which *would* have occurred as the result of a free decision, provided certain conditions had been fulfilled; the conditions, however, have not been fulfilled, and so these free acts *will never* actually happen. God must know such acts. All that is at stake in this proof is the establishment of the *fact* that God knows all conditionally free acts which will not occur, even though man may never understand 'how' God knows them. And now for the proof.

The infinitely perfect knowledge of God's intellect must embrace *everything true and knowable.* Now, even the free, conditionally future acts are true and knowable. Consider these two judgments: 'If the American Revolution in 1776 had miscarried, this country would be a colony of England today,' and 'If the American Revolution in 1776 had miscarried, this country would not be a colony of England today.' It is evident that one of the members of this disjunction is true and one is false, even though the condition has not been fulfilled. The two judgments are *contradictory.* Both simply cannot be true; one must be *true,* and the other must be *false.* We do not know which is the true judgment and which the false; but we do know that only one, and that a definite one, of these judgments must be true, while the other judgment must be false.

But now, since God knows all that is *objectively true and knowable,* He must, in virtue of the infinite perfection of His knowledge, also know which of these two judgments is true and which false. This, however, is only possible if He knows what event would happen in the hypothetical case mentioned above, *if* the condition given were verified, even though it was not and never would be verified. The fact itself is clear. In every case of conditionally free acts, though they will never actually occur because of the nonfulfillment of the conditions involved, something of a definite character *would have* occurred *if* the condition *had been* fulfilled. The truth contained in such conditionally free acts cannot be unknown to God.

Summing up, it is clear that *everything,* which in any way is *knowable,* must be known by God. If anything knowable escaped his knowledge, He would not be infinitely perfect.

Nature of God's Will

Will is a form of appetency, and an appetency (or, appetite), generally speaking, is the inclination or propensity of a being for something which is good for it. In a more special sense, appetency is the inclination or propensity of a being for an apprehended good. In this sense, it follows a cognition of the good, and this cognition may be either sensory or intellectual. In man, the appetency of an intellectually apprehended good is termed 'will,' so that the human will is defined as 'rational' appetency. In speaking of the human will as a 'rational' appetency, consideration is given to the fact that man possesses rationality and that man's intellect is a reasoning power or 'reason.'

God, as we have seen, does not 'reason' from premises to conclusions. His intellectual knowledge is pure insight, pure understanding, not reasoning. Reason concludes from the known to the unknown. For God's intellect, however, there is nothing unknown. In attributing 'will' to God, the imperfection of knowledge implied in 'reasoning' must be excluded. Intellectual knowledge, strictly as such, does not necessarily involve knowledge due to 'reasoning'; intellectual knowledge is more perfect when it is pure 'understanding' than when it is 'reason.' God's knowledge, being infinitely perfect, must be pure intellectual insight and intellectual understanding. Hence, God's *will* must be described as *an infinitely perfect intellectual appetency*.

Like the divine intellect, the divine will is an attribute of God's being. Entitatively it is one with God's essence. The essence of a being is conceived to be prior to anything which flows from the essence, and both intellect and will follow the constitution of the essence. Hence, although the 'will' in God is entitatively one with His essence, according to man's way of knowing God the will flows from His essence, and as such it is an 'attribute' of God. It is not a quiescent, but an active, attribute. Just as the intellect is the principle of knowledge (intellection) in God, so God's will is the principle of His volition. God's will, therefore, is an *operational attribute*.

The volition of God is identical with His being, as are all attributes of God. It is, therefore, self-subsistent. There is no real distinction between God's will, viewed as a 'power,' and His volition, viewed as an 'operation'; God's will is conceived as a 'logical power' with respect to its operation, so that there is only a 'logical distinction' between them. The volition of God is absolutely *simple,* because everything in God consists of one indivisible pure act; hence, God *is* His will and His volition. His volition is also *infinite* in perfection; this follows necessarily from the fact that His volition is one reality with His infinitely perfect being. Since volition always proceeds from the conscious apprehension of the good on the part of the intellect, it is obvious that there can be nothing blind and instinctive about the volition of God; it must be intellectually *conscious*. Similarly, there is nothing arbitrary about God's volition; it is essentially *well ordered,* so that He wills or loves Himself because of His infinite perfection and all other beings because of their similitude to His perfection.

The *object* of intellectual volition is the intellectually apprehended *good*. Man, as we know, may be in error regarding the nature of things and strive for an 'apparent' good rather than a 'real' good. God's intellect can neither be deceived nor be mistaken in its knowledge of what is good and what is evil; God knows all things as they actually are. God's will follows His intellectual knowledge. Now, the proper object of the will is the 'good,' just as the proper object of the intellect is the 'true.' There can, therefore, be no error in the object of God's operations of the will. If God has volition at all, it can only be centered on the 'good' as known by His intellect. God wills or loves all beings according to their intrinsic goodness and in proportion to their worth. He thus loves Himself as the Supreme Good supremely, and this love is a *necessary love,* without choice and with infinite intensity. His love for creatural beings, on the other hand, is a matter of *free choice,* so far as their existence and their amount of reality is concerned.

Existence of God's Volition

That God has a will and volition follows from His spirituality and intellectuality. According to sound psychology, an intellectual being, when in the presence of the 'good,' perceives that it is suitable to its own being and naturally desires it as an object to be sought and enjoyed. But 'seeking' and 'enjoying' are acts of a will in an intellectual being. Hence, unless this volition contains imperfection in some manner, it is a *pure perfection* and as such must be present in God. Naturally, man's volition is an operation superadded as a new reality to the power of the will and as such is an 'accident'; the will of man is 'dependent' on the objects with which it deals, because it cannot desire a good except under the condition that the good be presented to the will by the intellect. These imperfections, however, are not inherent in the will and its operations strictly as a 'will' and 'volition'; they pertain to man, because man is a being in which composition is a normal part of his nature. These imperfections removed, volition is a 'pure perfection.' God, however, possesses all 'pure perfections,' and in His being there can be no imperfections for the simple reason that everything in God is one infinitely perfect reality without accidents and without composition. Therefore, God has a will and volition capable of desiring the good presented by the intellect.

Furthermore, God would be *imperfect,* if He did not possess a will and volition. If God had no will, He could not control things or dispose of them as He wished; He could not issue any commands or prohibitions; He could not love anything, not even Himself. Under such circumstances, however, God would be very imperfect, less perfect than the ruler of a nation or the father of a family. Now, God cannot be imperfect from any standpoint. Consequently, He must possess a will and volition.

Finally, the very fact that *man* has a will and volition, is a clear proof that God must also have a will and volition. Man's nature is a contingent and caused reality given to him by God as the cause. Now, the cause must precontain the perfection of the effect either formally or eminently. Man, however, does not possess a will because he is an organic being; he is a 'man' and more than an animal, plant, or mineral precisely on account of his *spirituality*. Hence, man's spirituality and his *will resulting therefrom* are not 'mixed' but 'pure perfections' which must exist *formally* (strictly as such) in God. Consequently, will and volition are formally, not merely eminently, present in God.

There must be an *object* toward which the will and its volition is directed, and this object must be some *good*. From this it follows that God loves Himself and all other beings distinct from Himself.

God loves *Himself*.

The will of God is not a power or faculty; it is absolute and pure act, infinite in perfection. Since the divine will is an infinite act, it must also love an infinite object. Now, God alone is infinite in His reality. Therefore, God is the infinite object of the divine will and its volition. Hence, God loves Himself with an infinite love.

God loves *all other beings*.

All beings other than God are contingent in their essence and existence. The sufficient reason for their essence and existence does not lie in them but in God. God gives them their essence and existence. Hence, all beings which actually exist, have existed, or will exist, receive their existence ultimately from God, because He *wished* them to exist. But to 'wish' is to 'will' and 'love.' Consequently, God loves all beings distinct from Himself. This follows also from the fact that all creatural beings, whether they be *actual* or merely *possible,* can have essence and existence only in so far as they are (actual or possible) imitations of His own perfections. Now, God loves His own perfections, because His perfections are absolutely identical with Himself, and He loves Himself. Hence, God loves all other beings; otherwise He would not love His own being infinitely.

Only *being* can be a *good.* Only 'being' is something which is knowable in itself, and only the 'knowable' can be known in itself. Hence, only 'being' can be proposed by the intellect to the will as a 'good.' It is evident, then, that God's will *cannot love privations, defects, and evils* as an object, because such things (if we wish to call them 'things') are nonentities, nonbeings, nothing; 'nothing,' however, since it is a negation of being, cannot be the object of volitional activity: there is nothing to will.

Necessity and Freedom in God

'Necessity' and 'freedom' are opposing concepts. What is 'necessary' cannot be 'free,' and what is 'free' cannot be 'necessary.' In a general way, freedom is the absence of necessity. In order to understand the question of 'necessity and freedom in God,' it will be advisable to clarify their meaning.

In a *wide* sense, freedom is the absence of external coercion or restraint which hinders an appetency from expressing itself in external action. Thus, a shackled person lacks the freedom of movement; when the restraining shackles are removed, he has 'freedom from coercion.'

In a *strict* sense, freedom is the absence of intrinsic necessity or determination in the performance of an act. Something is 'intrinsically necessary' when it is determined by its very nature to be what it is and to act as it does. Applied to the will, 'freedom' means that the will is not necessitated by its nature to act in a determined manner, but is capable of choice even when all the conditions for acting are present.

There are *three types of freedom* in the acts of the will, so far as human volition is concerned. First, there is the *freedom of exercise* or contradiction; the will can choose freely between willing and not willing, between acting and not acting. For instance, a person can freely choose to read or not to read. Second, there is the *freedom of specification;* the will can freely choose between one object and another object and therefore also between one act of the will and another act of the will. Thus, a person can freely choose between the act of reading and the act of taking a walk. Third, there is the *freedom of contrariety;* the will can freely choose between a moral good and a moral evil. A person, for example, can choose between telling the truth and telling a lie. The 'freedom of contrariety' is reducible to one or the other of the first two types, since it is a choice either between acting or not acting or between one object or another object.

The *freedom of the will* is thus defined as *the ability of the will, all conditions for action being present, to decide whether to act or not to act and whether to act in this manner or in that manner.*

The essence of the freedom of the will, as just defined, consists in *indetermination,* so that the will, no matter what the nature of the antecedent external and internal conditions for action may be, is not determined to act by necessity. The absence of the freedom of the will is what is meant by *necessity,* so that the will, the conditions for action being present, *must act* in a determined manner.

After these preliminary explanations of 'necessity' and 'freedom,' the problem of their presence in God's volition should not be difficult to solve.

God loves *Himself necessarily.*

God's willing is purest act. As such, it demands an *adequate* object. This adequate object is God Himself, since He alone is infinite, and the adequate object of an infinite act must be infinite. But now, since the infinite volition of God is identical with God's essence, it must be as necessary as God's essence is. And since the act of volition consists in love, God loves Himself *necessarily;* that is to say, His love of Himself is *not free,* but determined by His very nature.

God loves *all other things freely.*

All beings other than God are *finite* regarding their *number* and the *amount of perfection* present in their being. This is evident. There must be a sufficient reason for this number and amount of perfection. The sufficient reason cannot lie in the *essence of the beings.* Their essence being the same, all the 'possible' individuals of the same essence would have to have received existence also. Experience, however, shows that this is not so; for instance, there could be more human beings in existence than actually exist. Nor can the sufficient reason be found in the *necessity of creation* on the part of God. This necessity on the part of God could find its proper explanation only in a *need* of God for creatural beings; unless this 'need' were present, there would be no 'necessity' for creation. However, God, as the infinitely perfect and self-sufficient Being, cannot have a 'need' for anything outside Himself. Since, therefore, we find the necessity for creation neither in God nor in the creatures, the sufficient reason for the definite number and amount of perfections in creatural beings must reside in the *free decision* of God. Hence, God wills, and therefore loves, all creatures freely.

Again, if there were a *necessary relation* between God's will and the existence of creatural beings, He would of necessity be constrained to create either nothing at all or everything possible or some beings to the exclusion of the rest. None of these alternatives is true.

The first alternative, that God would be necessitated to give existence to *nothing at all,* is manifestly *false.* We ourselves and many other creatural beings actually exist.

The second alternative, that God of necessity gave existence to *everything possible,* is also manifestly *untrue.* More things are possible and could, absolutely speaking, exist than actually do exist.

The third alternative, that God was necessitated to give existence to *some things to the exclusion of the rest,* is also *untenable.* Why should God be compelled to give existence to the limited number? At one time all creatural beings were merely possible and not actually existing. As 'possible' beings, they were all on a footing of equality. There can, then, be no reason in the possible beings *themselves* why God should be necessitated to create just some, and not more or less. Since all possible beings can imitate God's perfections, all have the possibility of receiving existence, so far as they themselves are concerned. If, then, a necessity exists to give some existence rather than others, the reason for this necessity must be *in God.* But what could constrain God? Certainly, the infinite imitability of God's infinite perfections cannot be exhausted by the existence of some creatural beings to the exclusion of others, because all possible beings are imitable of God's perfections. If there were any reason for this necessity in God, it could only be that He were constrained by His nature to make the *best* things His power could produce. Such a supposition implies that the present world is the *best possible world.* But this is not the best possible world. To leave all other beings out of consideration, man knows from his own personal experience that he himself labors under many physical, intellectual, and moral defects; he could be better than he actually is. And that is also true of other beings. But if the necessity for creating the present world as it is lies neither in the creatural beings themselves nor in God, then there can be no necessity for God to create this world as it is, giving some beings existence to the exclusion of the rest. Now, 'necessity' and 'freedom' are opposites; if there is no 'necessity,' there must be 'freedom.' Consequently, God's will is *free* in relation to the existence of creatural beings. But if God wills them freely, He also loves them freely.

The conclusion, therefore, is inevitable that He loves *Himself* with an absolutely *necessary* love and *all other beings* with an absolutely *free* love.

Liberty and Immutability

The activity of the free will in man is connected with potentiality. The freedom of man's will is the result of a power or faculty which is indifferent to different acts and objects. Every act of man's will is an added perfection, an accidental determination, and this addition of perfection involves a change in the will. On account of His absolute simplicity, a change or a superadded perfection in God is an impossibility. Since God is *ens a se,* a self-subsistent being, He is pure actuality, and His infinite perfection is an absolutely *necessary* perfection.

God's will-acts being identical with His *necessary* essence, *how can they be free?* Must not His will-acts be just as necessary as the divine essence? But can a free reality be necessary and a necessary reality free? Is not a *contradiction* involved in the very concept of the freedom of God's will?

That the *reconcilation* of God's freedom and immutability presents a grave difficulty, is apparent. Immutability seems to exclude all self-determination. Can a higher unity be effected between them?

We must bear in mind first of all, that there must be many things in an infinitely perfect being which cannot be grasped and comprehended by man's finite mind; there must be many *natural mysteries.* Man would have to have an infinite mind to encompass infinite perfection. Man's inability to fathom certain truths, so long as these truths are firmly established, cannot as such shake their validity. The inability to understand something is no criterion of its truth or untruth. *Contradictions,* of course, are not and cannot be true; and whenever contradictions are irrefutably shown to exist, man knows that an error must have been committed. But when speaking of the infinitely perfect being, we must be very careful in our assertions. Many things, when applied to creatures, may involve a contradiction in the very terms and would be physically and metaphysically impossible; but they need not be a contradiction in an infinitely perfect being. Thus, to speak of absolute simplicity or infinite perfection in a creatural being, or of free will in a brute, is a contradiction. When applied to a higher being, however, we perceive that no contradiction is necessarily involved.

Then how about God's *freedom* and *immutability?* Is no satisfactory explanation available? The following explanation, given by St. Thomas,[3] is offered as a *solution* of the problem. He says: "Sometimes a necessary cause has a non-necessary relation to an effect; owing to a deficiency in the effect, and not in the cause. Even so, the sun's power has a non-necessary relation to some contingent events on this earth, owing to a defect not in the solar power, but in the effect that proceeds not necessarily from the cause. In the same way, that God does not necessarily will some of the things that He wills, does not result from defect in the divine will, but from a defect belonging to the nature of the thing willed, namely, that the perfect goodness of God can be without it; and such defect accompanies all created good. . . . As the divine existence is necessary of itself, so is the divine will and the divine knowledge; but the divine knowledge has a necessary relation to the thing known; not the divine will to the thing willed. The reason for this is that knowledge is of the things as they exist in the knower; but the will is directed to things as they exist in themselves. Since then all other things have necessary existence inasmuch as they exist in God; but no absolute necessity so as to be necessary in themselves, in so far as they exist in themselves; it follows that God knows necessarily whatever He knows, but does not will necessarily whatever He wills."

The solution of St. Thomas can be expressed in a somewhat different way, as follows. The free act of the divine will, considered *entitatively,* is *necessary,* because it is identical with God's essence which is self-subsistent and necessary. This same act of the divine will is *free* in its *relation to the contingent object* to which it is directed. The reason for the freedom of the act of the divine will lies in the 'direction' of the act, and this direction brings in a *logical relation* between the act of the divine will and the contingent being. There can be no question

---

[3] *Summa Theologica* (New York: Benziger Bros.), I, qu. 19, art. 3, ad 4 et 5.

of a physical or metaphysical composition or change in God on this account, because this relation is only 'logical.' In the human will there is an indifference of the 'faculty' (the will) in regard to its respective acts, and through its acts it is indifferent to the 'objects,' and thus the will is free. In God, however, the will is not a 'faculty' but a *pure act,* and this pure act is *indifferent directly in regard to the contingent objects.* Man has one faculty and a real multiplicity of acts; God has one act and a *virtual* multiplicity of acts. In other words, *entitatively* (in so far as the act has 'being') the act of the divine will is one with God's essence and therefore *necessary; terminatively* (in so far as the contingent being is the 'object' or 'term' of the act), the act of the divine will is *free.*

Is the mystery hereby explained? It is not. But it is a solution which removes the apparent contradiction involved in the concepts of God's freedom and immutability. After all, a contradiction exists when one affirms and denies the same thing in the same respect of the same subject. Thus, if one were to say that 'God is immutable' and that 'God is not immutable,' that would be a contradiction; or, if one were to say that 'God is free' and 'God is not free,' that would be a contradiction. In both instances, however, it would be necessary to maintain the same respect or standpoint in the affirmation and denial; otherwise there might be only an *apparent* contradiction. The solution of St. Thomas is acceptable, because it leaves intact the established truth of God's necessity and immutability and also preserves the equally established truth of the freedom of God's will. At any rate, his solution avoids an open contradiction, and that is sufficient for a solution to be acceptable in a matter so deep and mysterious.

Much more could be said about God's intellection and volition. So much, however, should be clear from what has been given above: God has an intellect and a will and also their corresponding operations of knowledge and volition. But intellect and will and their respective acts must ultimately be identified with God's infinitely perfect essence. *That* this is so, is manifest; *how* this is so, exceeds the capacity of the human mind.

Summary of Chapter XII

This chapter deals with God's internal operational attributes of *intellection* and *volition*.

1. *Nature of God's Intellection.* — God, being spiritual in essence, possesses intellectual life. God's *act* of knowledge is identical with His substance, self-subsistent, immutable, simple, infinitely perfect; it is an absolute understanding, true, infallible, and independent of creatures.

2. *The Object of God's Knowledge.* — The *formal principle* of knowledge contains a double element: the 'external' element of the 'known object' and the 'internal' element of the 'intelligible species.' The 'intelligible species' of God's knowledge is the divine intellect itself; the 'object known' is God Himself as the primary object and all things distinct from God as the secondary object.

3. *Kinds of Divine Knowledge.* — Man distinguishes various kinds of knowledge in God's intellect: simple intelligence and vision, and (as many claim) intermediate knowledge (*scientia media*); abstractive and intuitive; speculative, practical, and speculative-practical; knowledge of approbation and simple cognition without approbation.

4. *Existence of God's Knowledge.* — *General argument.* Knowledge is a perfection, because it is a vital activity. Since God is infinitely perfect, He must know absolutely everything knowable.

Special argument. Truth is contained in everything that is 'being.' It is therefore contained in the purely possible realities, in the actual realities, in the future free acts which will actually occur, and in the conditionally free acts which will not occur because the condition of their existence was not fulfilled. Now, infinitely perfect knowledge must embrace everything true and knowable. Therefore, God knows all these objects of knowledge.

5. *Nature of God's Will.* — God's will is an infinitely perfect intellectual appetency. It is self-subsistent, absolutely simple, infinitely perfect, conscious, and well ordered. Its object is the intellectually apprehended 'good.'

6. *Existence of God's Volition.* — That God has a will and volition follows from His spirituality and intellectuality. God would be imperfect without a will and volition. Volition is not a 'mixed' perfection but a 'pure' perfection, because 'love' is a pure perfection.

There must be an 'object' toward which God's volition is directed, and this object must be some 'good.' God thus loves *Himself* and *all other beings.*

7. *Necessity and Freedom in God.* — 'Necessity' and 'freedom' are opposing concepts. Applied to the will, freedom is the ability, all conditions for action being present, to decide whether to act or not to act and whether to act in this manner or in that manner.

God loves *Himself necessarily,* because His will and volition are identical with His essence, and His essence is necessary.

God loves all *other beings freely.* The sufficient reason for the number and the amount of perfection present in contingent beings cannot be due to their 'essence'; otherwise all possible beings of the same essence would also have to exist. Nor can the sufficient reason lie in the 'necessity of creation,' because God does not 'need' creatures; He is absolutely perfect and self-sufficient. Again, if there were a necessary relation between God's will and the existence of creatural beings, He would of necessity be constrained to create either nothing at all or everything possible or some beings to the exclusion of the rest. None of these alternatives, however, is tenable. Therefore, God loves (wills) all creatural beings freely.

8. *Liberty and Immutability.* — God's will-acts being identical with His necessary essence, how can they be free? *Entitatively,* the act of the divine will is one with God's essence and therefore *necessary; terminatively,* the act is indifferent toward creatural objects and therefore *free.* The whole matter is a natural mystery.

Readings

Boedder, Bernard, *Natural Theology,* Bk. II, Chaps. IV, V. — Joyce, George Hayward, *Principles of Natural Theology,* Chaps. XI, XII. — Brosnan, William J., *God Infinite, the World, and Reason,* pp. 37–67. — Mercier, D. Card., *A Manual of Modern Scholastic Philosophy,* Vol. II, 'Natural Theology,' Part III, Chaps. I, II. — Garrigou-Lagrange, R., *God: His Existence and His Nature,* Vol. II, Chaps. III, IV. — Smith, Gerard, *Natural Theology,* Chaps. XIII, XIV.

CHAPTER XIII

OMNIPOTENCE AND CREATION

BESIDES the immanently operational attributes, which produce no external effects, there are also present in God *virtually transitive* operational attributes and activities, which produce (or, at least, 'can' produce) external effects. Chief among these are omnipotence and creation, concurrence and conservation, providence and governance.

God, of course, need not have made any creatures. As the supreme and infinite good, He is absolutely and infinitely sufficient unto Himself. He is and would eternally have been 'omnipotent' even under the supposition that no creatures exist, because He could always have given them essence and existence had He so desired and decided.

As a matter of fact, creatural beings do exist. We ourselves, for instance, and many other beings have existence. The problem, therefore, arises: How did creatural beings come into existence *originally?* The solution to this problem is: through the omnipotent, creative activity of God. *Omnipotence* and *creation,* then, must now be discussed.

The Notion of Omnipotence

The core of 'omnipotence' is the concept of 'power,' and *power* is the ability to do something or produce something. Power is the principle of action. Action may be either performance or production. Action always results in some effect, either in doing something or in producing something. It is in creatural beings that man first notices effects; and from such effects he concludes to the existence of 'power' capable of producing effects, because every effect demands a corresponding cause. Some effects are primarily 'immanent,' perfecting the active subject, as in the case of thinking, willing, and other vital operations; or, they may be primarily 'transient,' perfecting the passive recipient, as in the case of making steel out of iron or of throwing a ball. Whether the effects be the result of mere performance ('doing something' immanently) or efficient causality ('producing something' transiently), power is necessary to bring about the result.

In speaking of God's 'omnipotence,' reference is not made to His immanent (vital) activity but to His power to *produce* something transiently through efficient causality.

Omnipotence, as the word indicates (Lat., *omne,* all, everything; *potentia,* power), means that *God can produce everything.* Since there can be no 'passive power' in God, namely, the power to receive some perfection from some other being, omnipotence necessarily means 'active power,' namely, the power to produce all effects through efficient causality. And when it is stated that God can produce 'everything,' it is well to note the word 'thing.' The word *thing* is equivalent to *being,* and 'being' means whatever can exist. Omnipotence, therefore, implies that God can give existence to whatever can exist. In other words, God can produce whatever is *possible.*

The opposite of 'possible' is 'impossible.' Impossibility is either relative or absolute. Impossibility is *relative* when something exceeds the capability of a particular power; it does not involve a contradiction in itself, but the power in question is lacking or is too feeble to produce it. Thus, an ordinary man cannot lift an object weighing a ton; it is not a contradiction in itself to lift a ton, but the power of an ordinary man is incapable of doing it. What is impossible for the ordinary man need not be impossible for a machine with hydraulic equipment. Relative to an ordinary man, then, the lifting of an object weighing a ton is an impossibility; relative to a greater power, however, it need not be an impossibility. Impossibility is *absolute* when something exceeds the capability of every power; it involves a contradiction in its very concept, so that it is really a non-being, a 'nothing.' God, for instance, cannot sneeze or cough, blush or have indigestion, become weak or grow old, and so forth.

If God did any of these things He would be a 'material' being, while in reality He is a 'spiritual' being; a 'material-spiritual being,' however, is a contradiction and as such a not-being which cannot exist. Similarly, God cannot make a square circle or a stick with only one end or a stone so heavy that He cannot lift it. A 'square' consists of straight lines, and that excludes the round line of a circle; a 'circle' consists of a round line, and that excludes the straight lines of a square: since both the 'square' and the 'circle' are eliminated, there is nothing for God to make. In all such cases, the fault is not with God's power; the fault is with the supposed thing, because such a thing, involving a contradiction in itself, is a non-entity; where there is nothing to make, God cannot make it; where the effect cannot exist, no cause can give it existence. The only thing opposed to 'being' is 'absolute non-being,' sheer 'nothingness.' Anything that is a 'being' at all can exist, and such a being is 'possible.'

The statement that *God is omnipotent* means that he can give existence to *any possible being without exception,* and a 'possible being' is one that does not contain a contradiction in its very concept or term.

Like other perfections of God, His omnipotence is *formally immanent* but *virtually transient;* that is to say, His omnipotence, considered from the viewpoint of its reality, is identical with God's essence, but it can produce beings distinct from the divine essence. God's omnipotence is 'extensively' and 'intensively' infinite. It is *extensive* because God's power can bring into existence anything and everything 'possible' and because it can never be exhausted. In other words, God can never come to a point where there would be nothing more to make, since there is absolutely no limit to His efficient causality. The *intensive* infinity of God's power consists in this that He produces beings with perfect independence; hence, He causes them without the assistance of an instrumental cause, without the influence of any extraneous causality, without difficulty or exertion. Having specified the meaning of omnipotence, its existence in God must be proved.

Existence of God's Omnipotence

God is omnipotent.

In God there can be no composition of power and essence. God's power is identical with the divine essence; and since the divine essence is infinite, the divine power must be infinite. Now, infinite power must be *omnipotent;* that is, it must be able to bring to existence whatever can intrinsically have existence. Everything, however, which does not involve a contradiction in its concept is absolutely possible and as such can intrinsically have existence. God's infinite power, therefore, must be able to give existence to all that is absolutely possible. But to give existence to a thing is to produce it. Consequently, God's infinite power must be able to produce all that is absolutely possible. And that is the meaning of 'omnipotence.'

This capability on the part of God's power to produce all possible beings must be present in God. If God could not produce *everything* that is possible, He would be able only to produce *some* things, no matter how large the number might be, to the exclusion of at least one other possible thing. Evidently, that power would be greater and more perfect which would also include this one other possible thing. Consequently, a power that cannot produce *all* possibles is not the greatest and most perfect conceivable; it would surely not be infinitely perfect, because it would lack some perfection. But God's power is infinitely perfect, because it is identical with His infinitely perfect essence. God's power, therefore, must be able and is capable of producing all things which are intrinsically possible. Hence, God is truly omnipotent.

God's power is inexhaustible.

If ever God reached a point where His power would be exhausted in its productivity, so that nothing more could come into existence through His efficient causality, the power of God would be gone. However, together with the cessation of God's power, His essence would be gone and cease to exist. This would be inevitable, because the divine power is identical with the divine essence. Hence, if God's power would be exhausted, *God Himself would cease to exist.* That, however, is impossible. Consequently, God's power cannot be exhausted in its productivity.

One cannot say that God's power would be exhausted if there were *no more objects to produce.* In such a case the divine power would not really be exhausted; the store of possibles would simply be exhausted. However, even this latter assumption cannot be consistently maintained. Since the divine essence is infinite in perfection, its imitability by creatural realities must also be without limit. As a result, the store of possibles could be exhausted only if the divine essence were limited in its perfections (and its imitability limited in consequence of this condition) or if the actual number of imitations were infinite. But either alternative involves a contradiction. The 'infinite' perfection of God cannot be 'limited'; if it were, the 'infinite' would be 'finite'; and that is a contradiction. That an 'actually infinite number' of creatural imitations also involves a contradiction, will be shown in a later section. Therefore, the store of possibles is inexhaustible, and God's power is also inexhaustible.

It follows, then, that God's power can produce whatever is intrinsically possible, and it is inexhaustible in its productivity. God, therefore, is truly *omnipotent in power.*

From the omnipotence of God one cannot legitimately conclude that He must be capable of producing an *infinite effect.* An 'infinite effect,' like a square circle, belongs to the category of the absolutely impossibles; it involves a contradiction in its very concept. Since an 'infinite effect' is an *effect,* it is something that is *produced* and *dependent.* Now, 'being produced' and 'dependence' are absolutely incompatible with 'infinity'; a produced and dependent being is by the very fact of its production and dependence essentially 'finite.' The contradiction is evident. Being an 'effect,' it is finite; being an 'infinite' effect, it is 'infinite.' But a finite-infinite being is a contradiction, and as such it is an impossibility; it is a nonentity, a nothing, which cannot receive existence.

The Foundation of Possibles

A thing is said to possess *external* possibility when a power exists which can produce it. It possesses *internal* possibility, when the thing as such can have or receive existence, without regard to the actual existence of a power which can, as a matter of fact, actually produce it. The question now to be discussed is this: What is the *reason,* the *foundation,* for this 'internal possibility'? What is the reason, the foundation, why some things are intrinsically possible (and therefore 'can' exist) while other things are intrinsically impossible (and therefore 'cannot' exist under any circumstances)?

The answer to this question will be different, depending upon whether one asks for the *immediate* or *ultimate* foundation of internal possibility. Both answers will be given.

The *immediate foundation* of the internal possibility of the possibles lies in the *compatibility of the elements* which constitute the *essence* of a thing.

This is shown by the *idea* of 'internal possibility.' That thing is said to be intrinsically possible whose constituting elements do not contradict one another, but which can exist together; in other words, whose constituting elements are compatible and sociable. If one asks why a 'man' is intrinsically (internally) possible, it is because 'animality' and 'rationality' (the constitutive elements of the idea of 'man') can be united in one concept and realized as one being; these elements of man's nature are thus compatible and sociable.

Reversely, a thing is intrinsically or absolutely impossible whose constituting elements contradict one another and so cannot exist together; such contradictory elements are incompatible and insociable. Thus, a 'square circle' is intrinsically impossible, because 'square' and 'circle' contradict and mutually exclude each other; because of the incompatibility and insociability of the elements of 'square' and 'circle,' a 'square circle' is neither a square nor a circle, but absolutely nothing.

The immediate reason or foundation of internal possibility,

therefore, is the *non-contradiction, the compatibility,* of the thought-elements constituting the idea of a thing. This is called the *formal principle* of internal possibility.

There must be a reason, a foundation, for the intrinsic possibility of the possibles which lies deeper than the essence of the possible things themselves. The question is: What is the *ultimate* reason and ground why some constitutive elements are compatible, thereby making a being intrinsically possible, while other elements are incompatible, so that a being is intrinsically impossible?

God is the *ultimate* ground of the intrinsic possibility in all possible things.

This must be so. The intrinsic possibility of things must have its ultimate reason and foundation *outside the entire class of possibles.* Being only 'possible,' they themselves cannot give to themselves constitutive elements which would be either compatible or incompatible. If the ultimate ground for the compatibility or incompatibility of the constituting elements of their being were found in them, they themselves would be the reason or principle why some things are intrinsically possible (for example, a mountain of gold) and others intrinsically impossible (for example, a square circle). The possibles, however, are *subject* to the law of contradiction and non-contradiction (intrinsic possibility), regarding both their essence and their existence, and as such must *conform* to this law in order to be 'possible' at all. They cannot, then, be the reason or principle of this law. Hence, there must be some being outside the entire class of possible beings, which is the ultimate reason or foundation of their intrinsic possibility. Now, there is only one being outside the entire class of possible beings, existent and non-existent, and that is God. God, therefore, is the ultimate ground of the intrinsic possibility of all things.

What, precisely, is it in God that must be conceived to be the ultimate foundation of intrinsic possibility?[1]

---

[1] See the author's *The Domain of Being* (Milwaukee: The Bruce Publishing Co., 1939), Chap. VII.

God's essence is the ultimate ground of intrinsic possibility.
God is the ultimate ground for all possibility. But there must be something in God which is logically prior and deeper than His omnipotence, will, and intelligence, which is the ultimate reason why some constitutive elements of creatural essences are compatible or incompatible. This can only be God's *essence.*

A possible thing is fundamentally a 'being,' an 'essence,' while an impossible thing is fundamentally a 'non-being,' a 'non-essence.' Now 'being' ('essence') cannot have its ultimate ground in anything but 'being' ('essence'), because 'being' can proceed only from 'being' and 'existence' from an 'existent.' Consequently, God's existing *being* or *essence* is the ultimate foundation for the intrinsic possibility of things. Because God possesses 'being' to the fullness of infinite perfection, other things can obtain 'being' from Him in a limited and participated degree; they are *creatural imitations* of God's essence which He can *produce.* Thus, they are capable of receiving existence (that is to say, they are 'possible') from His omnipotence, through an act of His will, guided by His intelligence. On the other hand, a 'non-being,' a 'non-essence,' a 'nothing,' is the antithesis of God's being and essence and can, therefore, not imitate God in any way; for that reason such a thing is incapable of receiving existence from Him, that is, it is 'impossible.' Anything, consequently, which involves a contradiction in its very concept, is 'nothing'; and 'nothing' cannot exist. God could never make it either extrinsically or intrinsically possible without contradicting His own intelligence and essence.

God's essence is thus seen to be the *ultimate* reason, or ground, or *foundation of all intrinsic possibility,* just as His omnipotence, guided by His will and intelligence, is the ultimate ground for all extrinsic possibility. This is equivalent to saying that God's essence is the ultimate reason why the constitutive elements of creatural essences are compatible among themselves; and God's omnipotence is the ultimate reason why creatural beings can be produced and thereby receive actual existence. The only thing which God cannot produce through His efficient causality is that which is 'nothing,' and 'nothing' imposes no kind of limitation on either God's being or His power.

The Notion of Creation

Closely related to God's omnipotence is the concept of *creation*. First, though, it will be necessary to obtain an accurate notion of what 'creation' means.

Creation is a type of productive action, and productive action always terminates in an effect. Correspondingly, creation may be defined either with emphasis on production as the starting point of the action (*terminus a quo*) or with emphasis on the produced reality as the goal or termination-point of the action (*terminus ad quem*). Some philosophers prefer the first method; others, the second. One thus finds different definitions of 'creation.'

St. Thomas uses both methods in his works. Thus, he says: "The proper mode of His action is to produce a whole subsistent thing"[2]; "Creation is the production of a being"[3]; "to create is to make something from nothing"[4]; "creation is the production of the whole being."[5] In these definitions he begins with the productive action as it proceeds from God. In the following definitions he places the emphasis on the produced thing: "Creation, which is the emanation of all being (*totius esse*), is from the *not-being* which is *nothing*"[6]; "Creation, whereby a thing is made according to its whole substance."[7]

Later scholastics have combined the two standpoints into one comprehensive definition. 'Creation' is thus defined technically as *the production of a thing hitherto not existing, without the use of any subject-matter from which it is produced (productio rei ex nihilo sui et subjecti).*

Creation is said to be *productio rei*, 'the production of a

---

[2] St. Thomas Aquinas, *Summa Contra Gentiles,* tr. by the English Dominican Fathers (New York: Benziger Bros., 1925), Bk. II, Chap. XVI.

[3] *Ibid.,* Bk. II, Chap. XVIII.

[4] *Summa Theologica* (New York: Benziger Bros.), I, qu. 45, art. 2, ad 2.

[5] *Ibid.,* art. 4, ad 3.

[6] *Ibid.,* art. 1.

[7] *Ibid.,* art. 3.

thing.' It is a 'production,' and this word signifies the making of something through the positive action of an efficient cause. It is the production of a 'thing,' and 'thing' here means as much as a 'being' or a 'reality.' Creation is said to be *productio rei ex nihilo sui,* 'the production of a thing hitherto not existing.' This means that the 'being' in question is something new, something that did not have existence before the productive action gave it existence; it simply begins 'to-be,' to exist, in virtue of the efficient causality of the producing cause; before this cause gave it existence, it was a relative 'nothing,' something merely possible, but not as yet an actuality in the realm of existent beings. Creation is said to be *productio rei ex nihilo sui et subjecti,* 'the production of a thing hitherto not existing, without employing any subject-matter from which to produce it.' The phrase *ex nihilo subjecti* excludes any and every kind of pre-existent substrate, such as matter, out of which the new being might be produced. In other words, creation is not a 'change' or 'generation' of one being out of another being. When parents beget a child, for example, their productive action is not a 'creation' in the technical sense of the term, because their action presupposes the previous existence of a material substrate (ovum and semen) as necessary conditions for the process of fecundation; this process is therefore called 'generation' or 'procreation' rather than 'creation' strictly as such. Similarly, when an organism changes nonliving food into its own living substance in digestion, its action is a 'productive action,' but it is not 'creation,' because the food is already in existence at the time. In order that a productive action be truly a 'creative' action, the new thing, both from the standpoint of its own being and from the standpoint of any kind of pre-existing substrate from which it could derive existence, must be 'nothing.' It is this *productio rei ex nihilo subjecti* which properly characterizes creation. That is what St. Thomas meant when he spoke of "the whole subsistent being," "substantial being," "whole being," "all being (*totius esse*)," "whole substance"; and that is why he defined 'creation' as "making something from nothing."

By 'creative power' is thus understood the power to produce
something *out of nothing*. The phrase 'out of nothing' does not
imply that 'nothing' is some sort of material or substratum out
of which something is made, as a statue is carved out of a
shapeless mass of marble or a cup is molded out of formless
clay; the phrase means that there is *no pre-existent material of
any kind out of which* the (created) thing is made, but that
the 'total being' of the thing is produced by the creative power.

No one, except an out-and-out occasionalist or phenomenalist,
denies that creatural beings exercise true productivity through
efficient causality. Chemical compounds, plants, animals, and
men are being continuously produced through causal action.
The earth, the solar system, and the galaxies are constantly in
a process of change through the interaction of bodies. Man
unceasingly produces physical changes in himself and in other
beings. In all these changes the effects observed are the results
of *transmutative action*. These effects are either accidental or
substantial, as the case may be, but they are always a *changing*
of one kind of existing being into a different kind of existing
being. Creation, as the production of the 'total being' out of
nothing, is never observed to happen.

The problem of the divine action of creation is not concerned with *organic* or *cosmic evolution*. 'Organic' evolution
pertains to the probable development of organisms here on
earth or wherever they may be found to exist. 'Cosmic' evolution pertains to the probable development of the universe, as it
presently exists, from a former state. Both types of evolution
interest the philosopher because of the Principles of Sufficient
Reason and Causality. Evolution is a factual problem which
must be solved primarily by the natural sciences. Even if one
accepts the fact of evolution, evolution *presupposes* the things
which evolve, whether these things be organisms or celestial
matter: evolution cannot occur unless something exists which
can evolve.

What is at stake is the *origin*, the *first beginning*, of things,
not their subsequent change and development. If the universe
is a development of matter which has existed from eternity

without a beginning, it is evidently not a created universe; on the other hand, however, if it had a beginning in time, it is evidently a created universe. The question, therefore, is this: Must we accept 'creation' as the logical explanation of the existence of the universe?

Opponents of Creation

The *Jews* always maintained that the world was created by God. The first line of the Book of Genesis states expressly: "In the beginning God created heaven and earth." To 'create' was understood in the sense of a 'production out of nothing.' This can be seen from the words of the mother[8] of the Machabees, addressed to her youngest son just before his martyrdom: "I beseech thee, my son, look upon heaven and earth and all that is in them: and consider that God made them out of nothing, and mankind also." The *Christians,* too, have defended creation at all times, both in their religious doctrines and in their philosophic dissertations.

To the *pagans* of antiquity creation was practically unknown. *Polytheism* is essentially an anthropomorphic religion, and its anthropomorphism is reflected in its doctrines concerning the limited power of the deities. Even the greatest of the *Greek philosophers* (not to speak of the lesser ones) never quite succeeded in arriving at the concept of creation as a 'production out of nothing.' Plato expressly taught that matter was eternal. Aristotle, although he argued to the existence of a personal God, presupposed the eternity of matter; matter became 'transformed,' but it never had a real beginning.

It remained for the modern *pantheists* and *finitists* to have the dubious distinction of reviving the pagan concept of God by eliminating creation entirely or by reducing the creative action of God to a production of limited effectiveness. Ever since Spinoza, Fichte, Schelling, and Hegel launched their pantheistic systems, many thinkers, tired of the superficiality of materialism, have found mental refuge in the identification

---

[8] 2 Mach. 7:28.

of divinity with the world. God, in their view, is 'immanent' to the world, in the sense that God and the world are one ultimate reality. A goodly number of modern scientists, weaned away from their Christian heritage, subscribe to the doctrine of a modified pantheism. Science, strictly as such, is neither pantheistic nor theistic, for the simple reason that the field of scientific research is limited to the physical facts which are observable and measurable. Scientists, however, are not so restricted, and thus it frequently happens that scientists leave their field of science (in which they are recognized as authorities) and enter the field of philosophy (in which they are not authorities). But they think they can justifiably carry their scientific ideas over into the domain of philosophy. Many scientists are now convinced that the universe is limited, finite; the universe also shows intelligent purposiveness, and so they are also convinced of the existence of 'mind' in the universe. Not being able (or willing) to dissociate this mind from the reality of the universe, they identify Mind or God with the universe as a whole. The result is a *finite God*. Edgar Sheffield Brightman[9] gives expression to the view of modern finitists when he says: "We need a temporalistic rather than a purely eternalistic view of God. . . . Thus our finite God is not one of finished perfection; his perfection and the perfection of this world consist in their perfectibility."

Pantheists and finitists find the concept of creation as a 'production out of nothing' unpalatable. As Eddington[10] says: "Philosophically the notion of an abrupt beginning of the present order of Nature is repugnant to me, as I think it must be to most." Or, as James Ward puts it:[11] "The ordinary notion of creation — viz. that at a given moment there was no world and at a subsequent moment the world was there — is rejected as having no sort of analogy with experience, and as therefore

---

[9] *The Problem of God* (Nashville, Tenn.: Abingdon-Cokesbury Press, 1930), p. 129 f.

[10] *New Pathways in Science* (Ithaca, N. Y.: Cornell University Press, 1934), p. 59.

[11] *The Realm of Ends* (New York: G. P. Putnam's Sons, 1911), p. 191.

unthinkable." Pringle-Pattison[12] has the following to say: "The more thoughtfully we consider the idea of creation, as a special act or event that took place once upon a time, the more inapplicable does it appear. . . . God exists as creatively realizing Himself in the world, just as the true Infinite is not a mere Beyond, but is present in the finite as its sustaining and including life." One can quote many modern authors expressing themselves in a similar vein.

All we are interested in from the standpoint of philosophy is the establishment of the *ultimate cause* of the world. Neither the age of the world nor its original arrangement (whether as 'formed' or as 'chaotic') is a philosophic problem. God's existence has already been established; now His creatorship must be established.

Proof of Creation

In proving creation, the purpose is not to prove *how* God produced things out of nothing, but simply to prove *that* God produced them in this manner. The *fact* of creation is what must be proved, and this fact is proved as follows.

God is omnipotent; and to be omnipotent means that the infinite power of God can produce (give existence to) whatever is *intrinsically possible,* that is, to anything which does not involve a contradiction in the constitutive elements of its concept. Now, the concept of 'producing a thing out of nothing' *involves no contradiction.* The crux of the whole problem resides in this last statement; hence, it cannot be accepted without proof, and this proof must now be given.

The concept of creation is *not self-contradictory,* like the idea of a square circle or of an animate-inanimate organism. The 'production' of things is a common occurrence in the world. New beings are continually being produced, as is evidenced by daily experience. They originate through change and generation through the causal efficiency of other beings. Atoms are made and unmade; chemical compounds are formed

---

[12] *The Idea of God* (New York: Oxford University Press, 1917), pp. 302, 312.

and dissolved; plants, animals, and men come into existence and die. In every such instance of 'production,' of course, a pre-existent substrate of some kind is present. 'Production' itself, therefore, offers no difficulty: 'What is, can be.' But production 'out of nothing' contains no more contradiction than mere 'production' itself, when it is a question of the *first origin* of finite beings. Everything in this world is *finite* and *contingent;* that was shown in the proof for God's existence. Now, 'finite' and 'contingent' being does not have the sufficient reason for its existence in itself; or such a being would be 'infinite' and 'necessary.' Since all beings in this world are 'finite' and 'contingent,' they must have the sufficient reason for their existence in a being outside the world, namely, in the infinite and necessary being of God. But if they have the sufficient reason of their existence in God, that means that God *gave* them existence, that God *brought* them from non-existence to existence. However, outside of 'everything in this world' there is nothing but God. Therefore, God, if He gives them existence, can give them existence by 'producing them without a pre-existing subject,' that is to say, 'out of nothing.' In fact, there is no other way that God *can* bring about the *first origin* of the contingent beings of this world. 'Production,' in the strict sense of the word as 'giving existence to a new being,' necessarily includes the concept of 'efficient cause'; but the concept of a 'pre-existent subject (material cause)' out of which the new being is effected is neither included nor excluded. The elements of 'efficient cause' and 'absence of a pre-existing subject' are thus seen to be compatible, at least in the omnipotence of God. It follows, then, that 'efficient cause' and 'production out of nothing,' since they are not contradictory, *may be united* into the single concept of 'creation' without contradiction. Creation, therefore, must be intrinsically possible because it involves no contradiction in the concept.

Now, omnipotence can perform anything intrinsically possible. Creation, however, is intrinsically possible, as has just been shown. Consequently, creation is possible to God.

God, therefore, *can create.*

The entire universe is contingent, because the universe is nothing more than the sum of all the beings which form the parts of it, and all the single beings in the universe are not necessary but contingent. Hence, the entire universe must have had its *first origin* from God. In other words, the entire universe must have been 'produced out of nothing.' One cannot say that the entire universe was made out of pre-existent matter, because matter is an essential part of the universe. If, then, the entire universe, together with its constituent matter, had to be given existence through the efficient causality of God's omnipotence, it had to be produced 'out of nothing.' But the universe exists. Therefore, its *first origin* could not have been achieved except through a production out of nothing. That, however, is 'creation.' Consequently, *creation is a fact.*

The fact of creation also follows from the infinite perfection of God's power. Being infinitely perfect, it must be *absolutely independent* of any assistance in the exercise of its efficient causality. Hence, God's power must have been absolutely independent of any pre-existent subject, such as primordial matter.

God, therefore, *created the world out of nothing.*

The reason why creation is necessary for the first origin of things is not difficult to find. Whenever creatural beings produce something, production is always the result of *changing* one kind of thing into another kind of thing; it is the changing of a 'this' to a 'that.' But in the case of the first origin of things, the *whole being* of these things is involved, not merely a 'this' and a 'that.' Hence, in the case of the first origin of things, they cannot be produced by a mere 'change.'

St. Thomas expressed this truth very admirably, when he said:[13] "We must consider not only the emanation of a particular being from a particular agent, but also the emanation of all being from the universal cause, which is God; and this emanation we designate by the name of creation. Now what

---

[13] *Summa Theologica* (New York: Benziger Bros.), I, qu. 45, art. 1 et 2.

proceeds by particular emanation, is not presupposed to that emanation; as when a man is generated, he was not before, but man is made from *not-man,* and white from *not-white.* Hence, if the emanation of the whole universal being from the first principle be considered, it is impossible that any being should be presupposed before this emanation. For nothing is the same as no being. Therefore as the generation of a man is from the *not-being* which is *not-man,* so creation, which is the emanation of all being (*emanatio totius esse*), is from the *not-being* which is *nothing.* . . . If therefore God did only act from something presupposed, it would follow that the thing pre-supposed would not be caused by Him. Now it has been shown above (Q. 44, AA1, 2), that nothing can be unless it is from God, Who is the universal cause of all being. Hence, it is necessary to say that God brings things into being from nothing."

God Alone Can Create

The questions to be answered are these: Can God alone create? Can a creature act as the principal cause of creation? Can a creature act as an instrumental cause of creation? The pertinent terms are obviously 'principal cause' and 'instrumental cause.'

A *principal cause* is one which has a fully proportionate and sufficient power to produce the entire effect either alone or by using something else as instrumental cause in its pro-ductive action. An *instrumental cause* is insufficient of itself to produce the entire effect but causally influences the production of the effect under the direction and in the service of another (the principal) cause. A normal person, for instance, has the power to open his eyes in order to see; his own power is fully proportionate and sufficient to produce the effect of opening his eyes, and he does not need the assistance of any other thing to produce this effect. This same person, in order to drive a nail into a board, uses the instrumentality of a hammer; he is the 'principal cause' of this effect, because without his causality the hammer would not function. The hammer is the 'instrumental cause,' because its own peculiar causality of driving the nail into the board is used under the direction and in the service of the person acting as the principal cause.

God, of course, can create; that has been established. The *question* then arises: Can a creature be either the 'principal' or the 'instrumental' cause of creation? In answering this question, the matter under consideration refers to the *natural* power of a creature to be either the principal or instrumental cause of creation. Whether a creature can exert instrumental creative power in the 'supernatural' field is a disputed question which does not properly belong to philosophy.

The *Arians* taught that God created the Logos (Word), and the Logos in turn created all else. *Avicenna* maintained that the material world was created by the angels. *Frohschammer* defended the theory that parents create the souls of the children they generate. *Durandus* and *Arriaga* claimed that creation was at least possible to creatures.

No creature can be the *principal* cause of creation.

Creative power does not produce a particular kind of being, but *being as such* (*esse quâ esse*). This is clear, whether we view the creative act in its starting-point or in its terminal point.

Viewed in its *starting-point* (*terminus a quo*), the creative act begins with *not-being as such,* because there is nothing present from which the created being is produced. To this 'not-being as such' is opposed, not a specific kind of being, a 'this' or 'that,' but simply and absolutely 'being as such.' Viewed in its *terminal point* (*terminus ad quem*), namely, in the effect of the creative act, the effect is *being as such,* because that which is produced is always 'being as such' and not merely a particular kind of being. True, creation produces 'this' or 'that' kind of reality, so that a definite, specific kind of being receives existence; but the peculiar and proper effect of creation is the production of the *first being* (*primum esse*) of the whole thing, since the latter existed in no way and in no part before. Change and generation can produce a definite, specific kind of being (for instance, man can generate man), but it cannot confer 'being as such' to the new reality.

Now, the most universal effect demands as its sufficient reason the most universal cause. But 'being as such' (*ens quâ ens,* or *esse quâ esse*) is the most universal effect, because it enters in the concept and essence of everything *real* and *possible.* Hence, creative power must be able to produce everything that is real and possible. Such a power, however, must be *infinite,* because the store of possible imitations of God's infinite perfections is inexhaustible. Hence, if a creatural being could be the principal cause of the creative act, it would have to be capable of giving existence to everything real and possible. That, however, necessarily exceeds the power of any and every creatural thing, because its very being, and consequently also its power, is something essentially finite and limited. God alone is infinite, and there can be no more than one infinite being. Hence, no creatural thing can possess infinite power, so that it would or could be the principal cause of creation. It follows, therefore, that no creature can, in its natural capacity, be the *principal* cause in the creative production of any reality.

Nor can the creature be the *instrumental* cause of creation.

In order that something be an 'instrumental' cause in a productive action, it would really have to *influence the effect causally,* according to whatever way it acts as an instrument. A hammer, for instance, contributes its share toward the production of the total effect by pounding; a knife by cutting; and so with every type of instrument acting as a partial cause. An instrumental cause acts only under the direction of, and in the service of, a principal cause; but it must contribute its influence, in its own characteristic way, according to its nature.

Now, in the creative act this effect of the instrumental causality of the creature would have to either precede or follow or accompany the effect of the principal cause (God). But none of these alternatives is possible. The characteristic effect of the instrumental causality of the creature *cannot precede* the effect of the divine principal cause, because before creation there is nothing to which its causality could be directed. It *cannot follow,* because, once God as the principal cause has effected creation, there is nothing afterward for the instrumental cause to effect. It *cannot accompany* God's creative action: it would have to produce the entire existence of the created being, since existence is an indivisible reality, and then it would be the principal cause; or, it would not produce existence at all, since existence is an indivisible reality, and then it is no cause whatsoever. Now, a creatural being cannot be the principal cause of creation. Consequently, no creature can be the instrumental cause of creation.

This argument follows the line of St. Thomas[14] on this matter. To quote: "It happens that something participates in the proper action of another, not by its own power, but instrumentally, inasmuch as it acts by the power of another; as air can heat and ignite by the power of fire. And so some have supposed that although creation is the proper act of the universal cause, still some inferior cause, acting by the power of the first cause, can create. . . . But such a thing cannot be, because the secondary instrumental cause does not participate in the action of the superior cause, except inasmuch as by something proper to itself it acts dispositively to the effect of the principal agent. If therefore it effects nothing, according to what is proper to itself, it is used to no purpose; nor would there be any need of certain instruments for certain actions. Thus we see that a saw, in cutting wood, which it does by the property of its own form, produces the form of a bench, which is the proper effect of the principal agent. Now the proper effect of God creating is what is presupposed to all other effects, and that is absolute being. Hence nothing else can act dispositively and instrumentally to this effect, since creation is not from anything presupposed, which can be disposed by the action of the instrumental agent. So therefore it is impossible for any creature to create, either by its own power, or instrumentally that is, ministerially."

---

14 *Ibid.,* I, qu. 45, art. 5.

God alone can create.

This conclusion is a necessary consequence from what has just been said. If a creatural being is neither the principal nor the instrumental cause of creation, it simply cannot create. But it is neither the principal nor the instrumental cause of creation. Therefore, a creatural being cannot create. God, however, can create. And since no other being can create, *He alone can create.* Creation, therefore, is the essential and incommunicable privilege of the omnipotent power of God.

As St. Thomas[15] states: "If a greater power is required in the agent in proportion to the distance of the potentiality from the act, it follows that the power of that which produces something from no presupposed potentiality is infinite, because there is no proportion between *no potentiality* and the potentiality presupposed by the power of a natural agent, as there is no proportion between *not being and being.*"

Eternity of Creation

God exists from eternity. The question, therefore, naturally arises: Can God create from all eternity? This question leads to the next: *Can a created thing exist from eternity?*

God being omnipotent, it is manifest that He can give existence to anything which is intrinsically possible. Whatever is intrinsically impossible (that is, is contradictory in its very concept), cannot receive existence from God because it is essentially 'nothing'; and 'nothing,' of course, cannot exist. The problem thus simmers down to the question: Is an 'eternal creation' a contradiction in terms, or not? If not, God can create an 'eternal creature'; if it is, God cannot create it. God could not create it, not because of a lack of power on His part, but because there would be nothing positive on the part of the creature which He could produce.

The problem has puzzled philosophers a great deal, and *three opinions* have been advanced in an effort to solve it. The *first* view affirms the possibility of an eternal creation of

---

15 *Ibid.*, I, qu. 45, art. 5, ad 3,

things, both of those things which form a 'successive series' and of those which are 'permanent.' Among the advocates of this view are St. Thomas[16] (who claimed that the impossibility of an eternal creation cannot be 'demonstrated' by reason, although it is clear from revelation that the world had a beginning in time), Vasquez, the nominalists, and many thomists. The *second* view affirms the possibility of an eternal creation regarding 'permanent' things, but denies the possibility regarding 'successive' things. This view is defended by Suarez, Molina, John of S. Thomas, Urráburu, and others. The *third* view denies the possibility of an eternal creation regarding every type of created being, 'successive' or 'permanent'; they claim that an 'eternal creature' is a contradiction in terms, because of the contingency of the creature, and so an 'eternal creation' is intrinsically impossible. The majority of scholastics adhere to this third view.

The *third* view seems the *more probable,* both with regard to 'successive' and 'permanent' things.

An eternal creation of successive things is impossible.

The supposition is twofold: there is a series of successive realities, and this series is created. In this series of members, one succeeds the other. Since these members of the series succeed one another, some are later and some are earlier than the others in this succession. Such a succession, however, must inevitably lead to one member before which there was no other and after which all the others follow. This first member of the series is the *beginning of the succession,* and the entire series can thus be measured according to a *before* and *after* in its *succession.* But a succession measured according to 'before' and 'after' is the characteristic of *time.* Consequently, the first member of the series represents the *beginning of time.* Eternity, however, is not time and has no beginning. Hence, such a series would have creatures which are in time and are not in time, are eternal and not eternal, are arranged according to a

---

[16] *Ibid.,* I, qu. 46, art. 2.

'before' and 'after' and are not arranged according to a 'before'
and 'after,' have a beginning and have no beginning. In other
words, an 'eternal creature,' created by God in eternity, is a
contradiction in terms and as such impossible. God, therefore,
cannot create from eternity; and this impossibility is due to
the nature of the 'creature' as a creature, not to God as
omnipotent.

An eternal creation of permanent things is impossible.

An eternal 'permanent' being, one in which there is no
change, must be indestructible. Eternity means duration without beginning and without end. Therefore, an eternal being
is one which has all possible duration simultaneously. Now,
what the omnipotence of God creates it can also destroy; if He
is capable of giving existence, He must also be capable of
taking existence away. No created being has necessary existence; this is clear from the very fact of its creation. Hence, it
can be destroyed by God in any moment of its duration. A
being, however, which can be destroyed by God and lose its
existence in any moment of its duration, can have an *end to
its duration*. But where there is an *end* to duration, there must
also be a *beginning* to duration; a duration, however, which
has a beginning and (or) an end, is not eternity but *time*.
Either, then, God does not have the power to destroy such
a creature, or the creature is not eternal. But it is evident that
God possesses this power of destruction. Therefore, the supposedly 'permanent' creature is not eternal. But if the creature
cannot be eternal, God cannot create a creature from eternity
without contradiction. Consequently, an *eternal creation* of any
kind is *impossible* because it is contradictory to the very nature
of a created being.

Infinite Number of Creatures

God is infinitely perfect, and He can, absolutely speaking,
be imitated by creatures in any number of ways. It is, therefore, pertinent to ask: *Can God create an actually infinite number of creatures?* The answer is very much like the one given
in the foregoing section. There is no limit to God's omnipotent

power or to His imitability by creatures. But an 'actually infinite number' of creatures involves a contradiction in terms
and as such is impossible. It makes no difference whether one
postulates the simultaneous or successive existence of these
creatures; the number would exist simultaneously or successively, but it would be 'actually infinite' in either case.

An actually infinite number of creatures is impossible.

That an actually infinite number of *successive* beings or
events implies an actually infinite number of *simultaneously
existing* beings, is clear. God could, for example, create an
immortal soul every time one being or event succeeds the
other. And thus there would exist an actually infinite number
of 'successive' and 'simultaneous' things at the same time.

Now, it is intrinsically impossible that an actually infinite
number of beings exist simultaneously.

An actually infinite number is limitless and inexhaustible.
If it were limited, or if it could be exhausted, it would obviously
not be infinite but finite. Now, the concept of an infinite
number or multitude ends in a *contradiction*. Any number is
made up of units; it is also made up of couples and tens, etc.
Consider the result. There must be twice as many units as
there are couples in such a number, and ten times as many
units as there are groups of ten. For example, if an actually
infinite number of human persons were created by God, the
number of arms would be twice the number of human beings,
and the number of fingers would be ten times the number of
human beings. But the number of human beings is supposedly
'infinite,' that is, limitless and inexhaustible; and yet the number of human beings is only half as large as the number of
arms and one tenth as large as the number of fingers. It
follows that there are *different infinities,* some smaller and
some larger, some half and some twice the amount of the
other, some one tenth and some ten times the amount of the
other; and yet they are *the same,* because all are infinite.
Halving the infinite number would result in two infinites, and
yet only one, because two finite numbers cannot add up to
infinity; since two finite numbers are limited and each is ex-

haustible, their addition cannot result in an infinite number, and still they would. In fact, since an actually infinite number is limitless and inexhaustible, it would remain the same notwithstanding an infinite number of divisions and subtractions. All this, of course, is *self-contradictory.*

Hence, an actually infinite number of created beings is *intrinsically impossible.* In other words, no matter how many creatures God produces, His being can still always be imitated by other creatures without limit; other creatures are possible, and their possibility is inexhaustible. This means that the number of creatures which can exist, either simultaneously or successively, is *negatively infinite;* that is to say, the existing number can only be *actually finite,* but it is *potentially without limit.*

Therefore, God cannot create an infinite number of actually existing creatures, due to the fact that such a number is intrinsically impossible in actuality. God being actually infinite in perfection, his imitability by creatural beings, and as a consequence also their *creability,* is limitless and inexhaustible.

A few more strokes have now been added to the portrait of God's nature: His power is almighty and creative. Obviously, God does nothing aimlessly, because He is an intelligent being. The *reason* why God created the world at all, and the reason why He created just this amount of beings in the world, cannot lie in the creatures themselves, but must lie wholly in Himself. He did not create because He needed them; He is absolutely self-sufficient, and He was infinitely happy from all eternity. The only assignable reason for creation, therefore, can be this: God, being *infinite goodness,* freely decided, under the guidance of His intelligence, to communicate being to creatures in order that they might *share* in His infinite being and goodness. *Bonum est diffusivum sui,* goodness tends to diffuse itself.

Summary of Chapter XIII

This chapter treats of two virtually transitive (or transient) operational attributes of God, namely, *omnipotence* and *creation.*

1. *The Notion of Omnipotence.* — The basic concept underlying omnipotence is 'power.' Omnipotence means the power to produce everything which is possible (can exist); and something is 'possible' whose existence does not involve a contradiction in its very concept.

2. *Existence of God's Omnipotence.* — Since the divine essence is infinite, the divine power is also infinite. God's omnipotence, therefore, must be able to produce everything existible, without exception. Hence, God is *omnipotent.*

God's power is *inexhaustible.* His power is identical with His essence. If His power would or could be exhausted, God Himself would cease to exist and He would not be infinitely perfect.

God cannot produce an *infinite effect.* An 'effect' is something produced and dependent; as such it is finite. An 'infinite effect,' therefore, involves the contradiction of a being which is 'finite-infinite.'

3. *The Foundation of Possibles.* — The *ultimate reason* (or foundation) why some beings are non-contradictory (possible) and others contradictory (impossible) lies in *God;* not in the creatures themselves, because they are subject to the law of contradiction and non-contradiction.

God's *essence* is this ultimate ground. A thing is possible because it denotes a 'being,' and something is a being because it is an imitation of the 'being' of God.

4. *The Notion of Creation.* — Creation is the production of a thing hitherto not existing, without the use of any subject matter from which it is produced (*productio rei ex nihilo sui et subjecti*). It means, therefore, the production of a thing out of nothing.

5. *Opponents of Creation.* — The opponents of creation are the ancient pagans and modern pantheists and finitists.

6. *Proof of Creation.* — The problem is that of the *first origin* of the universe. The concept of creation does not involve a contradiction. 'Production' itself occurs constantly. Production 'out of nothing' is not self-contradictory, when it is a question of the first origin of creatural beings on the part of God's productive power. There is no other way that God can give existence to the first things than by producing them 'out of nothing.' Therefore, God *can* create.

If the universe exists, it must, therefore, have been produced by God out of nothing. But it exists. Consequently, creation is a *fact.*

7. *God Alone Can Create.* — If a creature can be neither the principal cause nor the instrumental cause of creation, then God

alone can create. The creature, however, can be neither the principal nor the instrumental cause of creation.

No creature can be the *principal* cause, because the effect of creation is 'being as such,' and no creature has the power to give existence to 'being' absolutely; it can only change a 'this' to a 'that.' It takes infinite power to bring something from a not-being to being. Nor can a creature be the *instrumental* cause of creation. If it were, its own proper causality would have to either precede, follow, or accompany the effect of the divine principal cause; none of the alternatives is possible. Therefore, *God alone can create.*

8. *Eternity of Creation.* — An eternal creation of *successive* things is impossible. Where there is such a succession, there is a 'before' and 'after' in succession; that, however, is *time, not eternity.*

Neither is an eternal creation of *permanent* things possible. If such a creature is eternal, it is indestructible; if it is a creature, it can be destroyed by God, and then its duration would not be eternal.

9. *Infinite Number of Creatures.* — God cannot create an actually infinite number of creatures, because an actually infinite number would involve a *contradiction in terms.*

Readings

Garrigou-Lagrange, R., *God: His Existence and His Nature,* Vol. II, Chap. 52. — Boedder, Bernard, *Natural Theology,* Bk. II, Chap. VI. — Joyce, George Hayward, *Principles of Natural Theology,* Chaps. XIV, XV. — Brosnan, William J., *God Infinite, the World, and Reason,* pp. 67–89. — Glenn, Paul J., *Theodicy,* pp. 245–258. — St. Thomas Aquinas, *Summa Theologica,* I, qq. 45 et 46.

CHAPTER XIV

CONSERVATION AND CONCURRENCE

OMNIPOTENT power is creative power. Because creatural beings are contingent, they do not have the reason for their essence and existence in themselves. Of themselves, they are nothing. The sufficient reason both for their essence and existence must reside in the necessary being, in the self-existent essence, in God. God *is* His existence; all other beings have *received* existence. They were 'created,' and for this reason they are rightly termed 'creatures.'

What most people do not realize, however, is the fact that creatures are dependent on God for more than the initial giving of existence. They seem to think that, once created, all creatural beings are capable of enduring in their existence and of performing their proper functions without any further action on the part of God. This view is erroneous.

For continued endurance in existence, creatures need the active *conservation* of God, and for the performance of all their functions they need the active *concurrence* of God. While the conservation and concurrence of God are not as clear to the average mind as the dependence of all creatures for their initial existence on God, a little thought will show their necessity.

Notion of Conservation

By *conservation,* in general, one understands continuation in existence through dependence on a cause. Taken 'passively,' it means that a being continues in its existence through some cause; taken 'actively,' it means that something is the reason why a being continues in its existence. Since we are concerned here with God as the cause of the continued existence of creatures, conservation is taken in its meaning of *active* conservation.

Active conservation can be either 'negative' or 'positive.' *Negative* conservation occurs when a being continues in existence *by not being destroyed* by another, although the other has the power to destroy it. Thus, a person negatively conserves a building by not demolishing it; or, a person conserves some papers by not throwing them into the furnace to be consumed by fire. In all such instances, the 'negative' conservation consists in refraining from performing the action required to make the thing cease to exist, although the person could execute the required action if he so desired.

Positive conservation occurs when a being is made to remain in existence *through some action* which is performed. This action may be either 'indirect' or 'direct' in its conservative power. *Indirect* positive conservation takes place when the action *hinders* destructive causes from destroying a thing or *provides the means* needed for the thing to remain what it is. Thus, rescuing a drowning person is indirectly the cause of preserving this person's life by hindering the water from filling his lungs and making breathing impossible; or, giving food to a starving person enables him to continue living and not to die of starvation. *Direct* positive conservation takes place when the continued duration of a thing is the *immediate effect of the positive action* of a cause. In such a case the thing in question cannot continue in existence without the continuation of the influence of the cause. Thus, color vision is possible only so long as the causal influence of light persists; vital activity in a living body is dependent on the immediate action of the soul, the principle of life in the body.

In speaking of divine conservation, it is necessary to guard against certain misconceptions. That God does not preserve in existence all things in their specific nature for all time, is clear from the mere fact that very many beings (for example, individual atoms and compounds, plants, animals, and men) come into existence, remain for a while, and then disappear as specific entities. That He preserves all things for the time of their actual existence with a 'negative' conservation, is evident from the fact that many things actually do exist at the present moment and actually have existed during the past; God certainly could annihilate them at any time in the past or present, but He does not do so. That not all beings which exist are preserved in their existence by God with a positive 'indirect' conservation (in the sense mentioned above), is manifest in the case of spiritual beings, such as immaterial human souls; spiritual beings, since they are simple in essence, cannot be dissolved and destroyed by natural agencies, and thus they need no 'indirect' conservation on the part of God to keep them in existence.

Proof of Divine Conservation

In recent years *E. Iglesias* proposed that divine conservation need not extend to all creatures without exception. According to him, God conserves in existence all subsistent beings which He has created; these 'subsistent' beings are primordial matter, angelic spirits, and human souls. On the other hand, 'nonsubsistent' beings, such as 'material forms' and 'accidents' (the latter are qualifications or determinations of substances), are not necessarily conserved by God in their existence; they can be conserved by other natural causes without any direct operation of God's conservative power.

This view is in opposition to the doctrine of all scholastic philosophers. *St Thomas* summarizes[1] the common doctrine on divine conservation in the following manner: "The being of every creature depends on God, so that not for a moment could it subsist, but would fall into nothingness were it not kept in being by the operation of the divine power."

We agree with St. Thomas and contend that *God preserves all things without exception by a positive and direct influence.* The proof rests upon the *contingency* of all beings distinct from God.

Every being, distinct from God, must be one of three types:

---

[1] *Summa Theologica* (New York: Benziger Bros.), I, qu. 104, art. 1.

it must be either a 'spirit' or a 'material being' or a 'compound of matter and spirit.' But these things are all *contingent,* that is to say, they have been created and have not the reason for their existence in their own essence; of themselves and in virtue of their own essence they are nothing. Consequently, they must have the sufficient reason for their essence and existence in another. So long as they have a contingent essence, they have the sufficient reason for their existence in another. Now, they retain their contingent essence during the entire period of their existence, from the first moment until the last. Therefore, during the entire period of their existence, from the first moment until the last, they are contingent and have the reason for their existence in another. Hence, they owe the entire period of their existence, from the first moment to the last, not to themselves, but to another.

This sufficient reason for existence cannot be found in their 'spiritual substance' or in their 'matter,' because both this spiritual substance and this matter are contingent and constitute the contingent essence of the being; hence, since they are totally contingent, they must also have the sufficient reason for their existence in another. And this truth applies to the entire universe and every being in it, because every created being as such is contingent. It follows, then, that the sufficient reason for the existence of the entire universe and of every being in it and of every created being as such, from the first moment to the last, must be found in a *noncontingent being.*

Now, there is no 'noncontingent being' except the *ens a se,* because the self-subsistent being alone has the reason for its existence in its own essence. But the *ens a se* is God. Consequently, just as the *initial* existence of the creatural being is contingent and, because of this contingency, needs the positive and direct activity of God to give actual existence to the being, so also its *continued existence,* because it remains contingent from the first moment until the last, demands the same *positive* and *direct influence* of God's activity. Hence, all creatural beings are preserved in their existence, from the first moment until the last, by the positive and direct influence of God's activity. That, however, is what is meant by divine *conservation.* Divine conservation, therefore, is a necessity.

One cannot validly say that a created *substance* can *preserve itself,* once it has acquired existence. This existence is contingent, not necessary, and as such demands a *cause.* The substance itself cannot be this cause; if it were, a patent contradiction would be involved, since such a situation would presuppose existence as well as non-existence at the same time in the same thing. It presupposes *existence;* because, if a being is the cause of its own continued existence, it must exist in order to exert its causality. It presupposes *non-existence;* because existence is the effect and result of the being's preserving action. Hence, the cause for the being's 'continuation' in existence must be in another, just as the cause of its 'beginning' had to be in another. Now, the entire universe is but the sum-total of creatural beings. Consequently, the entire universe (and every single being in it) must have the cause of its continuation in existence in the extra-mundane Being, namely, in *God.*

Nor can one validly say that the cause of the continuance of a being in existence lies in some *force* or *faculty.* Every force and faculty needs a substance as its basis. Every substance, however, owes its existence to God's positive and direct influence, as was just shown. Hence, since every force or faculty is by nature posterior to its substance and depends for its existence on the existence of the substance, it is incapable of preserving the substance in existence. In other words, both the substance and its force or faculty demand the positive and direct influence of God's conserving power in order to receive existence and to remain in existence.

Just as God has the power to create, He has the power to *annihilate.* He is the Supreme Lord over all things. He gives existence, and He can also make a thing cease to exist. Since annihilation means to 'make a thing cease to exist,' it cannot consist in any sort of positive activity. Every positive activity must have as the term of its influence a positive effect. Annihilation, however, has as its term a 'nothing,' a 'nil.' Hence, it cannot consist in a positive action on the part of God. Still, annihilation is something. Consequently, since it is no positive activity itself and still must be something on the part of God, it must consist in the *withdrawal of some positive activity* on the part of God. Now, if annihilation ('making a thing cease to exist') consists in the withdrawal of some positive activity of God, then the *perseverance* in existence on the part of the creatural being must be due to the *positive activity* of God which is withdrawn in annihilation. Hence, perseverance in existence, or continued existence, must be due to a positive activity of God; and that is divine conservation.

Creatural beings can neither create nor annihilate. All that creatural beings are capable of doing through the influence of their efficient causality is to *change already existing bodies.* Such changes are either accidental or substantial; but in every such change *matter* is always present as the existing subject of change. Since creatural beings cannot give existence to matter, they are incapable of producing anything *ex nihilo sui et subjecti;* that is to say, they are capable of generation and corruption, so that they can change a 'this' into a 'that,' but they cannot produce the *total reality* of the thing. The existence of this 'total reality' is not due to creatural beings but to God alone. And since creatural beings cannot *produce* the total reality of any being, they cannot *preserve* this total reality in existence either. This preservation in existence, or conservation, must be due to the uncreated being who produced the total reality by creation in the first place, namely, to God. This agrees with what St. Thomas[2] writes: "God cannot grant to a creature to be preserved in being after the cessation of the Divine influence: as neither can He make it not to have received its being from Himself. For the creature needs to be preserved by God in so far as the being of an effect depends on the cause of its being. So that there is no comparison with an agent that is not the cause of *being* but only of becoming."

---

[2] *Ibid.,* qu. 104, art. 1, ad 2.

Creatures, of course, also possess the power of conservation and exercise it in behalf of other beings. But it must be remembered that whatever creatures can accomplish in the line of conservation depends on the specific essence they have; they themselves, however, are not the real reason why they have this essence rather than another. It is God who gave the specific essence to things and who established the order between things. Hence, *God* is the *principal cause* of creatural conservation in *all* beings, while *creatures* are only the *secondary causes* (*concauses,* together with God as the principal cause) of conservation in a *limited* measure.

What is the *relation* between God's power of *creation* and His power of *conservation?* Fundamentally they are one, with a logical distinction between them. As St. Thomas[3] expresses this truth: "The preservation of things by God is a continuation of that action whereby He gives existence." For this reason conservation is often called a 'continued creation.' The phrase must not be confused with 'iterated creation,' as Pierre Bayle (1647–1706) interpreted conservation. An 'iterated creation' would mean that creatures fall back from moment to moment into nothingness and then are continuously recalled from moment to moment into existence by God. That such an interpretation is false, is evident, because man knows from his own conscious experience that he remains constantly in existence from moment to moment.

The *nature* of the conservative action on the part of God consists in the *omnipotent will-act* of God which, after creating a being, makes a being already created *remain* in existence.

Notion of Divine Concurrence

Divine *concurrence* (*concursus*) is defined as God's influence operating with the creatures in producing the same effect as they produce through their own activity. This concurrence or co-operation may be of different kinds.

---

[3] *Ibid.,* qu. 104, art. 1, ad 4.

Concurrence is either 'moral' or 'physical.' *Moral* concurrence consists in some sort of moral action, such as commands, exhortations, promises, rewards, and punishments. The 'moral' concurrence of God is not in question here. God's *physical* concurrence consists in a physical action through which He co-operates with the actions of creatures, so that He influences the effects produced by creatures through their actions.

The divine 'physical' concurrence will be either 'mediate' or 'immediate.' God's physical concurrence is *mediate* in so far as He *prepares* the creatures in such a way that they are fit for action and *preserves* them in that condition. Thus, God creates a thing with certain powers of action (operative powers); He preserves the thing and its operative powers, so that it is capable of action; He is the ultimate cause that the thing in its own proper order is the sufficient cause for a certain action. In mediate concurrence God sees to it that the 'causes' of action are present and fit to operate under proper conditions, but mediate concurrence does not bring about the effects of creatural actions strictly as 'effects.'

By means of His *immediate* physical concurrence, in the very moment when the creature acts in the production of an effect, God *effectively* and *directly* influences the creature in the production of the action itself. In other words, God and the creature are the two coefficient principles in every creatural action; every creatural action owes its efficacy and existence to God as the *primary* and *superior* cause and to the creature as the *secondary* and *subordinate* cause. The meaning of this statement is not, of course, that the action of the creature is due under all respects to the immediate concurrent action of God; that would be 'occasionalism,' which denies any real action of the creature, and occasionalism is false.

The *real meaning* of the immediate physical concurrence of God in all creatural actions has been well expressed by B. Boedder:[4] "What we do assert is that, although under one aspect the action of a creature is truly its own action depending on its own

---

[4] *Natural Theology* (New York: Longmans, Green & Co., Inc., 1927), p. 361 f.

activity, under another it is at the same time dependent on God, and this not only mediately but immediately. In other words, the creature in action depends upon a causal exercise of the omnipotent Divine Will, not only for the existence and preservation of its nature and faculties, but also for the actual exercise of those faculties; so much so that it can use none of them unless the Creator, in the very moment when the faculty is used, supports it with the efficacy of His Divine power. To this power the creature owes not only its faculties as applicable for action, but also as applied to act."

Both together, God and creature, produce the *totality* of the action, and the action could not occur without the causality of both effectively influencing the action. Each assists in the production of the effect to such an extent that the effect simply would not exist if either cause would not operate. Illustrations for this principle are readily available. In order, for example, to have an organ recital, a player, a wind pumper, and organ pipes are required; each agent contributes toward the totality of the effect (the music), and without the effective contribution of each cause the entire effect would be absent. Similarly, for every creatural action without exception divine concurrence is necessary for the totality of the effect. And this divine concurrence is not merely moral but *physical* in character.

The creature is really active, according to the nature and powers it has ultimately received from God the Creator of all. It stands to reason that the creature's nature and powers must first of all be 'conserved' by God, so that the creature is 'fit to act' under proper conditions. Besides conservation, however, 'physical concurrence' on the part of God is required so that the creature can pass from potentiality (power) to actuality (action); then, and only then, can the creature really produce the action natural to its power.

Proof of Physical Concurrence

Scholastic philosophers universally accept the fact of God's physical concurrence as a necessary agent in the production of every type of creatural action. However, in the fourteenth cen-

tury *Durandus* of St. Pourçain (he died probably in 1332) maintained that God's conservation of the creature's power to act is
required, but there is no immediate physical influence of God's
causality on the action itself; so long as the creature has the
power to act, it can proceed to the action without assistance
from God. In recent times, *E. Iglesias* and *J. Stufler* have sided
with Durandus on this question.

In opposition to Durandus and his modern followers, we
maintain that *an immediate physical concurrence of God is
necessary for all creatural action,* whether this creatural action
be necessary or free.

The relationship between creature and Creator in this regard
is that of an essentially 'subordinate' and 'secondary' cause to
the absolutely 'superior' and 'primary' cause. Two 'coequal'
causes cannot produce an identically same effect through their
respective actions, because each of the two causes would produce
its own effect through its respective action. The result would
be that each cause would produce only a *part of the effect,* but
would not be the cause of the *total effect.* It would be like two
horses pulling a load too heavy for either one to move alone;
jointly they can move the load, because each horse pulls a part
of it. Such a situation does not happen in divine concurrence.
The *superior* cause can concur with the *subordinate* cause in
the production of the same action and its effect. Both causes,
superior and subordinate, co-operate in the production of the
total effect, but each agent is responsible for the 'total effect'
under a different respect: the Creator-cause attains it under the
respect of a 'contingent' being considered strictly in its contingency, while the creature-cause attains it under the respect of
a being restricted to a definite class of effects (not to 'being
as such'). The combination of Creator-cause and creature-cause
then brings about an effect whose *totality* is dependent on God
as the 'superior' and 'primary' cause of its *contingent* being and
also dependent on the creature as the 'subordinate' and 'secondary' cause of its *specific* being (inasmuch as the effect is 'this'
or 'that' particular reality, and not 'being as such'). The creature-cause really and truly produces the effect, but with the

immediate and physical co-operation of God who, through His assisting action, also really and truly produces the effect. This immediate and physical co-operation of God with the action of the creature-cause in producing an effect is what is meant by God's *concurrence.*

And now for the *proof.*

The proof is based on the *complete contingency of the creature.* The creature is contingent in every respect. In no phase of its being, whether in its nature or in its action, is it self-sufficient. Nothing that it is or has or does is due to its own self; everything in a creatural being is 'contingent.' Contingency implies the ultimate and absolute dependence of the creature on God as the first and necessary cause. God as Creator is the supreme cause of all that has existence outside Himself. Since every creatural being is contingent in its very essence and nature, it can exist only in perfect and absolute dependence on God. Action follows nature. Consequently, also in its *action* the creature is dependent on God in a perfect and absolute manner; otherwise the creature's dependence on God (and God's dominion over the creature because of the latter's complete contingency) would not be perfect and absolute. But now, in its essence and existence the creature is dependent on God intrinsically, essentially, and immediately. Hence, the dependence of the creatural action and its effect must also be intrinsic, essential, and immediate. However, there will be an immediate dependence of the creature's action upon God only if God gives His divine *concurrence* to the action. Any other assistance of God would not be 'immediate' at all; because, if God gave and conserved only the nature and operative powers of the creature, the action itself would be immediately dependent only on the creature and not on God. It follows, therefore, that the complete contingency of the creature demands the *immediate assistance* (concurrence) of God *in its actions.*

Again, whatever exists depends for its *existence* directly on the power of God. God alone is self-existing and exists necessarily; all other beings (creatures) exist contingently and as such cannot have the *adequate reason* for their existence in themselves or in any other creatural being, but in God alone. Now all *actions* and *effects* of creatures are a positive reality in the order of existence. Hence, they are, as existing realities, dependent on God for their existence. This dependence must be *immediate*. If this dependence were only 'mediate,' namely, if the creatural actions were dependent on God only through the intermediation of some other being, they would not be dependent on God just inasmuch as they are *existing*. No being can be dependent on a finite being inasmuch as it has 'existence'; otherwise whatever has 'existence,' and in whatever the concept of 'being' is verified, would have to be dependent on this finite being. This, however, is manifestly impossible. Consequently, every creatural action must be immediately dependent on God in its existence.

Finally. God can *hinder* any creatural being from performing an *action,* and that without destroying the creature's power of action or the object to which the creature's action might be applied. Since God has absolute dominion over all beings distinct from Himself, He can do anything which does not involve a contradiction. Now, it certainly involves no contradiction if a creature's power of action does not go into operation, even when all the requisite conditions for action are present. Hence, God can hinder any creatural being from performing an action, even when all the requisite conditions for action are present. This hindrance of creatural action, however, would be impossible for God, if He did not *co-operate* in the creatural action *in a positive manner*. The reason is obvious. Unless God withdrew His immediate, physical assistance (concurrence) accompanying the creature's action, there would be nothing to stop the creature from performing the action, if the power fit for action and the required conditions for action remained intact. Hence, every creatural action also demands God's concurrence.

A number of *objections* have been raised against the doctrine of divine concurrence. The more important ones will be discussed.

First objection. According to the view expressed above, God must also be a *coefficient principle in sin.* But it is against God's infinite sanctity to give active assistance to sin. Hence, He gives no concurrence.

Answer. God in His concurrence is a coefficient principle in the production of the *reality* of the sinful act, but *not of the sin itself.* Sinfulness is not a positive entity but the absence of conformity of the act to the moral law; sin is, therefore, no reality in the strict sense of the term, but something negative. The real cause of sin is that which is the 'determining' cause of the sinful act, namely, the human will. God wills the act in so far as it is a positive reality; only if He were the determining cause of the sinful act, could the sin (sinful act) be imputed to Him. God gives an *indifferent* assistance for the act with regard to its positive reality, not with regard to its sinfulness as such (deviation from the moral law). The physical and physiological act is not wrong as a physical and physiological reality; otherwise such an act (for instance, killing a person, sexual excitement, pronouncing sacred names, etc.) could never be allowed. The sinfulness of such an act lies in its disagreement with the demands of morality.

Second objection. God created beings with the necessary *powers of operation.* Then why should divine concurrence be necessary? Divine concurrence is *superfluous.*

Answer. God gave operative powers, and they are used by the creature in its actions. But nothing can take away the *contingency* of the creature in its entire being; it is and will always remain essentially contingent and therefore an essentially dependent principle of action.

Third objection. If divine concurrence were a fact, God would be only a *partial cause* in the action. However, it would be an *imperfection* in God to be a partial cause.

Answer. To be a 'partial cause' would be an imperfection for God only if He could not perform an act by Himself; not, however, if He *gives* a creature power to act itself, since that is a sign of divine benevolence. God is still always the *total cause* of the totality of the effect.

Mode of Divine Concurrence

With very few exceptions, noted above, scholastic philosophers agree in maintaining the necessity of God's immediate
physical concurrence in creatural actions. It is in the discussion
of the particular *mode of divine concurrence* that agreement
ceases. A heated controversy arose in the sixteenth century concerning the 'mode' of divine concurrence, and the controversy
is still very much alive in our day. This discussion gave rise
to two main schools of thought — *bannesianism* and *molinism*.
Previously, some philosophers expressed ideas akin to those
incorporated in these two rival theories, but they did not even-
tuate into distinct schools of thought.

The system of 'bannesianism' derives its name from *Domingo
Bañez* (1528–1604), while that of 'molinism' had its origin with
Luiz de Molina (1535–1600). Bañez was a Dominican and
Molina a Jesuit; historically, the Dominicans generally have
followed Bañez, and the Jesuits, Molina. Similarly, the *thomists*
usually defend the doctrines of bannesianism.

In the beginning, the controversy centered on the theological
problem of 'grace' and 'free will.' The operation of 'grace' is an
instance of supernatural divine concurrence. Supernatural concurrence has its counterpart in the general concurrence of God
with creatural action in the field of natural activity. Even in
the field of natural activity, however, the crux of the problem
is found in the action of man's free will.

The chief point of the controversy thus resides in the answer
to the question: How reconcile the *absolute dominion of God*
over all creatural actions (including the free acts of man's
will) with the *self-determination of man's free will*? Both the
'absolute dominion' of God and the 'freedom of the will' must
be maintained and safeguarded. But how should this be done?

The bannesianists and the molinists attempt to give the
answer. And their attempt at an adequate answer has precipi-
tated a never ending controversy. Some of the greatest minds
have attempted a solution and failed. Here an explanation of
the rival systems will be given.

The Answer of Bannesianism

Leaving aside the question of grace as not germane to philosophy, the answer of the bannesians to the problem indicated above is briefly as follows.

The bannesians (and, generally speaking, the thomistic school) contend that a mere simultaneous concurrence on the part of God is insufficient to maintain His supreme dominion over creatures. They therefore claim that God applies a *physical premotion,* a *physical predetermination* (*concursus praevius*) directly to the creature's operative power. This 'physical premotion' is not an act of the divine will or of divine power or anything else identical with God's nature; it is a *finite created entity,* a quality (according to the general view), which is applied to the creatural faculty and gives it the immediate preparation for action (places it in *actu primo proximo* for action). Only when the creatural operative power has received this physical assistance ('physical premotion, determination') from God, can the power perform its proper action (*actus secundus*); without it, it cannot pass from potentiality (of action) to act.

The physical predetermination is *prior* to the activity of the creature, not with a priority in time, but with a priority of nature; it is prior in nature as the cause is always prior to the effect. This physical premotion removes the creature's indifference to action, thereby determining it to act (hence the terms '*pre*motion' and '*pre*determination'). Premotion is not merely a 'moral' influence whereby God 'induces' the creature to act; it is a 'physical' assistance and influence *determining* the finite cause to its last actuality, so that the act naturally results of itself. This physical premotion (predetermination) is necessary for every creature's every activity and therefore also for man's free acts of the will.

This teaching on physical premotion and predetermination leads to some interesting results. Physical premotion, by its very nature, *infallibly* brings the operative power of the creature into act. Not only 'can' the power act in virtue of this physical divine assistance; it infallibly does act, and that not in any manner and direction, but in that particular *manner and direction* which corresponds to the nature of the predetermination given by God. That is also true of the *free acts* of the rational creature. As long as the will is not predetermined, it is absolutely impossible for the will to act; if and when it is predetermined by God, it is absolutely impossible for the will to produce any kind of act except that to which it is predetermined.

The will has no means of *choosing* a certain predetermination in preference to another, because without a *previous* determination it cannot be active at all. Hence, the will cannot decide for or against predetermination, nor for or against any particular kind of predetermination. *Whether* and *when* and *how* it be predetermined lies alone in the *decree of God's will;* and if and when the free will of the creature is predetermined, it *infallibly performs* the act for which the predetermination is given by God.

Nevertheless, the bannesians (and thomists) say, man's *will does not* thereby *become unfree.* God predetermines every creature according to its particular kind of nature. If the creature, because its constitution is such, acts necessarily, the predetermination is given by God so that it acts necessarily. If the creature possesses a free will, the will is predetermined so that it acts infallibly, but it still acts in a perfectly free manner.

One can now understand the position of the bannesians (and thomists) with regard to *God's knowledge* of the future free acts of man. God knows what the free will of man can and will decide by simply knowing the *predetermining decrees* of His own will concerning these acts of man's will. Just as there are only two classes of acts, namely, those which will not occur in the future and those which will (depending on God's physical premotion), so there are but two kinds of divine knowledge, namely, *simple intelligence* and *vision.* As a consequence, the bannesianists reject absolutely all 'intermediate knowledge.'

The Answer of Molinism

The answer of *molinism* to the problem of the mode of divine concurrence differs radically from that of bannesianism (and thomism).

The molinists, in order to distinguish their doctrine of immediate divine concurrence from that of the bannesians (and thomists), call it *simultaneous concurrence.* In doing this, they want to express their rejection of any kind of an immediate 'previous' assistance (physical premotion, physical predetermination) to creatural activity on the part of God. According to the molinistic view, God has *decreed from all eternity* to give His concurrence to a certain creatural act which will take place in time; however, the concurrence itself is *given in time,* at the very moment when the act is performed. This decree is one of the prerequisite conditions placing the creature in immediate preparation to act *(in actu primo proximo).* Since the concurrence is given, not prior to the act, but at the time when the act is performed, it is 'simultaneous' and not 'previous.'

From the standpoint of God it is a 'readiness to concur' with the creature's activity, and this is termed the *offered concurrence (concursus oblatus).* The act of the creature, if it is a necessary act, will now proceed with necessity from the creature's nature; thereby the 'offered' concurrence becomes *actual (concursus collatus, concursus in actu secundo).*

Concerning creatural *free* acts (as in the case of man's free choosing) God's concurrence will be *indifferent;* that is to say, it will not be 'determined,' as is the case with beings acting necessarily. God's decree of concurrence, therefore, with regard to 'free' acts will not be: "I will give this creatural action my determined concurrence"; such a decree applies only to the 'necessary' actions of creatural beings. In 'free' acts, God's decree will be: "I will give this creature in its free acts such a concurrence which does not compel it to act, but which *enables* it to act and that in any of the different ways which it *can choose* under the circumstances." Divine concurrence is thus, with regard to the free acts, eternally and entitatively one but indifferent and virtually multiple.

Only such an 'indifferent' divine concurrence, molinists claim, is compatible with that active indifference and self-determination which is the essence of the freedom of the creature's will. Only under the supposition of an 'indifferent' concurrence is the creatural will capable of *omitting* an act which it could otherwise perform or of *performing* one particular act instead of another. By omitting an act (although it could perform it) or by performing one kind of act (although it could omit it or set a different act), the will makes use of its God-given freedom of action; thereby it determines both itself and the actual concurrence of God. God is thus a partial cause of the creatural free act; and so also is the free will a partial cause of the same act. Every free act of the will thus has two partial causes, two coefficient principles; but only one is the 'determining' cause, and that is the creatural will itself. The totality of the effect, however, depends on each of these two partial causes, so that, if either one were missing, the total effect (the act in its entirety) would also be missing.

The molinists strenuously oppose the doctrine of the bannesians (and thomists) that God knows all actually and conditionally future free acts of man in His predetermining decrees; they claim that in such a view the freedom of man's will is sacrificed. God's decrees, they say, are not the source of His knowledge. And yet it must also be maintained that God's knowledge of the free acts of man is absolute and eternal; it cannot be conditioned by man's free will, so that God would know of man's free decisions only at the time they are made. To solve this very great difficulty, the molinists have recourse to *intermediate knowledge (scientia media)*, in virtue of which God infallibly and eternally knows all that a free will *can* or *would do* in every combination of circumstances. By means of this 'intermediate knowledge' God foresees every actually or conditionally free act of the will, because each such act contains within itself a *formal* and *objective truth* which must be known to the omniscient mind of God prior to any decision of His own will regarding it. This 'intermediate knowledge' of God is independent of any divine decrees and is logically prior to them. In this manner the molinists seek to harmonize the eternal and infallible foreknowledge of God and the freedom of the created will.

The Defense of Thomism

At the present time the *thomists* defend the tenets of the bannesian theory.

Two main questions are constantly in the foreground of the controversy: the question of divine physical premotion in general concerning all creatural activity; and the question of maintaining the freedom of the human will during divine physical premotion.

The question of *physical premotion in general.*

The thomists, who are the chief defenders of Bañez and bannesianism, base their argument for divine physical premotion on the 'principle of motion.' This principle reads: *Quidquid movetur ab alio movetur: Whatever is moved is moved by another.*

The 'principle of motion,' say the thomists, is a strictly universal principle and law, and it admits of no exceptions. Now, all creatures are 'moved' in their actions, since they pass from *potentiality* to *actuality* (from 'potency' to 'act') in their activities. The passage from potentiality to actuality in creatural beings always implies the acquisition of some new reality; if they possessed the reality already, they could not acquire it by passing from potentiality to actuality. Consequently, the new reality is not present in the creatural being beforehand. Yet the new reality cannot come from nothing, because 'nothing is nothing' and has nothing to give. The new reality must, therefore, come from a being already 'in act,' and this being must be 'other' than the being acquiring the new reality by passing from potentiality to actuality. However, *all* creatural beings pass from potentiality to actuality and thereby constantly acquire new reality, and so they must be 'moved' in this acquisition by

'another.' But there is only one 'being in act' outside the sum
of 'all creatural beings,' namely, God. Therefore, whatever new
reality creatural beings acquire must be received from God.
God is the mover.

To be 'moved by another' means to be *'educed* from potency
to act by another,' because the very action of the 'passage' from
potentiality to actuality is a new reality which was not previously present in the being. It follows that the creatural being
must be *intrinsically dependent* in its passage from potency to
act on the *action of the mover,* so that there exists a priority of
nature between the action of the mover and the transition from
potentiality to actuality. But a merely 'collateral' or 'simultaneous' concurrence, as the molinists interpret God's concurrence,
is insufficient to account for the *entire* transition. The molinistic
theory always supposes the creature to move itself at least in
some part of the action, namely, when the creature, in passing
into act, makes the 'offered concurrence' become 'actual concurrence.' Such an action on the part of the creature is against
the above-mentioned 'principle of motion' and therefore impossible. More, then, is needed than a 'simultaneous' concurrence. God must give a physical *premotion* in order that a creature can really act.

George Hayward Joyce[5] (a Jesuit, by the way) expresses this
view admirably: "Inasmuch as all action is a transition from
potency to actuality, it is totally impossible that it can take
place without the continuous agency of a cause external to the
immediate agent: that otherwise we should be driven to admit
that a being can confer on itself a new reality which it does
not possess, giving to itself that which it has not got to give.
The principle that the transition from potency to actuality
supposes the operation of a cause which itself possesses the perfection actualized, is, we maintain, self-evident — though, of
course, the perfection may exist in the cause in a higher manner, and not in the manner in which it is found in the effect.

---

[5] *Principles of Natural Theology,* 2 ed. (New York: Longmans, Green & Co., Inc.,
1924), pp. 537, 538.

It follows that the operations of a finite agent can only take place in virtue of a premotion, ultimately referable to the First Cause. The finite cause is instrumental in regard of the Prime Mover: and apart from a 'previous' concurrence, its efficient powers lack their final complement."

Since every act of man's *free will* entails a transition from potentiality to actuality, the free will in its action is also moved by God by means of a *physical premotion* into action.

The free will, under the influence of the physical premotion of God, *wills infallibly* that to which it is predetermined. It does *not follow* from this, thomists contend, that the will is moved with *necessity* to act as it does; rather, it is placed by God in the act of *freely willing* something. The will of God not merely sees to it that something comes into existence by the thing which it moves, but it also sees to it that this is done in the manner which agrees with the thing's nature and is demanded by the thing's nature. Now, it is demanded by the nature of the will that it be moved *freely*. Hence, it must be held that the human will, in virtue of this physical premotion, is placed by God in the act of willing something 'freely.'

Garrigou-Lagrange[6] (a thomist) says in this connection: "Who could demonstrate that there is any *contradiction* in maintaining that the *Creator of the free will,* who is *more intimately associated* with the *will than freedom itself is,* can *infallibly move the will to determine itself freely to act?* Infallibility is not necessity." In a footnote to this passage Garrigou-Lagrange remarks: "Thus in the case of a regularly constructed syllogism, in which the major is a necessary proposition and the minor is contingent, the conclusion follows *infallibly* though being at the same time in itself a contingent statement. In other words, there is *necessity of consequence* and not necessity of *consequent,* as in the following example: The virtuous person is deserving of credit. Now the Apostles were models of virtue. Therefore they were deserving of credit." A little

---

⁶ *God: His Existence and His Nature,* tr. by Dom. Bede Rose, 4 print. (St. Louis: B. Herder Book Co., 1947), Vol. II, p. 76. (Italics by Garrigou-Lagrange.)

farther on[7] he says: "How can the finite being exist apart from the infinite Being? It can exist only on condition that it is caused by Him and remains absolutely dependent upon Him. How can a secondary liberty exist apart from the primary liberty [of God]? It can exist only on condition that it is caused and moved by the latter, so that the faculty of willing passes from a state of *passive indifference* to one of *active indifference* contained in the very choice made by the faculty. Thus all the perfections of this secondary liberty pre-exist eminently from all eternity in the primary liberty. Why would God not have the power to produce infallibly in us and with us the freedom of our acts? . . . To maintain that God, as first cause, cannot produce with us and in us the free mode of our acts, is to maintain that a *mode of being* cannot be produced by the prime Being, who is the Creator of all the being there is outside Himself."

The reason, therefore, why the thomists insist on a 'physical premotion' for all creatural activity, including that of man's free will, is the *absolute dependence* of the creature on the Creator. God is the Lord and Master of all, and this, they feel, would not be so unless God *predetermined* all creatural activity by means of a 'physical premotion.'

The Defense of Molinism

The molinists take as the starting-point of their discussion of the problem the *freedom of the will*. The freedom of the will is admitted, at least in principle, by both the thomists (bannesians) and the molinists; the fact itself, whether viewed from a theological or philosophical point of view, is indubitable, and the freedom of man's will must be safeguarded against all attacks. But the thomistic position, molinists contend, destroys free will in their doctrine of 'physical premotion (physical predetermination).' As a result of this conviction, the molinists attack the doctrine of 'physical premotion' as the proper interpretation of 'divine concurrence'; in its stead they advocate *simultaneous concurrence*.

---

[7] *Ibid.*, pp. 78, 79.

Physical predetermination, molinists claim, is not necessary. And the freedom of man's will cannot be upheld under the influence of physical premotion.

Physical premotion is superfluous for the purpose intended.

The thomists demand this physical premotion, first of all, in order to make it clear that God is the absolute *Prime Mover* of all creatures and to show their *complete dependence* on Him in all actions. However, the molinists say, all this will be upheld, and God can do everything described above, without 'physical premotion.' Hence, physical predetermination is superfluous for the purpose.

The *absolute dependence* of every creature on God is sufficiently clear and safeguarded when the following points are accepted:

The creature owes its entire *being* and all its *powers* directly to God; thereby its absolute dependence on God is assured under all circumstances.

No creature can pass from the state of *insufficient preparation* for action to the state of sufficient preparation, unless God (either alone or through creatures entirely dependent on Him) brings the creature into a state of immediate preparedness for action.

No creature, even when in a state of immediate preparedness for action, can pass from potency to act *unless assisted by divine concurrence* in the very act, that is to say, unless God, as a coefficient principle, produces (together with the creature) the actual application of the operative power to its connatural and proportionate action by willing this action to be produced and to proceed from the creature's operative power.

For all this, however, 'simultaneous' concurrence is sufficient, and 'physical premotion' is not required. Hence, physical premotion (predetermination) is not necessary for *complete dependence* of the creature on God.

Furthermore, thomists demand the existence of 'physical premotion (predetermination)' so that God *can direct all creatural actions to His purposes and ends.* Certainly God must be able to do this if He is the Master of all things. Molinists agree that God must be able to direct all creatural actions so that His supreme purposes and ends will prevail, but God can do this *without a physical premotion.*

With regard to the creatures which act *necessarily,* God knows from all eternity just what forces for action lie in them. By giving them their particular nature and powers and by arranging the order existing in the universe, God can produce, through 'simultaneous' concurrence (without which they cannot operate), any result that He wishes and direct them to any purpose that He desires by the very fact that He arranges them in their respective order and that they act with necessity. More is not needed.

With regard to the creatures which *act with freedom of the will,* God, since he created the will with freedom of action, leaves the free will intact. Still, He can direct the free will of men to any particular purpose that He wishes. Through His 'intermediate knowledge' God knows from eternity what every person *will actually* decide to do and what he *would* decide to do under any and every possible condition. God thus knows, infallibly and eternally, that this or that person will actually and freely do something in the circumstances as given. Consequently God knows with absolute certainty what He should decree and what circumstances He should bring about, in order that the free will of man fulfill His own purpose in a free manner; all this should cause no difficulty for the omniscient and omnipotent Creator of man's free will.

There is, therefore, *no necessity* for any kind of 'physical premotion (physical predetermination),' so that God can bring about any result He wishes. 'Physical premotion' is thus superfluous for the purpose intended; 'simultaneous concurrence' is all that is required. Why, then, postulate physical predetermination of the will, especially when the theory presents insurmountable difficulties in maintaining the will's freedom?

Physical premotion contradicts free will.
The freedom of the will consists essentially in an *active in-*

difference which makes the will master of its own acts and places it in its power to act or not to act (freedom of exercise), to will 'this' or 'that' (freedom of specification), and that even if all the requisite conditions for action are present. But this 'active indifference' is made impossible by physical premotion, whether one considers the will as predetermined or not as yet predetermined.

The *will as predetermined* by God has no active indifference. Under the influence of physical premotion it is metaphysically impossible, as the thomists and bannesians assert, for the will to *omit* the act to which it has been predetermined by God or to *change* it. The will simply *cannot* act in a manner *different* from that to which it has been predetermined by God. Hence, it has no active indifference or choice, so that it could perform or omit the act or choose 'this' rather than 'that.'

The *will not as yet predetermined* has no active indifference either. This physical premotion, according to the thomists, is a necessary *prerequisite condition* for every act of the will, and as such the will, without physical premotion, is absolutely *incapable* of performing an act at all.

Now, if the human will lacks active indifference before and in and after predetermination, then it cannot be said to be free in its choice. Hence, free will is incompatible with physical premotion (predetermination). And yet, the human *will is free in its choice*. Consequently, physical premotion (predetermination) must be said to destroy free will. Physical premotion, therefore, must be rejected as the proper interpretation of the 'mode' of divine concurrence.

Thomists, of course, assert that God applies His physical premotion according to the nature of the agent, and He therefore applies it in such a manner to the will that it acts freely under the influence of the predetermination. Molinists say to this that the thomists uphold free will *in words,* but their *explanation really destroys* the will's indifference and thereby its *freedom* also. Their explanation involves, not a mystery (as some of them claim), but a *contradiction:* man's will would be actively indifferent and undetermined (because the will is 'free,' which implies *self*-determination) and yet be determined through physical premotion. Now, an 'undetermined-determined' will is a contradiction pure and simple.

Physical premotion contradicts God's sanctity.

For all acts without exception, thomists and bannesians claim, God must give His physical premotion, or they cannot be performed. Molinists contend that such a view makes *God the author of sinful acts;* and they argue in this manner.

God alone is the *author* of physical predetermination, and the influence of this premotion on the will is such that it has an irresistible, infallible effect. Hence, God is the 'determining cause' in every concrete act according to its entire concrete being, while the position of man is that he *cannot omit* the act. God's will in this respect is to man's will as the irresistibly determining to the irresistibly determined. But one who is the determining factor in a concrete act which, under the circumstances of time, person, etc., is sinful, is in the real sense of the word the *cause of the sin;* otherwise there is no cause for sin at all. For example. Some person likes a 'drink.' He has drunk to the limit of soberness and realizes that he ought to stop; but he continues to drink until completely intoxicated. For every glass he needed a physical premotion from God; with a physical premotion he could not possibly have stopped to drink. In virtue of the physical premotion and predetermination given to his will by God, he simply had to drink on to intoxication; he not only could drink on, but he could not possibly have prevented it. Without physical premotion the very possibility to drink was taken away, and with it the very possibility of avoiding intoxication was excluded. The cause of intoxication, therefore, is the influence of the physical predetermination; rather, God, the author of physical premotion, is the responsible author of the sinful act of intoxication. And so with all other sinful acts. Now, God, the infinitely holy, cannot be the author of anything sinful. But He would be, according to the theory of physical premotion. Therefore, the theory is wrong. Thomists resent this interpretation of their theory. God, they say, merely predetermines man to the *material* sin (to the positive reality found in the sinful act), *not to formal sin* (to the sinfulness of the act precisely as sinful). To this the molinists answer that it is true that God predetermines the creatural will merely to the physical reality of the act. However, we impute the physical act as 'sinful' to the creatural will because the will *actively determines itself* to this concrete physical act which, considering all the circumstances, does not agree with the moral law. When, therefore, God actively *predetermines* the will by means of physical premotion to this same act, He is, even more than the creature, the responsible agent of the sinful act.

That thomists dislike this imputation and its conclusion, is obvious. As Garrigou-Lagrange[8] writes: "The opponents of the Thomist thesis would have it that we say: 'God determines our choice,' whereas we say: 'God *moves* our will to *determine itself* freely in a certain manner.' After thus misrepresenting our thesis, they find it easy to add that, like Calvinism, it destroys liberty because it leads to the conclusion that free will, moved and prompted by God, cannot resist." For this reason the thomists constantly repeat their distinction between the 'infallibility' and the 'necessity' of the creatural act proceeding under the influence of God's physical premotion.

The molinists counter by claiming that the thomists are guilty of *inconsistency* when, in view of their doctrine of physical premotion and predetermination, they ascribe the sinful act to the will of the creature. In their explanation of the sinfulness of an act, and in order to make the creature responsible instead of God, they *surreptitiously introduce self-determination into the creatural will*. So they *do* admit (contrary to their avowed principles) that the will of man can 'actively determine itself,' irrespective of the divine premotion. But then why postulate physical premotion and predetermination? 'Simultaneous concurrence' suffices. In any case, molinists insist, *self*-determination on the part of the creatural will is incompatible with complete *pre*determination.

---

[8] *Ibid.,* p. 358.

Evaluation

Both thomism and molinism have their good points and also their obscurities. The two theories approach the problem from different angles, due to the emphasis on certain truths.

Thomism stresses the *absolute sovereignty of God* over the creature and, as a consequence, the absolute dependence of the creature on God. God is the creator of everything outside Himself, so that everything, including the action of creatures, owes its existence to the almighty power of God. Without God the creature is nothing. And since God does not act blindly but with evident purpose for all things, it is clear that creatures cannot frustrate the ultimate purpose of God. In order to safeguard the infinite sovereignty of God, thomists are convinced that it is necessary to make all creatural action (and that includes the action of the free will) dependent on a divine *physical premotion* and *predetermination*.

Molinism, on the other hand, while admitting the absolute sovereignty of God, emphasizes the *freedom of man's will*. The freedom of the will is the basis of all morality, for without this freedom there can be no responsibility, no reward, no punishment, no commandment. Take away man's effective freedom and man is lowered to the level of a beast or of an automaton. The freedom of man's will must be safeguarded at all costs. And so also must God's absolute sovereignty. God cannot force man's free will, because in His infinite goodness He decided to create man as a free agent capable of good and evil through active self-determination. As they see it, physical premotion and predetermination would destroy this freedom of man's will. *Simultaneous concurrence,* based on intermediate knowledge, suffices to safeguard God's absolute sovereignty and also man's freedom. And thus complete harmony is established between God's sovereignty and man's freedom of the will.

No reference to the teaching of St. Thomas Aquinas has been made in the foregoing sections outlining the views of thomism and molinism. The reason for the omission is simple: both schools of thought quote passages of St. Thomas in support of their theory, and their interpretations are naturally influenced by their respective views.

Summary of Chapter XIV

The divine *conservation* of creatures and the divine *concurrence* in creatural action is the subject of the present chapter.

1. *Notion of Conservation.* — By *conservation* one understands continuation in existence through dependence on a cause. It is either 'passive' or 'active.' The issue in question here is the 'active' conservation of creatures on the part of God, namely, that He is the cause of the continued existence of creatures. Active conservation is either 'negative' or 'positive,' and positive conservation is either 'indirect' or 'direct.'

2. *Proof of Divine Conservation.* — We claim that God preserves all things without exception by a *positive and direct influence* (direct conservation).

All creatural beings are *contingent* and as such do not have the sufficient reason for their being in themselves but in God. This insufficiency pertains to the entire period of their existence. Hence, the sufficient reason for the entire period of their existence (not merely for their beginning in existence) lies in the noncontingent being, in God. Hence, their *continued existence,* because it is contingent like their beginning, demands the same positive and direct influence of God's activity. That, however, is what is meant by *divine conservation.*

God has the power to *annihilate,* that is, to make a being cease to exist. But annihilation, since it is no positive activity directed toward a positive result, must consist in the withdrawal of some positive activity of God. Consequently, the perseverance in existence on the part of the creature must be due to a positive activity of God; and this positive activity is divine 'conservation.'

3. *Notion of Divine Concurrence.* — Divine *concurrence* is the influence of God operating with creatures in producing the same effect as they produce through their own activity. It is either 'moral' or 'physical,' and physical concurrence is either 'mediate' or 'immediate.' God's concurrence to creatural action is *physical* and *immediate.*

4. *Proof of Physical Concurrence.* — The complete *contingency* of the creature affects not only its nature but also its *action.* Hence, also the action of the creature is dependent on God intrinsically,

essentially, and immediately. Consequently, God must give His physical and immediate concurrence to the action of the creature.

Again. Whatever exists depends for its *existence* directly on the power of God. Now, all actions and effects of creatures are a positive reality in the order of existence, and as such depend directly on the power of God for their existence.

Finally. God can *hinder* creatural *action*, because no contradiction is involved. This hindrance, however, would be impossible for God, if He did not co-operate in the creatural action in a positive manner.

5. *Mode of Divine Concurrence.* — Bannesianism (and thomism) and molinism attempt to give an explanation of the *mode* or manner of divine concurrence. The problem is how to reconcile the *absolute dominion* of God over all creatural actions (including the free act of man's will) with the *self-determination* of man's free will.

6. *The Answer of Bannesianism.* — The bannesians (and thomists) claim that God applies a physical *premotion* (predetermination) to the creature's operative power, thereby determining the finite cause to its last actuality so that the act naturally results of itself. The action 'infallibly' follows the kind of premotion given. But 'infallibility' is not the same as 'necessity'; the free acts of man follow 'infallibly' but 'freely,' because God premoves according to the nature of the being He assists in its action. God's *knowledge* of the creature's free acts is based on His predetermining *decrees.*

7. *The Answer of Molinism.* — Molinism rejects physical premotion and in its stead advocates *simultaneous concurrence.* In actions of the free will this concurrence is 'indifferent,' enabling the will to choose and determine itself. Instead of God's knowledge resulting from His predetermining decrees, molinists postulate an *intermediate knowledge (scientia media)* in connection with the free acts; each such act contains a formal and objective truth which must be known to God's omniscient mind prior to any decision of His will regarding it. Only in this way, molinists are convinced, can the freedom of man's will be safeguarded.

8. *The Defense of Thomism.* — As regards *physical premotion* in general, thomists base it on the universal principle that 'Whatever is moved is moved by another.' Every creatural action is a passage from potentiality to actuality, and as such the new reality acquired can come only from the *Prime Mover, God.* This principle applies

also to the *free* acts of man. Since 'infallibility' is not 'necessity,' the free will acts infallibly but freely under the influence of physical premotion.

9. *The Defense of Molinism.* — Physical premotion, the molinists contend, is *superflous* for the purpose intended. The thomists assert that physical premotion is required in order to make it clear that God is the Prime Mover of all creatures and to show their complete dependence on Him in all actions. Both purposes are achieved with 'simultaneous concurrence.'

Physical premotion *contradicts free will* because it deprives the human will of the 'freedom of exercise' and the 'freedom of specification.' A physically determined will has not the 'active indifference' necessary for freedom.

Physical premotion *contradicts God's sanctity,* because it makes God the author of sinful acts. Thomists say that God premoves the will to act freely. But, the molinists assert, what the thomists say in words they contradict in their explanation, or they surreptitiously introduce, contrary to their avowed principles, *self*-determination into the creatural will.

10. *Evaluation.* — Thomism stresses the *absolute sovereignty of God;* molinism emphasizes the *freedom of man's will* in its actions.

Readings

Brosnan, William J., *God Infinite, the World, and Reason,* pp. 90–153. — Boedder, Bernard, *Natural Theology,* Bk. III, Chap. I. — Joyce, George Hayward, *Principles of Natural Theology,* Chap. XVI. — Garrigou-Lagrange, R., *God: His Existence and His Nature,* Vol. II, pp. 144–161, 306–338, 354–396. — Mercier, D. Card., *A Manual of Modern Scholastic Philosophy,* Vol. II, 'Natural Theology,' pp. 124–128. — Glenn, Paul J., *Theodicy,* pp. 259–280.

Chapter XV

PROVIDENCE AND GOVERNANCE

ALL creatures owe their existence to God. God created them because He is infinitely good and wished them to share in His goodness. Creatures thereby imitate the perfections of God in a limited fashion.

More, however, is required than creation. For creatures to endure in their being and existence, they need the 'conservation' of God; without this, they would immediately return to nothingness. For them to be active, both with regard to their own being and in relation to others, they need the 'concurrence' of God. Under all circumstances and conditions, creatures are thus dependent on the First Cause for their being and activity.

Another transient activity of God, relative to creatures, is His *providence* and *governance*. All theists agree in this. Even the pagans in their religious observances manifest a belief in the providence and governance of God, at least implicitly, because they pray and offer sacrifices to their deities for protection and assistance.

Belief alone, however, is insufficient to establish the providence and governance of God; solid reasons are required, in order to establish this activity of God to the satisfaction of the philosophic inquirer.

Notion of Providence

Etymologically (Lat., *pro,* for; *videre,* to see, to look) the term *providence* means as much as 'to look out (care) for something.' And that is the common significance of the word. From a philosophical standpoint, all that is further required is a deepening and broadening of the term.

St. Thomas[1] *defines* God's providence as the "type (plan) of the order in things towards an end." And in another passage[2] he calls it "the type (plan) of the order of things foreordained towards an end." What St. Thomas wants to say is that God has *in His mind* a definite plan of the order which He intends and foreordains in His creatures, so that the particular purpose of their being will be in accordance with the universal purpose of all creation. In other words, God did not give existence to His creatures and then let them fend for themselves, without bothering about them and their future in any special manner. On the contrary, God not only gave them their being, but also 'foreordained' the order of their being in themselves and in relation to other beings in this world; and He sees to it that this order is directed toward an end and is carried out toward the end He desires.

Two things, therefore, are involved in the providence of God: an act of His intellect containing the *plan* of the order which shall exist in creatural beings; and an act of the will containing the *decree* that this order shall prevail according to the particular and ultimate purpose (end) He has assigned for them.

So far as the *purpose* of creatural beings is concerned, a distinction is necessary. Each individual being has its own inherent purpose, namely its own particular fitness and well-being. But each individual is also a member of a wider group and of the universe at large, and as a member it is subordinated to the purpose of the entire universe as a whole, namely, to the order of the universe as God has foreordained this order. And all beings, whether considered as individuals or as members of the entire universe, have as their ultimate purpose the manifestation of God's perfections, namely, the external glory of God.

The *whole* has more intrinsic value than the parts constituting the whole. In the designs of God's providence, therefore, the well-being of the parts of an individual being are subordinated to the well-being of the total individual, and the well-

---

[1] *Summa Theologica* (New York: Benziger Bros.), I, qu. 22, art. 1.
[2] *Ibid.*, art. 3.

being of the individuals is subordinated to the well-being of the universe as a whole; all, however, whether viewed as individuals or as a universe, have as the ultimate purpose of their being and existence the manifestation and exaltation of God. This arrangement of creatural beings, both in themselves and in their relation to other beings as members of the entire universe, is what is meant by 'the order of things' foreseen and decreed by God in the designs of His providence. We maintain that every being, nonliving and living, material and spiritual, is subject to the loving direction of God's providence.

God's providence thus extends to the well-being of the individual beings and of the universe at large. Correspondingly, a distinction is made between 'particular' and 'universal' providence. God's *particular* providence is the practical ordering of the individual beings for the achievement of the various ends proper to them. His *universal* providence is the practical ordering of the universe of things for the attainment of the end proper to the universe as a whole.

Now, if an 'end' is intended, the 'means' required to achieve the end also must be intended. God, then, through the plan of His providence supplies each creature with the means needed for its physical well-being; this is *physical* providence. Man, however, is also a moral being, and God gives man the means needed by him to live in conformity with his moral nature; this is the *moral* providence of God.

Notion of Governance

The *governance* of God is the execution of the plan of providence among existing beings; in other words, whereas providence pertains to the 'plan' of the order among things in the mind of God, governance is the 'actual direction' of things toward the end established for them by God.

Providence, considered as the plan of the order of things, is an exemplary idea present in the intellect of God which the divine will decrees shall be carried out; as such it is identical ultimately with God's infinite essence and exists in Him from all eternity. Governance (or 'government'), on the other hand, considered as the execution of the plan of providence, presupposes the fact of creation and of the existence of creatural beings, so that, if creatures did not actually exist, there would be no governance on the part of God. As St. Thomas[3] expresses the matter: "Two things pertain to the care of providence — namely, the reason of order, which is called providence and disposition; and the execution of order, which is termed government. Of these, the first is eternal, and the second is temporal."

In a *strict* sense, therefore, providence and governance are by no means identical. Providence exists in the mind of God *prior* to the existence of creatures, while governance is *posterior* to (that is, follows) their existence.

In a *wider* sense, however, providence may be considered, as a matter of actual fact under present circumstances, to include governance. Creation need not have occurred; if it had not occurred, there would have been providence but not governance. Creation, however, actually having occurred, the providence of God involves its execution in fact. For this reason most authors include governance in the general concept of providence.

Henceforth in this chapter, since creatural beings actually exist, the concept of 'providence' will be used in the wider sense as including 'governance.'

Proof of God's Providence

The fact of divine providence is denied by the materialists, pantheists, finitists, fatalists, and many deists. We maintain that *God, through His providence, directs the world in general and man in particular* in a most wise manner toward the end He has decreed.

First, God's *general providence.*

The general providence of God can be proved either indirectly or directly. Both proofs will be given.

Indirectly, God's general providence is proved by showing the *absurdities* which necessarily follow its denial. A person

---

[3] *Ibid.,* qu. 22, art. 1, ad 2.

could deny the existence of divine providence, only by maintaining that God either does not know how to direct all
things to their proper and ultimate end, or that He has not
the power to do it, or that He could do it but does not care
to do it. None of these alternatives can be reasonably defended.
God is infinite in His wisdom, His power, and His goodness.
The first alternative is contrary to His infinite wisdom; the
second, contrary to His infinite power; the third, contrary to
His infinite goodness. Consequently, God's general providence
directs the world and all creatures toward the end He has
decreed.

Directly, God's general providence is proved from the *nature
of God and of His creatures.* The nature of every single creatural being is such that it is immediately dependent in essence
and operation on God as the First Cause. The end and purpose
of each creature has been designed by the Creator. The creature
attains its proper and ultimate end through action, and action
follows nature and essence. As a result, creatural action necessarily requires not only that God give the creature a nature
capable of, and fit for, action, but also immediately and directly
assist it in the realization of its actions. This assistance on the
part of God is conservation and concurrence. Now, to assist a
creature immediately and directly in the achievement of its end
and purpose of being through concurrence in its every action
is the same as to 'direct' it toward its end and purpose of being,
because without God the creature can do nothing. Therefore,
God directs all beings, from the smallest to the largest, toward
the end and purpose of their being. That He does this in a
most wise manner is evident from the fact that every act of
God is infinitely perfect and consequently infinitely wise. Now,
such an infinitely wise direction of all creatures toward the end
and purpose of their being is what is meant by 'general providence.' God, therefore, directs the entire universe by means of
His general providence.

It is obvious that every single being has its own *proper end*
and purpose. Its 'proper end' is indicated by the specific nature
it possesses, and every being has its specific nature. Man, because

of the constitutional limitation of his mind, may and, in most cases, will be ignorant of the specific nature of the beings he encounters in the world; but this ignorance does not alter the fact that such a specificity is present. By the very fact that God gave a specific nature to each being He *intends* the realization of this specific nature as the proper end and purpose of the individual being; and what God 'intends' He realizes.

Besides the proper end and purpose inherent in its nature, each individual being and all together have an *ultimate end* and purpose. Whatever is inseparably connected with something that is intended must be intended with it. Now, the manifestation of God's goodness is inseparably connected with creation, inasmuch as creatures are things which are 'good.' Therefore, the manifestation of God's goodness in His creatures is *intended* by God. But this manifestation of God's goodness is what is understood by God's 'external glory.' Consequently, the ultimate end and purpose of all creatural beings, singly and collectively, is God's external glory. God, therefore, intended His external glory as the ultimate end and purpose of all creatural beings. What God intends, however, will and must eventually come about; God's will cannot be frustrated by creatures. Hence, whether creatural beings know it or do not know it, consciously strive for it or do not consciously strive for it, they actually manifest the goodness of God and thus carry out the 'ultimate end' and purpose of their existence.

Since it is the 'intention' of God that all creatures, singly and collectively, realize the particular and ultimate end and purpose of their being, and since God's intention is always effective, His providence extends over the entire universe and every being in it. In other words, God's providence is truly *universal*.

Next, God's *special providence concerning man.*

Moral philosophy, or ethics, shows that man strives naturally and necessarily for *perfect happiness;* it also shows that man cannot find this perfect happiness in creatural goods, but only in God the supreme good. Man is unable to achieve this goal in his life here on earth. Hence, the perfect happiness of man can consist only in an intimate union with God in eternity through contemplation and love of God.

Now, the entire world and every creature in it is by its very nature *fit to dispose* man for this final happiness. Hence, it must be the *intention* of God that all creatural beings do this.

Man uses the things within his reach for food, shelter, clothing, ornamentation, and the commodities of life. Directly or indirectly, the world has the natural function of ministering to man's vegetative and sentient life. Man's vegetative and sentient life, however, is the foundation of his intellectual life, and this intellectual life is the preparation for his ultimate happiness. The things present in the universe thus give occasion to man to develop his intellectual powers by study and contemplation, and thus man can mediately dispose himself for a more perfect knowledge and love of God by acquiring a deep knowledge of God's creatures. The world leads man's mind to God. Creatural beings furnish man with abundant material to know God, acknowledge His dominion, love Him above all things, and to show his complete dependence on God in many ways. In this manner all things conspire to man's benefit.

After all, man is a *moral* being, subject directly to God as the eternal lawgiver. Morality can exist only when there is a conformity of man's actions with the norms of moral living. Man's ultimate happiness is closely bound up with the observance of the moral law. And since the moral law has God as its author, it is evident that God *intended* man to live according to the dictates of the moral law and also *intended* to be the supreme object of man's ultimate happiness. God, therefore, in making man a moral being and in giving him an eternal goal of happiness to strive for, has *ordered* the things of this world in such a way that the inferior beings are in existence for the *well-being and happiness of man.* Man, consequently, is not subordinated in any way to the material things of this world, but they are subordinated to him; man is *subordinated to God,* inasmuch as all things should lead him to know and love God as the ultimate truth and the supreme good. Man may, of course, violate the moral law and thus frustrate the innermost purpose of his being, but he cannot thereby frustrate the purposes of God. Man, too, exists for the external glory of God. He will glorify God either in His goodness or in His justice.

God having intended that man observe the moral law here on earth and thereby find his eternal happiness in union with God, it is evident that He has *given man a special end* and purpose. Man is thereby a special object of God's providence. According to his bodily nature, man is a part of the universe at large; according to his spiritual nature, man has a purpose in life which is much nobler than that of the whole physical universe. Mere size means nothing in the eyes of God. It is man's moral well-being that counts in the estimation and intention of God. And because God loves man with a special predilection of His providence and governance, man must love God with his whole heart, his whole mind, his whole soul, and with all his strength. Only in this way will man make himself worthy of God's special providence and achieve his eternal happiness.

God does not do things by halves. Just as a wise architect, in contemplating the erection of a building, not only designs the plan but also makes provision for all the requisite materials and then supervises the actual construction; so, too, God in His infinite wisdom not only plans the nature of each individual being and of the universe as a whole, but also orders the requisite means for them to realize their particular and ultimate end. Any other procedure would reveal a lack of wisdom. Man, therefore, since he occupies a special position in the scheme of things and has a special purpose as a spiritual and moral being, can be sure that the providence of God directs all things in such a manner that his specific and ultimate end can be realized. God will never abandon man to be a mere piece of driftwood tossed about aimlessly on the sea of the world.

St. Thomas[4] proposes the argument for divine providence

[4] *Ibid.*, qu. 22, art. 1.

in the following clear and succinct manner: "It is necessary to attribute providence to God. For all the good that is in created things has been created by God, as was shown above (Q.6, A.4). In created things good is found not only as regards their substance, but also as regards their order towards an end and especially their last end, which, as was said above, is the divine goodness (Q.21, A.4). This good of order existing in created things, is itself created by God. Since, however, God is the cause of things by His intellect, and thus it behooves that the type of every effect should pre-exist in Him, as is clear from what has gone before (Q.19, A.4), it is necessary that the type of the order of things towards their end should pre-exist in the divine mind: and the type of things ordered towards an end is, properly speaking, providence."

Providence, therefore, is a fact.

Physical Evil

The problem of the existence of physical and moral evil in the world is by no means modern. It has exasperated the mind of man from time immemorial. The *existence of evil* has always been adduced as an argument against divine providence.

Already the *epicureans* denied divine providence and governance because of the presence of evil. But that was like spilling the child out of the tub in spilling out the water of the bath; then the manifest order existing in the universe could not be explained. Later on, the *manicheans,* taking over the two supreme principles of light and darkness from the Persian religion, maintained that all the good in the world owed its existence to the 'principle of light' as the source of good and that all the evil owed its existence to the 'principle of darkness' as the source of evil. Both principles are supreme in their respective spheres and are in perpetual war with each other, but eventually the 'principle of light' will conquer the 'principle of darkness' and the good will triumph over the evil. They overlooked the fact that 'darkness' and 'evil' are negative in concept and being and that the 'principle of darkness' can have no existence as such without it being a 'good.' *Pluralists* and *finitists,* like William James and many moderns, identify God with the finite world and consider Him to be subject to all the limitations and defects present in the things of this world; God, in their view, is continuously combating evil through self-improvement. That their 'God' is not the infinitely perfect God of the theists, is obvious; in fact, this world-god is not God at all, at least in the traditional sense of the term. There is no need of proving here the existence of the Supreme Being as distinct from finite beings.

The existence of *physical evil is admitted* unreservedly. The fact is too evident to be denied. What is not admitted, however, is that the existence of physical evil in the world is a valid argument against the providence of an all-wise Creator. Man's mind, of course, is very limited in its power and knowledge, and man cannot expect to penetrate the depths of God's infinite wisdom; many things, therefore, will always remain obscure and mysterious to man.

Unfortunately, too, the real force of the argument of physical evil lies in its emotional appeal, particularly if someone has suffered personal loss or injury. The problem, of course, must be met on a *rational, not an emotional, basis.* If this is done, much of the difficulty vanishes.

Of primary importance in properly judging the presence of physical evil is the fact that *God freely created the world as it is.* He was under no compulsion to create at all; nor was He under compulsion to create this particular world rather than another. Much less was He under compulsion to create the best possible world. Undoubtedly, God could have created a world without physical evil in it, had He so desired. The fact is, He created this particular world with a *hierarchy of inferior and superior beings,* and to these beings He gave the power of action. The individual being is a member of a group, and the various groups constitute the universe. In this way each individual being has a definite place in the *order of the universe as a whole,* just as the constituent parts of the individual have a definite place in the order of each being as an individual.

Now the parts, although they have their own proper being, exist for the whole; the inferior is subordinate to the superior. The well-being of the whole may well require the sacrifice of the well-being of the parts, and the well-being of the superior may well require the sacrifice of the well-being of the inferior. Subatomic particles furnish the material for the elements; the elements, for the compounds; the compounds, for the plants; the plants, for the animals; the animals, for man; and all, for the order of the universe as a whole. In this *hierarchy of order,* therefore, the lower beings must give way to the higher. And so it happens that in the interplay of action between lower and higher beings some lose their physical integrity, and *physical evil results.*

What is wrong with such an arrangement? Nothing whatsoever. The individual being thus has its own proper end as an individual and also an end in the order of the group and of the universe. As an individual being it is less important than as a member of the group and of the universe. God's providence extends to all beings, whether they be considered as individuals or as members of a higher order. But if God wanted the order of the physical world to be such that the inferior beings exist for the superior and that the well-being of the individuals be subordinated to the well-being of the groups and of the universe as a whole, then that is the way the world should be. And that means that *physical evil is a normal feature of the world.*

St. Thomas[5] develops this point very plainly, when he writes: "The perfection of the universe requires that there should be inequality in things, so that every grade of goodness may be realized. Now, one grade of goodness is that of the good which cannot fail. Another grade of goodness is that of the good which can fail in goodness, and this grade is to be found in existence itself; for some things there are which cannot lose their existence, as incorruptible things, while some there are which can lose it, as things corruptible. As, therefore, the

---

[5] *Ibid.,* qu. 48, art. 2.

perfection of the universe requires that there should be not only beings incorruptible, but also corruptible beings; so the perfection of the universe requires that there should be some which can fail in goodness, and thence it follows that sometimes they do fail. Now it is in this that evil consists, namely, in the fact that a thing fails in goodness. Hence, it is clear that evil is found in things, as corruption also is found; for corruption is itself an evil. . . . God and nature and any other agent make what is best in the whole, but not what is best in every single part, except in order to the whole, as was said above (Q.47, A.2). And the whole itself, which is the universe of creatures, is all the better and more perfect if some things in it can fail in goodness, and do sometimes fail, God not preventing this. This happens, firstly, because 'it belongs to Providence not to destroy, but to save nature,' as Dionysius says (Div. Nom. IV); but it belongs to nature that what may fail should sometimes fail; secondly, because, as Augustine says (Enchir. 11), 'God is so powerful that He can even make good out of evil.' Hence many good things would be taken away if God permitted no evil to exist; for fire would not be generated if air was not corrupted, nor would the life of a lion be preserved unless the ass were killed. Neither would avenging justice nor the patience of a sufferer be praised if there were no injustice."

Physical evil is thus no valid argument against the providence of God. The deficiencies of nature are the necessary result of the *limited perfection* of created nature and its powers. There must be some limitation and some deficiency somewhere. Hence, God can permit physical evil and indirectly will it as a normal feature of the order of the universe.

But what about *pain* in brute and man? Physical pain is real; not a mere illusion, as Christian Science claims. Does not the presence of pain bespeak cruelty in the Creator? Not at all. In organic sentient beings pain has a normal function in the economy of their system.

Brutes have two classes of supreme tendencies — the preservation of the individual and the conservation of the species. For this purpose brutes possess senses and instinct. Together with these powers they have *pleasure* and *pain,* and they are the sanction of the preservation or violation of their fundamental natural tendencies. Since brutes do not possess reason, they have pleasure and pain to guide them in the preservation of the order stamped upon their nature.

Physical *pleasure* accompanies the normal exercise of every natural faculty in the service of the well-being of the individual animal and in the service of the conservation of the race. Physical *pain* is the natural result of the overuse or the lesion of some bodily organ; as such, pain prompts the animal nature to repair the damage suffered. Since the brute by its very nature seeks pleasure and avoids pain, the natural order is maintained or restored. Organic disorder would become a permanent disability, if there were no pain to force it to seek relief. To suffer no pain under any condition of life would be equivalent to destroying the animal itself. Pain is never present for itself; it is merely an indication that something is wrong, and its function is the restoration of normal function. That is why *pain is exceptional;* it is never the rule.

The same principle applies to *man,* taken according to his sentient nature. Man would refrain from doing many things conducive to his physical well-being, if it were not for pain. But here, too, pain is a means of preservation, of preventing injury, and of restoring proper function and structure. Every pain indicates some kind of organic need, and thus physical pain is a wise ordination of providence.

From an *ethical standpoint,* pain has an even greater significance. It *prevents* moral evil and *stimulates* moral good. It is an occasion for great virtue. Self-control, self-sacrifice, fortitude, patience, forbearance, charity — all are hardly possible without a certain amount of suffering and pain. Pain also shows the *value of life.* It plainly and persistently calls to man's mind the truth that he is not made for this life, that the earth is no playground and life no play, that he was created for something nobler than this transient world, that there is a better existence to come for which he must prepare himself. Pain is also a *means of penance,* a restoration of the violated moral order which demands satisfaction and atonement.

But what about the *calamities* and *catastrophes* which destroy human life? An earthquake, for example, occurs in a thickly populated territory. All are sleeping. In a moment the walls of the home rock and crash. There is a shriek, a gasp, a groan — and hundreds and thousands of persons die a violent death. To the unthinking such an occurrence may seem to be against the providence of an all-good God. The answer, however, is relatively simple and clear. Man's ultimate happiness and destiny does not consist in this earthly life; it consists in his *eternal happiness* after death, and the sudden cessation of man's earthly existence does not affect his eternity. Hence, God is in no way obligated to suspend the established laws of nature for the sake of saving human lives, since this does not really influence man's eternal soul and does not hinder him from attaining the ultimate purpose of his existence — happiness in eternal union with God. Besides, such fatalities are a great warning which may deter many from sin and keep hundreds of thousands on the path of righteousness. If some human beings thereby lose their destiny, the fault is not God's but man's. Death is by no means the greatest evil; sin is.

The fact of an eternal life also explains why many good people suffer misfortune on earth, while the wicked frequently prosper: the latter have their reward here; the former are to receive it in the life to come.

Physical evil, therefore, cannot be adduced as a valid argument against the providence of God.

Moral Evil

In relation to divine providence, some thinkers find an insoluble difficulty in the *existence of moral evil,* of sin, in the world. Yet, like physical evil, moral evil is no valid argument against God's providence.

There is a great difference between *permitting* sin to happen and *approving* sin when it does happen. The 'approval' of sin on the part of God would indeed be contrary to His infinite holiness. To 'permit' sin to occur means merely 'not to hinder' it from occurring, although one could, *per se,* hinder it from taking place. In committing sin, the created will is the sole cause of the transgression; God merely gives His concurrence to the physical or physiological act of man, and thus He does 'not hinder' man from setting the act, but He does 'not approve' of the act in so far as it involves a violation of the moral order.

Specifically, moral evil is neither against God's goodness nor against His wisdom.

It is not against *God's goodness.*

So long as man has a *free will,* he can choose to perform an action or refrain from an action which is in conformity or in disconformity with the moral law. Man knows this from personal experience: he is forced neither to obey nor to disobey the dictates of conscience. The *possibility* of moral evil (sin) is thus necessarily connected with the created will because of its 'freedom.' Where there is necessity, there is no freedom; and where there is no freedom, there is no possibility of sin. God could, of course, have decided to make moral evil impossible by simply *abstaining from creating* the human will as free; but in that case such a creature would not be 'man.' Man as man is a being endowed with freedom of choice; man as man, therefore, will always be able to decide to act contrary to his conscience and disobey the moral law. Consequently, if God decided to create man, He foresaw the possibility of moral evil in the free will of man. Or, God could have decided to give *such assistance* to man's free will that he would, as a matter of fact, never disobey the moral law. Such an assistance, however, cannot be demanded of God's goodness, because God gives *enough* assistance (conscience, promises of reward, threats of punishment) to deter man from committing sin. Besides, man is not compelled to sin; sin is a *free* act, and it can always be avoided by a person of good will. So long, then, as God gives man the power and the means to avoid sin, there is no fault on His side. If man sins, the fault is entirely his. Hence, moral evil is not against God's goodness.

Nor is it against *God's wisdom*.

The truly wise person always acts for a definite *end* and uses the proper *means* to achieve the end. The final end to be achieved by creation and by man is the greater glory of God. The existence of moral evil would be contrary to God's wisdom only if moral evil would frustrate this final end. But it cannot and it does not. Even if a human will obstinately persists in moral evil unto death, God's wisdom triumphs. For God directs even moral evil to the ultimate purpose of creation, because, by means of his sanctions in the life to come, God leads man to glorify His infinite *justice*. Even in this life God's wisdom uses moral evil for the *welfare of man:* He does this for the welfare of those who have done evil by leading them to repentance, as in the case of St. Paul, St. Augustine, and of countless others; and for the welfare of those who suffer the ill effects of moral evil at the hands of others, by leading them to greater virtue, as in the misfortunes of the martyrs and in general of those who are persecuted unjustly. In this way God uses the presence of moral evil, which He never approves but tolerates, as a means of showing His infinite *mercy* to man. Sin thus is the condition and occasion for much moral good; and this good is a sufficient reason for God to *permit* sin to occur. Ultimately, the ways of God's wisdom are vindicated.

The following quotation from St. Thomas[6] is pertinent to the matter under discussion: "Providence multiplies good things among the subjects of its government. Therefore any thing that would deprive things of many good things does not belong to providence. Now if the will were deprived of freedom, many good things would be done away: for no praise would be given to human virtue; since virtue would be of no account if man acted not freely: there would be no justice in rewarding or punishing, if man were not free in acting well

---

[6] *Summa Contra Gentiles,* tr. by English Dominican Fathers (New York: Benziger Bros., 1925), Bk. III, Chap. LXXIII, 4.

or ill: and there would be no prudence in taking advice, which would be of no use if things occurred of necessity. Therefore it would be inconsistent with providence to deprive the will of liberty.

"Hence it is said (Ecclus. XV, 14): 'God made man from the beginning and left him in the hand of his own counsel'; and again (*ibid.*, 18): 'Before man is life and death, good and evil, that which he shall choose shall be given him.'

"Hereby we refute the opinion of the Stoics who held that all things happen of necessity according to the order of infallible causes, which order the Greeks called εἱμαρμένη."

The evidence for the existence of Providence, as seen especially in the order prevailing in the universe, is so great that it would be unphilosophic to doubt or deny providence merely because some facts seem to be irreconcilable with it. Isolated facts, particularly when not too well understood, can never be a valid argument against a well-established law. In our shortsightedness we see only the immediate causes, effects, and purposes of things, and we are unable to penetrate into the deeper meanings of God's wisdom and knowledge. Ignorance is neither an excuse nor a fit argument.

Fate and Chance

Is there such a thing as *fate*?

The answer will depend on what meaning is given to the term. Seneca[7] defines 'fate' as "the necessity of all things and actions which no force can break." If 'fate' is taken in an *absolute* sense, namely, in the sense that all creatures and their actions are so controlled by other creatures and creatural forces (for example, by the stars) that the course of their existence is absolutely determined for them beforehand, then fate is non-existent. Fate in such an absolute sense implies the denial of the freedom of God and man and leaves no room for divine providence and governance in the affairs of men and of the world. But if 'fate' is taken in a *relative* sense, its existence

---

[7] *Natur. Quaest.*, l. 3, c. 36: "Necessitas omnium rerum actionumque, quae nulla vis rumpat."

can be readily admitted. In this relative sense 'fate' would merely mean the arrangement of secondary (creatural) causes so as to produce the effects foreseen by God and decreed by Him according to the purpose of His providence. It is in this sense that St. Thomas[8] speaks of 'fate.' Generally speaking, however, it is better not to use the term 'fate,' because people usually take the word in an absolute sense.

Is there such a thing as *chance*?

The term 'chance' can be taken in one of two ways: either with regard to the intellect or with regard to the cause. With regard to the *intellect* something is said to happen 'by chance' when the intellect is ignorant of the cause producing the effect. With regard to the *cause* something happens 'by chance' when it occurs outside of the intention and arrangement of the cause. Taken in the first meaning, many things can be said to happen 'by chance' in so far as man's intellect is concerned, because man is naturally ignorant of many of the causes which operate in nature; God being omniscient, however, nothing can happen 'by chance' with regard to His intellect. From the standpoint of the operating causes, it is evident that many things can and do happen 'by chance' where particular causes are concerned. For example, when a brick slips from the hand of a bricklayer high up on a scaffold and in falling hits a passerby on the head, it does so by chance, because it does not lie in the nature of the brick to strike a passerby on the head. However, with regard to God as the provident universal cause concurring in all creatural actions, nothing can ever happen 'by chance.' Chance, therefore, occurs with respect to creatural beings, both from the standpoint of knowledge and causality, but never with respect to the providence of God.

It is, therefore, a grave error of judgment to speak of *good fortune* and *misfortune* as if they occurred independent of the rule of divine providence: whatever happens, happens either according to God's intention or at least with His permission.

---

8 *Summa Theologica* (New York: Benziger Bros.), qu. 116.

Optimism and Pessimism

Optimism, as a philosophic system of thought, is the doctrine that the present universe is the best of all possible worlds. G. W. Leibnitz (1646–1716) was an advocate of absolute optimism. He admitted the existence of evil, but attributed its ultimate source to the imperfection intrinsic to all limited existence. In order to vindicate God's absolute perfection, therefore, he maintained that the present world is the best which God could create.

While we assert that God is infinitely good and perfect in all that He does, so far as He Himself is concerned, we deny that the present world is *absolutely the best* which God could create. Not only does experience reveal many physical and moral evils in this universe as it is presently constituted, but an absolutely perfect world, the best which God could create, is a *contradiction in terms.* God being infinitely perfect is indefinitely imitable by creatural beings. Every creatural being, however, is necessarily finite in its perfections. More perfect beings must be possible to God's creative power; otherwise a limit is set either on God's power or on His perfections. God cannot be necessitated to create, much less to create beings with greater perfection than that which the present world contains. God freely created the present world, and it is *relatively perfect,* namely, as perfect as He intended it to be; but it is not the best possible world, because such a world is self-contradictory.

Pessimism, as a philosophic system of thought, is the opposite of optimism. Its doctrine contends, at least as far as man is concerned, that there is nothing good in life and in the world. Absolute pessimism is just as erroneous as absolute optimism.

Buddhism as expounded by Gautama (or Gotama) looks upon living as essentially full of sorrow. Existence itself is an evil, and the main problem of life is to obtain the extinction of all desire (the source of all pain and suffering) in nirvana and of all being in parinirvana. *Modern pessimism* owes its vogue mainly to the philosophies of Arthur Schopenhauer (1788–1860) and Eduard von Hartmann (1842–1906). From their writings pessimism was carried over into the field of literature.

That there is much suffering in life, is an evident fact. But that life is essentially a failure and an endless source of pain and sorrow, is contrary to all experience. Pantheism and finitism can never succeed in giving an adequate explanation of the existence of physical and moral evil in the life of man. Theism alone can. Just as this world is not absolutely the best, so it is also not the absolutely worst. The infinite goodness of God is reflected in His creatures; it cannot be otherwise. Hence, in so far as beings have essence and existence at all, they *must be good*. Now, if the world is essentially good, pessimism is false.

The ultimate explanation of life, of course, is not found in the natural order. It is found in the *supernatural destiny of man*.

Miracles

From the standpoint of its etymological derivation, a 'miracle' (Lat., *mirari,* to wonder) is anything that causes wonderment. Wonderment, however, can be caused in a person for reasons of ignorance. For instance, an electric storm or the rise and fall of the tides may produce wonderment in an uneducated rustic, although they are purely natural phenomena. More is needed for a 'miracle' properly so called.

In traditional usage, a *miracle* is defined as a perceptible event which exceeds the order and power of nature and has God as its author. The terms need clarification.

Miracles are viewed as a testimony of God's intervention in the course of nature on behalf of man. For this reason the definition of a 'miracle' is formulated as given above. A miracle is an *event,* that is, an occurrence, a happening, an effect of some sort. It must be a *perceptible* event. One could just as well say that it must be a 'sensible' event, because only something sensible is perceptible. Man derives his knowledge through the senses, and purely spiritual realities make no impression on the senses. For instance, the spiritual transformation of a soul is of a higher order than a sensible occurrence; but it is not classed as a 'miracle' in the strict sense of the term, because its existence cannot be proved by means of the regular channels of information. Then, a 'miracle' must *exceed the order and power of nature*. The word 'nature' here means the assemblage of all creatural beings, whether they be material or spiritual, together with all the powers flowing from their essence. The phenomena of spiritism (if they are genuine) would be performed by spirits; however, since such spirits are creatures belonging to the realm of 'nature,' such phenomena are not 'miracles' in the accepted meaning. The 'order of nature' is presupposed as existing; and on this account divine creation and conservation and concurrence are excluded from the concept of a 'miracle' since they are prerequisites for this order itself. To be a real 'miracle' the occurrence must exceed the powers of any and all creatural beings, so that it *has God as its author*. The mere fact that an event is rare and extraordinary does not make it miraculous; nor does the fact that man is ignorant of the forces at play. The circumstances must be such that man is certain that the existing forces of nature are incapable of producing the effect in question, so that recourse must be had to the omnipotence and wisdom of God as the only logical explanation of the occurrence. Every 'miracle' is thus a *suspension of the ordinary laws of nature* on the part of the Almighty.

Some events exceed the order and powers of nature *substantially* (*quoad substantiam*). Such effects simply do not occur at all in the realm of nature. Effects of this kind would be, for example, the restoration of life to a really dead person, the actual compenetration of material substances (physical bodies), the giving of sight to a person born blind because of some organic deficiency. These effects lie entirely beyond the range and power of natural causes and laws; only God can produce them. Other events exceed the order and power of nature because of the *manner* (*quoad modum*) in which they are performed. The events themselves occur in nature and are pro-

duced by natural causes and forces, but not in the particular
'manner' as in the miraculous occurrence. Thus, it is a natural
event that diseases are cured and broken bones mended. But
when such facts occur instantaneously, by means of a mere
word or command, then this 'manner' or 'mode' is not in
accordance with the procedure of natural causes and laws;
hence, in such cases it is the manner of the occurrence, not
the event itself, which must be ascribed to the omnipotent
power of God in whose name they are performed.

Miracles Are Possible

Whether miracles have ever actually occurred is a matter of
historical evidence. The philosopher is primarily concerned
with the twofold problem of the *possibility* and *cognoscibility*
of miracles.

Pantheists of all shades deny the possibility of miracles. To
be consistent, they must. According to their doctrine, God is
identified with the world; God (or nature) is the only reality
which exists. There can be nothing outside of, or above, or
contrary to, nature; that would be equivalent to saying that
something exists outside the entire range of being, or above,
or contrary to, all existing being. Granted their premise, the
possibility of miracles must certainly be denied. *Deists,* as a
rule, assert that God has indeed created the world, but after
that He leaves it entirely to the forces and laws which operate
in nature, so that no exceptions occur in the natural course of
events. *Fatalists* maintain that every being in the world, man
included, is controlled by the iron law of necessity which
nothing can abrogate or alter. *Materialists* admit of no beings
but those which are material. God, providence, and miracles
can have no place in their system. *Many physical scientists*
deny the possibility of miracles. They, perhaps more than
others, perceive the admirable order of the universe and the
complete reign of law in nature and in each single being, and
from this constancy of order and uniformity in nature they
argue that the possibility of miracles is precluded. A miracle,
they claim, would be a violation of nature's inflexible laws, and

to admit the possibility of that would be tantamount to the destruction of science. Others, like *Spinoza, Locke,* and *Kant,* admit the possibility of miracles in principle. Practically, however, they deny it. What man calls a miracle, they say, is really a natural event, only he does not and cannot discover the natural laws and causes that govern the phenomena.

We claim that *miracles are possible.*

If miracles were impossible, the reason would have to be sought either in *God* or in the *laws of nature.* But neither is true.

The reason does not lie *in God.*

Certainly, miracles would be impossible on the part of God, if they would imply an *imperfection* of some kind in God, either because of the 'fact' that a natural law has been suspended or because of the 'manner' of the action or because of the 'purpose' of the miracle. That, however, is not the case.

Every miracle, of course, is a suspension of a law of nature in a particular instance. But this *fact* does not oppose God's *immutability.* Together with the uniformity of nature which God has undoubtedly decreed, He also decreed the exception involved in the miracle. Hence, in wishing both the laws and the exception to some law, He does not change His plans and decrees, but merely His works. Nor does the fact of a miracle contradict His *wisdom.* If God worked a miracle in order to correct some mistakes in the creation of the world or to remedy a positive defect which He had somehow overlooked, then an imperfection in God would be implied. However, it is preposterous to think that the all-knowing and all-wise Supreme Being could make mistakes or overlook a defect. If, then, God decreed from all eternity that a miracle should occur at a particular point of time, the miracle would be a result of His wisdom and not contrary to it.

The same line of reasoning applies to the *manner* in which a miracle is worked. If a miracle were worked because of *arbitrariness* and *fickleness* in God's will, it would involve an imperfection in God's being and be impossible. But why would a miracle be the result of arbitrariness and fickleness on God's part? It certainly need not be so. And if it is not, a miracle must be, to say the least, in accordance with His perfection.

So far as the *purpose* of a miracle is concerned, a miracle would be impossible on the part of God if His purpose in working a miracle were against His *sanctity*. But that could only happen if God's purpose were contrary to holiness itself. God the all-holy, however, cannot have an unholy purpose in any of His operations. Hence, His purpose in working a miracle cannot be contrary to His sanctity.

The *laws of nature* do not make miracles impossible.

The present order of nature is not necessary. It is an effect of creation, and creation came about through an act of *free choice* on the part of God. God, therefore, was in no way constrained to create just this particular order. Consequently, in decreeing the present order God could also include exceptions to this order.

Of itself, the *order* of the world *could be different* from what it actually is. This order had to be known by the divine intellect before God's will brought it into being. Now, God's intellect could and did see in the imitability of His perfections other worlds and other natural orders capable of imitating His perfections. It is evident, therefore, that of itself the present order of nature could be different. Hence, exceptions to this order, that is, miracles, are not intrinsically impossible.

All creatural beings exist in *absolute dependence* on God as their creator. Because God gave to these beings their entire substance and all their powers, He can, immediately and most intimately, influence them in any way He desires. It follows that the order of nature and the laws governing nature are *not immutable* in relation to God. If He can annihilate the creatures completely, He can certainly change them in their substance and powers, and He can certainly also suspend their operations any time He so decrees.

One must never forget that a miracle is not an 'abrogation' of a natural law; rather, it is an *exception* to an existing law. When a miracle occurs, the law remains in full force throughout the universe except in this particular place and at this particular time and on this particular occasion. Fire, for instance, does not cease to burn and consume on earth, because the three youths were spared by God in the furnace of Babylon. Men are not cured instantaneously now, because Christ cured a man born blind in an instant by His mere word. A body heavier than water would sink into the water anywhere, even though Christ once walked on the waters of the Sea of Galilee. If God designs to work a miracle, the natural tendencies of creatural beings remain intact. God does not change the 'nature' of being through the performance of a miracle, nor does He disturb the uniformity of the order of nature; all He does is *suspend the effects* of nature and its forces in a particular instance.

It is thus evident that neither on the part of God nor on the part of the laws of nature is a miracle impossible. When, therefore, certain scientists fear that a miracle would tend to destroy science and scientific knowledge, their misgivings are utterly unfounded.

Miracles Can Be Known

The intrinsic possibility of miracles is thus established. However, it is one thing to say that miracles are possible, and quite another thing to claim that miracles can be objectively recognized as having actually occurred. Can this claim be established beyond reasonable doubt?

Two considerations enter the problem. The first is: Did such and such an occurrence actually happen? This is a question of *historical fact*. The second is: Does this occurrence exceed the order and powers of nature? This is a question of *philosophical judgment*.

So far as the actual occurrence of a miracle as a *historical fact* is concerned, its acceptance will be conditioned by the 'evidence' furnished by the witnesses. All events, whether miraculous or not, are on an equal footing as historical facts. They depend entirely on the competence of the witnesses, and this competence is determined by their *knowledge* of the facts and their *trustworthiness* as witnesses. Since a miracle is a 'perceptible' event, the knowledge required is simply the knowledge obtained through ordinary observation. That a man limps because his one leg is shorter than the other, is an ordinary observable fact; and that his walk is afterward normal because both legs are now of equal length, is also an ordinary observable fact. That a person has tuberculosis of the lungs in an advanced stage, any competent physician can verify with the help of X rays; that the destroyed tissue of the lungs is later restored, the physician can also verify with the help of X rays. The trustworthiness of the witnesses, as we see in courts of law, can also be established to the satisfaction of reason. Hence, the *fact* of a certain occurrence, considered to be miraculous, should not be too difficult to establish, provided one takes all the significant circumstances into account.

The miraculous character of an occurrence presents a more serious problem of *philosophical judgment*. For this judgment knowledge of the *cause* of the event is necessary: if the cause is a natural force, the event itself is natural; but if a natural force cannot have produced the observed effect, the event is miraculous. Some thinkers, especially some scientists, claim that man can never know that a miracle has actually occurred because some 'hidden force' of nature may have produced the effect. In order to be certain, they say, man would have to know *all* the forces of nature, and such a knowledge man can never acquire. This is an extravagant demand, one which these scientists never exact in their own field of research. All that is required is a knowledge of the *pertinent* forces, and such a knowledge man may have in many instances.

For example. *Decomposition* of the body and *rigor mortis* are true signs of the death of a person, and they are readily observable. Suppose they are present; death has most certainly overtaken the organism. Everybody, especially the scientist and physician, knows that no pertinent natural force can restore life to the corpse. The restoration of life to a dead person, therefore, cannot be the effect of a natural power. If then, this dead person is restored to life, the restoration must be adjudged a miraculous event. Another example. Every physician is aware that *muscular atrophy,* resulting in paralysis, may possibly be cured through prolonged exercise; but he also knows that a mere verbal command will not be a sufficient cause to restore the atrophied tissue. Yet it is done. What must be his verdict in the case? That some 'hidden natural force' produced the effect? Not at all. He knows that no 'pertinent' force of nature was present in the verbal command, and the cure was therefore 'miraculous.'[9]

Miraculous events, therefore, are possible and their occurrence can be verified under proper conditions. That is all that logically pertains to philosophy.

God and Man

Philosophy, by its very nature, is restricted to the findings of unaided, natural reason. The supernatural is thus excluded from philosophical investigation. It is on this foundation that the science of theodicy has been built.

But the supernatural is also a fact, although philosophy is incapable of proving it. God has given man a *supernatural destiny,* culminating in the Beatific Vision in heaven. This is the sublime purpose of man's existence. It explains everything. And the supernatural means which God gave man to attain his eternal goal is sanctifying grace. Grace makes man truly a son of God by adoption; and God is truly man's Father. But if man is a son, then he is also an heir. His inheritance is the immortal possession of God in never ending glory and in everlasting bliss. This is an end eminently worth striving for and living for through a lifetime of loving God. Therein lies the wisdom of the ages.

As it is said in the Book of Wisdom:[10] "Wisdom is glorious, and never fadeth away, and is easily seen by them that love her, and is found by them that seek her. . . . For she goeth about seeking such as are worthy of her, and she showeth her-

---

[9] Read the account of the cure of the blind man in St. John, Chap. 9, and of the lame man in Acts, Chap. 3. On the presumption that these narratives are historically true, the cures are 'miracles.'

[10] Wisd. 6.

self to them cheerfully in the ways, and meeteth them with all providence. For the beginning of her is the most true desire of discipline. And the care of discipline is love: and love is the keeping of her laws: and the keeping of her laws is the firm foundation of incorruption: and incorruption bringeth near to God. Therefore the desire of wisdom bringeth to the everlasting kingdom."

Summary of Chapter XV

God's *providence* and *governance* are the subject of this chapter.

1. *Notion of Providence.* — *Providence* is "the type (plan) of the order of things foreordained towards an end." God's intellect has the 'plan,' and His will decrees that this order shall prevail. As an individual, each being has its 'proper' end; and as a member of the universe at large, it has an 'ultimate' end. The providence of God is thus 'particular' (pertaining to the 'proper' end of each individual being) and 'universal' (pertaining to the ultimate end of all beings in the universe at large).

2. *Notion of Governance.* — *Governance* is the execution of the plan of providence among existing beings. Since the world actually exists, governance is often viewed as an integral part of divine providence.

3. *Proof of God's Providence.* — As regards *general providence,* it can be proved 'indirectly' and 'directly.' *Indirectly,* God's providence is proved by the absurdities which follow the denial of it; such a denial involves the denial either of God's wisdom or power or goodness. *Directly,* God's providence is proved from the nature of God and of His creatures. Since God created each being and the universe and the order prevailing in them, He had to 'intend' this order and its execution.

As regards God's *special providence concerning man,* it is proved by the nature of man as God created him. Man seeks 'perfect happiness' naturally and necessarily, and this happiness can be found only in the life to come after death. Man is a 'moral' being, and his happiness is dependent on the observance of the moral law. This being man's nature, God *intended* that man observe the moral law and find his eternal happiness in the union with God. God, therefore, has created man with a special end and purpose. That man can fulfill this end and purpose, demands a special providence which directs all things so that his special end will be realized.

4. *Physical Evil.* — The presence of physical evil in the world is no valid argument against God's providence. God created this world *freely* and with it the *hierarchy of order* consisting of inferior and superior beings. In this order the interplay of action is such that some beings lose their physical integrity, and physical evil results. Physical evil is thus a normal feature of the world, due to the limited perfection of created nature and its powers.

5. *Moral Evil.* — The presence of moral evil is also no valid argument against God's providence. God 'permits' moral evil, but He does not 'approve' it. If moral evil were contrary to God's providence, it would have to be either against His goodness or His wisdom. It is neither.

Moral evil is not against *God's goodness.* The possibility of moral evil (sin) is necessarily given with the *freedom* of man's will. If God wanted to create man, then He had to give him a free will; and 'free will' involves the free choice of man to choose sin. That God created man, is a sign of His goodness. Nor is moral evil against God's *wisdom.* God gave to man a definite end and the proper means to achieve this end; that is wisdom. Moral evil does not frustrate the ultimate end of man; if he does not glorify God's goodness, he glorifies His justice.

6. *Fate and Chance.* — *Fate* in an 'absolute' sense is non-existent, because it would be contrary to the freedom of God and man. It exists in a 'relative' sense, as the arrangement of creatural causes so as to produce the effects intended by God's providence.

Chance occurs with respect to creatural beings, both from the standpoint of knowledge and causality; but with respect to God's providence, nothing ever happens 'by chance.'

7. *Optimism and Pessimism.* — *Optimism* is false. The present world is not the best of all possible worlds. God, because of His infinite perfection and power, could always create a better world. The 'best possible world' is a contradiction.

Pessimism contends that there is nothing good in life and in the world. This system is false. In so far as beings have essence and existence at all, they must be good.

8. *Miracles.* — A *miracle* is a perceptible event which exceeds the order and power of nature and has God as its author. It may exceed nature either 'substantially' or in the 'manner' of its occurrence.

9. **Miracles Are Possible.** — They are possible from the stand-

point both of God and of the laws of nature. In no case do they imply an *imperfection in God*. From the standpoint of the *laws of nature,* these laws are not absolutely but only relatively necessary.

10. *Miracles Can Be Known.* — Two things are involved: the *historical fact* of the occurrence, and this depends on the knowledge and trustworthiness of witnesses; the *philosophical judgment* that the effect cannot have been brought about by a natural cause, and for this a knowledge of the 'pertinent' laws of natural causes is sufficient.

11. *God and Man.* — Although theodicy, as a department of philosophy, is restricted to the 'natural,' the 'supernatural destiny of man' is all-important.

Readings

Driscoll, John T., *God,* Chaps. XII–XV. — Joyce, George H., *Principles of Natural Theology,* Chap. XVII. — Boedder, Bernard, *Natural Theology,* Bk. III, Chap. II. — Mercier, D. Card., *A Manual of Modern Scholastic Philosophy,* Vol. II, 'Natural Theology,' Part III, Chap. III, n. III. — McCormick, John F., *Scholastic Metaphysics,* Vol. II, Chaps. XIV, XV. — Brosnan, William J., *God Infinite, the World, and Reason,* pp. 154–236. — Garrigou-Lagrange, R., *Providence.* — Smith, Gerard, *Natural Theology,* Chap. XVI. — Aquinas, St. Thomas, *Summa Theologica,* I, qu. 22; *Contra Gentiles,* Bk. III, Chap. 71 ff.

GLOSSARY

ABIOGENESIS. The theory that living beings ultimately came into existence through a development on the part of the forces indigenous to nonliving matter. Spontaneous generation.

ABSOLUTE. The unconditioned, the ultimate ground of all reality.

ACCIDENT. A being, incapable of existing in itself, which needs another being in which to inhere.

ACT. The condition or state of existing; whatever exists is 'actual being.' Act, therefore, is the perfection, determination, or degree of reality present in a thing as it exists.

ACTUAL. See Act.

ACTUALITY. See Act.

AGNOSTICISM. The doctrine which denies or doubts the constitutional ability of the human mind to know ultimate reality. It usually concludes with the recognition of an intrinsically Unknowable.

ANNIHILATION. The reduction of an existing being into non-existence; the complete destruction of a being.

APPETENCY. The inclination or propensity of a being for something which is good for it.

APPROBATION. See Knowledge of Approbation of God.

ASEITY. The state of God considered as not owing His existence to another but to Himself, so that existence is of His essence; He is, therefore, 'of Himself' (a se).

ATHEISM. The doctrine that no divinity or God exists.

ATTRIBUTE. That which follows by natural necessity upon a fully constituted essence. Another term for 'attribute,' practically synonymous with it, is property. The 'divine attributes' are all those perfections which flow necessarily from the divine essence and which are found in no other being but God.

ATTRIBUTE, ABSOLUTE. An attribute which pertains to God's essence as such.

ATTRIBUTE, RELATIVE. An attribute of God that has a relation to things other than God.

BANNESIANISM. The doctrine that God applies a physical premotion, a physical predetermination, directly to the creature's operative power, and therefore also to the will of man in making its free choice. The bannesians claim that such a physical premotion is required in order to safeguard God's absolute dominion over His creatures.

BECOMING. *See* Change.

BEING. Whatever exists or is capable of existence. Expressed negatively, 'being' is that which is opposed to 'absolute nothing'; expressed positively, 'being' is anything which has actual or possible existence.

BEING, RELATIVE. Anything which is 'capable of existence,' though now does not actually exist.

BEING, SELF-SUBSISTENT. A being which exists or subsists in virtue of its own essence.

BERGSONIANISM. *See* Evolution, Creative.

CAUSE. Anything which assists in the production of a thing through some positive influence.

CAUSE, EFFICIENT. Anything which produces something, that is, brings it from non-existence to existence by the positive influence of its own action.

CAUSE, INSTRUMENTAL. A cause which is insufficient of itself to produce the entire effect but influences the production of the effect under the direction and in the service of another (the principal) cause.

CAUSE, PRINCIPAL. A cause which has a fully proportionate and sufficient power to produce the entire effect either alone or with the use of an instrumental cause.

CHANCE. A mode of causal activity, not purposive in character, regarded as determining an event.

CHANGE. The actualization of something potential; it implies the passage of a being from one state to another.

CHANGE, EXTRINSIC. Change is extrinsic, when it is the result of an 'extrinsic denomination.'

CHANGE, INTRINSIC. Change is intrinsic when some reality is either acquired or lost in the passage of the subject from one state to another.

COGNITION, SIMPLE, IN GOD. *See* Knowledge of Simple Cognition in God.

CONCURRENCE, DIVINE. God's influence operating with creatures in producing the same effect as they produce through their own activity.

CONCURRENCE, IMMEDIATE PHYSICAL. As applied to divine concurrence, concurrence is physical in as far as God effectively and directly influences the creature in the production of the action itself.

CONCURRENCE, MEDIATE PHYSICAL. As applied to divine concurrence, concurrence is mediate in so far as God prepares the creatures in such a way that they are fit for action and preserves them in that condition.

CONCURRENCE, MORAL. Concurrence based on some sort of moral action, such as commands, exhortations, and promises.

CONCURRENCE, PHYSICAL. Concurrence based on some sort of physical action.

CONSERVATION. Continuation in existence through dependence on a cause.

CONSERVATION, ACTIVE. The activity of a cause producing continuation in existence.

CONSERVATION, DIRECT POSITIVE. Positive conservation is direct when the continued duration of a thing is the immediate effect of the positive action of a cause.

CONSERVATION, DIVINE. God's influence in the continuation in existence on the part of creatures.

CONSERVATION, INDIRECT POSITIVE. The conservation which occurs when an action hinders destructive causes from destroying a thing or provides the means needed for the thing to remain what it is.

CONSERVATION, NEGATIVE. Conservation is said to be negative when a being continues in existence by not being destroyed by another, although the other has the power to destroy it.

CONSERVATION, PASSIVE. Continuation in existence on the part of a being through the activity of some cause.

CONSERVATION, POSITIVE. Conservation is said to be positive when a being is made to remain in existence through some action which is performed.

CONTINGENCY. That state in virtue of which something can be otherwise than it is in its being or existence or both; if a contingent being actually exists, its non-existence would involve no contradiction because existence does not belong to the constitution of its essence.

CONTINGENT. Something is said to be 'contingent' when it actually exists but need not exist.

CONTRADICTION, FREEDOM OF. *See* Freedom of Exercise.

CREATION. The production of a thing hitherto not existing, without the use of any subject-matter from which it is made; *productio rei ex nihilo sui et subjecti.*

CREATION, ETERNAL. Creation from eternity, so that the created being has no actual beginning in time.

CREATOR. One who creates or produces something out of nothing.

CREATURE. Anything created; any being apart from God.

DEISM. A quasi-philosophic movement in opposition to revealed religion. Chiefly, deism defended a universal natural religion; it conceded that it could be proved on rational grounds that God exists and is the Creator. Many deists, however, contended that God, after creating the world, took no interest in mundane affairs.

DESIGN. The arrangement of various items into a system or whole, so that the order obtained is the result of plan and intention. The 'purpose' of design consists in the achievement of a definite end through the use of definite means.

DISTINCTION. The difference or diversity between various realities or between the concepts of the same reality. Distinction always implies an absence of identity between things or concepts.

DISTINCTION, MENTAL. The difference between concepts of the same reality.

DISTINCTION, PURELY MENTAL. The difference between concepts of the same reality without a foundation in the thing itself. *Distinctio rationis ratiocinantis.*

DISTINCTION, REAL. The difference between things that are not alike in their reality, independent of the consideration of the mind.

DISTINCTION, VIRTUAL. The difference between concepts of the same reality, with a foundation in the object itself for the distinction. *Distinctio virtualis, distinctio rationis ratiocinatae, distinctio rationis cum fundamento in re.*

DISTINCTION, VIRTUAL, WITH AN IMPERFECT FOUNDATION. A virtual distinction is said to have an imperfect foundation when the concepts of the same reality are distinct in such a manner that they are not mutually exclusive but rather include each other implicitly.

DISTINCTION, VIRTUAL, WITH A PERFECT FOUNDATION. A virtual distinction is said to have a perfect foundation when the concepts are so distinct in comparison to each other (although they apply to the same reality) that they are objectively different in content.

DURATION. The permanence of a being in its existence.

DURATION, PERMANENT. Duration which remains constant and intact.

DURATION, SUCCESSIVE. Duration in which one part continuously follows the other.

EMANATIONISM. *See* Pantheism, Transient Realistic.

EMINENTLY CONTAINED PERFECTION. A perfection present in a producing cause in such a manner that it is precontained in some higher perfection of the cause.

EMPIRICISM. The doctrine which denies or doubts the validity of all intellectual knowledge and admits only the certainty of sense-knowledge or 'experience.'

ENS A SE. Being independent of any other being; self-subsistent being.

ESSENCE. That through which a being is just what it is (*id quo res est id quod est*).

ESSENCE, METAPHYSICAL. An essence consisting of all those elements which are necessary for the concept of the thing and without which this thing cannot be conceived. The 'metaphysical essence of God' is that perfection which is conceived by man as being the most basic to an understanding of God.

ESSENCE, METAPHYSICAL, OF GOD. 'Self-subsistent Being' is the metaphysical essence of God.

Essence, Physical. The complex of all the fundamental elements without which this thing cannot *exist* in the order of reality, independent of the consideration of the mind contemplating it.

Essence, Physical, of God. 'Omniperfection' is the physical essence of God.

Eternity. Duration in existence which is essentially without beginning and end and which is essentially without real succession and intrinsic change.

Evil. The privation of a good.

Evil, Moral. The privation of a good pertaining to the moral order; sin.

Evil, Physical. The privation of a good pertaining to the physical order.

Eviternity. The everlasting duration of a naturally incorruptible being in its existence.

Evolution. The gradual unfolding of something precontained.

Evolution, Creative. The doctrine of Bergson and his followers that everything is in a continuous flux of becoming and change, without any underlying subject which becomes and changes.

Evolution, Emergent. The theory that nature is the product of evolution in such a manner that entirely new and unpredictable properties originate through synthesis and thereby form new and higher levels of reality in a continuously ascending process of development.

Evolution, Organic. The theory that the various species and types of animals and plants derive their origin, not through distinct and separate creative acts of God, but through development from other pre-existing species and types, all differences being accounted for by modifications acquired in successive generations according to purely natural laws.

Evolution, Purposive. The theory that the Supreme Intelligence endowed nature with a purpose and with the necessary principles of action to realize this purpose through evolution.

Existence. Something is said to 'exist' or 'to have existence' when it is outside the producing power of a cause and is actually present in the world of reality, so that it has 'being' of its own; hence, the condition or state of being outside the mind and outside the productive power of an efficient cause.

Experience, Religious. The doctrine that man has an experience, either intellectual or emotional, of God's existence; this experience is supposed to be 'non-inferential.'

Extra-mundane. Not a part of the present universe, but existing apart from it.

Fate. Necessity controlling all creatural actions of whatever kind, so that these actions are predetermined.

FATE, ABSOLUTE. Fate is absolute, when all creatures and their actions are so controlled by other creatures and creatural forces that the course of their existence is necessarily determined for them beforehand.

FATE, RELATIVE. The arrangement of secondary (creatural) causes so as to produce the effects foreseen by God and decreed by Him according to the purpose of His providence.

FIDEISM. The theory or attitude that human reason is incapable, of its own native ability, of reaching certitude regarding any truth or at least regarding truth of the philosophic and religious order; it affirms that knowledge of truth consists in an act of *faith*.

FINITISM. The theory which holds that God is always in a process of becoming.

FORMALISM. The doctrine which holds that the necessity of judgments is due to native *a priori* mental forms.

FORMALLY CONTAINED PERFECTION. A perfection precontained in the producing cause in such a manner that the actuality of the perfection is present according to its real being in the efficient cause.

FREEDOM. In a wide sense, the absence of external coercion or restraint which hinders an appetency from expressing itself in external action; in a strict sense, the absence of intrinsic necessity or determination in the performance of an act.

FREEDOM OF CONTRADICTION. *See* Freedom of Exercise.

FREEDOM OF CONTRARIETY. The freedom to choose between a moral good and a moral evil.

FREEDOM OF EXERCISE. The freedom to will or not to will, to act or not to act. Also called *freedom of contradiction*.

FREEDOM OF SPECIFICATION. The freedom to choose between one act of the will and another act of the will, between one object and another object.

FREEDOM OF THE WILL. The ability of the will, all conditions for action being present, to decide whether to act or not to act, and whether to act in this manner or in that manner.

FUTURIBLES. Conditionally future events; events referring to acts which a man would do through free choice under certain unfulfilled conditions.

GENERATION, SPONTANEOUS. *See* Abiogenesis.

GNOSTICISM. The doctrine which maintains the origin of numberless 'aeons' through emanation from God.

GOD. God is the ultimate author of all change in the universe; the absolutely necessary being and the sufficient reason for the existence of all contingent beings; extra-mundane, unchanged and unchangeable; the uncaused cause, the *ens a se;* the intelligent designer of the order present in the universe; pure act and pure spirit, possessing unlimited perfection and life; a substance, absolutely simple, devoid of all potentiality and composition, without accidental determinations of any kind; absolutely unique; personal; omnipotent; omnipresent; the creator of the world; the supreme being, incomprehensible and ineffable.

GOOD. Something suitable for a being.

GOVERNANCE, DIVINE. The execution of the plan of divine providence among existing beings.

IMMENSITY. The intrinsic attribute of God in virtue of which He is necessarily present wherever any being exists which is not God.

IMMUTABILITY. The impossibility of undergoing change.

IMPOSSIBILITY, ABSOLUTE. Impossibility is absolute when something exceeds the capability of every power, because it involves a contradiction in its very concept.

IMPOSSIBILITY, RELATIVE. Impossibility is relative when something exceeds the capability of a particular power, but does not involve a contradiction in itself.

IMPOSSIBLE. Something is said to be 'impossible' when it does not exist and cannot exist. Such a being is either absolutely or relatively impossible.

INFINITE. Without limits or bounds.

INFINITE, ACTUALLY. A being is said to be actually infinite, or to possess actual infinity, if its reality exists without limitation.

INFINITE, POTENTIALLY. A finite being is said to be potentially infinite, or to possess potential infinity, if its reality can be increased without limit.

INTELLECTION. Exercise of the intellect; knowing.

INTELLIGENCE, SIMPLE. By the 'simple intelligence' of God one understands God's knowledge which has as its object those things that are merely possible.

KNOWLEDGE, ABSTRACTIVE, OF GOD. God's knowledge of events and things which never exist.

KNOWLEDGE, ANALOGICAL. Knowledge based on unlike, but related, realities, so that such knowledge is partly the same and partly different. Our knowledge of God is analogical, since the terms referring to the perfections common to God and creatures are neither absolutely identical nor absolutely equivocal in meaning.

KNOWLEDGE, INTERMEDIATE. With respect to God, intermediate knowledge pertains to conditionally future events dependent on the free will of man. *Scientia media.*

KNOWLEDGE, INTUITIVE, OF GOD. God's knowledge of events and things which actually exist at one time or another.

KNOWLEDGE, PRACTICAL, OF GOD. God's knowledge for the making of something, when the intention of making is present.

KNOWLEDGE, SPECULATIVE, OF GOD. God's knowledge which looks solely to the truth involved in knowing.

KNOWLEDGE, SPECULATIVE-PRACTICAL, OF GOD. God's knowledge required for making something, but the intention to make it being absent.

KNOWLEDGE OF APPROBATION OF GOD. God's knowledge of all that is good.

KNOWLEDGE OF SIMPLE COGNITION IN GOD. God's knowledge of evil.

LAW OF PROBABILITY. Probability, on the basis of chance, follows the ratio of geometrical progression.

LIBERTY. *See* Freedom.

LIFE. Immanence of action.

LOGICAL DISTINCTION. *See* Distinction, Mental.

MANICHEISM. The doctrine that there are two supreme principles governing the world, one good and one bad.

MATERIALISM. The philosophic system of thought which considers matter to be the only reality and attempts to explain everything in the universe as the result of the conditions and activities of matter.

MIRACLE. A perceptible event which exceeds the order and power of nature and has God as its author.

MODERNISM. The doctrine which holds that God is present in man through 'vital immanence,' in consequence of which man is emotionally conscious of God's presence and has a 'vital experience' of God dwelling and working in him.

MOLINISM. The doctrine, opposed to bannesianism and its theory of physical premotion, of simultaneous concurrence on the part of God in free actions. The molinists claim that a simultaneous concurrence is required to safeguard the freedom of man's will.

MONISM. The doctrine which seeks to deduce all phenomena from a single principle; specifically, the doctrine which holds that there exists but one fundamental reality or being, either mind (idealism), or matter (materialism), or a neutral reality that is neither mind nor matter but is the substantial ground of both: opposed to dualism and pluralism.

MONOTHEISM. The doctrine that there exists only one divinity; the worship of a single Deity.

MOTION. In reference to the existence of God, motion means the same as 'movement.' *See* Movement.

MOTUS. *See* Movement.

MOVEMENT. In Aristotelian and scholastic technical language, movement is 'the act of a being in potency in so far as it is in potency.' Substantial or accidental change; the reception or loss of any reality in the process of change.

NATURAL THEOLOGY. *See* Theology, Natural.

NATURE. A 'nature' is an essence considered as the ultimate principle of operation in a being.

NECESSARY. Something is said to be 'necessary' when it actually exists and also must exist.

NECESSITY. That state in virtue of which something cannot be otherwise than it is. With regard to existence, a thing is said to be 'necessary' when it must exist and cannot not exist.

NECESSITY, ABSOLUTE. Necessity for a being is absolute when it exists in such a manner that it must exist, independent of any condition; the non-existence of such a being would imply a contradiction.

NECESSITY, HYPOTHETICAL. Necessity for a being is hypothetical when its existence is dependent on a cause, but which, once the condition of its existence is given, must be (cannot not be) a definite reality.

NON-BEING. Whatever does not exist or is incapable of existence.

NON-BEING, ABSOLUTE. The total absence of being, so that it neither actually exists nor is it 'capable of existence'; its very idea involves the impossibility of existing. Absolute nothing.

NON-BEING, RELATIVE. Something which does not now actually exist, either because it has ceased to exist or has not as yet received existence although it is 'capable of existence.' Such a being, because it is 'capable of existence,' is also by that fact a 'relative being.'

NOTHING, ABSOLUTE. *See* Non-Being, Absolute.

NUMBER, ACTUALLY INFINITE. An existing number greater than which none can be conceived, so that it is incapable of increase and cannot be exhausted by successive subtractions.

NUMBER, POTENTIALLY INFINITE. A number which is finite and limited in itself, but is capable of being increased indefinitely, without limit.

OBJECT, FORMAL. The formal object of a science is that special aspect of the common (material) object which is distinctive for a particular science. In theodicy it is 'God as known by natural human reason.'

OBJECT, MATERIAL. The material object of a science is the general subject-matter which it treats. In theodicy it is 'God.'

OMNIPOTENCE. The capability to produce anything intrinsically possible, *i.e.,* which does not involve a contradiction; the ability to give existence to whatever can receive existence.

OMNIPRESENCE. The relation of God's presence to the beings which actually exist and to the real space which they occupy. Ubiquity.

ONTOLOGISM. The doctrine which holds that God and Divine Ideas are the first object of our intelligence and the intuition of God the first act of our intellectual knowledge.

OPTIMISM. The philosophic doctrine that the present universe is the best of all possible worlds.

ORDER. The arrangement of various items into a system or whole according to some relationship existing or placed between them. It is 'static,' if the items are ordered with regard to their entity; it is 'dynamic,' if the items are ordered with respect to the performance of a unified function.

ORGANISM. Biologically, an organism is an individual constituted to carry on the activities of life by means of parts and organs more or less separate in function but mutually dependent.

PANTHEISM. The theory which holds that God is identical with either a part or the whole of the physical world.

PANTHEISM, EVOLUTIONISTIC. A form of realistic pantheism which maintains the evolution of the Deity into the world.

PANTHEISM, IDEALISTIC TOTAL. The form of total pantheism which holds that all being, including God or the Absolute, is actually thought-being, so that things have existence only in a mind and only in so far as they are thought.

PANTHEISM, IMMANENT, TOTAL. A form of pantheism which applies the principle of evolution to God and maintains that the divine reality has evolved into the present world, so that world-beings are modifications of the divine reality and that God is 'immanent' in the world.

PANTHEISM, PARTIAL. The type of pantheism which maintains that God is not the totality of world-beings, but only a part of the world.

PANTHEISM, REALISTIC TOTAL. The type of pantheism which holds that the reality which is identified with God is a physical entity (not a mere product of mind or thought).

PANTHEISM, TOTAL. The theory which maintains that all reality is but one, so that God is identified with total reality.

PANTHEISM, TRANSIENT REALISTIC. The form of realistic pantheism which holds that all beings in the world emanate or flow from the divine substance, so that they originate, not by means of God's causal action, but through a transformation of God's substance. Emanationism.

PERFECTION. Any reality or real entity which is present in any kind of being. It may be potential or actual, mixed or simple.

PERFECTION, ABSOLUTE. Perfection which pertains, not to a certain type of being, but to every line of being without restriction.

PERFECTION, ACCIDENTAL. Perfection which does not belong to the essence or nature of a being, but is connected with the essence or nature as a superadded modification or determination.

PERFECTION, ACTUAL. Perfection which exists in reality.

PERFECTION, ESSENTIAL. Perfection referring to the essence or nature of beings.

PERFECTION, EXTENSIVE INFINITE. Possession of all perfections possible.

PERFECTION, INFINITE. Perfection which is actually and absolutely without limit.

PERFECTION, INTENSIVE INFINITE. Possession in the supreme degree of all perfections possible.

PERFECTION, MIXED. Perfection which in its very concept implies limitation or imperfection.

PERFECTION, POTENTIAL. Perfection which does not exist but is capable of being brought into existence.

PERFECTION, PREDICAMENTAL. Perfection representing generic concepts; for example, 'animal,' 'body,' 'plant.'

PERFECTION, RADICAL INFINITE. A being is said to possess radical infinite perfection when it is intrinsically determined in such a manner that it demands both extensive and intensive infinity of perfection.

PERFECTION, RELATIVE. Perfection that pertains to a certain type of being.

PERFECTION, SIMPLE. Perfection which does not include in its concept limitation or imperfection.

PERFECTION, TRANSCENDENTAL. Perfection which is found in, or can be applied to, all beings; for example, 'one,' 'being,' 'good,' 'true.'

PERFECT PANTHEISM. See Pantheism, Total.

PESSIMISM. The philosophic doctrine which contends, at least as far as man is concerned, that there is nothing good in life and in the world.

PHILOSOPHY. The science of beings in their ultimate reasons, causes, and principles, acquired by the aid of human reason.

POLYTHEISM. The philosophic and religious doctrine which maintains that a plurality of deities exists.

POSITIVISM. The theory which holds that man's knowledge cannot reach beyond the phenomenal.

POSSIBILITY, EXTERNAL. A thing is said to possess external possibility when a power exists which can produce it.

POSSIBILITY, INTERNAL. A thing is said to possess internal possibility, when it can have or receive existence, without regard to the actual existence of a power which can, as a matter of fact, actually produce it.

POSSIBLE. Something is said to be 'possible' when it does not actually exist but is capable of existence.

POSSIBLE, FOUNDATION OF. The reason or ultimate ground for internal possibility; the imitability of God's essence.

POSTULATE. A proposition which is either self-evident or which is taken over without proof by one science from another science because it has been proved by this other science. The postulates of theodicy are the existence of the physical world and the trustworthiness of human reason in its search for facts and truths.

POTENCY. The condition or state of 'being possible'; capable of receiving existence, though not actually existing as yet. It is the aptitude to receive a perfection, determination, or degree of reality.

POTENCY, OPERATIVE. The capacity for doing something.

POTENCY, RECEPTIVE. The capacity for receiving an act.

POTENTIAL. *See* Potency.

POTENTIALITY. *See* Potency.

PRAGMATISM. The doctrine, or rather attitude, which places all knowledge and truth in a direct relation to life and action; it judges the value of ideas, judgments, hypotheses, theories, and systems, according to their capacity to satisfy human needs and interests in a social way. Truth is thus 'made,' not 'discovered.'

PRIME MOVER. God, as the ultimate author of change in the universe.

PRINCIPLE OF CAUSALITY. 'Whatever happens or becomes must have a cause for its happening or becoming.'

PRINCIPLE OF CONTRADICTION. 'A thing cannot be and not be the same thing at the same time under the same respect.'

PRINCIPLE OF EFFICIENT CAUSALITY. 'That which begins to exist demands a cause (an efficient cause) for its beginning; that is to say, it demands an existing being to bring it from non-existence to existence.'

PRINCIPLE OF EXCLUDED MIDDLE. 'A thing either is or is not (something).'

PRINCIPLE OF IDENTITY. 'Whatever a thing is, it is'; 'Everything is identical with itself.'

PRINCIPLE OF NON-CONTRADICTION. *See* Principle of Contradiction.

PRINCIPLE OF SUFFICIENT REASON. 'A thing must have a sufficient reason for its being and existence.'

PRINCIPLES, FIRST. The ultimate, most fundamental principles of thought and being. Such are the Principles of Identity, Contradiction, Excluded Middle, Sufficient Reason, and Causality.

PRODUCTION. The positive influence of an efficient cause making a being or perfection pass from non-existence to existence.

Proof, Ontological. A proof for God's existence, based on the idea of God as the most perfect being.

Providence, Divine. The plan of the order of things in the world foreordained by God toward an end.

Providence, Moral. The plan of God's providence providing man with the means needed by him to live in conformity with his moral nature.

Providence, Particular. The practical ordering of the individual beings for the achievement of the various ends proper to them.

Providence, Physical. The plan of God's providence providing each creature with the means needed for its physical well-being.

Providence, Universal. The practical ordering of the universe of things for the attainment of the end proper to the universe as a whole.

Science. A body of proved truths concerning a general subject-matter, resting on fundamental principles and arranged into a system.

Scientia Media. See Knowledge, Intermediate.

Series, Finite. A series which is limited in the number comprising it, so that it can be counted. A finite series always presupposes a first number.

Series, Infinite. A series without beginning and end; a series consisting of a number of items in such a manner that no amount of subtraction or division will be able to exhaust it.

Simple Cognition in God. See Knowledge of Simple Cognition in God.

Simplicity. The absence of composition in the reality of a being.

Simplicity, Absolute. Simplicity is said to be absolute, when the being excludes all parts of whatever nature, be they real or conceptual. Such a being is not only actually undivided but also potentially indivisible.

Simplicity, Relative. Simplicity is said to be relative when the being in question excludes parts of one kind but has parts of another kind. Such a being is indivisible in one respect but divisible in another.

Spinozism. The immanent evolutionistic pantheism propounded by B. Spinoza.

Spontaneous Generation. See Abiogenesis.

Substance. A being which exists in itself and needs no other being in which it must inhere.

Temporal. Pertaining to time.

Theodicy. The philosophical science of God, or the science of God acquired by means of natural reason. Same as 'natural theology.'

THEOLOGY, DOGMATIC. The science of God acquired by the application of reason and of the reasoning process to truths furnished by supernatural revelation.

THEOLOGY, NATURAL. The philosophical science of God, or the science of God acquired by means of natural reason. Same as 'theodicy.'

THEOLOGY, SUPERNATURAL. *See* Theology, Dogmatic.

THEOSOPHY. A modern version of Indian pantheism, a form of immanent pantheism.

TIME. The measure of movement according to 'before' and 'after.'

TRADITIONALISM. The theory or attitude which holds that human reason is incapable, of its own native ability, of reaching certitude regarding any truth 'or at least regarding truth of the philosophical or religious order; it maintains that the supreme criterion of certitude is the authority of revelation as given to man through *tradition*.

TRANSCENDENTALISM. The name given to Kant's philosophy, which maintained that all human knowledge is conditioned by certain innate *a priori forms* present in the mind antecedently to all experience. Such innate forms, on the level of reasoning, are 'God,' 'World,' and 'Soul'; we can *think* these Ideas, but we cannot *know* them.

UBICATION. Presence in a place. Whereness.

UBICATION, CIRCUMSCRIPTIVE. The presence of an extended corporeal substance, so that it has parts outside parts quantitatively extended in the place which it occupies.

UBICATION, DEFINITIVE. The presence of a spatially unextended substance in such a manner that it can exercise its activity only within certain limits of space.

UBICATION, REPLETIVE. The presence of a spatially unextended ('spiritual') substance in all places and spaces, past, present, and future.

UBIQUITY. *See* Omnipresence.

UNICITY. Singleness or uniqueness, the absence of plurality.

UNICITY, IMPERFECT. Unicity is imperfect when no other being of the same kind actually exists, but another being of the same kind is possible.

UNICITY, PERFECT. Unicity is perfect when no other being of the same kind actually exists, and another being of the same kind is impossible.

VIRTUALLY CONTAINED PERFECTION. A perfection precontained in the actuality of an efficient cause in such a manner that the latter can produce it.

VISION. With respect to God's knowledge, 'vision' pertains to objects which at sometime, either in the past, or present or future, will have existence.

VOLITION. The exercise of the power of the will; willing.

WAY OF AFFIRMATION. The affirmative predication of 'pure perfections' of God.

WAY OF EMINENCE. Affirmatively ascribing to God a 'pure perfection' and then raising the perfection to the highest degree conceivable.

WAY OF NEGATION. Denying of God every sort of imperfection and attributing to Him the corresponding perfections in such a manner that they apply to Him alone.

WHERENESS. *See* Ubication.

WILL. Rational, intellectual, appetency.

WILL OF GOD. An infinitely perfect intellectual appetency.

BIBLIOGRAPHY

AITKEN, ROBERT GRANT, "Behold the Stars," in *The Great Design* (New York, Macmillan, 1934).

ALEXANDER, SAMUEL, *Space, Time, and Deity* (London: Macmillan, 1927).

ANSELM, ST., *Proslogium and Monologium*, tr. by Sidney Norton Deane (Chicago: Open Court Publishing Co., 1926).

ANTWEILER, ANTON, *Unendlich* (Freiburg: B. Herder, 1934).

ARMSTRONG, HENRY E., "The Chemical Romance of the Green Leaf," in *The Great Design* (New York: Macmillan, 1934).

AUGUSTINE, ST., *Enchiridion*, tr. by M. Dods (Edinburgh: T. and T. Clark, 1873).

AVELING, FRANCIS, *The God of Philosophy* (London and Edinburgh: Sands, 1906).

BAÑEZ, D., *Schol. Comment. in Iam Partem*, ed. Douai, 1614.

Basic Writings of St. Thomas Aquinas, 2 vols., ed. A. C. Pegis (New York: Random House, 1945).

BASKFIELD, GERALD THOMAS, *The Idea of God in British and American Personal Idealism* (Washington, D. C.: Catholic University of America, 1933).

BAUER, JOHANNES, *Kausalität und Schöpfung* (München: Schnell und Steiner, 1947).

BENNET, LINCOLN, *The Universe and Einstein* (New York: William Sloane Association, 1948).

BERG, ERNST, *Das Problem der Kausalität* (Berlin: L. Simion, 1920).

BERGSON, HENRI, *Creative Evolution*, tr. A. Mitchell (New York: H. Holt & Co., 1911).

———— *The Two Sources of Morality and Religion*, tr. R. Audra and C. Brereton (New York: H. Holt & Co., 1935).

BOEDDER, BERNARD, *Natural Theology*, 2nd ed. (New York and London: Longmans, Green, 1927).

———— *Theologia Naturalis* (Breisgau: Herder, 1900).

BOUQUET, ALAN COATES, *The Doctrine of God* (Cambridge, England: W. Heffer and Sons, 1934).

BOWMAN, A. A., *A Sacramental Universe* (London: Milford, Oxford University Press, 1939).

BRAUN, HEINRICH SUSO, *Der Namenlose Gott*, 3rd ed. (Heidelberg: F. H. Kerle, 1946).

BRIGHTMAN, EDGAR SHEFFIELD, *The Finding of God* (New York and Cincinnati: The Abington Press, 1931).

—— *The Problem of God* (New York and Cincinnati: The Abington Press, 1930).

BROSNAN, WILLIAM J., *God and Reason*, 9th printing (New York: Fordham University Press, 1941).

—— *God Infinite and Reason* (New York: The America Press, 1928).

—— *God Infinite, the World, and Reason* (New York: Fordham University Press, 1943).

BRUNSCHWICG, LEON, *L'Expérience humaine et la causalité physique* (Paris: Alcan, 1922).

BRYAR, WILLIAM, *St. Thomas and the Existence of God* (Chicago: Regnery Co., 1951).

Causality. Lectures delivered before the Philosophical Union, University of California, 1932 (Berkeley, Calif.: University of California Press, 1932).

CLAUDEL, P., *Letters to a Doubter*, tr. by Henry L. Stuart (London: Burns, Oates, and Washburne, 1929).

COMPTON, ARTHUR H., lecture in *Man's Destiny in Eternity* (Boston: Beacon Press, 1949).

CRANNY, TITUS F., *Saint Bonaventure's Teaching on the Immediate Evidence for the Existence of God* (Washington, D. C.: Catholic University of America, 1948).

CROWTHER, JAMES ARNOLD, "Radiation," in *The Great Design* (New York: Macmillan, 1934).

D'ARCY, M. C., *Pain and the Providence of God* (Milwaukee: The Bruce Publishing Co., 1935).

DEBURGH, W. G., *From Morality to Religion* (London: Macdonald and Evans, 1938).

—— *Towards a Religious Philosophy* (London: Macdonald and Evans, 1937).

DECOCQS, PEDRO, *Praelectiones Theologiae Naturalis* (Paris: Gabriel Beauchesne, 1932).

—— *Schema Theodiceae* (Paris: Beauchesne, 1941).

DECOURSEY, SISTER MARY EDWIN, *The Theory of Evil in the Metaphysics of St. Thomas and Its Contemporary Significance* (Washington, D. C.: Catholic University of America Press, 1948).

DESCARTES, RENÉ, *The Philosophical Works of Descartes*, 2 vols., ed. E. Haldane and G. Ross (Cambridge: The University Press, 1911–1912).

DONAT, J., *The Freedom of Science* (New York: J. F. Wagner, 1914).

—— *Theodicea* (Innsbruck: F. Rauch, 1936).

DRIESCH, HANS ADOLF EDUARD, *Man and the Universe,* tr. by W. H. Johnston (London: G. Allen and Unwin, 1929).

——— "The Breakdown of Materialism," in *The Great Design* (New York: Macmillan, 1934).

DRISCOLL, JOHN T., *God* (New York: Benziger Bros., 1904).

DU NOÜY, LECOMTE, *Human Destiny* (New York and London: Longmans, Green, 1947).

ENRIQUES, FEDERIGO, *Causalité et Déterminisme dans la philosophie et l'histoire* (Paris: Hermann, 1941).

ESSER, GERARD, *Theologia Naturalis* (Techny, Ill.: Typis Domus Missionum ad St. Mariam, 1949).

EVE, ARTHUR STEWART, "The Universe as a Whole," in *The Great Design* (New York: Macmillan, 1934).

FARRAR, A., *Finite and Infinite* (Westminster: Dacre Press, 1943).

FARRELL, WALTER, *A Companion to the Summa,* 4 vols. (New York: Sheed and Ward, 1945–1947).

FRASER-HARRIS, D. F., "Unity and Intelligence in Nature," in *The Great Design* (New York: Macmillan, 1934).

GAGER, C. STUART, "Adaptations in the Plant World," in *The Great Design* (New York: Macmillan, 1934).

GARRIGOU-LAGRANGE, R., *God: His Existence and His Nature,* 2 vols., tr. from the 5th French ed. by Bede Rose (St. Louis: B. Herder Book Co., 1947–1948).

——— *The One God,* tr. by Bede Rose (St. Louis and London: B. Herder Book Co., 1943).

——— *Providence,* tr. by Bede Rose (St. Louis: B. Herder Book Co., 1946).

——— *Le Réalisme du Principe de Finalité* (Paris: Desclée de Brouwer, 1932).

GILSON, ÉTIENNE, *God and Philosophy,* 5th printing (New Haven: Yale University Press, 1949).

——— *The Philosophy of St. Thomas Aquinas,* tr. from the 3rd rev. and enlarged ed. of *Le Thomisme* by E. Bullough, ed. by G. A. Erlington (Cambridge: W. Heffer and Sons, 1929).

GLENN, PAUL J., *Theodicy* (St. Louis: B. Herder Book Co., 1938).

GRANT, FRANCIS, *Oriental Philosophy* (New York: The Dial Press, 1936).

HALDANE, J. B. S., *What is Life?* (London: Lindsay Drummond, 1949).

HART, HORNELL, lecture in *Man's Destiny in Eternity* (Boston: Beacon Press, 1949).

HARTSHORNE, CHARLES, *The Divine Relitivity, a Social Conception of God* (New Haven: Yale University Press, 1948).

HAWKINS, D. J. B., *The Essentials of Theism* (London and New York: Sheed and Ward, 1949).

—— *Causality and Implication* (London: Sheed and Ward, 1937).

HEARD, GERALD, *Is God in History?* (New York: Harper, 1950).

HELLIN, JOSEPHUS, *Theologia Naturalis* (Madrid: Biblioteca de Autores Cristianos, 1950).

HEMINGHAUS, HENRY J., *Internal Finality as an Indirect Proof of Divine Providence* (Washington, D. C.: Catholic University of America, 1948).

HENGSTENBERG, HANS EDUARD, *Das Band Zwischen Gott und Schöpfung*, 2 Aufl. (Regensburg: J. Habbel, 1948).

HEYDON, J. K., *The God of Reason* (New York: Sheed and Ward, 1940).

HILL, OWEN A., *Psychology and Natural Theology* (New York: Macmillan, 1921).

HOCKING, WILLIAM ERNEST, lecture in *Man's Destiny in Eternity* (Boston: Beacon Press, 1949).

—— *Science and the Idea of God* (Chapel Hill: University of North Carolina Press, 1944).

HONTHEIM, JOSEPHUS, *Institutiones Theodicaeae* (Fribourg: B. Herder, 1893).

HOOPER, CHARLES E., *The Fallacies of Fatalism* (London: Watts, 1930).

HUGHES, SISTER MARY COSMAS, *The Intelligibility of the Universe* (Washington, D. C.: Catholic University of America Press, 1946).

JAMES, WILLIAM, *A Pluralistic Universe* (New York: Longmans, Green, 1925).

—— *The Varieties of Religious Experience* (New York: Longmans, Green, 1925).

—— *The Will to Believe and Other Essays* (New York: Longmans, Green, 1923).

JEANS, SIR JAMES, *Mysterious Universe* (London: Macmillan, 1932).

JOYCE, GEORGE HAYWARD, *Principles of Natural Theology*, 2nd ed. (New York and London: Longmans, Green, 1924).

KANE, ROBERT, *God or Chaos* (New York: P. J. Kenedy, 1912).

KANT, IMMANUEL, *The Critique of Pure Reason*, tr. Max Müller (New York: Macmillan, 1925).

LAIRD, J., *Theism and Cosmology* (London: G. Allen and Unwin, 1940; New York: Philosophical Library and Alliance Book Corp., 1942).

LEIBNITZ, GOTTFRIED WILHELM, *Essais de Theodicée sur la bonté de Dieu, la liberté de l'homme et l'origine du mal,* 2nd ed. (Amsterdam: I. Troyel, 1712).

LEWIS, CLIVE STAPLES, *Beyond Personality,* 2nd pr. (New York: Macmillan, 1945).

LEWIS, EDWIN, *The Creator and the Adversary* (New York: Abington-Cokesbury Press, 1948).

LIBERATORI-CORSI, *Theodicea,* 2 vols., rev. ed. (Neapoli: Ex Typographia Commerciali, 1931).

LODGE, SIR OLIVER, "Design and Purpose in the Universe," in *The Great Design* (New York: Macmillan, 1934).

MACBRIDE, ERNEST WILLIAM, "The Oneness and Uniqueness of Life," in *The Great Design* (New York: Macmillan, 1934).

Man's Destiny in Eternity, by Arthur H. Compton and others (Boston: Beacon Press, 1949).

MARITAIN, JACQUES, *The Dream of Descartes,* tr. M. Anderson (New York: New York Philosophical Library, 1944).

―――― *La philosophie Bergsonienne* (Paris: Desclée de Brouwer, 1931).

―――― lecture in *Man's Destiny in Eternity* (Boston: Beacon Press, 1949).

―――― *St. Thomas and the Problem of Evil* (Milwaukee: Marquette University Press, 1942).

MARLING, JOSEPH M., *The Order of Nature in the Philosophy of St. Thomas Aquinas* (Washington, D. C.: Catholic University of America Press, 1934).

MASCALL, E. L., *He Who Is* (New York: Longmans, Green, 1945).

MATTHEWS, WALTER ROBERT, *The Purpose of God* (New York: C. Scribner's Sons, 1936).

MERCIER, D. CARD., *A Manual of Modern Scholastic Philosophy,* 2 vols., tr. by T. L. Parker and S. A. Parker, 8th ed. (St. Louis: B. Herder Book Co., 1917).

METCALF, MAYNARD M., "Intelligent Plan in Nature," in *The Great Design* (New York: Macmillan, 1934).

MILLER, THEODORE AUGUSTUS, *The Mind behind the Universe* (New York: Frederick A. Stokes, 1928).

MORGAN, C. LLOYD, "The Ascent of Mind," in *The Great Design* (New York: Macmillan, 1934).

MORRISON, A. CRESSY, *Man Does Not Stand Alone* (New York: Fleming H. Revell, 1944).

NIEBUHR, REINHOLD, lecture in *Man's Destiny in Eternity* (Boston: Beacon Press, 1949).

NORTHROP, F. S. C., lecture in *Man's Destiny in Eternity* (Boston: Beacon Press, 1949).

NOYES, ALFRED, *The Unknown God* (New York: Sheed and Ward, 1940).

O'BRIEN, SISTER MARY CONSILIA, *The Antecedents of Being* (Washington, D. C.: Catholic University of America Press, 1939).

O'TOOLE, CHRISTOPHER J., *The Philosophy of Creation in the Writings of St. Augustine* (Washington, D. C.: Catholic University of America Press, 1944).

OURSLER, FULTON, *Why I Know There is a God* (Garden City: Doubleday, 1950).

PARK, CHARLES E., lecture in *Man's Destiny in Eternity* (Boston: Beacon Press, 1949).

PATTERSON, ROBERT LEET, *The Conception of God in the Philosophy of Aquinas* (London: G. Allen and Unwin, 1933).

PRINGLE-PATTISON, A. SETH, *The Idea of God in the Light of Recent Philosophy,* 2nd rev. ed. (New York and London: Oxford University Press, 1920).

REMER, V., *Theologia Naturalis,* ed. 4 emendata et aucta (Romae: Sumptibus Universitatis Gregorianae, 1922).

RENARD, HENRI, *The Philosophy of God* (Milwaukee: The Bruce Publishing Co., 1951).

RING, GEORGE C., *The Religions of the Far East* (Milwaukee: The Bruce Publishing Co., 1950).

ROCHE, EVAN, *The De Primo Principio of John Duns Scotus* (St. Bonaventure, N. Y.: The Franciscan Institute, 1949).

ROYCE, JOSIAH, *The Conception of God* (New York: Macmillan, 1897).

—— *The World and the Individual* (New York and London: Macmillan, 1900).

ROYDEN, MAUDE, lecture in *Man's Destiny in Eternity* (Boston: Beacon Press, 1949).

RUSSELL, HENRY NORRIS, *Fate and Freedom* (New Haven: Yale University Press, 1927).

SCOTUS, JOHN DUNS, *The De Primo Principio,* tr. and rev. by Evan Roche (St. Bonaventure, N. Y.: The Franciscan Institute, 1949).

SERTILLANGES, ANTONIN GILBERT, *Dieu ou Rien?* (Paris: Flammarion, 1933).

—— *L'Idée de Création et ses retentissements en philosophie* (Paris: Aubier, 1945).

SHEEN, FULTON J., *God and Intelligence in Modern Philosophy* (London: Longmans, Green, 1925).

———— *Religion Without God* (New York: Longmans, Green, 1928).

SMITH, GERARD, *Natural Theology* (New York: Macmillan, 1951).

SPERRY, WILLARD L., lecture in *Man's Destiny in Eternity* (Boston: Beacon Press, 1949).

STANDEN, ANTHONY, *Science is a Sacred Cow* (New York: E. P. Dutton, 1950).

STRAUBINGER, HEINRICH, *Religionsphilosophie mit Theodizee* (Freiburg: B. Herder, 1949).

STRONG, JOHN HENRY, *A Man Can Know God* (Chicago: Judson Press, 1949).

STUFLER, JOHANN, *Gott, der erste Beweger aller Dinge* (Innsbruck: F. Rauch, 1936).

SULLIVAN, JAMES BACON, *First Principles in Thought and Being* (Washington, D. C.: Catholic University of America Press, 1939).

TAYLOR, A. E., *Does God Exist?* (New York: Macmillan, 1947).

The Basic Works of Aristotle, ed. R. McKeon (New York: Random House, 1941).

The Great Design, ed. by Frances Mason (New York: Macmillan, 1934).

The Works of Aristotle Translated into English, 11 vols., ed. W. D. Ross and others (Oxford: Clarendon Press, 1928–1931).

THOMAS AQUINAS, ST., *Concerning Being and Essence (De Ente et Essentia),* tr. by George G. Leckie (New York and London: D. Appleton-Century Co., 1937).

———— *Of God and His Creatures,* a translation (with some abridgement) of the *Summa Contra Gentiles* by Joseph Rickaby (London: Burns and Oates, 1905; Westminster, Md.: The Carroll Press, 1950).

———— *Summa Contra Gentiles,* 5 vols., tr. by the Dominican Fathers (New York: Benziger Bros., 1928–1929).

———— *Summa Contra Gentiles,* tr. by the Fathers of the English Dominican province (London: Burns, Oates, and Washburne, 1923).

———— *Summa Theologica,* 22 vols., tr. by the Dominican Fathers (London: Burns, Oates, and Washburne, 1920–1922).

———— *Summa Theologica,* 3 vols., tr. by the Fathers of the English Dominican province (New York: Benziger Bros., 1947–1948).

THOMSON, SIR J. ARTHUR, "The Wonder of Life," in *The Great Design* (New York: Macmillan, 1934).

VAN NUYS, KELVIN, *Science and Cosmic Purpose* (New York: Harper, 1949).

WAND, JOHN WILLIAM CHARLES, *God and His Goodness* (London: Eyre and Spottiswoods, 1947).

WHITTAKER, SIR EDMUND, *Space and Spirit* (Hinsdale, Ill.: Henry Regnery Co., 1948).

WILLIS, BAILEY, "The Earth as the Home of Man," in *The Great Design* (New York: Macmillan, 1934).

WOODS, H., *The Creator Operating in the Creature* (San Francisco: The Gilmartin Co., 1928).

YOUNGHUSBAND, SIR FRANCIS, "The Mystery of Nature," in *The Great Design* (New York: Macmillan, 1934).

ZIMMERMAN, O., *The Problem of Evil and Human Destiny*, tr. by J. S. Zybura (St. Louis: B. Herder Book Co., 1924).

INDEX

ABIOGENESIS, atheistic scientists and philosophers on, 137; in history, 136; not a scientific postulate, 138; opinions on, 136; a philosophic postulate of materialism, 138; problem of, 135 ff; scientifically untenable, 136

ACCIDENT, God has no, 223; and substance, 222

ACT (ACTUALITY), in change, 61; God is pure act, 159, 231; notion, 62

ACTION, 133

ACTUALITY (ACT), in change, 61; and compound, 221; God is pure act, 231; notion, 62; perfection, 151, 225

ACTUALIZATION, partial, 151; *see also* Movement

AFFINITY, chemical, 91

AFFIRMATION, way of, in knowing God, 190

AGNOSTICISM, advocates, 40; based on Hume's empiricism, 41; man's knowledge of God, 188; meaning, 40; modern, 40; refutation of, 41

AITKEN, ROBERT GRANT, organic unity in the universe, 88

ALBERT THE GREAT, ST., ontological proof, 45

ALEXANDER, S., emergent evolution, 143 f

AMAURY (AMALRIC), of BÈNE, partial pantheism, 256

ANALOGY, of intrinsic attribution, 195; man's knowledge of God by means of, 193 ff; proper proportionality, 195

ANIMALS, order in world of, 93 ff

ANNIHILATION, change, improperly so-called, 241; defined, 324; God's power of, 323 f

ANSELM, ST., ontological proof, 45 f

ANTHROPOMORPHISM, denies absolute simplicity in God, 220; divine and human knowledge, 272; meaning, 105; in popular knowledge of God, 5

ANTI-CHANCE, 85

ANTWEILER, A., God's metaphysical essence, 200

APPETITION and life, 139

APPROBATION, knowledge of, 274

AQUINAS, ST. THOMAS, argument from causality, 125; argument from change, 74 f; argument from contingency, 115; argument from the grades of perfection, 158; argument from order and design, 101; conservation, 321, 324; conservation and creation, 325; creation, 300, 307; creative power infinite, 312; creatures as cause of creation, 311; eternal creation, 313; fate, 367; generation and corruption, 116; God's knowledge of Himself and of other things, 269; governance, 353; intelligible species in God's knowledge, 269; man's way of knowing God, 240; movement, 66; and ontological proof, 45, 46; origin of life as proof of God's existence, 157; physical evil a normal feature of universe, 360; providence defined, 351; providence proved, 357; providence and sin, 365; self-subsistence as the metaphysical essence of God, 208; terrestrial elements, 158; union of diverse perfections, 154; way of negation in knowing God, 191; on will of God, 288

ARIANISM on creation, 309

ARISTOTLE, act (actuality), 61; actuality (act), 61; chance, 85; change, 61 ff; corruption and generation, 116; creation unknown to, 303; definition of movement (actualization), 62; finality in nature, 86; generation and corruption, 116; God's immensity, 252; and Heraclitus, 63; and Parmenides, 63; permanence, 61 ff; potency (potentiality), 61; potentiality (potency), 61; subject of change, 63; terrestrial elements, 158

ARRHENIUS, SVANTE AUGUST, origin of life on earth, 137

ASEITY as God's metaphysical essence, 201, 205

ASSOCIATION OF IDEAS, Hume's empiricism, 26

ATHEISM, individuals and peoples, 3

ATOM, authorities on, nature of, 88 f

ATTRIBUTE, absolute, 187; absolute, in God, 214; divine, 199; essential, in God, 214; eternity of God, 240; immanently operational, 292; immensity of God, 240; immutability of God, 240; intellect of God, 266; internal operational, of God, 266; notion, 198; omnipotence, 292 ff; pertaining to God's essence, 214; pertaining to God's operations, 214; property, 198; relative, 187; relative, in God, 214; transient, 350; virtually transitive operational, 292; will of God, 266

AUGUSTINUS STEUCHUS EUGUBINUS, God's immensity, 253

AVERAGE, STATISTICAL, and chance, 82

AVICENNA, creation, 309

BANEZ, D., God's metaphysical essence, 201; mode of divine concurrence, 332

BANNESIANISM, defense of, 337 f; evaluation, 346; and free will, 340; as a mode of divine concurrence, 332 ff; physical predetermination, 333; physical premotion, 333; and predetermining decrees, of God's, 336

BAUTAIN, L., fideism and traditionalism, 42

BAYLE, PIERRE, conservation, 325

BECOMING, 61 ff

BECQUEREL, ANTOINE HENRI, experiments on living germs, 137

BEING, expressed negatively and positively, 16; includes all reality, 228; and nought, identified by Hegel, 30; possible, 19

BELIEF, universal, in God, 3

BELMOND, God's metaphysical essence, 200

BERGSON, HENRI, change, the whole of reality, 64 ff; creation, 65; Creator, 65; denial of the validity of the Principles of Identity and Contradiction, 65; intellect, 64; intuition, 64; refutation of, 66

BIEL, GABRIEL, nominalism, 234

BILLUART, intelligence the metaphysical essence of God, 201

BIOLOGY, causality, 118

BLOUNT, CHARLES, deism, 39

BOEDDER, B., concurrence, 326; God's metaphysical essence, 201

BOETHIUS, definition of eternity, 248

BOHR, N., concept of the atom, 89

BOLINGBROKE, VISCOUNT, see St. John, Henry

BONNETTY, A., fideism and traditionalism, 42

BORN, M., concept of the atom, 89

BOUTROUX, God's metaphysical essence, 201

BRANCA, W., abiogenesis, 138

BRIGHTMAN, EDGAR SHEFFIELD, finitist, 304

BROSNAN, WILLIAM J., idealistic pantheism, 260

BÜCHNER, LUDWIG, materialism, 175, 227

BUDDHISM, pessimism, 368

BURKE, JOHN BUTLER, and abiogenesis, 136

CABANIS, PIERRE J. G., materialism, 175

CALKINS, M., finitism, 227

CAPREOLUS, God's metaphysical essence, 201

CARREL, ALEXIS, embryological development of man, 96; human hand, 96; thinking does not increase metabolism, 180

CATEGORIES in Kant's formalism, 53

CAUSALITY, actually infinite series of causes, 122 ff; an a priori category in Kant's formalism, 53; argument of Aquinas, 125; circle of causes, 124; demands a First Uncaused Cause, 120; fact of, 118; infinite or finite series of causes, 119 ff; and life, 139; meaning of, as a proof of God's existence, 117; and the natural sciences, 118; and nature of God, 126; Principle of, see Principle of Causality; proof of God's existence from efficient causality, 125

CAUSE, adequate, as sufficient reason for transcendental perfections, 156; chance, 367; definition, 117; effect precontained in efficient, 68; efficient, and change, 67; efficient, precontains the perfection of the effect, 68; efficient, meaning, 22; efficient, passage from non-existence to existence, 23;

efficient, real production, 22; one, of universe, 187; proper proportion between cause and effect, 139; uncaused, possessing unlimited perfection, 157; unchangeable, 73; *see also* Causality

CELL, and life, 132; man's origin from a single fecundated cell, 96; and order in plants, 91, 92

CHANCE, anti-chance, 85; Aristotle on design, 85; cannot explain uniformity, regularity, constancy, 98; and cause, 367; end (purpose), 86; excludes predictability, 82; existence of, 367; finality in nature, 86; and intellect, 367; and the intricate structure and inherently purposive function of organisms, 139; and law, 82; meaning, 82; notion, 367; and order, 82, 105; order, an observable fact in nature, 87; and the organic world, 148; and probability, 83 f; purpose (end), 86; ratio of geometrical progression in, 83; regularity, a characteristic of law, 82; scientific attitude, 83; and statistical average, 82

CHANGE, accidental, 62; analysis of, 67; as applied to God, 242; argument of Aquinas, 74; Aristotle, analysis of change and permanence, 60; becoming, 61 ff; and causality, 67 ff; ceaseless, according to Heraclitus, 59; consequences of argument from change, 76; creatures power of, 324; of energy, 70; and eternal existence of the universe, 72; extra-mundane cause of, 71 f; extrinsic, 241; extrinsic, in God, 242; extrinsic, involves no change in God Himself, 246; an illusion, according to Parmenides, 59; immutability in God, 241; improperly so-called, 241; infinite series of changes, 72; intellectual, 242; intrinsic, 241; in living beings, 70; moral, 242; in motion, 71; in nonliving beings, 70; notion, 62; physical, 242; Prime Mover, an eternal, living, intellectual, spiritual, personal being, 76 f; as a proof for God's existence, 58 ff; properly so-called, 242; qualitative, 62; quantitative, 62; relative real production, 23; subject of, 63; substantial, 61; and sufficient reason, 67; unchangeable cause, 73 f; universality of, 70

CHEMISTRY, causality, 118

CHRISTIANITY, creation, 303

CIRCLE OF CAUSES, 124

CO-ADAPTATION, of structure and activity in an organism, 132

COGNITION, simple, of God, 274

COMPATIBILITY, and intrinsic possibility, 297

COMPOSITION, the Absolute, 221; accidental, 218; of actuality and potentiality in created beings, 151; in creatures, 155; demands a pre-existing cause, 222; distinction, 215; in individual beings, 150; kinds, 215; logical, 218; mental, 218; metaphysical, 219; metaphysical composition in God excluded, 224; nature, 221; not found in God, 223; opposite of simplicity, 214; physical, 219; real, 218; substantial, 218

COMPOUND, notion, 214; order in a chemical, 90; *see also* Composition

COMPTON, ARTHUR H., intelligence implied in the plan of nature, 99

CONCURRENCE, actual, 335; Bañez, 332; bannesianism, *see* Bannesianism; *concursus praevius,* 333; and contingency of creatures, 329; and creatures as causes of creatural action, 326; defense of thomism and bannesianism, 337 f; and free acts, according to molinism, 335; God as the cause of creatural action, 326; God and creature produce creatural action, 327; immediate, 326; indifferent, 335; intermediate knowledge (*scientia media*), according to molinism, 336; mediate, 326; mode, 332 ff; Molina, 332; molinism defended, 340 ff; molinism, *see* Molinism; moral, 326; notion, 325; objections to, 331; offered, according to molinism, 335; physical, 326; physical predetermination, 333; physical premotion, 333; physical premotion contradicts God's sanctity, according to molinists, 344 f; physical premotion and free will, 339, 342; physical premotion superfluous, according to molinists, 341 f; predetermining decrees of God, according to bannesianism, 336; problem stated, 332; proof of God physical, 327 ff; simultaneous, according to molinism, 340; thomists,

332; virtually transitive operational attribute, 292

CONSCIOUSNESS, in animals and men, 135; excessive dualism of Descartes, 14; life, 139

CONSERVATION, active, 319; and annihilation, 323 f; Aquinas, 321, 324, 325; and contingency, 321 ff; and creation, 324, 325; creatures, secondary causes of, 325; direct, 320; faculty, 323; force, 323; God, the principal cause of, 325; indirect, 320; and matter, 322; nature of, 325; negative, 320; notion, 319; opinions on, 321; passive, 319; positive, 320; proof of divine, 321 ff; and spiritual substance, 322; of substances, 323; virtually transitive operational attribute, 292

CONTENSON, on God's metaphysical essence, 201

CONTINGENCY, argument of Aquinas, 115; atoms, 109; of creatures demands divine concurrence, 329; definition, 107; of the earth, 108; existence of contingent beings is caused, 107; matter, 110; matter is not eternal, 111; nature of God as a corollary of, 126 f; and necessity, 105 ff; notion, 107; organisms, 108; proof of God's existence, 105 ff; proves God's existence, 113 ff; supposed infinite number of contingent beings, 114; universality of, 107 ff; and the world, 107; see also Contingent; Necessity

CONTINGENT, meaning, 25; notion, 107

CONTRADICTION, see Principle of Contradiction

CONTRARIETY, freedom of, 284

CREABILITY, of creatures is limitless and inexhaustible, 316

CREATION, absolute real production, 23; Aquinas, 300, 307, 311, 312; Aquinas on eternal, 313; Aristotle, 303; change, improperly so-called, 241; Christians, 303; and conservation, 325; creatures as cause of, 309; definition, 300; eternal, 312; eternal, impossibility of, 313; finitists, 303; first beginnings of things, 302; infinite number of creatures, 314; instrumental cause of, 308; intrinsically possible, 305; Jews, 303; no pre-existing matter,

301; not concerned with organic or cosmic evolution, 302; notion, 300; opponents, 303; origin of things, 302; pagans, 303; polytheists, 303; principal cause of, 308; proof of, 305 ff; reason for, 316; time, 303; virtually transitive operational attribute, 292

CREATURE, as cause of creatural action, 326; one, but composite, 155; proper end of, 354; secondary cause of conservation, 325; ultimate end of, 355

DARWIN, CHARLES R., organic evolution, 176

DAVID OF DINANT, partial pantheism, 256

DEATH, and life, 134; shows the contingency of organisms, 109

DE BONALD, LOUIS G., fideism and traditionalism, 42

DEDUCTION, 10

DEISM, advocates, 39; meaning, 39; miracles do not occur, 371; refutation, 39

DE LAMENNAIS, FÉLICITÉ R., fideism and traditionalism, 42

DE LA METTRIE, JULIAN O., materialism, 175

DEL PRADO, God's metaphysical essence, 201

DEMOCRITUS, systematic materialism, 174

DESCARTES, RENÉ, empiricism, 26; excessive dualism of mind and body, 14; on God's metaphysical essence, 200; and the idealistic monism of Hegel, 29; influence on Kant, 168; and Kant's formalism, 53; ontological argument of, 47; and the ontological proof, 45; and ontologism, 42; theory of knowledge, 53

DESIGN, Aquinas, 101; Aristotle, 85; conclusions drawn from design in the world, 98 f; definition, 81; and intelligence, 85; and order, 80 f; and organic evolution, 176; in plants, 91 f; proof for God's existence, 80 ff, 100 f; purpose in, 81; in the universe shows intelligence, 99; in the world of atoms, 88 ff; in the world of men, 95 ff

DEWEY, JOHN, pragmatism, 31

D'HOLBACH, BARON PAUL H., materialism, 175

DIRAC, P., concept of the atom, 89

DISTINCTION, based on differences in concepts, 234; between divine attributes among themselves, 234; between God's essence and perfections, 234; concerning God's perfections and attributes, 233 ff; in God, theories concerning, 234; God's essence and His attributes, 235; kinds, 215; logical, 215; mental, 216; notion, 215; purely mental, 216; real, 215; virtual, 216; virtual, with an imperfect foundation, 217; virtual, with a perfect foundation, 217

DUALISM, excessive, of Descartes, 14

DU NOÜY, PIERRE LE COMTE, probability in chance effects, 84

DURANDUS OF ST. POURÇAIN, concurrence, 328

DURATION, creatural, 247; definition, 246; divine, 247; everlasting, 248; eviternity, 248; permanent, 247; proof of God's eternity, 249 f; successive, 247; temporal, 247

EARTH, see World

EDDINGTON, SIR ARTHUR S., on creation, 304

EFFECT, immanent, 292; possibility of an infinite, 296; proper proportion between effect and cause, 139; transient, 293; see also Cause; Causality

EINSTEIN, ALBERT, curved space, 181

ELECTRON, 89

ELEMENT, constancy of properties, 89; natural kinds of elements, 89; periodic law, 89; Rydberg Series, 89; same kinds on the earth and in the stars, 88

EMANATIONISM, 257

EMINENCE, way of, in knowing God, 192

EMPIRICISM, doctrine on substance, 222; Heraclitus, 59; meaning, 26; preconceived tenet of, 37; refutation of, 28

END, Aristotle on, 85; finality in nature, 86; in God's providence, 351; proper, of creatures, and providence, 354; relations of means to, 87; ultimate, of creatures, and providence, 355

ENERGY, 70

ENS A SE, absolutely necessary being, 115; infinitely perfect, 227; and the logical concept of universal being, 260; self-existence of, 115

EPICURIANISM, physical evil and divine providence, 358

EPICURUS, materialism, 174

ESSENCE, attributes, of the divine, 214; God's metaphysical, 199 ff; God's metaphysical, differentiating elements, 206 f; God's metaphysical, theories evaluated, 202 ff; God's physical, 210; God's physical and metaphysical, 211; God's, the ultimate foundation of intrinsic possibility, 299; metaphysical, 197; notion, 196; physical, 197; self-subsistence as the metaphysical essence of God, 206 ff

ETERNITY, Boethius, 248; duration, see Duration; notion, 246; of Prime Mover, 76; proof of God's, 249 f

EUNOMIUS THE ARIAN, distinctions in God, 234

EVIL, Aquinas, 360, 365; finitism, and physical and moral evil, 369; moral, 363 ff; Moral, see Sin; pain in brute and man, 361; pantheism, and physical and moral evil, 369; physical, natural to the hierarchy of order present in the universe, 359 f; and providence, 358 ff; simple cognition, on the part of God, 274

EVITERNITY, definition, 248

EVOLUTION, creation not concerned with organic or cosmic evolution, 302; creative, of Bergson, 64 f; Darwin, 176; of the Deity, as total immanent pantheism, 257; emergent, 141; emergent, evaluation of, 143 f; emergent, notion of, 143; Fallacy of Begging the Question, 142; Fallacy of False Consequent, 142; intervention of God in, 143; organic, 141; organic, and design, 176; pantheistic, of God, 227; purposive, 146 ff; and theism, 141

EVOLUTIONISM, denies the absolute simplicity of God, 221

EXCLUDED MIDDLE, see Principle of Excluded Middle

EXERCISE, freedom of, 284

EXISTENCE, eternal, of universe, in change, 72; meaning, negatively and positively, 58

EXISTENCE, GOD'S, *a posteriori* demonstration, 55; can be demonstrated, 49 ff; life, proof of, *see* Life; method of proving, 54; necessity of proof, 48 f; not self-evident, 48; ontological proof for, 45 ff; perfection, as a proof of God's existence, 149 ff; proof from causality, *see* Causality; proof from design, 100 f; proved from change, 58 ff; proved from contingency, 113 ff; proved from efficient causality, 125; proved by grades and limitation of perfections, 157; views opposing the traditional proofs of, 163 ff

EXPERIENCE, as distinguished from science, 5; vital immanent, in modernism, 44

EXPERIENCE, RELIGIOUS, 44

EYE and order, 93

FACTS in science, 37

FAITH, cannot precede reason, 42; *see also* Fideism

FATALISM, miracles do not occur, 371

FATE, 366 f

FICHTE, J. H., pantheism, 227; total idealistic pantheism, 258

FIDEISM, 41 f

FINALITY, 86

FINITISM, denies the absolute simplicity of God, 221; denies creation, 303; and many modern scientists, 304; opposed to God's infinite perfection, 227; physical evil and divine providence, 359; physical and moral evil, 369

FIRST PRINCIPLES, *see* Principles, First

FORMALISM of Kant, 51 ff

FORMS, *a priori*, of Kant, 52

FREEDOM, kinds, 284; notion, 283

FREE WILL, Aquinas, 365; and physical premotion, according to bannesianism, 339; thomists and bannesians on, 340

FUTURIBLES, knowledge of, in God's intellection, 273

GARRIGOU-LAGRANGE, R., on free will, 339; on God's metaphysical essence, 201; on physical premotion and free will, 345

GAUTAMA, expounder of Buddhism, 368

GENERATION, SPONTANEOUS, 135 ff

GEOPHYSICS, causality, 118

GILBERT DE LA PORRÉE, distinctions in God, 234

GIOBERTI, V., ontologism, 43

GNOSTICISM, a form of emanationism, 257

GOD, absolute attributes, 187; Absolute Being, 131; absolute immutability, 242 ff; absolutely one reality, 224; absolutely simple, 23, 220; accidents not in, 223; analogy of intrinsic attribution, 195; analogy of proper proportionality, 195; can produce whatever is possible, 293; causality as a proof of God's existence, *see* Causality; change, *see* Change; changeless, 126 f; composition not found in, 231; concurrence, *see* Concurrence; conservation, *see* Conservation; creation, *see* Creation; and creatural action, 326; distinctions concerning, 233 ff; divine attributes, 199; *ens a se,* 115, 260; essence of, the ultimate foundation of intrinsic possibility, 299; eternity, 240 ff; eternity of, and all other types of duration, 248; eternity proved, 249 f; and evil, 283; evolution, 141 ff; existence, *see* Existence of God; extrinsic change, 246; a finite being according to finitism, 304; first cause, 126 f; governance, *see* Governance; "He Who Is," 209; imitability by creatural beings, 296; immanently operational attributes, 292; immensity, *see* Immensity; immutability, 240 ff; incomprehensible, 196; ineffable, 196; infinite perfection, 226 ff; infinite perfection proved, 227 ff; infinite perfection (reality), 231; infinitely perfect, 224 ff; infinity, 214 ff; intellect, 266 ff; intellect, in providence, 351; intellection, 266 ff; intellectually immutable, 245; intelligence, 127; intelligent, 126 f; intervention of, in evolution, 143; knowledge, *see* Knowledge of God; knows Himself and all other things, 270; life, proof of God's existence from, 131 ff; loves all things distinct from Himself freely, 285 f; loves Himself necessarily, 284; and man, 376; man's knowledge of, 188 ff; man's knowledge of, indirect and discursive, 189; man's soul produced by, 147; metaphysical composition impossible, 224; metaphysical essence, 197, 199 ff; metaphysical essence, theories analyzed, 202 ff; morally immutable, 245; name of, 209; nature, 8, 187 ff; nature of, as shown by contingency and causality, 126 f; necessary, 126 f; no potentiality, 159; object of God's knowledge, 268 ff; omnipotence, see Omnipotence; omnipresence, 254; operations, 8; opponents of His absolute simplicity, 220; opponents of His infinite perfection, 227; opponents of the traditional proofs of God's existence, 163 ff; pantheism, see Pantheism; and perfection, 153 ff; perfection as a proof of God's existence, 149 ff; a personal being, 262; physical essence, 210; physical and metaphysical essence, 211; physically immutable, 244; possesses spiritual life, 159; potentiality not found in, 231; power, 127; power is inexhaustible, 295; providence, see Providence; provisional notion, 58; pure act, 159; pure act (actuality), 231; pure spirit, 159, 223; purposive evolution, 146 ff; and reasoning, 279; relative attributes, 187, 292 ff; self-subsistence as the metaphysical essence of, 206 ff; simplicity, 214 ff; special object of theodicy, 5; a spirit, 223; spiritual being, 159; a substance, 222; a substance devoid of composition, 231; supernatural destiny of man, 376; Supreme Being, 160; terms signifying perfections common to God and creatures, 193; time, as applied to, 250; transient activity of, 350; ubiquity, 254; the ultimate cause of the origin of life, 138 ff; ultimate foundation of intrinsic possibility, 298; the Uncaused Cause possessing unlimited perfection, 157; unicity, 214 ff, 231 ff; unicity proved, 232 f; unlimitedly perfect, 159; virtually transitive operational attributes, 292; volition, see Will; ways of knowing, 190 ff; will, see Will of God; without composition, 159; without limitation, 159

GONET, intelligence the metaphysical essence of God, 201

GOOD, approbation, on the part of God, 274; diffusive of itself, 316; object of God's volition, 280
GOTAMA, see Gautama
GOTTI, God's metaphysical essence, 201
GOVERNANCE, Aquinas, 353; notion, 352; presupposes the fact of creation, 353; and providence, 353; relation to providence, 353; virtually transitive operational attribute, 292
GRADATION, of perfection, 150; of reality, 154
GREGORY OF RIMINI, nominalism, 234

HAECKEL, ERNST, materialism, 175, 227; pantheism is nothing but "polite atheism," 259
HAMILTON, SIR WILLIAM, agnosticism, 40
HEAT, an irreversible process in nature, 111
HEGEL, GEORG, Absolute Idea, 29; and Descartes, 29; and First Principles, 29 f; an idealistic monist, 29 f; pantheism, 227; refutation of, 30; total idealistic pantheism, 258
HEISENBERG, W., concept of the atom, 89
HELLIN, J., God's metaphysical essence, 201
HERACLITUS, and Aristotle, 63; on change, 59 f; denial of permanence, 59; empiricist, 59; pantheism of, 257
HERBERT OF CHERBURY, LORD, deism, 39
HOBBES, T., materialism, 227
HONTHEIM, J., God's metaphysical essence, 201
HUME, DAVID, and agnosticism, 41; on causality, 27; and Descartes's theory of knowledge, 52; doctrine on substance, 222; empiricism, 26; on First Principles, 26; his empiricism gave rise to materialism, 175; influence on Kant, 168; the Principle of Causality as an expression of "invariable sequence," 26
HUXLEY, THOMAS, agnosticism, 40; materialism, 175
HYPOTHESIS, purpose of, 37

IDEALISM, concerning the absolute

simplicity of God, 221; total pantheism, 258

IDENTITY, PRINCIPLE OF, see Principle of Identity

IGLESIAS, E., on concurrence, 328; conservation, 321

IMMANENCE, of action, characteristic of life, 133; of action, superior to nonliving matter, 139; as a form of total pantheism, 257

IMITABILITY, of God, inexhaustible, 296; of God's essence, the ultimate foundation of intrinsic possibility, 299

IMMENSITY, absolute attribute of God, 251; and absolute space, 251; eternal attribute of God, 251; infinite attribute of God, 251; intrinsic attribute of God, 251; Mercier, 253; notion, 250; omnipresence, 252; opponents, 252; presence in a place, 255; proof of God's, 252 f; relation of God's presence to extended space, 252; ubication, 255; ubiquity, 252; whereness, 255

IMMUTABILITY, intellectual, of God, 245; liberty and immutability in God's volition, 287 ff; moral, of God, 245; notion, 241; of God, opponents of, 242; physical, of God, 244; proof of God's, 242 ff

IMPERFECTION, see Perfection

IMPOSSIBILITY, absolute, 293; of an infinite effect, 296; relative, 293

IMPOSSIBLE, meaning of, 25

IN ACT, see Act

INDIA, immanent evolutionistic pantheism, 258

INDUCTION, as used in theodicy, 10; definition, 9

INFINITE, see Infinity

INFINITE NUMBER, see Number, infinite

INFINITE SERIES, see Series, infinite

INFINITY, actual, 226; extensive, 200; extensive, of perfection, 226; as God's metaphysical essence, 200; infinite number of creatures, 314; intensive, 200; intensive, of perfection, 226; as the metaphysical essence of God, analysis of, 202; negative, 316; not the result of a summation of finite realities, 226; notion, 225; of perfection, 224; potential, 226; proof of

God's, 227 ff; radical, 200; radical, of perfection, 226

IN POTENCY, see Potency

INTELLECT, chance, with respect to, 367; divine, in providence, 351; of God, see Knowledge of God; God's intellection, 266 ff; objective element of intellection, 267; possessed by Prime Mover, 77; subjective element, 267

INTELLECTION, see Intellect

INTELLIGENCE, and chance, 85; in the finality present in nature, 86; as the metaphysical essence of God, analysis of, 203; responsible for the order and design present in the universe, 99; simple, in God's knowledge, 272

JAMES, WILLIAM, finitism, 227; physical evil and divine providence, 359; pragmatism, 31

JEWS, creation, 303

JOHN OF ST. THOMAS, eternal creation, 313; intelligence, the metaphysical essence of God, 201

JOHN SCOTUS ERIUGENA, pantheism, 257

JOULE, J. P., Law of the Conservation of Energy, 176

JOYCE, GEORGE HAYWARD, defense of bannesianism, 338; on the metaphysical essence of God, 201, 205

JUDGMENT, binding force of, 14; contingent, 14; necessary, 15

KANT, IMMANUEL, agnosticism, 40; a priori forms demand the existence of God, 172; and Aquinas, 164; and the argument from order and design, 173; category, 169; causality, a mental category, 167; and cosmological argument for God's existence, 165 ff; Descartes's ontological argument, 173; doctrine of phenomenon (appearance) and noumenon (thing-in-itself) in regard to the argument for God's existence, 167; existence of God not provable, 53; experience, 169; formalism, 51 ff; on miracles, 372; misunderstood Aquinas' arguments, 173; objections to the traditional arguments for God's existence, 163 ff; ontological argument for God's existence, 164; ontological argument of Leibnitz, 173; ontological argument of St. Anselm, 173; phenomenon and noumenon distinguished, 169; physico-theological argument for God's existence, 167; postulate, in his system, 11; and Principle of Causality, 169 f; theory of knowledge, 168; transcendent inference from phenomena to noumena, 173; transcendentalism, 163 ff; transcendentalism of, contrary to the principles of reason, 171; transcendentalism criticized, 170; transcendentalism refuted, 168 ff

KELVIN, WILLIAM THOMSON, LORD, origin of life on earth, 137

KNOWLEDGE, analogical, 193; analogical, of God, 193 ff; analogy of intrinsic attribution, 195; analogy of proper proportionality, 195; Aquinas on, 269; Aquinas, on the way of negation, 191; equivocal, 193; of God, according to Aquinas, 240; of God and Principle of Causality, 189; God's, see Knowledge of God; intelligible species in human and divine intellection, 269; intermediate (scientia media), of molinism, 336; life, 139; man's, of God, 188 ff; mediate and discursive, of God's existence, 49; objective element, 267; pantheism, 271; subjective element, 267; terms signifying perfections common to God and creatures, 193; from things, 266; univocal, 193; way of affirmation in knowing God, 190; way of eminence in knowing God, 192; way of negation in knowing God, 191; ways of knowing God, 190 ff

KNOWLEDGE OF GOD, absolutely simple, 268; absolutely true, 268; abstractive, 273; of actual realities, 276; all things known without exception, 275; of approbation, 274; conditionally free acts, 278; creatural reality does not determine, 271; existence of, 275 ff; external formal principle, 268 f; formal principle, 268 f; future free acts, 277; futuribles, 273; of Himself and all other things, 269, 270; identical with His substance, 267; immutable, 267; infallible, 268; infinitely perfect, 268; intelligible species, 269; intermediate, 272; internal formal principle, 268 f; intuitive, 273; kinds, 272 ff; knower and the object known, 272; and man's, 267; object, 268 ff; of possible realities, 276; practical, 274; primary object, 269; secondary object, 269; self-subsistent, 267; sheer understanding, 268; of simple cognition, 274; simple intelligence, 272; speculative, 274; speculative-practical, in God, 274; unconditionally independent, 268; vision, 272

KÜLPE, OSCAR, partial pantheism, 256

LADD, G. T., prediction of future events, 179

LAW, and chance, 82; characteristic of science, 37; governs the universe, 98; of probability in chance effects, 83; regularity a characteristic of, 82; same laws operate throughout the world, 88

LE BROGLIE, L., concept of the atom, 89

LEDESMA, God's metaphysical essence, 201

LEIBNITZ, GOTTFRIED WILHELM, God's metaphysical essence, 200; meaning of theodicy, 4; ontological argument, 47; and the ontological proof, 45; optimism, 368; Principle of Determining (Sufficient) Reason, 21

LEQUIER, God's metaphysical essence, 201

LIBERTY, as the metaphysical essence of God, 201; as the metaphysical essence of God, analysis of, 204

LIFE, abiogenesis, 135 ff; appetition, 139; consciousness, 135, 139; death, 134; difference between living and non-living beings, 131; evolution, organic and emergent, 141 ff; exceeds the inherent causality of inorganic substances, 139; exigency, 132; functions of organisms, 132; God, the ultimate cause of, 138 ff; immanent action, 133; inherent natural purposiveness, 134; knowledge, 139; lifeless condition of the globe in former times, 137; manifestations, and inorganic matter, 139; materialists, 131; metaphysical essence of God, according to a few authors, 201; as the metaphysical essence of

God, analysis of, 204; opinions on, 237 f; organism, *see* Organism; in organisms, 133; origin, 135 ff; perception, 135; in plants, 91 f; possessed by Prime Mover, 77; preservation of the species, 134; principle of, 134; and the Principles of Sufficient Reason and Causality, 138; problem of, 131 ff; purposive evolution, 146 ff; rational, of man, 135; spiritual, in man, 135; spontaneous generation, 135; structure of organisms, 132

LIMITATION of perfection, 151 f, 229

LOCKE, JOHN, empiricism, 26; empiricism of, gave rise to materialism, 175; on miracles, 372; the rise of deism, 39

LODGE, SIR OLIVER, order, 91

LOVE, metaphysical essence of God, according to a few authors, 201; as the metaphysical essence of God, analysis of, 204

LUCRETIUS, materialism, 174

MALEBRANCHE, N., ontologism, 42

MAN, design in, 95 ff; end of, 376; and God, 376; as a moral being, object of special providence, 355 ff; order in, 95 ff; pain and providence, 362; rational life, 135; spiritual life, 135; supernatural end, 376

MANICHAEANISM, denies God's unicity, 232; physical evil and divine providence, 358

MANSEL, HENRY L., agnosticism, 40

MATERIALISM, abiogenesis, 138; activities of life, 131; Darwin's organic evolution and design, 176; English, 175; eternity of matter, 181; expanding universe, 181; exponents, 174 ff; Fallacy of False Exclusion, 177; God's existence, 174 ff; infinity of time not in accord with the findings of science, 181; Law of the Conservation of Energy no longer valid for modern physicists, 180; miracles are impossible, 371; nature as a closed system of causation is indemonstrable by induction, 181; notion, 174; opposed to God's infinite perfection, 227; oversimplification, 177; prediction of future events, 179; progress of the natural sciences, 175; psychic factor denied, 178; reaction against, 177; refutation

of, 177 ff; systematic, of Democritus, 174; and thinking, 180

MATTER, contingency of, 110; eternity of, refuted, 111, 181; inorganic, and life, 139; not found in God, 223; notion, 110; pre-existing, and creation, 301

MAYER, R., Law of the Conservation of Energy, 176

McGIFFERT, A. C., finitism, 227

MEANS and end, 87

MELISSUS, pantheism of, 257

MERCIER, D. CARD., proof for God's immensity, 253

METAPHYSICS and scientific knowledge, 14

MIDDLE, EXCLUDED, *see* Principle of Excluded Middle

MILL, JOHN STUART, on causality, 28; empiricism, 28; positivism, 227

MILLIKAN, ROBERT A., God's existence proved by the orderliness of nature, 102

MINGES, God's metaphysical essence, 200

MIRACLE, cognoscibility of, 374 f; exceeding the order and power of nature substantially or because of its manner, 370; an exception to an existing natural law, 373; not an abrogation of a natural law, 373; not impossible on the part of God, 372; not impossible on the part of the laws of nature, 373; notion, 369; possibility of, 371 ff; suspension of the ordinary laws of nature, 370; views on, 371

MODERNISM, 44

MOLESCHOTT, JAKOB, materialism, 175, 227

MOLINA, LUIZ, eternal creation, 313; on God's metaphysical essence, 201; mode of divine concurrence, 332

MOLINISM, defense of, 340 ff; evaluation, 346; free acts and concurrence, 335; indifferent concurrence, 335; intermediate knowledge (*scientia media*), 336; as a mode of divine concurrence, 332; on mode of divine concurrence, 335 ff; offered concurrence, 335; physical premotion contradicts free will, 342; physical premotion contradicts God's sanctity, 344 f; physical premotion superfluous, 341 f; on self-determination, 345; simultaneous concurrence, 335

MONISM, idealistic, 29; idealistic, refutation of, 30; materialistic, 29; meaning, 29

MONOTHEISM, notion, 3

MORGAN, C. LLOYD, emergent evolution, 143 ff

MOSELY, H., concept of the atom, 88

MOTION, change in, 71; contingency of matter, 110; see also Change

MOVEMENT, analysis, 62; Aquinas, 66; Aristotle's definition, 62

MOVER, PRIME, 76 f

MULTIPLICITY, an illusion, according to Parmenides, 59

MUTABILITY, definition, 241; see also Immutability

NATURAL THEOLOGY, derivation of term, 4

NATURE, a goal-directed cause, according to Aristotle, 86

NECESSARY, meaning, 25; see also Necessity

NECESSARY BEING, existence of, 106

NECESSITY, and contingency, 105 ff; definition, 105; kinds, 105 f; see also Contingency; Necessary

NEGATION, way of, in knowing God, 191

NEO-PLATONISM, advocated emanationism, 257

NEURON and order, 93

NEUTRON in the atom, 89

NIRVANA, extinction of all desire, 368

NOMINALISM, distinctions in God, 234; on eternal creation, 313; metaphysical essence of God, 200; on the metaphysical essence of God, analysis of, 203; Ockham, 200

NON-BEING, 16

NON-CONTRADICTION, PRINCIPLE OF, see Principle of Contradiction

NOTHING, see Non-Being

NOUGHT and Being identified by Hegel, 30

NOUMENON in Kant's formalism, 52

NUCLEUS of atom, 89

NUMBER, actually infinite, 122 ff; of beings demands an outside intelligence, 155; of beings in the universe limited, 155; definition, 122; implies limitation in the universe, 151; infinite, of changes in the universe, 74; infinite, of creatures, 314; limitation in, involves limitation of perfection in an absolute sense, 152; negatively infinite, of creatures, 316; notion, 122; potentially infinite, 122; supposed infinite, of contingent beings, 114

OCKHAM, WILLIAM OF, God's metaphysical essence, 201; nominalism, 234

OMNIPOTENCE, definition, 293; existence of God's, 295 f; extensively infinite, 294; formally immanent but virtually transient, 294; imitability of God, 296; impossibility, see Impossibility; inexhaustible, 295; intensively infinite, 294; notion, 292 ff; possibility, see Possibility; as related to power, 292; ultimate foundation of intrinsic possibility is God's essence, 298; virtually transitive operational attributes, 292

OMNIPRESENCE, follows God's absolute immensity, 254; notion, 252; relative attribute of God, 252; repletive, on the part of God, 255; temporal attribute of God, 252; ubiquity, 252

ONENESS, see Unicity

ONTOLOGISM, 42 f

OPTIMISM, 368 f

ORDER, Aquinas, 101; Aristotle, 85; artificial, 81; and chance, see Chance; in chemical affinity, 91; in chemical compounds, 90; conclusions drawn from the order of the world, 98 f; definition, 80; and design, 80 f; designed, 81; dynamic, 80; and intelligence, 85 f; natural, 81; observable fact in nature, 87; in plants, 91 f; proof of God's existence, 100 f; random, 81; static, 80; in the universe, shows intelligence, 99; in the world of animals, 93 ff; in the world of atoms, 88 ff; in the world of men, 95 ff; in the world of stars, 87; see also Design

ORGAN and life, 132

ORGANISM, first, 146; and life, 132, 134, 135; inherent natural purposiveness of, 134; life and chance, 140

OVERSTREET, H. A., finitism, 227

PAGANISM, creation practically unknown to, 303; providence, 350
PAIN in brute and man, 361
PANTHEISM, of the Absolute, 258; denies absolute simplicity in God, 220; emanationism, 257; evolution of the Deity, 257; exponents of, 256 ff; fallacy underlying idealistic immanent pantheism, 260; gnostics, 257; on God's immensity, 253; imperfect, same as partial, 256; kinds, 256 ff; and knowledge in God, 271; miracles impossible, 371; notion, 255; opposed to God's absolute immutability, 242; opposed to God's infinite perfection, 227; opposed to theism, 255; partial, 256; perfect, same as total, 256; philosophy of India, 258; physical and moral evil, 369; realistic total pantheism, 256; refutation of, 259 ff; School of Elia, 257; theosophy, 258; total, 256; total idealistic, 258; total immanent evolutionistic, 257
PARINIRVANA, extinction of all being, 368
PARMENIDES, and Aristotle, 63; denial of change, 58 f; pantheism of, 257
PASTEUR, LOUIS, experiments on abiogenesis, 136
PEIRCE, CHARLES S., pragmatism, 31
PERFECTIBILITY, 151 f
PERFECTION, absolute, 225; accidental, 149; acquired through change, 69; actual, 149; actuality, 225; Aquinas on, 154; argument of Aquinas for God's existence, based on perfections, 157; composition, 150; in creatural beings, 151; degrees, 151; diverse perfections combined into a unity, 154; as effect, 68; essential, 149; extensive infinity of, 226; and God, 153 ff; grades of, 150; graduated series, 225; infinite, 224; infinite, intrinsically possible of realization, 229; infinite, proof of God's immutability, 244; intensive infinity of, 226; limitation of, 151 f, 229; limitation of, demands an efficient cause, 155; limitation in an absolute sense, implied in the limitation in number, 152; limitation means imperfection, 152; as the metaphysical

essence of God, analysis of, 203; mixed, 149; notion, 149, 225; number of beings in universe limited, 155; number implies limitation of, 151; objections against the possibility of infinite perfection, 230 f; omniperfection, the physical essence of God, 210; opponents of God's infinite, 227; perfectibility, 151; potential, 149; predicamental, 149; problem of God's infinite, 226; proof of God's infinite, 227 ff; radical infinity of, 226; reality, 225; relative, 152, 225; series of perfections, 154; simple, 149; transcendental, 150; transcendental perfections are simple, 156; uncaused cause, possessing unlimited, 157; unlimited, in God, 159
PERMANENCE, Parmenides, 59
PERSON, 260
PERSONALITY, Prime Mover, personal, 76
PESSIMISM, 368 f
PHENOMENON, in agnosticism, 40; in Kant's formalism, 52
PHILOSOPHY, competency of reason, 39; definition, 6; and special natural sciences, 7; theodicy, a department of, 7; theodicy, the philosophical science of God, 4
PHYSICS, causality, 118
PLANCK, M., concept of the atom, 89
PLANTS, order in, 91 ff
PLATO, eternity of matter, 303
PLOTINUS, advocated emanationism, 257
PLURALISM, physical evil and divine providence, 358
POLYTHEISM, creation unknown to, 303; denies absolute simplicity in God, 220; denies God's unicity, 232; on God's immensity, 253; idols, 3; notion, 3; opposed to God's absolute immutability, 242
POSITIVISM, opposed to God's infinite perfection, 227
POSSIBILITY, foundation of, 297 ff; immediate foundation of internal, 297; of an infinite effect, 296
POSSIBLE, God can produce whatever is possible, 293; meaning, 25; potential being, 61 ff; see also Possibility
POSSIBLE BEING, 19 f

POSTULATE, Kantian, 11; meaning, 11

POTENCY (POTENTIALITY), in change, 61; notion, 62; receptive, 68

POTENTIALITY (POTENCY), in change, 61; and compound, 221; implies imperfection, 152; notion, 62; not present in God's nature, 159; perfection, 151; receptive, 68; without limit in the number of creatural beings possible, 316

POWER, as related to omnipotence, 292

PRAGMATISM, 31 f

PREDETERMINATION, physical, in the theory of bannesianism, 333

PREDICTABILITY, of chance effects, 82

PREMOTION, physical, and free will, according to bannesianism, 339; physical, in the theory of bannesianism, 333

PRESENCE, circumscriptive, 255; definitive, 255; repletive, 255

PRIME MOVER, see Mover, Prime

PRINCIPLE, formal, of thinking, 267; vital, 135

PRINCIPLE OF CAUSALITY, analysis, 22 ff; analytical principle, 117; change, 68; and 'invariable sequence,' 26; not an a priori form of the mind, 172; and the origin of life, 138; stated, 15; underlies man's knowledge of God, 189

PRINCIPLE OF CONTRADICTION, 15; analysis of, 17 f

PRINCIPLE OF EXCLUDED MIDDLE, analysis of, 19 f; stated, 15; validity of, 20

PRINCIPLE OF IDENTITY, 15 f

PRINCIPLE OF SUFFICIENT REASON, analysis of, 20 ff; causality, 131; change, 68; contingency, 131; and the origin of life, 138; stated, 15

PRINCIPLES, FIRST, 14 ff; analytical, not empirical, 32; and basic concepts, 25; binding force, 14; of Causality, see Principle of Causality; contingent judgments, 14; of Contradiction, see Principle of Contradiction; Descartes, 14; empiricism, 26 ff; of Excluded Middle, see Principle of Excluded Middle; and experience, 15; foundation of reality and thought, 15; of Identity, see Principle of Identity;

kinds, 15; necessary judgments, 15; self-evident, 16; of Sufficient Reason, see Principle of Sufficient Reason; validity must be established, 14

PRINGLE-PATTISON, on creation, 305

PROBABILITY, and chance, 83 f

PRODUCTION, absolute and relative, 23; creation and change, 23

PROGRESSION, GEOMETRICAL, of probability on the basis of chance, 83

PROOF, ONTOLOGICAL, 45

PROPERTY, see Attribute

PROVIDENCE, Aquinas, 351, 353, 357, 360, 365; chance, 366, 367; fate, 366; and governance, 353; moral, 352; moral evil, 363 ff; notion, 350; and pain, 361; particular, 352; physical, 352; physical evil, 358 ff; physical evil natural to hierarchy of order present in the universe, 359 f; plan of God's intellect, 351; proof of, for general providence, 353 ff; proof of, for special providence concerning man, 355 ff; proper end of creature, 354; relation to governance, 353; ultimate end of creature, 355; universal, 352; views on, 358; virtually transitive operational attribute, 292

PSYCHOLOGY, causality, 119

PURPOSE, in design, 81; in God's providence, 351; see also End

PURPOSIVENESS, inherent and natural, in every organism, 134

RADIATION, same kinds everywhere, 88

RAMSAY, SIR WILLIAM, refutation of John Butler Burke, 136

REALITY, gradation of, 154; perfection, 225; unknowable, in the theory of agnosticism, 40

REASON, cannot be preceded by faith, 42; competency of, in science and philosophy, 39; man's instrument for proving God's existence, 54; may be capable of discovering the ultimate causes of things, 38; natural, instrument used in theodicy, 9; and order, 105

REDI, FRANCESCO, abiogenesis, 136

REGRESS, infinite, involves a contradiction, 131

REGULARITY, characteristic of law, and chance, 82

RELIGIOUS EXPERIENCE, see Experience, Religious

REVELATION, and theodicy, 7

ROSMINI, A., ontologism, 43

RUTHERFORD, E., concept of the atom, 88

RYDBERG SERIES, nature of, 89

ST. JOHN, HENRY, VISCOUNT BOLINGBROKE, deism, 39

SCHELLING, F., pantheism, 227; total idealistic pantheism, 258

SCHILLER, F. C. S., finitism, 227; pragmatism, 31

SCHOLASTICISM, on concurrence, 327; conservation, 321; on eternal creation, 313

SCHOPENHAUER, ARTHUR, pessimism, 369

SCHRÖDINGER, E., concept of the atom, 89

SCIENCE, abiogenesis, 138; causal explanation, 37; causality, as a universal fact in nature, 118; and chance, 83, 84; description of facts, 37; as distinct from philosophy, 7; as distinguished from experience, 5; eternity of matter not in accord with the findings of, 181; and facts, 37; infinity of time not in accord with the findings of, 181; and materialism, 175; meaning, 5; and metaphysics, 14; and miracles, 371; neither theistic nor pantheistic, 304; often only approximation, 38; physical sciences, 5; reason's place in, 38; scientific explanation, 36 ff; scientific knowledge, 14; shows that the universe is not eternal, 111

SCIENTIA MEDIA, in God's knowledge, 272; of molinism, 336

SCOTISTS, theory of God's metaphysical essence, 200

SCOTUS, DUNS, and the ontological proof, 45

SECRÉTAN, on God's metaphysical essence, 201

SELF-EXISTENCE, of ens a se, 115

SELF-SUBSISTENCE, Aquinas, 208; as the metaphysical essence of God, 201, 206 ff

SELF-SUFFICIENCY of ens a se, 115

SENECA, definition of fate, 366

SENSISM, theory of, 26

SERIES, infinite, of causes, 119 ff; infinite, of changes in the universe, 72; infinite, intrinsically impossible, 122 f; infinite, involves an actually infinite number, 122; of perfection, 154

SIMPLICITY, absolute, 218; the Absolute, 221; absolute, in God, 220; definition, 215; distinction, 215; of God, 223; kinds, 215; metaphysical composition in God excluded, 224; notion, 214; notions of God's, 221; opponents of God's absolute simplicity, 220; problem of God's, 219 ff; proof of God's, 221; proof of God's absolute immutability, 244; relative, 219

SIN, Aquinas, 365; not against God's goodness and wisdom, 364 f; permitted by God, 363

SOUL, origin of, 147

SPACE, absolute, 251; imaginary, 251; in Kant's formalism, 52

SPECIFICATION, freedom of, 284

SPECTOGRAPHY, 87

SPENCER, HERBERT, agnosticism, 40; materialism, 175; positivism, 227

SPINOZA, B., immanent evolutionistic pantheism, 258; on miracles, 372; pantheism, 227

SPIRIT, Prime Mover, 77

SPONTANEOUS GENERATION, see Generation, Spontaneous

STATISTICAL AVERAGE, see Average, Statistical

STOICISM, advocated partial pantheism, 256

STOICS, denied simplicity in God, 220

STRUCTURE of the galaxies, 88

STUFLER, J., concurrence, 328

SUAREZ, F., eternal creation, 313; God's metaphysical essence, 201

SUBJECTIVISM, involved in Kant's formalism, 53

SUBSTANCE, 222

SUFFICIENT REASON, see Principle of Sufficient Reason

TAYLOR, A. E., Descartes's ontological argument, 164; view on Kant, 164

THEISM and evolution, 141

THEODICY, current meaning, 4; definition, 7; a department of philosophy,

7; derivation of term, 4; difficulties, 7; dogmatic (supernatural) theology, 6; First Principles, 15; formal object, 9; God, the special object of, 5; material object, 9; and metaphysics, 6; method, 9 f; natural theology, 3 f; necessity of proving God's existence, 8; notion, 3 ff; a philosophical science, 6 f; philosophical science of God, 4; postulates, 11; and revelation, 7; science of, 5, 6; scope, 3 ff, 7 ff; starting-point, 7

THEOLOGY, dogmatic, 4; natural, 4; natural, see Natural Theology and Theodicy; philosophical, 4; supernatural, 4; and theodicy, 6

THEOSOPHY, 258

THERMODYNAMICS, shows the irreversible process of heat, 111

THOMISM, defense of bannesianism, 337 f; divine concurrence, 332; on eternal creation, 313; evaluation, with regard to the mode of divine concurrence, 346; and free will, 340

THOMISTS, on metaphysical essence of God, 201; proper proportionality, 195

THOMSON, J. J., concept of the atom, 88

THOMSON, SIR J. ARTHUR, God, the Author of life, 148

TIME, as applied to God, 250; and beginning of material reality, 112; creation, 303; infinity of, and science, 181; in Kant's formalism, 52; origin of organisms, 109

TINDAL, MATTHEW, deism, 39

TOLAND, JOHN, deism, 39

TORRES, on God's metaphysical essence, 201

TRADITION, see Traditionalism

TRADITIONALISM, 41 f

TRANSCENDENTALISM, arbitrary and subjective, 170; contrary to the principles of reason, 171; Kant's criticism of the argument from order and design unfounded, 173; and proofs of God's existence, 163 ff

TRUTH, God is Truth, 270

TYNDALL, JOHN, materialism, 175

UBAGHS, C., fideism and traditionalism, 42

UBICATION, 255

UBIQUITY, follows God's absolute immensity, 254; omnipresence, 252

UNICITY of God, 231 f

UNIVERSE, age, 111; expanding, implies limited space, 181; intelligible and rational, 182; same laws operate everywhere, 88; a unitary system demanding a single cause, 73; see also World

URRÁBURU, on eternal creation, 313

VAN DE WOESTYNE, God's metaphysical essence, 200

VAN TIEGHAM, origin of life on earth, 137

VASQUEZ, eternal creation, 313; God's metaphysical essence, 201

VENTURA, G., fideism and traditionalism, 42

VERIFICATION, purpose of, 37

VISION in God's knowledge, 272

VOGT, KARL, materialism, 175

VOLITION, see Will

VOLUNTARISTS, God's metaphysical essence, 201

VON HARTMANN, EDUARD, pessimism, 369

VON HELMHOLTZ, HERMAN L. F., Law of the Conservation of Energy, 176; origin of life on earth, 137

VORSTIUS, God's omnipresence, 253

WALLACE, ALFRED RUSSELL, on the wing and feather of a bird, 94 f

WARD, JAMES, creation unthinkable, 304

WELLS, H. G., finitism, 227

WHITTAKER, SIR EDMUND, duration of the world, 182

WILL, Aquinas, 288; divine, in providence, 351; God is infinitely perfect, 280; kinds of freedom, 284; notion, 279

WILL OF GOD, absolutely simple, 280; essentially well-ordered, 280; and evil, 283; existence, 281 ff; God loves all beings distinct from Himself, 282; God loves all things distinct from Himself freely, 285; God loves Himself, 282; God loves Himself necessarily, 284; intellectually conscious, 280; liberty, 287 ff; necessity and freedom, 283 ff; object, 280; an operational attribute, 280

WISDOM and man's supernatural destiny, 376

WORLD, contingency, 107; governed by law, 98; one cause of, 187; same laws operate everywhere, 88; should reveal its cause, 50; truly a cosmos, 98; a unitary system demanding a single cause, 73

XENOPHANES, pantheism of, 257

ZENO OF ELIA, pantheism of, 257